After Yorktown

To Greg —
Many thanks
Don Glickstein 1-19-19

After Yorktown

THE FINAL STRUGGLE
FOR AMERICAN
INDEPENDENCE

Don Glickstein

WESTHOLME
Yardley

To my mom, Lillian Hamlin Glickstein (1915–1965), an immigrants' child and proper Bostonian who inspired me to love history, politics, and the arts, and who took me to my first baseball game.

And to Alvin F. Oickle, who, when I was a young journalist, challenged me to be fearless and creative. Thirty-five years later, he challenged me to write this book.

Westholme Publishing, LLC
904 Edgewood Road
Yardley, Pennsylvania 19067
Visit our Web site at www.westholmepublishing.com

ISBN: 978-1-59416-261-9
Also available as an eBook.

Printed in the United States of America.

"Wild, tormenting rumours of an armistice and peace are in the air, they lay hold on our hearts and make the return to the front harder than ever. . . . Breath of hope that sweeps over the scorched fields, raging fever of impatience, of disappointment, of the most agonizing terror of death, insensate question: Why? Why do they make an end? And why do these rumours of an end fly about?"

–Erich Maria Remarque, *All Quiet on the Western Front*

CONTENTS

Reference Maps   x–xiii

Introduction: How to End a War   xv

Part One Surrender

   1. The Treaty   3

   2. O'Hara's Wars   6

   3. Rochambeau and Washington   16

Part Two The South

   4. Rice and the Low Country   29

   5. General Leslie Comes to Charlestown   32

   6. The Deputy Savior   38

   7. The "Bloodiest, Cruel War"   43

   8. North Carolina: Two Combustible Commanders   50

   9. Georgia: "Making Bricks Without Straw"   60

10. Leslie's Work   74

11. "Howlings of a Triple-Headed Monster"   80

12. The Swamp Fox Meets His Match   88

13. "Bloody Bill" Cunningham Raids the Backcountry   99

14. Laurens and His Glory   104

15. At Last, the Evacuation   113

Part Three   The Frontier

16. Indians   127

17. The Death of Captain Butler   137

18. Massacre and Revenge   149

19. Ambush at Blue Licks   166

20. Final Fights on the Ohio   173

21. Sevier Hunts for Dragging Canoe   182

22. Arkansas Post and the Spanish Frontier   189

23. Between Two Hells   204

Part Four   The Caribbean

24. Riches   213

25. The Golden Rock   221

26. More British Humiliations   229

27. Battle of the Saintes   238

28. Flip-flops in Central America   245

29. A Future Hero   249

Part Five   The Sea and the Raiders

30. Britannia Doesn't Rule the Waves   259

31. French Disaster, British Tragedy   264

32. Secret Mission to the Arctic   268

33. Coastal War: Halifax to Boston   273

34. Coastal War: Delaware to Chesapeake   278

Part Six The Mediterranean

35. "Calamity Has Come On Us"   291
36. The Great Siege of Gibraltar   296

Part Seven The Battle for India

37. Hyder Ali: The "Most Formidable Enemy"   311
38. Coote and Hughes to the Rescue   318
39. Suffren's "Lust for Action"   323
40. The Final Battles   328

Part Eight Washington and Carleton

41. New Leader, Old Leader   343
42. Refugees and the *Book of Negroes*   351
43. Evacuation Day   359

Notes   363
Bibliography and Acknowledgments   403
Index   421

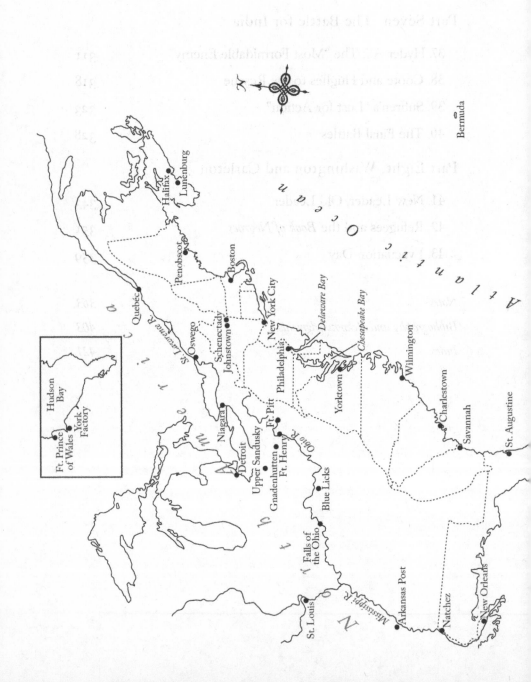

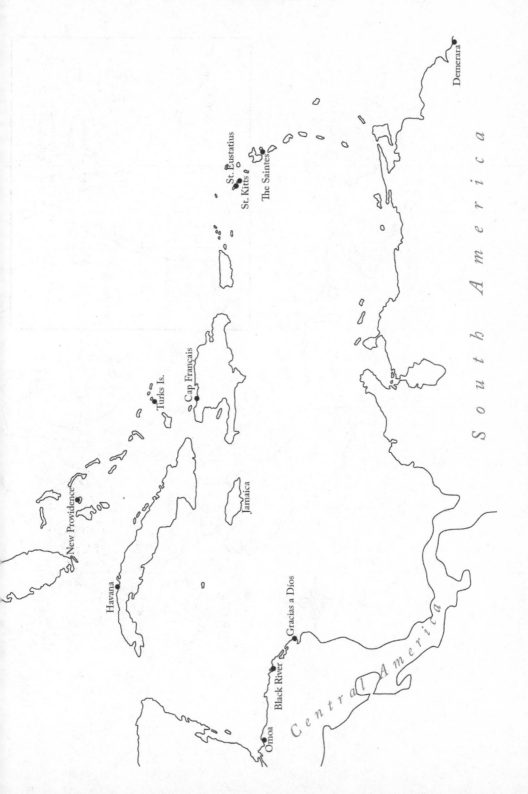

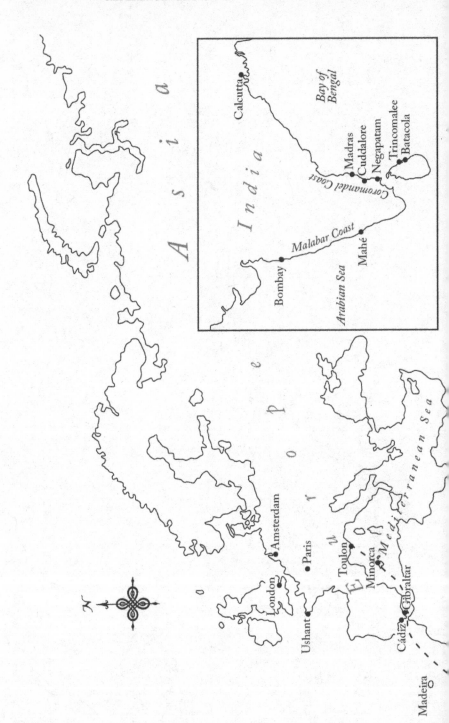

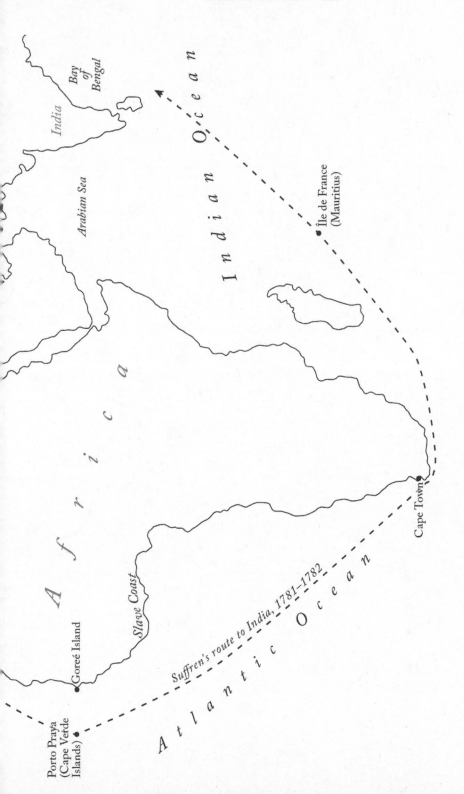

INTRODUCTION

How to End a War

I N 1966, GEORGE D. AIKEN, 74, A FRUIT GROWER AND U.S. Senator from Vermont, made what he called "a far-fetched proposal" to end the Vietnam War. Vietnam was a "quagmire," said one Pulitzer Prize–winning reporter; many adopted the metaphor. "Waist deep in the Big Muddy," sang antiwar activist Pete Seeger. Even President Lyndon B. Johnson complained: "A man can fight if he can see daylight down the road somewhere. But there ain't no daylight in Vietnam."[1]

Now, Aiken offered his proposal because "nothing else has worked." He proposed that the U.S. "declare unilaterally that this stage of the Vietnam War is over." Then, without losing face, the U.S. could regroup to strategic, defensible enclaves.[2]

Others summarized Aiken's words with less nuance. In 2009, for example, a columnist applied Aiken's concept to Afghanistan: "Some folks sneered and laughed when Sen. Aiken said the U.S. should quickly get out of a growing quagmire in Southeast Asia. Afghanistan is rapidly becoming a similar quagmire." Two years later, a different columnist talked about the continued fighting: "We should declare victory and leave."[3]

Many American wars—perhaps most, depending on how you define "war"—have been similar to Vietnam and Afghanistan. They were quagmires, with no clear path to victory, just exhausted, endless fighting. President James Polk, for example, in 1847, defended his quagmire in Mexico as that war's popularity plummeted: "The continued successes of our arms may fail to secure a satisfactory peace. . . . [But] to withdraw our Army without a peace, would not only leave all the wrongs of which we complain unredressed, but would be the signal for new and fierce civil dissensions and new revolutions."[4]

Senator Aiken delivered his proposal on October 19, 1966—185 years to the day that the British surrendered to French and rebel American armies at Yorktown, Virginia. The mythology of the surrender is that the American Revolution ended there and then, with Americans victorious.

Mason Locke Weems, an Episcopal parson from Maryland, was twenty-two when the British surrendered. In his bestselling, fictional biography of Washington, he wrote that the Yorktown surrender "was justly considered as the close of the war." It is a hindsight that has endured. On the surrender's 229th anniversary in 2010, comic-strip readers saw Beetle Bailey, an army private, chat with his fellow soldiers. "This is the anniversary of the British General Cornwallis surrendering," Beetle says. "It was a very important event. It was 1781. The end of the war with England." Even the U.S. National Park Service maintains the surrender meant the war was over. "And it was. The victory secured independence for the United States."[5]

The reality was that nearly seven years after insurgent American colonists killed seventy-three royal infantry along a road from Concord to Boston, on what the British perceived to be a peacekeeping mission—seizing caches of rebel weapons—the war remained inconclusive with no end in sight, no pathway to peace. A quagmire.

This is the story of the people who continued to fight after Yorktown for nearly two more years because they had no orders to stop.

It is an important story in the twenty-first century, not because history predicts the future, but because it cautions us about the present. "If the study of history does nothing more than teach us humility, skepticism and awareness of ourselves, then it has done something useful," said historian Margaret MacMillan. Acknowledging an enemy's perspective doesn't impugn one's patriotism. Each data point of events obscure or known—enhances the pool of knowledge, the "big data" that strengthen our ability to make wiser decisions.[6]

A style note: Eighteenth-century writers spelled, punctuated, and wrote inconsistently. I embrace the editors of Nathanael Greene's papers who tried to make such manuscripts "intelligible to the present-day reader while retaining the essential form and spirit of the writer." Likewise, Colin G. Calloway, a leading scholar of Native Americans, kept "the names of individuals and groups in the form I thought would be most readily identifiable for most readers." Finally, I avoid terms like "patriot" and "traitor" that could be applied to both sides. There's no question American Whigs were in rebellion—and thus, "rebels"—while Tories were "loyalists" to Britain. The term "American" applied to both Loyalists and rebels. As one exiled Loyalist said, "I am sometimes tempted to endeavor to forget that I am an American . . . but the passion for my native country returns."[7]

PART ONE

Surrender

i. The Treaty

THE AMERICAN REVOLUTION ENDED ON WEDNESDAY EVENING, May 12, 1784, in Passy, a village near Paris.

Two and a half years had passed since a British army surrendered at Yorktown, Virginia. For thirteen months, enemy diplomats and politicians circled each other before agreeing to an armistice. Another sixteen months passed before three diplomats and their aides gathered in Passy, on a large estate "in a pretty house situated in a fine amphitheater-like garden." There, one of the diplomats, an American named Benjamin Franklin, 78, lived as a guest of an international trader and arms dealer who had supplied gunpowder to the American rebel army.[1]

Franklin's partner that evening was John Jay, 39, a thin, balding, hook-nosed lawyer from New York, former president of the Continental Congress, and minister to Spain. He was, said a diplomat, reserved, taciturn, and grave, all of which "give him greater regard than he seems to merit." The future chief justice and New York governor made "a poor figure, being rather of a small size, remarkably thin," said an acquaintance. But "this proves the falsity of judging by appearances." A former law partner turned political enemy told Jay: "Your cold heart, graduated like a thermometer, finds the freezing point nearest the bulb." Yet Jay would become a trusted advisor to two presidents.[2]

Franklin and Jay were in Passy to exchange peace treaty documents signed by Congressional leaders. Their British counterpart was David Hartley, a member of Parliament who had with him the treaty documents signed by George III.

Hartley, 52, had been an outspoken opponent of the war. Like Franklin, who was an acquaintance, Hartley wore glasses, opposed slavery, and was both a politician and a practical scientist. His noted contribution showed how to make buildings fire resistant by using iron and copper plates between floors. Unlike Franklin—celebrated for his wit, writing, discoveries, and inventions—Hartley was celebrated for boring people. "In Parliament," wrote a fellow MP, "the intolerable length, when increased by the dullness of his speeches, rendered him an absolute nuisance, even to his own friends. His rising always operated like a dinner-bell." Still, Hartley "possessed some talent, with unsullied probity, added to indefatigable perseverance and labor."[3]

Why had it taken so long to reach this point when Franklin, Jay, and Hartley exchanged the ratification documents?

While George III insisted in the days after Yorktown that the war would continue, Parliamentary opposition grew. In February 1782, it voted to end an offensive war in North America. The prime minister resigned; the government fell. In fits and spurts, the enemies talked informally, but the American rebels refused formal negotiations unless the British first acknowledged their independence, which the British preferred to grant rather than assume. The new prime minister, the Marquess of Rockingham, dropped dead suddenly in July 1782. His successor, William Petty Fitzmaurice, Earl of Shelburne, agreed to the American terms of recognizing independence three months later.

Meanwhile, the diplomats crossed and double-crossed their own people and each other. American negotiators ignored their instructions from Congress to defer to the French. They discussed a separate deal with the British, who would be generous if it meant splitting the Americans from their French, Spanish, and Dutch allies. The French, Spanish, and Dutch, for their part, would sell out their American ally if it strengthened their interests in Europe, the Caribbean, the Mediterranean, and India.

The British and Americans reached a preliminary treaty on November 30, 1782. Given their spies' abilities, it's doubtful the French were blindsided, except by the quantity of British concessions. Nevertheless, Franklin apologized to his chief ally, and assured France that the treaty wouldn't take effect until all the parties had reached an agreement. Then, Franklin asked France for yet another loan.

France, Spain, and Britain signed their preliminary peace treaty on January 20, 1783, when they also agreed to an armistice. (The Dutch continued to negotiate for another seven months.) A month later, Parliament approved the American treaty while censuring Shelburne for its generous terms—"more calamitous, more dreadful, more ruinous than war could possibly be," said one MP. Shelburne's government didn't survive the censure.[4]

The final approved treaties were signed in September 1783 by the Americans in Hartley's rooms in Paris, and by the French and Spanish at the Versailles palace. All that was left was ratification of the treaties by each government. Congress wasn't able to accomplish this until mid-January 1784, and then, only at the last minute because it couldn't get a quorum. Once the documents made their way across the wintry Atlantic, George III, in late March, signed his copies, and sent them to Hartley in Paris. (Hartley's career ended after this mission. He retired from politics, continued to study mechanics and chemistry.)[5]

The day after Franklin and Jay exchanged papers with Hartley, Franklin celebrated in a letter to his friend, Charles Thomson, the secretary of Congress: "Thus, the great hazardous enterprise we have been engaged in is, God be praised, happily completed—an event I hardly expected I should live to see."[6]

During these lengthy diplomatic maneuvers, the American army got sparse and often conflicting information. Its commander, George Washington, worried that negotiations could fall apart. As late as February 1783, he ordered one of his generals to prepare to besiege New York as "a probable operation." In America, in the Caribbean, around the world—for it had become a world war—the fighting continued for months after Yorktown.[7]

One of those fighters was Charles O'Hara, the British second-in-command at Yorktown. He had been fighting the war since 1777.

2. O'Hara's Wars

TEN YEARS LATER . . . FRANCE, NOVEMBER 1793. THE PEACE treaty that ended the American Revolution was a decade in the past. Now, in 1793, Great Britain was again fighting a revolution, this time against America's old ally, France, and its regicidal, republican government.

In late December, the terse first reports from France stunned Britain: The enemy had captured Lieutenant General Charles O'Hara, commander-in-chief of the allied armies in France and governor of the besieged Mediterranean naval port, Toulon. The circumstances of the capture, as reported in French newspapers, were unlikely. O'Hara had been with frontline troops attacking an enemy position.

"It appears so improbable that a commander-in-chief should so expose his person in a sortie, as to be taken prisoner, that we give no credit to the intelligence," *The Times* reported. A French correspondent asked if O'Hara had exercised "imprudence, ineptitude, or something worse?" The British naval commander wrote London, "The governor promised not to go out himself, but unfortunately did not keep his word."[1]

This War of the First Coalition was not going well for Britain and its allies. The war was the thirty-first England and France had fought dating back to 1066, and O'Hara's third. It began in 1792 when revolutionary France declared war on Austria and Prussia. Over the next two years, the revolutionaries guillotined their former king, occupied Brussels, and fought against most of a Europe allied in name, but divided by future advantage: Britain, Spain, Portugal,

Sardinia, Naples and Sicily, and Holland. Those were the enemies outside. Within France, a civil war with shifting alliances and ideologies: federalists, royalists, republicans, Brissontins, Septembriseurs, Feuillants, Hébertists, Dantonists, Girondists, Jacobins, Les Enragés, Paris against Bordeaux, radical against reactionary, xenophobes, paranoids, terrorists.[2]

In Marseilles and Toulon, French federalists and royalists rebelled against the Paris regime, and asked Britain and Spain for support. The allies obliged. A British fleet arrived in Toulon in August 1793; other allies soon joined. A growing revolutionary Republican army met them and converged on the outskirts of Toulon.

O'Hara, 53, Gibraltar's lieutenant governor and an experienced general, was ordered to take command in Toulon. He arrived in late October and sensed a debacle. His allied troops were unreliable, inexperienced, and undisciplined, giving "no very encouraging prospects in any attempts we may make."[3]

Gilbert Elliot, the civil administrator, also newly arrived, said O'Hara was too pessimistic: "I never saw a man half so nervous, or half so blind to every side but the black one, as O'Hara. His strange rattling, and to all appearance, absurd and wrong-headed manner of talking, and indeed acting on some points, is more alarming in my eyes than any other circumstance. He is not without sense in his profession, and he has considerable military experience and knowledge, with personal courage in the highest degree, but he sees all the difficulties and can think and talk of nothing else."[4]

Beyond the quality of his troops, O'Hara's biggest concern was strategic. Ridges and hills of up to 1,900 feet nearly encircle Toulon's harbor. If an enemy seized the heights, cannon could pummel the city and ships in the inner harbor.

A French revolutionary artillery captain did exactly that. Backed by political connections in Paris, Captain Napoleon Bonaparte, 24, assumed authority for the artillery placement. "Artillery persistently served with red-hot cannon-balls is terrible against a fleet," he said.[5]

On November 28, the French completed a crucial battery on one of the high ridges, and began firing on an allied fort at a lower elevation. O'Hara ordered an attack on the French position for November 30. "The night before the action he was as nervous as it is possible to conceive, and was wretched about the whole business and its possible issue," Elliot said.[6]

But the attack was successful. About 2,350 allied soldiers stormed and overran the French position. "We succeeded in surprising and forcing the enemy, and were soon in full possession of the battery and height," said O'Hara's second-in-command.[7]

Then things went wrong. The undisciplined allied troops chased the French instead of securing their success. They met overwhelming numbers of French soldiers, and were not only forced to retreat, but also forced to give up the position they had captured. Bonaparte helped lead the successful counterattack. He later described how he and his men advanced unperceived through an olive-tree grove, and began "a terrible fire" on the allied troops. The French "poured down with great superiority of numbers," Elliot said next day, and it was during the British retreat that "so many were killed and wounded." It was "a bad day for us."[8]

One of the casualties was O'Hara. At the first success, he joined his troops on the ridge, and, like his men, was surprised by the counterattack. As he tried to rally them, a bullet wounded his hand. Losing blood, he sat at the foot of a wall, and there, French soldiers seized him. Bonaparte took credit for the capture:

> I . . . seized him by the coat, and threw him back amongst my own men, thinking that he was a colonel. . . . He cried out that he was the commander-in-chief of the English. . . . I ran up and prevented the soldiers from ill-treating him. He spoke very bad French; and as I saw that he imagined they intended to butcher him, I did everything in my power to console him; and gave directions that his wound should be immediately dressed, and every attention paid to him.[9]

Bonaparte's secretary—not an eyewitness—didn't credit him, but corroborated the gist of his account. "General O'Hara . . . was wounded in the hand by a musket-ball, and a sergeant seized and dragged him prisoner."[10]

O'Hara spent twenty-one months as a prisoner of war. Classified as a political criminal—this was the Reign of Terror—he was forced to watch mass executions. Mobs paraded him through the streets, and he suffered from his wounded hand, which never healed properly. He was brought to the Luxembourg Palace in Paris, once a symbol of luxury but now "a huge loathsome prison."[11]

He was exchanged in 1795 for a French lieutenant general, Donatien Marie Joseph de Vimeur, the Viscount de Rochambeau. Ironically, Rochambeau's father, Jean-Baptiste, had been detained by the revolutionary regime for six months.

O'Hara had met the Rochambeaus fourteen years earlier. They had even dined together. The day before they met, O'Hara had surrendered a British army to the French and their American allies at Yorktown, Virginia.

O'Hara may have been born in 1740, probably in Lisbon, Portugal. He was one of at least fourteen bastard children by any of three mothers and the "singularly licentious" James O'Hara, a British soldier and diplomat.[12]

James was close to Charles, and he mentored and championed him. Charles started his military career around the not-unusual age of eleven, in 1751, when he became an infantry ensign. The next year, James bought Charles a commission as cornet in a dragoon regiment. Charles joined the Coldstream Guards as a lieutenant in 1756; his father was regimental colonel. At nineteen, he fought in his first major battle, Minden, in Germany, where the British and allies defeated the French and their allies. The experience gave O'Hara what later generations would call networking opportunities. He became acquainted with two other future generals, Henry Clinton and Charles Cornwallis, whose careers became linked two decades later in the American war.[13]

More postings and promotions ensued. By 1765, he was commander and governor of Gorée (now part of Dakar, Senegal). There, he commanded pardoned military criminals who had agreed to serve the rest of their lives in Africa—a Hobson's choice given the likelihood of contracting fatal tropical diseases.

O'Hara was commissioned as a regimental captain and army lieutenant colonel in 1773, but by 1776, his career was at a dead end. He was an obscure officer in an obscure location, and reports of administrative incompetence led to an investigation and his firing. The next year, with the rebellion in America unresolved, O'Hara was posted to New York. There, he was assigned administrative duties, including arranging prisoner exchanges. "O'Hara was a very agreeable man, very talented and witty—in fact, a specimen of a well-bred Irish gentleman," said one colleague.[14]

He was "remarkably handsome . . . a *bon vivant*, an unrivalled boon companion, one to whom society was as necessary as the air he breathed." A friend said O'Hara's face was "as ruddy and black and his teeth as white as ever."[15]

In New York, the new commander, Henry Clinton, was O'Hara's acquaintance from Minden. Clinton recognized O'Hara's military engineering ability, promoted him to brigadier general, and gave him command of "a few battalions" to defend Sandy Hook, New Jersey. A barren, fishhook-shaped sandspit, Sandy Hook pierced New York's outer harbor for five miles. Sandbars, shoals, and inevitable shipwrecks surrounded the strategically crucial position. Its defense, Clinton said, was needed "to deter the French fleet from entering the harbor." France had joined the rebelling Americans fighting the British three months earlier.[16]

O'Hara's command was short-lived. "I soon found he was the last man I should have sent with a detached corps—plans upon plans for defense; never easy, satisfied, or safe; a great, nay plausible, talker," Clinton said. In February 1779, O'Hara returned to Britain on leave. Again, his career had little future.[17]

Perhaps with the help of political friends—including a former prime minister, Augustus Henry Fitzroy, Duke of Grafton—he returned to America twenty months later commanding a brigade. His letters to Grafton from the colonies were angry, hardline, and pessimistic. He advocated a scorched-earth policy:

> America in every respect is hostile to the interests of Great Britain, as when I left this place two years since. . . . England has not only lost this country forever, but must forever consider the people of this continent as the most inveterate of her enemies. . . . Our experience should now produce an immediate resolution, either to give over so ruinous and fruitless a pursuit, or adopt that mode of war that might probably lead to permanent advantages. . . . I mean a war of desolation, as every part of the continent is exposed to invasion, where the object is only to ruin and devastate and not make establishments. This idea is shocking to humanity, but however dreadful, it must be undertaken upon the principle that I am persuaded either this country or England must be sacrificed; that they never can, or will exist at the same time.[18]

Lieutenant General Charles Cornwallis and O'Hara, both Minden veterans, renewed their acquaintance in January 1781 when O'Hara reported for duty about 145 miles upcountry from Charlestown, South Carolina (renamed Charleston after the war). Cornwallis believed that O'Hara's strength was as a field general, not as an administrator: O'Hara's brigade became the army's advance column as part of Cornwallis's new, risky strategy: He would jettison the bulk of his train—all but medical supplies, salt, and ammunition—and turn his army into a fast-moving predator that would catch and destroy the southern rebel army, led by a Rhode Island forge owner-turned-general, Nathanael Greene.

"In this situation," O'Hara wrote Grafton, "without baggage, necessaries, or provisions of any sort for officer or soldier, in the most barren inhospitable unhealthy part of North America, opposed to the most savage, inveterate perfidious cruel enemy, with zeal and with bayonets only, it was resolved to follow Greene's army to the end of the world."[19]

O'Hara's first major fight was on February 1, at Cowan's Ford, twenty miles north of Charlotte, North Carolina. He led the army in crossing the swollen Catawba River in the early hours of a "very dark and rainy" morning. The river was "broad, deep, and rapid water, full of very large rocks, the opposite shore exceedingly high and steep . . . [with] a powerful current that carried many of the strongest men down the stream, under a very heavy fire." O'Hara's horse lost its footing in the riverbed, and the current swept man and horse downstream for forty yards. But the crossing succeeded, despite four men killed and thirty-six wounded. The Americans—self-described as "Whigs"—retreated, and their commander, a militia general, was killed.[20]

The next month, deeper in North Carolina backcountry, more than two hundred miles from the coast, O'Hara fought at Guilford Courthouse. It was a two-hour battle, in dense woods, tangled underbrush, gullies, hills, and muddy cornfields, through three rebel lines spread over three-quarters of a mile. At the end of the day, the Whigs retreated, but British casualties were heavier than the rebels'. One of the fatalities was Artillery lieutenant Augustus O'Hara, described by different sources as Charles's half-brother, out-of-wedlock son, or nephew. Nearly half of O'Hara's regiment were killed or wounded. O'Hara himself suffered severe injuries to his chest and thigh. Cornwallis praised him: "After receiving two dangerous wounds, he continued in the field whilst the action lasted."[21]

O'Hara gave Grafton a blunt assessment about Guilford Courthouse: "Every part of our army was beat repeatedly. . . . The rebels were so exceedingly numerous as to be able constantly to oppose fresh troops to us, and be in force in our front, flanks, and rear." For two days after the battle, "we remained on the very ground on which it had been fought covered with dead, with dying, and with hundreds of wounded, rebels as well as our own. A violent and constant rain that lasted above forty hours made it equally impracticable to remove or administer the smallest comfort to many of the wounded."[22]

O'Hara recovered from his own wounds over the summer and rejoined Cornwallis as second-in-command. With the strategy to secure the Carolinas thwarted by the constant resupply of the rebels from Virginia, Cornwallis decided to go after those supply bases. He and his army left North Carolina in late April for Virginia—a 260-mile march to the rebel capital—leaving behind ten garrisons in the Carolinas and Georgia, including Charlestown and Savannah. A month later, he joined other British troops near Richmond.

Cornwallis was smart, daring, and tough. An enemy general described him as "a modern Hannibal." In Britain, the public recognized him as one who "fights away and beats his enemies, be they few or many."[23]

With skill and brutality, Cornwallis turned Virginia into a laboratory for O'Hara's "war of desolation." His army moved quickly and unpredictably, destroying rebel camps, property, food, and supplies, terrorizing the civilian population. One modern scholar talked of "how close Cornwallis came to subduing Virginia."[24]

Whig governor Thomas Jefferson's experience was typical. Cornwallis, he said, "destroyed all my growing crops of corn and tobacco. He burned all my barns. . . . He used . . . all my stocks of cattle, sheep, and hogs for the sustenance of his army, and carried off all the horses capable of service: Of those too young for service he cut the throats, and he burnt all the fences on the plantation, so as to leave it an absolute waste."[25]

Helping the British, "employed in different branches of the public service," were African Americans—at least three thousand.

Some, the British conscripted. Many more volunteered, having "flocked to the enemy" to escape slavery. The British used them for stealing horses for the cavalry; serving as orderlies, cooks, personal servants, spies, guides, and foragers; and building fortifications.[26]

Those who were sick were also useful—for biological warfare. About seven hundred former slaves infected with smallpox escaped to British general Alexander Leslie's lines. "I shall distribute them about the rebel plantations," he wrote Cornwallis. Black corpses and animal carcasses also were useful; they were tossed down wells to contaminate them for rebel use.[27]

In June, Clinton, concerned about a French attack on New York, ordered Cornwallis to seek and secure a safe harbor from which the British navy could operate. "With regard to a station for the protection of the king's ships," Clinton said, "I know of no place so proper as Yorktown," on the York River near the entrance to Chesapeake Bay. Cornwallis concurred, and, in August, began fortifying the town.[28]

O'Hara commanded the rear guard. His duties included making arrangements for white Loyalist refugees and figuring out what to do with the hundreds of black refugees. Both groups burdened the army's resources, but the blacks were especially problematic. Not only were they less likely to have been inoculated against smallpox, and almost certain to be returned to slavery if recaptured by their rebel "owners" and possibly punished, but they were . . . black.

O'Hara and Cornwallis traded letters trying to figure out a solution:

O'Hara: "What will you have done with the hundreds of infected Negroes, that are dying by scores every day?"

Cornwallis: "It is shocking to think of the state of the Negroes, but we cannot bring a number of sick and useless ones to this place [Yorktown]; some place must be left for them and some person of the country appointed to take charge of them to prevent their perishing."

O'Hara: "I will continue to victual [feed] the sick Negroes, above 1,000 in number. They would inevitably perish if our support was withdrawn. The people of this country are more inclined to fire upon than receive and protect a Negro whose complaint is the smallpox. The abandoning of these unfortunate beings to disease and famine, and what is worse than either, the resentment of their enraged master, I should conceive ought not to be done."

Cornwallis: "I leave it to your humanity to do the best you can for the poor Negroes . . ."

O'Hara: "We shall be obliged to leave near 400 wretched Negroes; I have passed them all over to the Norfolk side [of the river], which is the most friendly quarter in our neighbor and have begged of the people of Princess Ann and Norfolk counties to take them."[29]

O'Hara, his troops, and his refugees—minus the sick blacks—arrived in Yorktown on August 22. Cornwallis assumed his army and refugees would be supplied, if not evacuated, by the British fleet. It didn't happen.

Soon, Cornwallis was surrounded by the rebel and French armies, as well as the French fleet. Cut off from supplies, soldiers and refugees survived on "putrid meat and wormy biscuits." Half the cavalry were without weapons, and what weapons they had were mostly inferior, taken from captured or killed soldiers of the "ill-appointed" rebels. As for infantry, they "are much reduced in numbers by desertion, . . . unremitting fatigues, and by death; while those remaining are much shattered in point of constitution," a commander reported.[30]

Within the camp, smallpox, typhus, typhoid, malaria, and hunger plagued them. Sick soldiers were given "stinking salted meat and some flour or worm-eaten biscuit. These unfortunates die like flies from want, and the amputated arms and legs lay around in every corner and were eaten by dogs." Throughout the siege, a deafening, constant effective cannonade. "We had no rest or sleep, for the enemy kept up heavy firing," one soldier wrote.[31]

When the siege began, Yorktown had about sixty empty houses, its residents having been imprisoned or ordered to leave. Now, the buildings were "prodigiously shattered." Cornwallis moved his headquarters to a bunker dug into the thirty-foot-high river cliffs that Yorktown was built upon.[32]

The bombardment killed many. Everywhere, a French chaplain reported soon after the surrender, lay "carcasses of men and horses, half covered with dirt, whose moldering limbs, while they poisoned the air, struck dread and horror to the soul." Outside the camp, "almost every thicket affords you the disagreeable prospects of a wretched Negro's carcass brought to the earth by disease and famine," said a rebel officer.[33]

As for the black survivors, "We had used them to good advantage and set them free, and now, with fear and trembling, they had to face the rewards of their cruel masters," said a Hessian captain. "This harsh act had to be carried out, however, because of the scarcity of provisions."[34]

3. Rochambeau and Washington

B ESIEGED, CORNWALLIS'S ARMY SURRENDERED ON FRIDAY, October 19, 1781.

It was a French victory, made possible by a French strategy; two French fleets; French siege engineers; French artillery that pounded the British; fought largely by French soldiers, marines, and sailors who outnumbered their American allies four-to-one; and set up by a French expatriate, the Marquis de Lafayette, who commanded a small rebel force that had shadowed Cornwallis since the summer. During the siege, Whig troops captured one of two key British fortifications; the French took the other. It was a victory financed by French money that paid, armed, clothed, and propped up the Whigs.[1]

And it was French diplomacy that ordered its commander-in-chief, Jean-Baptiste Donatien de Vimeur, Comte [Count] de Rochambeau, 56, to publicly defer to the Whig general, George Washington, 49, without overtly ceding him any authority. Washington had no choice but to accept the implicit French terms.

Before his overt campaign in 1775 to become the Whig commander—he wore an army uniform to Congress to announce his availability—Washington's previous military experience included triggering a world war: In 1754, leading a small force of Virginia militia, Washington ambushed a then-enemy French army officer on a diplomatic mission to the British. Washington then failed to stop the scalping and murder by his Indian allies of several French soldiers who had surrendered. It became an international incident, setting off the Seven Years' War (French and Indian War, in America). He later surrendered to pursuing French troops after building a crude fort in an indefensible meadow. The next year, to his credit, Washington warned British general Edward Braddock about the danger of a French and Indian ambush; Braddock ignored the advice, was ambushed, and killed. Washington helped regroup the fleeing troops. In 1758, he was one of the commanders of the successful effort to retake French-held territory in the Ohio River Valley.

He was "no harum-scarum, ranting, swearing fellow, but sober, steady, and calm," said a Connecticut congressman.[2]

After the war, Washington grew wealthy. He inherited wealth, married into it, innovated productive farming techniques, used slave labor on his farms, diversified with entrepreneurial ventures, and speculated in land. He eventually owned tens of thousands of acres from the Great Dismal Swamp on the North Carolina–Virginia border to farmland in the Ohio River Valley. The greatest fortunes, he said, were made by buying low and selling high, "taking up and purchasing at very low rates the rich back lands which were thought nothing of in those days, but are now the most valuable lands we possess." Throughout his life, Washington's most frequent theme in his letters was land—"more precisely, his own land," said the editor of his papers.[3]

John Adams, who, as a congressman, promoted Washington's bid to become commander in 1775, later became a sometime critic. He asked, "Would Washington have ever been commander of the revolutionary army or president of the United States, if he had not married the rich widow of Mr. Custis?"[4]

As commanding general of the rebellion against the British, Washington had a mixed record. His deployment of troops and artillery around Boston forced the British to evacuate. His well-executed raids on Trenton and Princeton in the early years strengthened him politically, and strategically helped the rebellion survive. Once it became clear the French wanted to move against Cornwallis, Washington created the diversions and feints that allowed the two allied armies to slip past the British stronghold in New York. But he lost or failed to win every other battle: Long Island, Kip's Bay, White Plains, Fort Washington, Brandywine, Germantown, Monmouth.

He was an average general, but a superb politician, logistician, and administrator, a "spiritual and managerial genius." He outmaneuvered rivals, suppressed mutinies, chose aides and generals who were abler than he was, and somehow kept his army intact despite enlistment expirations, starvation, epidemics, and the bankruptcy of what passed for a government.[5]

But 1781 was the war's seventh year, and for most of it, Washington despaired. His army had been decimated by desertions, casualties, and lack of supplies. The rebels were broke. They engaged in check-kiting schemes to thwart creditors and buy supplies. The chief Whig financier, Robert Morris, listed the problems: "The derangement of our money affairs. The enormity of our public expenditures. The confusion in all our departments. The languor of our general system. The complexity and consequent inefficacy of our operations."[6]

In secret, Washington laid out the situation to John Laurens, 27, an aide whom Congress chose to go to France to pry away more money: "Without a foreign loan, our present force (which is but the remnant of an army) cannot be kept together . . . We are at the end of our tether, and [therefore] now or never our deliverance must come."[7]

Rochambeau also needed money. His troops couldn't diplomatically forage or steal from allied civilians. Since the American Continental army couldn't get enough food and supplies for its own use, the French needed periodic infusions of silver and other hard money. Some was supplied by his son, Donatien Marie Joseph de Vimeur, the Viscount of Rochambeau, who would later become O'Hara's prisoner-exchange counterpart. The younger Rochambeau, the assistant adjutant general, was sent back to France with his father's plea for reinforcements and money. He returned with money, but no reinforcements.[8]

That there was a strategy to rendezvous in Yorktown was no thanks to Washington. Washington obsessed about a joint land-sea attack against the British in New York, something Rochambeau and the French admiral, Grasse, thought bad strategy for reasons ranging from impregnable British positions to the difficulty of low-draft French ships entering New York's harbor. Washington,

Rochambeau said, "had scarcely another object in view but an expedition against the island of New York." When the French made it clear that their fleet would only go to Chesapeake Bay, Washington became enraged in private. An eyewitness later described Washington's "intemperate passion (which I shall not repeat)," an anger "so strikingly singular that I shall never forget it."[9]

Like O'Hara, Rochambeau had entered his country's army at an early age, fought in many battles, including Minden, and was seriously wounded several times. With Washington, he showed a diplomatic veneer; with his own men, he was gruff. One of his officers offered a mixed portrait:

"He mistrusts every one and always believes that he sees himself surrounded by rogues and idiots. This character, combined with manners far from courteous, makes him disagreeable to everybody." Still, the officer conceded "that he is wise, that he desires what is good, and that, if he is not an able administrator, he is generally very active, having an excellent glance, readily becoming acquainted with a country, and understanding war perfectly. . . . [In America], people expected to see a French fop, and they saw a thoughtful man."[10]

Washington named aide John Laurens as the Whig representative of the team that negotiated surrender terms at Yorktown. It was Laurens's reward for what had turned out to be a successful mission to France, but it also sent a symbolic message to the British: Laurens had been captured in May 1780 when a Whig army under General Benjamin Lincoln surrendered Charlestown to Henry Clinton. Clinton imposed on the rebels what were, by eighteenth-century standards, humiliating terms: The enemy's flags and banners couldn't be unfurled as they marched into imprisonment or, for officers like Laurens, paroled. Washington, through Laurens, ordered these same terms.

Laurens represented another symbolic message. The British navy had captured Laurens's father, Henry, a former president of Congress, while en route to a diplomatic mission to Holland. He was held under such harsh conditions in a British prison that he became "much emaciated." The younger Laurens hoped that Congress would demand that his father be exchanged for Cornwallis.[11]

The surrender terms required the British army and their Hessian mercenary allies to march out from Yorktown at 2 P.M. to lay down their arms. They marched past a silent, mile-long gauntlet of French soldiers and marines on the southwest side of the road, and the rebels on the northeast. "Through these lines," an officer wrote, "the whole British army marched, their drums in front beating a slow march, their colors furled and cased."[12]

Now, it was the British who sent the symbolic messages. Protocol and tradition dictated that the defeated general, Cornwallis, lead his troops to the surrender field. The British emerged from Yorktown, but without their commander.

Instead, O'Hara led the column. Cornwallis, he explained, was indisposed. Some biographers suggest that Cornwallis might indeed have been ill, "perhaps a recurrence of the fever he had contracted in North Carolina." Yorktown was "a hotbed of disease," and both Rochambeau and Lafayette had been ill at various times during the siege.[13]

Contemporaries weren't as generous. Cornwallis's absence was seen as a deliberate snub. "Cornwallis held himself back from the humiliating scene, obeying sensations which his great character ought to have stifled," said one Whig officer. A Rochambeau aide called Cornwallis's illness a "pretext." Besides, the British troops "showed the greatest scorn for the Americans." A Whig military physician felt Cornwallis was "pretending."[14]

"Elegantly mounted," O'Hara was met by Rochambeau's aide, Lieutenant Colonel Guillaume Mathieu, Comte de Dumas. O'Hara asked Dumas to point him toward Rochambeau. "The English general urged his horse forward to present his sword to the French general," Dumas remembered. This was no innocent error. The articles of capitulation specified that Washington was "commander in chief of the combined forces of America and France."[15]

Rochambeau himself guessed O'Hara's intent and nodded toward the Americans across the road. Simultaneously, Dumas intercepted O'Hara and accompanied him to Washington. Washington wasn't going to be one-upped by accepting a sword of surrender from a second-in-command. He pointed to O'Hara's counterpart, Major General Benjamin Lincoln, 48, "fat, lame, and undramatic." Lincoln, a Washington loyalist from Massachusetts, had led troops during the Boston siege, at White Plains, Saratoga, and Charlestown, South Carolina (where he surrendered). O'Hara offered Lincoln his sword; Lincoln touched it, and returned it. (Lincoln showed similar political savvy in his career after the war, suppressing, mostly peacefully, Shay's Rebellion in 1786, serving as lieutenant governor, and, finally, collector of the Port of Boston.)[16]

For the rest of the day, British soldiers—drunk, angry, melancholy, miserable, disorderly, unsoldierly, sullen, humiliated—grounded their arms. About six thousand British regulars and Hessian mercenaries became prisoners. Cornwallis was allowed to fill one ship that sailed to New York unhindered and uninspected. He filled it with Loyalists, including some blacks and deserters who feared for their lives from a vengeful rebel enemy. Most officers, including Cornwallis and O'Hara, were paroled, and returned to New York, Canada, the Caribbean, or Europe with a pledge not to fight unless and until they were exchanged for paroled or imprisoned enemy counterparts. All sides usually observed this honor system.[17]

Before parole, however, there was protocol: dining with the enemy the next day. Cornwallis continued to plead illness, so O'Hara represented him. By all accounts, he made an awkward situation easier. O'Hara is "very social and easy," said a Whig colonel. A French officer was "amazed" at how the British could be so sociable "the very day after such a catastrophe as had happened to them." He praised O'Hara who "talked a great deal and very intelligently. He has traveled wide and has an extensive acquaintance everywhere."[18]

For the foreseeable future, the war was over for Cornwallis and O'Hara. For Washington, it was only the celebration that ended.

Writing to Grafton the day after the surrender, O'Hara said, "America is irretrievably lost." But he recognized that the politicians still needed to be "persuaded," something he hoped the surrender would do. Even so, he predicted more fighting. The French would attack Charlestown. The French would take Britain's few remaining Caribbean colonies. The Spanish would join in.[19]

Clinton admitted, "This is a blow," and he expected the next round of fighting to be in South Carolina, Georgia, and the West Indies. He urged London to send "a superior fleet" to America.[20]

The Yorktown news reached London around noon on November 25, two days before George III was scheduled to speak before Parliament. George Sackville, Lord Germain, the hardline secretary of state for the colonies and day-to-day director of the war, brought the news to the prime minister, Frederick North.

North, 49, was "heavy, large, and much inclined to corpulency," a fellow MP said. "His tongue, being too large for his mouth, rendered his articulation somewhat thick, though not at all indistinct." He was nearsighted and possibly narcoleptic. Despite the frailties, he was smart, a policy wonk, "able and fluent in debate," blunting opponents' arguments with wit and humor. North was a man under pressure. The empire, a colleague wrote, "was shaken and convulsed in almost every quarter." Britain's finances were a mess because of war expenses. Enemy navies and privateers were preying on commerce.[21]

When Germain told North about Yorktown, the prime minister lost his poise and firmness "for a short time." Reacting "as he would have taken a ball in his breast," North "opened his arms, exclaiming wildly, as he paced up and down the apartment during a few minutes, 'Oh, God! It is all over!' "[22]

Germain then informed the king. Although he had "sentiments of the deepest concern," George III vowed that he and his government would continue "prosecution of the present contest."[23]

Two days later, the king expanded on that theme to Parliament. While Yorktown was "very unfortunate" and of "great concern," the cause was right, God was on their side, Britain would recover the initiative, and the war would continue: "I retain a firm confidence in the protection of Divine Providence, and a perfect conviction of the justice of my cause; and I have no doubt but that, by the concurrence and support of my parliament, by the valor of my fleets and armies, and by a vigorous, animated, and united execution of the faculties and resource of my people, I shall be enabled to restore the blessing of a safe and honorable peace to all my dominions."[24]

A new war strategy leaked to the media in the next few weeks. Instead of focusing on America—a military black hole—it would focus on America's enablers: the French especially, but also the Spanish and Dutch. It was, as one newspaper said, "the only means left for a renovation of our glory." It had the advantage of playing to Britain's strength, its navy. George III reinforced his intentions with

North on December 15: "Though internal continental operations in North America are not advisable, the prosecution of the war can alone preserve us from a most ignominious peace."[25]

Pro-government newspapers applauded the sentiment. "We must conquer America, or this country ceases to exist as a powerful commercial kingdom. The Americans are already exhausted in their finances," wrote one commentator. "This is a war of necessity." Another writer praised the new strategy. "Is the loss of Lord Cornwallis and a few thousand troops of such magnitude as to induce you to give up America? Is the loss of a finger, because it is painful, to justify the amputation of the arm? . . . It is no longer an American war, but a French war in America."[26]

In France, Holland, and Spain, the allies' belligerence was a mirror image of George III's. Vergennes, the French foreign minister, warned of complacency. "We'd make a mistake if we think that an era of peace is imminent," he wrote Lafayette. He told Lafayette that the Whigs must strengthen their army.[27]

In Holland, rebel diplomat John Adams reported that some Dutch believed that Yorktown would lead to an international peace conference. "But I cannot be of that sentiment," he said. "The English must have many more humiliations before they will agree to meet us upon equal terms, or upon any terms that we can approve."[28]

In Russia, the rebel envoy said speculation about mediation by the Russian empress was groundless. "We shall not hear much more of the mediation" until at least another year of military operations had concluded.[29]

In Paris, Franklin warned Congress to continue military efforts. The British, "tho' somewhat humbled at present," he said, might find that "a little success may make them as insolent as ever." And to Washington, Franklin wrote, "The English seem not to know either how to continue the war, or to make peace with us."[30]

In America, the reaction to Yorktown was three-fold: speculation about Britain's next military offensive; planning for an allied offensive; and concern that politicians—and potential new recruits— would grow complacent.

Whig general Nathanael Greene, in South Carolina, reminded the Virginia governor that the enlistments of Continental soldiers from that state expired in December. British troops in Charlestown outnumbered Greene's, and the enemy was "ready to take advantage of our weak state." To Congress, Greene said, "I cannot help dreading . . . some untoward blow." To a subordinate, Greene worried that the British might be reinforced, in which case, "we may have active operations again." To the governor of North Carolina, where the British still occupied Wilmington, Greene predicted that "the enemy . . . will be encouraged to prosecute the war."[31]

Washington shared Greene's concern about complacency: "My greatest fear [is that Congress] may think our work too nearly closed, and will fall into a state of languor and relaxation. . . . Our grand project is to be prepared in every point for war."[32]

He, Greene, and other military leaders shared a second concern—a diplomatic one. Eventually, there would be a truce. Without a complete British capitulation, a truce or treaty could result in an agreement that allowed Britain to keep the territory it held. This kind of agreement—in diplomatic language, *uti possidetis*—would mean the British would keep New York City, Charlestown, Savannah, Wilmington, strategic frontier forts from Detroit to upstate New York, East Florida, and a key post in Maine.[33]

Peace negotiations began in April 1782. But throughout the summer and fall, fighting and skepticism continued. Richard Henry Lee, a former Virginia congressman, said, "I fear that our enemies have not yet drank deep enough of the cup of misfortune." The British continued to interfere with inland water commerce. "These crews are made up of refugees, negroes, and such as fly from civil justice, who under the sanction of British commissions are warring upon women and children, stealing clothes and negroes, and committing every outrage."[34]

The Whig negotiators in Paris were also skeptical about peace, even in fall 1782. "We may, and we may not, have peace this winter," said Jay.[35]

Washington wrote John Laurens, then attached to Greene's army, that the British navy continued to capture American ships, while in the west the British and their "savage allies" were "scalping and burning the frontiers." To another former aide, he wrote that "the king will push the war as long as the nation will find men or money admits not of a doubt in my mind."[36]

Washington's own preparations for continued fighting began at Yorktown. He urged French admiral Grasse to participate in a joint land–sea attack against Wilmington and Charlestown. Grasse refused, citing the impending hurricane season and his commitments in the Caribbean. "Every argument and persuasive had been used with the French admiral to induce him to aid the combined army in an operation against Charlestown, I am obliged to submit," Washington told Greene."[37]

Another part of Washington's plan was for Congress to plead for more money and troops from the states, although he was skeptical the states had the "abilities and inclinations" to supply them. He told the French he would be grateful for the appearance in spring 1782 of a "decisive naval force" and, of course, more "pecuniary aid from your generous nation."[38]

Washington returned with most of his army to the New York area to keep Clinton in check. For Greene's southern army, the best Washington could do was to send "a respectable reinforcement."[39]

PART TWO

The South

4. Rice and the Low Country

THE GREAT DISMAL SWAMP, INTO WHICH LAND SPECULATOR George Washington had sunk money in the 1760s, starts about fifty miles south of Yorktown and spills over the North Carolina border. Soon after that, the coastline turns sharply to the southwest. The next five hundred miles, and for about fifty miles inland, is low country—a coastal plain. "It may be said of this place," a 1671 traveler reported, "as we read of the Land of Canaan . . . it is a land flowing with milk and honey."[1]

Scores of rivers—the Ashley, Stono, Combahee, Edisto, Pee Dee, Cape Fear, Neuse, Santee, Cooper, Ashepoo, Chehaw, Black, Coosawhatchie, and Savannah, among others—along with countless creeks flood and feed swamps and marshes, leaving rich soil and habitat. In estuaries, fresh waters mix with seawater, even thirty miles inland, raising and lowering the river levels. Between the rivers is dry ground, used as early as 1688 by white settlers for cattle and pigs, cowpens and pigpens. There are pine forests, live oak, palmettos, cypress trees. Indians grew corn, beans, squash, and ate seaweed and wild plants. Whites and Indians alike hunted quail, wild turkeys, deer, and ducks. They fished and picked oysters, shrimp, and clams.[2]

But the low country wasn't Canaan. It was a hot, humid land that got forty to fifty inches of rain a year. It bred thousands of insect species, many of them parasites, no-see-ums, greenhead and deer flies, and mosquitoes. Yellow fever and malaria devastated settlers. There were bobcats, foxes, rattlesnakes, water moccasins, alligators. Norway rats immigrated from ships. The earliest whites were "in fear of the wolves, which are too plenty."[3]

Descriptions from diaries of Whig soldiers from the North—the reinforcements Washington sent after Yorktown—complete the picture:

Lieutenant William Feltman: "We were obliged to cross a number of very disagreeable swamps. . . . We were obliged to wade through them knee-deep. . . . Camped in the wilderness among a fine parcel of pines and surrounded by swamps . . . The water here is very bad, no springs or rivulets, all ponds and swamps, which are full of little insects." Later, a servant "killed a very large rattlesnake. It was above six feet long, and of a prodigious thickness." Day after day of bad weather came in April, and Feltman's typical entry was "A very rainy and very disagreeable day. We were obliged to keep in our tents."[4]

Lieutenant John Bell Tilden: "The roads horrid bad the greater part of the way, with mud and water to the knees." The mosquito bites are "intolerable."[5]

Lieutenant William McDowell: "The roads exceedingly good and straight. See a number of elegant houses, a small distance from the road and fine avenues leading to them, and a large rice plantation."[6]

Major Ebenezer Denny: "Rice farms around this neighborhood—the fields almost all under water; immense quantities of ducks; excellent sport at times. . . . Was on picket the night before we reached Ashley [River]; got exceedingly wet—it rained all night. Marched next morning in wet clothes 12 miles . . . laid up with fever—carried to hospital. . . . Ashley River low; full of alligators."[7]

It had taken nearly a generation for settlers to understand the low country—dangerous and lush, impressive and harsh—tame it, and monetize it. Tenants and agents of the original seventeenth-century British landowners experimented with crops, trying to find the optimum commercial product that could survive the floods, weather, heat and humidity, and occasional frosts and droughts. They planted olives, almonds, dates, indigo, cocoa, tobacco, pepper, ginger, cotton, sugar, grapes, corn, capers, currants, oranges, mulberry, and fruit.[8]

By the mid-1720s, there was a clear winner: rice. It wasn't an obvious choice. The planters began by growing rice in dry, upland soil, relying on rainfall. With the help of West African-born slaves (some historians argue) who had grown rice in their native lands, planters eventually shifted to coastal swamps that could be irrigated using man-made—that is, *slave*-made—paddies, dikes, gates, and tidal flows. Once the planters and their slaves figured out how to grow and mill it efficiently, the rice economy grew exponentially. South Carolina exported ten thousand pounds of rice in 1698. By 1726, the colony exported ten million pounds.[9]

As rice production grew, so did African slave importation: Rice farming required labor-intensive work. A South Carolina doctor, unsympathetic with slavery, wrote that the "tilling, planting, hoeing, reaping, threshing, pounding have all been done merely by the poor slaves here." A white merchant believed in the logic of slavery: "I am positive that the commodity can't be produced by white people because the work is too laborious, the heat very intense, and the whites can't work in the wet at that season as Negroes do to weed rice." By 1765, about ninety thousand black slaves lived in South Carolina—nearly seventy percent of the population.[10]

This was the low country when the Revolution began: Wealthy white planters owned the land. They imported, bought, and bred black slaves, who grew the rice. They traded with merchants and shippers in Charlestown, Savannah, and Wilmington, who shipped and sold the rice to Europe.

5. General Leslie Comes
to Charlestown

WHILE CORNWALLIS AND O'HARA FOUGHT AND RAIDED IN Virginia during late summer and early fall 1781, Clinton, the British commander-in-chief, grew concerned about Charlestown and the rest of the South. The ranking officer who replaced Cornwallis was a colonel who had arrived with reinforcements only in June. This colonel, Clinton said, was "altogether deficient in local knowledge." Moreover, Clinton anticipated a "powerful" French-and-rebel offensive sometime in 1782.[1]

He ordered Lieutenant General Alexander Leslie, 51, to sail from New York and assume command in the Southern District. Unlike O'Hara, whose career lurched between lows and highs on three continents, Leslie's rise to command was linear and North American. The son of a Scottish peer, Leslie was named after an ancestor—a successful general who led armies in the seventeenth century. When he was twenty-nine, the then-Major Leslie married. His wife, Mary Tullidiph, died a year later after giving birth to a daughter.[2]

He received regular promotions in the army. He was a regimental commander and lieutenant colonel when he arrived in Boston, Massachusetts, in 1768. For the next fifteen years, he would live and fight in the American colonies.

He was, a fellow officer said, "a genteel little man, lives well, and drinks good claret." Leslie's gentility also impressed the sister of a Boston customs collector, who found him "an amiable and good man, the father of his choir and the soldiers who all look up to him with respect and affection. He's of a noble Scottish family, but distinguished more by his humanity and affability." These weren't idle words. The woman described Leslie's predecessor as "devoted to self and self-gratification . . . and universally despised." Even the rebels conceded his grace. A Boston newspaper publisher who certainly knew of Leslie, by reputation if not personally, said he was "brave, sensible, polite" and conducted himself "with a dispatch and propriety worthy of his character."3

At one point, Leslie was posted to Halifax, but by the summer of 1772, with anti-Crown agitators creating civil unrest, he returned to Boston. In late 1774, anti-British rebels secured some old cannon, smuggled in new artillery from Europe, and were converting old ships' cannon into field pieces. The British knew this because of their superb intelligence. If the rebels were a majority of the population, that majority wasn't yet overwhelming; many residents saw it as their duty to keep the government informed.4

So the British knew precisely where the cannon were: in a blacksmith's shop, separated by a single-span drawbridge on the North River immediately across from Salem, a wealthy port of five thousand people, twenty-five miles north of Boston. (In 1790, it was Massachusetts's second-largest city, and the nation's seventh largest.)

Lieutenant General Thomas Gage, the royal governor and commander, ordered Leslie and a 246-man detachment to make a surprise raid and seize the cannon. To achieve surprise, they sailed from Boston a little after midnight on February 25, 1775. They arrived off Marblehead, five miles from Salem, and timed their landing for when most residents would be at afternoon church services. The plan didn't work. By the time Leslie arrived at the North River, rebels had spread the alarm, raised the drawbridge, and dispersed the cannon.

Abusive Salem residents and rebel militia from as far as forty miles away soon outnumbered the British. According to one rebel account, when Leslie saw the raised bridge, "he stamped and swore, ordering the bridge to be immediately lowered." A rebel taunted him back: "You had better be damned than fire! You have no right to fire without further orders! If you do fire, you will all be dead men." A Quaker tried to calm Leslie by asking if he understood the seriousness of the situation. The mob shouted, "Soldiers, red jackets, lobster coats, cowards, damnation to your government!" Leslie threatened to take over homes to quarter his troops unless the mob lowered the bridge. One rebel prevented Leslie's troops from seizing a boat—the last on the Salem side of the river—by staving its bottom. Then, he bared his chest and invited a soldier to bayonet him. The soldier pricked him and drew a little blood.[5]

By now it was 5 P.M. The sun was going down. A Loyalist clergyman arrived and offered to mediate the standoff. Soon the parties reached a compromise: The rebels would lower the drawbridge—a useless symbol, since the cannon had been removed much earlier—and Leslie would uphold royal honor by marching across the bridge and back.

The start of the war would wait—for fifty-two days. Then, on April 19, during another mission to seize rebel arms (in which Leslie didn't participate), forty-nine rebels and seventy-three British soldiers would die along the road from Boston through Lexington, Concord, and back.

Leslie's career became a map of the war. He helped plan the defense of Boston, and in February 1776 led a raid, capturing six rebels. But the British finally evacuated the city, and after playing a key role, Leslie was promoted to brigadier general.

The war shifted to New York and New Jersey, where the British overwhelmed the rebels. Leslie led light infantry at the Battle of Long Island and the landing at Kip's Bay in Manhattan. He commanded troops on Harlem Heights, where, on September 16, his men were surprised by the rebels' flanking movement and forced to fall back until reinforcements arrived. The next month, in White Plains, Leslie's troops assaulted a strong rebel position, but were thrown back in heavy fighting. But the British won the field, and the rebels retreated to New Jersey. Leslie commanded troops in January 1777 at Maidenhead, New Jersey, where his men failed to detect Washington and his army passing nearby on the way to a successful attack on Princeton. (A Leslie nephew was killed there.)[6]

The next year, Leslie was in New York commanding the strategically important Staten Island. He was rewarded in April 1779 with another promotion, this time to major general. For the rest of the war, Leslie's assignments took him southward. He participated in the capture of Savannah and Charlestown in late 1779 and spring

1780, and briefly commanded Charlestown before returning to New York. Later in 1780, he commanded troops raiding rebel supply lines in Virginia, and he established a base in Portsmouth.

In the wake of a British debacle and defeat at King's Mountain on the inland border between North and South Carolina, Clinton ordered Leslie to the Carolinas. He arrived in Charlestown before Christmas, and joined Cornwallis's main army in mid-January 1781. He was with Cornwallis at Cowan's Ford on February 1. There, like O'Hara, Leslie nearly drowned. At the Guilford Courthouse in March, he commanded the British right wing. Although he didn't figure as prominently as O'Hara, Cornwallis praised him nonetheless: "I have been particularly indebted to Major General Leslie for his gallantry and exertion in the action, as well as his assistance in every other part of the service."[7]

As Cornwallis prepared to move north into Virginia, Leslie's health deteriorated, and he received permission to return to New York to recuperate. Once recovered, Clinton ordered him to assume command in Georgia and the Carolinas. He was experienced—and experienced in the South. On November 8, 1781, Leslie arrived by frigate in Charlestown to take command.[8]

With the defeat at Yorktown, the British occupied peripheries and enclaves.

In the north, their positions in Canada were secure; the last serious rebel incursion, in 1775–1776, ended in a debacle. On Penobscot Bay in Maine (then part of Massachusetts), the British manned a small fort. On the frontier—from Lake Ontario and upstate New York to Georgia—most Indians allied themselves with the British, who pledged to prevent incursions by land-greedy rebels. The British also controlled frontier forts on the Great Lakes. South of Georgia was the small colony of East Florida, centered in St. Augustine. Clinton's headquarters was in strongly fortified New York—although he maintained an ongoing fear of a coordinated operation by the rebels and the French navy.

By fall 1780, the British had largely pacified the South: not just the low country, but all of Georgia and the Carolinas. A battle-filled year later, when Leslie took command, the British maintained positions only within radii of Wilmington, North Carolina, Charlestown, and Savannah. Charlestown was the key. With more than twelve thousand residents in 1775, it was British North America's fourth-largest city, and the South's economic center.

Leslie found a dire situation. In North Carolina, the rebels threatened Wilmington. In Georgia, an aggressive enemy general, Anthony Wayne, was reported to be on his way. Wayne's superior, Nathanael Greene, had forced Cornwallis to leave the Carolinas, and now he threatened Charlestown itself. In East Florida, the governor told Leslie he anticipated an attack by Spain, the French ally that controlled the Gulf Coast and New Orleans. Another report said the Spanish would recruit Creek Indians as allies.[9]

The rebel armies were strong and growing—at least 2,500 Continental army regulars, according to British intelligence, plus experienced state militia. What the British didn't know was the whereabouts of key rebel generals and how many reinforcements they were getting post-Yorktown. If the French navy coordinated an assault with the rebels on any of the cities, the British positions would be untenable.[10]

Leslie found 3,500 regulars in South Carolina fit for duty. Savannah, Wilmington, and St. Augustine had roughly seven hundred, five hundred, and 450 regulars, respectively, plus small bands of Loyalist militia. The towns were indefensible at those troop levels. Wilmington's situation was urgent, as rebel troops were on the march. Throughout the low country, 2,300 British regulars in total were sick or recovering from wounds. Desertion caused more erosion. Hessian mercenaries, especially, deserted daily, and the British refused to trust them as advance guards. Loyalist militia disappeared.[11]

Refugees crowded into the four towns. Rebels plundered Loyalist plantations and seized Loyalist property—that is, the slaves who made the plantations profitable—for use as bounty: three slaves offered for every new rebel recruit. Food became scarce. The rebel forces pressured land the British used for forage. Rebel privateers squeezed supply ships.[12]

South Carolina's royal lieutenant governor said that while Leslie's arrival gave residents "fresh spirits," the rebels threatened a blockade and subjected Loyalists in the countryside to "violence and plunder." Spies abounded, and the purchases of food and wood "drains the town of ready money." Leslie reported the same to Clinton: "The numbers of loyal inhabitants and of helpless refugees, with their women and children, is very great. They are burdens that will soon become very serious . . . Provisions is an object of so great importance that unless the inhabitants get some supply, they must all leave the town[Charlestown]."[13]

A month later, Leslie went into greater detail: "The whole of the country is against us but some helpless [Loyalist] militia with a number of officers, women, children, Negroes, etc. Add to this the refugees from North Carolina and many from Virginia on parole to feed, clothe and support, many of them formerly in affluent circumstances and now are destitute. . . . I must get my heart steeled. It is a most unpleasant situation." Disease decimated Leslie's troops. He ran down the roll call of his senior officers: "Colonel Balfour expects to go away . . . General Gould has been confined to his room ever since my arrival . . . General Knoblock is also ill . . . General Bose (a most respectable man) manages his Hessians, and that is all. From wounds and sickness, a great many officers of the last-arrived regiments are going home."[14]

Three days into 1782, Leslie summarized his situation to London: "It is with much concern that I am obliged to inform your Lordship of the almost total revolt of this Province."[15]

6. The Deputy Savior

T
HE REBEL GENERAL, NATHANAEL GREENE, 40, HAD HIS OWN
problems. He was Washington's most trusted general, but not
because of military success. Greene was "neither the most wise, the
most brave, nor the most patriotic of counselors," said one rival.
Asthmatic, often ill, and with a bad leg that made him walk with a
limp, he didn't look like a soldier. To some, he disrespected civilian
authority. He left an impression of "belittling and sneering . . . not
only undignified and petulant, but unwise and most unfortunate. . . .
He assumed a grand air of importance, superiority, and patronage,
and in a manner somewhat at least as that of a dictator."[1]

Southern Whigs sarcastically called him "the Deputy Savior."
These complaints reached Congress. "Have you heard," asked one
congressman of another, "a report which has been whispered here,
and the truth of which I cannot assent to, concerning the unpopu-
larity of General Greene with his army?"[2]

Greene fought every year of the war and never won a battle. At
a crucial time on Long Island in August 1776, he had been a no-
show, suffering from a life-threatening fever. The Whigs were routed. While he argued that preservation of the army was more important than saving New York, he caused the surrender of its last
stronghold there. "I cannot conceive the garrison to be in any great
danger," he advised Washington. Six days later, its three-thousand
men surrendered to the British.[3]

His experience was shaped in a Rhode Island iron foundry that
specialized in forging anchors. It was a successful business, and the

extended Greene family was prominent. (A cousin was the Rhode Island governor.) Greene drifted from his family's Quaker religion, and at one point was suspended from his meetinghouse for going to a "public resort"—a tavern.[4]

While both Washington and Greene were unschooled and large-ly self-taught, Washington learned his military skills from the expe-rience of fighting in the Seven Years' War; Greene learned his from books. "I lament the want of a liberal education," he wrote. "I feel the mist [of] ignorance."[5]

He opposed the British for a traditional New England reason: The British cracked down on smugglers who avoided customs duties. In 1772, a revenue schooner, the *Gaspée*, seized a boat smuggling cargo for the Greene family business. Rhode Islanders later attacked the *Gaspée* and burned it. The action contributed to increasing tensions. As those tensions climaxed in the Boston area, Greene joined a local Rhode Island militia unit. To his "mortification," his fellow soldiers refused to elect him as an officer, citing his limp, which was "a blem-ish" to the unit. But Greene stayed with the unit as a private. When fighting began in April 1775, he found himself in a different position. Rhode Island formed a 1,500-man army to support the Massachusetts rebels, and the legislature named Greene, a private, to be its general. Family connections and his own service in the legisla-ture notwithstanding, Greene projected persuasive intangibles.[6]

It wasn't the first time. A year before, he had persuaded Catharine "Caty" Littlefield to marry him. Littlefield was about twenty; Greene, thirty-two. "Her power of fascination was absolute-ly irresistible," wrote an early biographer. During and after the war, she would attract men wherever she went, but to Greene, she would be "my dear angel." (A jealous Philadelphia matron suggested Caty's marriage to former ironmonger Nathanael was evidence of her class: "I think I hear the clink of the iron on the anvil at every step she takes.")[7]

Washington found other intangibles in Greene. He was "much in my confidence, so intimately acquainted with my ideas, with our strength and our weaknesses, with everything respecting the Army. . . . He deserves the greatest respect, and much regard is due to his opinions."[8]

The general of the Rhode Island Army became the youngest brigadier general in the Continental army. "His knowledge is intuitive," wrote General Henry Knox. "He came to us the rawest and most untutored being I ever met with; but in less than twelve months, he was equal in military knowledge to any general officer in the army, and very superior to most of them."[9]

After New York, he commanded troops at the battles in Trenton in 1776, and Princeton, Brandywine, and Germantown in 1777. In early 1778, Washington, desperate for supplies, named Greene quartermaster general. Greene reluctantly accepted. "Nobody ever heard of a quartermaster in history," he told Washington. He proved tough and competent.[10]

In fall 1780, Washington ordered Greene to take on a desperate situation. British generals Clinton and Cornwallis had defeated two Whig armies in the South. Britain controlled the backcountry and the low country. Greene became commander-in-chief of the Southern Department.

"I think I am giving you a general," Washington told South Carolina's Whig governor.[11]

When Greene arrived, he wrote Caty, and was only half-joking about what he found: "I arrived here the second of this month and have been in search of the Army I am to command, but without much success, having found nothing but a few half-starved soldiers who are remarkable for nothing but poverty and distress."[12]

Cornwallis found Greene to be "as dangerous as Washington; he is vigilant, enterprising, and full of resources. With but little hope of gaining any advantage over him, I never feel secure when encamped in his neighborhood."[13]

Greene's counterpunching, ill-provisioned, amateur army forced Cornwallis to retreat to Virginia and, eventually, Yorktown. "We fight, get beat, rise, and fight again," Greene said. "The whole country is one continued scene of blood and slaughter." He described his strategy: "There are few generals that run oftener or more lustily than I have done. But I have taken care not to run too far; and commonly have run as fast forward as backward to convince our enemy that we were like a crab that could run either way." General Knox summarized Greene's accomplishment: "Without an army, without means, without anything, he has performed wonders."[14]

Now, in November 1781, Greene faced a new opponent in Leslie, as well as the challenge of maintaining an army. The British outnumbered Continental army regulars. Indian and Tory raids discouraged residents from leaving home to join the Whig militia. Soldiers left the army to go home to plant crops. Those who stayed lacked muskets. They lacked salt, cattle, bacon, spirits. They lacked clothing. There was neither money to pay for provisions nor money to pay the soldiers. The air dripped of mutiny, and Greene executed one sergeant for inciting one. Men deserted daily. British and Loyalist cavalry raided the countryside, stealing (or foraging, depending on perspective) "every species of property, Negroes, plate, household furniture, horses, carriages, cattle, etc."[15]

"Our usual dish—a large plate of rice and little salt," wrote a lieutenant. "This morning, six of the 2nd Battalion deserted . . . but what can we expect in their situation, without clothes and pay for two years? . . . On the road I killed an alligator seven-feet long. . . . This day, I mounted guard and was almost eat up with the mosquitos."[16]

Greene's letters describe woe after woe, and he sent his complaints to anyone he thought might help:

To the secretary of war: "You can have little idea of the confusion and disorder which prevails among the southern states."[17]

To Washington: "We are in a poor situation to contend with a very superior force. Our men are almost naked for want of overalls and shirts, and the great part of the Army, barefoot. We have no rum or prospect of any. . . . We were four weeks without ammunition. . . .

"We are remote from support and supplies of every kind. No large bodies of militia can be hastily called together here, nor can supplies of any kind be had, but with the greatest difficulty. We have 300 men now without arms, and twice that number so naked as to be unfit for duty but in cases of desperation. Not a rag of clothing has arrived to us this winter. Indeed, our prospects are really deplorable."[18]

To Congress: "The enemy threaten us daily with an attack. What have we *not* to fear with a very inferior army . . . ? Our force is daily diminished . . . The picture is too disagreeable to dwell upon."[19]

To South Carolina's governor: "One day we are without beef, the next without rice, and some days without either."[20]

To the superintendent of finance: "The service in this country has become disagreeable even to the officers. The choking situation of the men . . . The badness of provision, the poorest of beef and rice, the exhausted state of the country, which affords them nothing but their rations and very bad water and the want of money, which prevents persons from bringing anything to the army for sale, are circumstances which keep the minds of the officers continually in a petulant and discontented disposition."[21]

To an army provisioner: "The states have taken up an idea that the Continental army can subsist upon air."[22]

To Pennsylvania's chief executive: "Virginia and North Carolina governors say they can't requisition supplies. They both appear like two great overgrown babies who have got out of temper and who have been accustomed to great indulgence."[23]

Greene's and Leslie's South was a dictionary of eigteenth-century horrors: impure water, infection, vermin-infested clothes, malnutrition, exhaustion, fear of inoculation, heat exhaustion, rheumatic fever, jaundice, pneumonia, pleurisy, dysentery, smallpox, flu, sexually transmitted diseases, typhus, scurvy, typhoid fever, tetanus, worms, yellow fever (the "black vomit"), scabies, and malaria. Treatments often made things worse, from physician bans on drinking water when sweating, to bleeding and use of mercury. Old and new armament technology—tomahawks, bayonets, grapeshot, soft lead musket bullets that shredded flesh, cannonballs, powder burns—created terrible wounds. While longtime residents had some immunity to yellow fever and resistance to malaria, most Whig and British regulars had none. They died in epidemic numbers.[24]

"Men die very fast," wrote a Whig major. "Hospitals crowded, and great many sick in camp. Deaths so frequent, the funeral ceremony dispensed with." Greene himself became "exceedingly sick" in September 1782. That month, he wrote Leslie seeking permission for another Whig general to pass through British lines to a coastal island for the "benefit of the sea air" to recover from his own "dangerous fever." Leslie granted the request. Leslie's own men were equally incapacitated. In one British unit of nearly 2,300, more than forty percent took ill.[25]

"This has been one of the sickliest seasons known this 30 years," Greene wrote in reporting the deaths of two hundred men. "The only consolation and security we have had [is] the enemy has suffered no less than we."[26]

7. The "Bloodiest, Cruel War"

GREENE AND LESLIE FACED ANOTHER MUTUAL CHALLENGE: unexpected, brutish fighting. The methodical terrorism that became the southern war between Tory and Whig militias obliterated the eighteenth-century courtesies and rules that regular armies observed.

Ten months before Yorktown—where the allies hosted dinners for the defeated generals—O'Hara wrote about the kind of war he had seen in the South. "I cannot even hint . . . upon the scene before me, which are beyond description wretched, every misery which the bloodiest cruel war ever produced . . . The violence of the passions of these people are beyond every curb of religion and humanity. They are unbounded, and every hour exhibits, dreadful, wanton mischiefs, murders, and violence of every kind, unheard of before."[1]

The British commander in Wilmington reported, "This country is in a glorious situation for cutting one another's throats." Rebel soldiers, said a Tory officer, were "Goths and Vandals," having "murdered every Loyalist they found whether in arms or at home." After an incident in which rebels burned a British hospital and reportedly forced injured soldiers to "expire in the swamps," Leslie's adjutant protested that this "is a species of barbarity hitherto unknown in civilized nations."[2]

Even a Whig officer conceded that "scarce a day passes but some poor deluded Tory is put to death at his door." A Yorktown veteran and Whig legislator said the brutality was mutual. "The outrage and cruelty of the British is beyond description, and the inveterate hatred and spirit of vengeance which they have excited in the breasts of our citizens is such as you can form no idea of," he wrote. "The very females talk as familiarly of shedding blood and destroying the Tories as the men do."[3]

South Carolina governor John Rutledge summarized the Whig grievances: Not only did South Carolinians feel the "common calamities" of war, but they suffered from "the wanton and savage manner in which it has been prosecuted." Many residents were confined on prison ships. Their properties were looted. "Many who had surrendered as prisoners of war were killed in cold blood." Others were turned over to Indians—"savages"—and tortured to death. The British raped women. They burned churches. They destroyed homes of "widows, the aged, and infirm." They "disgraced the profession of a British soldier, and fixed indelible stigmas of rapine cruelty, perfidy, and profaneness on the British name."[4]

"You can have little idea how the war has raged here. It has operated like a consuming fire and has hardly left a green thing," Greene wrote a friend. To Caty, he said: "With us, the difference between Whig and Tory is little more than a division of sentiment; but here they persecute each other with little less than savage fury."[5]

One account describes a Whig dragoon who was shot and killed. The British parade his scalp through Savannah, then mangle and disfigure his body, and order that it remain unburied. Black people, "more humanized," steal the corpse and bury it. The British offer a reward for the capture of these criminals. German Moravian settlers complain about Whigs who "seized oats, pottery, corn, and whatever came to hand," robbing and beating up farmers and their wives. A Whig general says the British treat prisoners poorly, holding them in cages without room to stand or sit, and without adequate food. The British respond with accusations in kind. Salisbury, North Carolina, residents testify about Whig militia who committed "numberless barbarities, assassinations, murders, and robberies." The rebels arbitrarily seize men and murder them on the spot or jail them. Others "have been hanged up two or three times until almost dead, and then shot by way of diversion. . . . Women and children have been tortured, hung up and strangled, cut down, and hung up again, sometimes branded with brands or other hot irons in order to extort confessions from them." A British officer stops a rebel woman in Charlestown "as she was innocently walking out one morning."

He orders a "Negro fellow" to kiss her. In Cross Creek, North Carolina, rebels exact revenge on a Loyalist widow. "They have taken every article of clothing and every means of subsistence from the widow and the children, and have left them to the cold merciless hand of charity." A boy is bayoneted by British troops who believe he's a spy. Whig soldiers find him the next day. As he dies, he explains he was looking at the soldiers out of curiosity. "The sight of this unoffending boy butchered," says one Whig, "relieved me of my distressful feelings for the slaughter of the Tories, and I desired nothing so much as the opportunity of participating in their destruction." Alexander Shannon, a Tory, is captured and killed by rebel militia in retaliation for a murder. Shannon's killing, concedes a militiaman, didn't follow "the rules of law" but was justified because "the country was almost drowned in the blood of her citizens by barbarous murders, not done by the British, but by the Tories."[6]

In another account, a Loyalist captain and his men seize fourteen rebel soldiers and execute them. The Loyalists decapitate the rebel captain, then sever both hands of another man before killing him. Whigs torture a Tory captain while hanging him. "In his struggles while dying, he attempted several times to take hold of the limbs of the tree on which he was hanged; and it afforded them high amusement to beat down his hands with their whips and sticks. His body remained hanging for three days." A wounded Whig lies on a battlefield for thirty hours before friends find him. As he dies, he tells them that a Tory came by—a neighbor—"and instead of giving him a little water, for which he craved, to quench his raging thirst, kicked him and cursed him as a rebel." In Charlestown, the British throw two women suspected of spying into the same cellar as rebel prisoners and British felons. It was "a damp, unwholesome place, which occasioned amongst the prisoners much sickness, and some deaths. It was a horrid place."[7]

The southern experience was a "war of extermination," said Whig John Marshall, a Valley Forge veteran (and future chief justice).[8]

Another Whig veteran, General William Moultrie, spent two years as a prisoner. "Each party oppressed the other as much as they possibly could . . . Although they had been friends, neighbors, and brothers, they had no feelings for each other, and no principles of humanity left. . . . The conduct of those two parties was a disgrace to human nature."[9]

The result: devastation, depopulation, desolation. "All was gloomy," said a traveling pastor. "Not a person was to be met with in the roads." Moultrie was struck by the absence of animals. "Not the vestiges of horses, cattle, hogs, or deer, etc., was to be found. The squirrels and birds of every kind were totally destroyed. . . . No living creature was to be seen except now and then a few [buzzards] . . . picking the bones of some unfortunate fellows who had been shot or cut down and left in the woods above the ground."[10]

This was the South that Greene and Leslie were ordered to command.

Greene based his military strategy on a simple principle: Distrust the British. Even after spring 1782, when rumors of peace agreements, evacuations, and ceasefires came to him from Congress and Washington in the North, and from Leslie and intelligence reports in Charlestown, Greene maintained three objectives: Preserve his army, "cover this country"—that is, pacify Loyalists—and "drive the enemy from their strongholds."[11]

Greene was concerned that a peace treaty would be negotiated on the basis of *uti possidetis*. He intended to force the British from the South before their positions were preserved by treaty. Greene also was concerned that easing military pressure on the British in America would allow the enemy to focus resources on defeating the French. If that happened, the British would return in force. Moreover, it would be "dishonorable and perfidious" to ally France.[12]

Two months after Washington reported that the British would end their offensive war and evacuate the South, Greene pushed back. "I am not agreed with your Excellency in opinion that the enemy mean to evacuate this country; on the contrary I am fully convinced they do not. They are repairing their works, have lately paid off their militia, and engaged them for a further term of service."[13]

By late summer 1782, Washington admitted that he had been too optimistic, and paraphrased Franklin: The British are "unable to carry on the war and too proud to make peace."[14]

But Greene would get no major reinforcements. Washington told him to focus solely on "confining the enemy to their lines, and preventing them from carrying their ravages into the country." Given the poor condition of Greene's army, there would be no major battles, no turning points, no sieges, no ousting the British from Charlestown. Greene shared his frustration with a friend: "Our operations this campaign are as insipid as they were important the last."[15]

In Charlestown, Leslie's strategies changed with his orders. Clinton had originally ordered Leslie to save Charlestown at all costs. To do this, Leslie pulled in his troops from far-flung, indefensible positions almost as soon as he arrived in November. He strengthened a defensive line at Quarter House, a narrow part of the Charlestown Peninsula six miles north of the city proper, and it became "one of the best-fortified field positions imaginable." And he abandoned outposts such as Monck's Corner, thirty-five miles north of the city. The day Leslie arrived, he ordered Wilmington to be abandoned. The troops there hadn't even heard about Cornwallis's surrender. And Leslie warned Clinton that he wouldn't be able to help Savannah or St. Augustine if they were attacked without jeopardizing Charlestown.[16]

Islands in the immediate Charlestown area, however, were important. Leslie established new posts on them and pledged "to keep the islands as long as I can, as our only hope of supplies to this town depends upon them."[17]

Anticipating that the contraction would cause an outcry among Loyalists, Leslie publicly pledged that the British were there to stay. He promised Loyalists they could rely on "speedy and effectual support" by the British army. "In every event and situation," he said, Loyalist "interests and security shall be considered as inseparably connected with those of his Majesty's troops." As for anyone who previously promised to support the Crown, but later became rebels, "the severest punishment shall be inflicted."[18]

To give his words credibility, he ordered "frequent excursions of cavalry, sustained by infantry, to irritate the enemy and harass their detached posts." He conceded these raids resulted in "no decided consequences," but they nonetheless "were distressing to the rebels, gave confidence to the King's troops, and served to animate a defensive situation."[19]

Leslie also had a personal strategy: After 14 years in America, ten of them consecutive, seven of them at war, he wanted out. He begged Clinton to relieve him of command. His health was "much impaired from having served the whole war. . . . From sickness and accidents, by falls, dislocations, etc., my health is unfit to stand the summer." The "perplexity" of problems related to Loyalist civilians was "so much beyond my abilities to arrange that I declare myself unequal to the task." The stress was fierce: "From morning to night I have memorials and petitions full of distress." His mother, 82, was "going into her grave, and only wishing to see me." His only daughter "now depends on my return to Europe" because she refused to get married until her father returns. "My country has got her full share out of me," Leslie said.[20]

Clinton was unsympathetic. Leslie stayed.

Leslie's orders to defend and maintain Charlestown suddenly changed in May 1782. Clinton had resigned, and the pro-war government was gone, both victims of Yorktown. The new commander, Lieutenant General Guy Carleton, arrived in New York with new orders: Abandon Charlestown, Savannah, and New York. Consolidate the British North American army in Halifax.[21]

For Leslie, evacuation posed complex questions. Will there be enough ships? When will they arrive? How do you break the news to Loyalists? What can they take with them? How do you handle slaves who escaped for British promises of freedom? Do you include the Loyalists' slaves? Slaves that British officers had stolen from rebel plantations? With Greene making it dangerous to forage, how do you feed and house the growing numbers of refugees? Are prisoner exchanges possible? Will Greene attack the troops as they leave Savannah and Charlestown? Will the evacuation be another massacre like the road from Concord to Boston in 1775?

At first, Leslie acted secretly and refused to confirm the evacuation rumors. "The people in town don't much believe it," he reported to Carleton in June. "When it happens it will be severely felt by many. I've taken no steps toward it yet, knowing the jealousy of the people."[22]

Meanwhile, refugees arrived daily, adding to the thousands already there. By the end of April, Leslie was trying to feed nearly eleven thousand men, both soldiers and civilians, along with 2,100 women, 1,600 children, and another 1,100 free or enslaved blacks.

"Their misery and helpless situation justifies our attention to them." Shortages of fresh meat and vegetables caused prices to spike. Rebels made it difficult to seize food from the countryside.[23]

But it wouldn't be until August that Leslie would publicly announce the evacuation.

8. North Carolina: Two Combustible Commanders

TWO DAYS BEFORE LESLIE'S NOVEMBER 8 ARRIVAL IN Charlestown, the British commander in Wilmington, North Carolina, 170 miles to the northeast, requested reinforcements and supplies. A 1,500-man rebel army was threatening; the 450 British troops in Wilmington were on two-thirds rations; and the commander, Lieutenant Colonel James Henry Craig, 33, reported he had grain for only twenty-five days.[1]

But the next week, Craig learned about Cornwallis's defeat at Yorktown. With Leslie's support, instead of organizing reinforcements, he began to organize an evacuation. Leslie hoped Craig wouldn't lose many troops in the process.[2]

Wilmington was the last British stand in North Carolina, a state they thought they had pacified the year before. It was a port town of two hundred houses and one thousand residents along the Cape Fear River, "confined to very narrow limits, the buildings concentrated in the hollow west of the sand hills, and resting on the river." The British had occupied Wilmington since late January 1781, when Cornwallis ordered Craig to secure a supply route from the coast to the interior.[3]

Craig, like Leslie and O'Hara, was a career army man. His Scottish father was a judge in Gibraltar, where James Henry was born. He joined the army at fifteen. By 1774, he commanded an infantry company in the Boston area. He fought in the war's first major battle, Bunker Hill; in Canada in 1776, helping to thwart a rebel invasion; in three battles that were part of the British northern invasion of New York in 1777; the successful 1779 Penobscot River campaign in Maine; another campaign in the Chesapeake Bay area the next year; and, finally, Clinton's invasion of the Carolinas in late 1780. He was wounded three times.

Unlike the "genteel" Leslie, Craig was an acquired taste—authoritarian, stubborn, manipulative, and easily offended, although friend and foe acknowledged his competence. A subordinate described him as "very short, broad, and muscular, a pocket Hercules, but with sharp, neat features as if chiseled in ivory. Not popular, for he was hot, peremptory, and pompous, yet extremely beloved by those whom he allowed to live in intimacy with him; clever, generous to a fault, and a warm unflinching friend to those he liked."[4]

After Craig overwhelmed Wilmington's two hundred defending rebel militia in January 1781, he turned the town into a support base and haven for Loyalists and Loyalist militia. He disarmed residents of questionable loyalty and built up Wilmington's defenses. He captured prominent rebels and put them in a notorious prison yard nicknamed "Major Craig's Bull Pen." One captured rebel congressman was brought to Wilmington "thrown across a horse like a sack of meal." Both he and a rebel militia brigadier general died during imprisonment—as a result of mistreatment, the Whigs said.[5]

Craig refused to negotiate prisoner exchanges. He lured slaves to leave their rebel masters and work for the British. Most important, he took the war to the rebels, supplying Loyalist militia, sometimes supporting them with regular troops, always encouraging them to raid the traitors and treat them harshly.

One Whig militiaman described a typical Craig-inspired raid: "Horses, cattle and sheep, and every kind of stock were driven off from every plantation; corn and forage taken for the supply of the army and no compensation given; houses plundered and robbed; chests, trunks, etc., broke; women and children's clothes, etc., as well as men's wearing apparel and every kind of household furniture taken away. The outrages were committed mostly by a train of loyal refugees."[6]

Wilmington was "the theatre of proscription, murder, and torture, in rapid succession and often under circumstance of atrocity utterly incompatible with the honor of a great and civilized society. . . . Every active and spirited Whig, within the range of their operations, was 'hunted like a partridge on the mountains,' and, if caught, was instantly put to death. Fathers, husbands, and brothers were murdered in cold blood, and their mothers, wives, and children were left without a home, without protection, and without even the means of subsistence," said an early nineteenth-century historian who interviewed veterans and other survivors.[7]

But the Whigs didn't passively give in. A militia major described their reaction: "A system of plunder and cruelty was practiced by the Tories . . . which soon produced a spirit of retaliation on the part of the Whigs, and devastation marked the track of both parties as they passed the dwellings of their adversaries."[8]

Craig himself said North Carolina had become "a glorious situation for cutting one another's throats." By summer 1781, the British and Loyalist militia controlled much of the colony. Craig's success gave Greene "pain and mortification to find the Tories so successful in their excursions. Wilmington is the root of the evil."[9]

In less than two months, everything would change. It began with a Whig militia general, Griffith Rutherford, as hated by the Tories as Craig was hated by the rebels. "A perfect savage," said a Loyalist colonel.[10]

"This villainous ruffian . . . butchered [Loyalists] in cold blood," and ordered his men to "wound with their swords every Loyalist they met," reported a Tory newspaper. The resulting scars were called "General Rutherford's mark." Even a fellow Whig, a Wilmington-area legislator, said Rutherford was a "bloodthirsty old scoundrel."[11]

Greene, knowing Rutherford's reputation, gently warned the militia general about the reports that Rutherford was treating Tories "with great severity, driving them indiscriminately from their dwellings without regard to age or sex, and laying waste [to] their possessions, destroying the produce and burning their houses. . . . But in national concerns as well as private life, passion is a bad counselor, and resentment an unsafe guide. . . . If we pursue the Tories indiscriminately and drive them to a state [of] desperation, we shall make them from a weak and feeble foe [to] a sure and determined enemy."[12]

Rutherford was neither a North Carolina native nor even American-born. Historians fill the first thirty years of his life with modifiers: "approximate," "around," "about," "apparently," "perhaps." He was born in Northern Ireland—about 1731. His mother had moved there from Wales, his father from Scotland. Around age eight, in 1739, he and his parents sailed to America, but his parents died aboard the ship, or perhaps soon after arriving. While he had family in Virginia, he appears to have been raised by an elderly German couple, possibly in Delaware. He might have been related to them. Around 1745—or 1750 or 1751—he lived in Virginia near or with his relatives. By 1753, he had moved to North Carolina, about two hundred miles upcountry from Wilmington. There, another set of relatives helped him get a job as a surveyor. He was about twenty-two.[13]

The next year, or possibly two years later, he married a local woman, with whom he had ten children. Both his relatives and his wife's family were apparently well connected, which helps explain why an orphan could later have the political and social success he did. Like Washington, Rutherford turned his surveying skills into profitable land speculation. While his wealth never rivaled that of low-country plantation owners, he was able to buy thousands of cheap acres, much of which he turned into productive farmland.[14]

In 1758, Rutherford began his military career as a militia member, and fought the French and Indians in the Seven Years' War. A different kind of fighting broke out in 1765. The "regulators," poorer, backcountry farmers, often indebted, protested the political and economic power of low-country planters, royal officials, lawyers, and land speculators. Their protests ranged from intimidation, refusal to pay taxes, disruption of court proceedings, to seizing repossessed property. The movement caught Rutherford in the middle. The royal governor had appointed him county sheriff, responsible for enforcing the law, and he earned a fee from collecting taxes. Rutherford balanced royal politics with local politics by supporting reform in the assembly, resigning as sheriff after a year, and endorsing a local agreement with the regulators—while participating in militia action against them.[15]

When the dispute between colonists and the British reached the tipping point, Rutherford chose rebellion. His neighbors elected him to the Whig legislature, and he was named colonel of his county militia. By the end of 1775, he helped relieve a Whig army besieged by Tories in South Carolina. In 1776, the legislature named him a state brigadier general.[16]

His first action as general was against the Cherokees, "that treacherous, barbarous nation of savages, with their white abettors [the British], who, lost to all sense of humanity, honor, and principle, mean to extinguish every spark of freedom in these United States." The Indians had escalated the defense of their land against encroaching white settlers. Rutherford's army of 2,400 men destroyed thirty-six Cherokee towns. When some of his men scalped a Cherokee woman and murdered a prisoner, Rutherford arrested the ringleader, but was forced by troops to release him. (The next year, the legislature began offering a bounty for Indian scalps.) Unable to resist the white army, the Indians sued for peace, and ceded large swaths of territory.[17]

During these years, Rutherford's neighbors continued to elect him to the assembly, and in 1777 to the state senate, where he remained a senator for eleven years. He advocated a strong legislative branch, a weak executive, religious freedom—no established church—and harsh policies toward Tories.

In 1780, the British captured Charlestown, forcing rebel general Lincoln into a humiliating surrender. Rutherford joined the new rebel general, Horatio Gates, in backcountry South Carolina in August. That month, in Camden—forty-five miles from the North Carolina border—Cornwallis routed the rebel army. Rutherford, who had multiple wounds, was taken prisoner. Cornwallis called out his capture: "The taking [of] that violent and cruel incendiary, Gen. Rutherford, has been a lucky circumstance."[18]

As an officer, Rutherford was treated well in his St. Augustine imprisonment, allowed to grow a garden, and to walk within certain limits of the town. He was exchanged after ten months, and arrived back in North Carolina in early September 1781. He immediately recruited an army. By October, he led 1,400 or 1,500 men.[19]

Now, he marched toward Wilmington. With little artillery, he didn't intend any frontal assaults on entrenched British regulars—a direct attack on Wilmington would have been suicidal—but he would do everything else: cut off supplies, try to starve Craig's garrison, intimidate Tory civilians, and fight Tory militia.

The first battle was on October 15, about ninety miles from Wilmington. Part of Rutherford's army surprised three hundred to six hundred Tory militia, routing them "entirely with sabre," and forcing them to flee into swamps and marshes. By the 20th,

Rutherford successfully confined British troops to the Wilmington area. Craig wrote his commander that Rutherford's only goal was to "subdue the Tories—and distress them they will." He hoped the Tories would elude the Whig army.[20]

On the 22nd, Rutherford moved to besiege Wilmington. He split his army, sending one force down the west side of the Cape Fear River, and the other approaching Wilmington on the north. By mid-November, Rutherford was on Wilmington's outskirts. At More's Plantation on the 14th, his troops surprised one hundred Loyalist militia, killing or wounding forty-two of them. The next day, the Whigs skirmished with British regulars at the heavily fortified Brick House, just outside the main Wilmington defenses. A militia captain demanded the British surrender. "I disregard your orders," the British officer replied. "I don't surrender." With no artillery to make good on their demand, the Whigs retreated.[21]

Tory militia attacked ninety Whigs on the 16th. The Whigs counterattacked, and the Tories retreated. The next day, Rutherford's main army was four miles from Wilmington, and learned about Cornwallis in Yorktown. But Craig had learned about Yorktown several days earlier and was already making plans to evacuate.

At sunrise on November 18, British troops marched to their transport boats, taking with them about one thousand Loyalist militia and families. "Boats lined the wharves, baggage upon baggage; dragged down and conveyed to the ships, riding at anchor in the stream," an eyewitness recalled. "The fife and drum were heard, and company after company, headed by their respective officers, marched in solid columns through the streets, leaving their horses behind."[22]

Suddenly, while the troops were still embarking, a small group of rebel cavalry rode into town "at full speed." One of the rebels recognized a Tory on the road. He rushed up to him, "and with one blow by a vertical cut laid his head open, the divided parts falling on each other." The dead man, the rebel said, had hanged his father with a grapevine. British regulars fired back, but the cavalry retreated quickly, receiving only slight wounds.[23]

Rutherford's army arrived after the British had sailed. Immediately, they began looting Whig and Tory property. A civilian representative begged Rutherford for protection. The general agreed, and placed a guard by all civilian houses. Over the next two weeks, the army broke up and went home.

Rutherford also returned home and was named commissioner of confiscated property. He showed little spirit of reconciliation. When a former Tory asked for help in reuniting his family, Rutherford told him he was an "open enemy" and suggested the man move to Canada. After voting against ratification of the Constitution in 1788, he lost his seat in the state senate. He retained large land holdings in North Carolina and Tennessee, and added more. In 1792, Rutherford moved to Tennessee, where he led the territorial legislature. Two counties, in Tennessee and North Carolina, are named in his honor.[24]

Craig continued his upward career track in the British army, serving in Holland, Cape Town, India, and Italy. His most well-known role was as governor and commander of Lower Canada, in 1807. It was a controversial tenure, and Craig worsened the tensions between French and British Canadians. Nor did Craig hesitate to interfere in American affairs, supporting Indian efforts on the frontier to counter American expansionism. He also hired a spy, which caused a Congressional stir. His health failing, he left Canada for England in 1811 and died the next year.

But there was a final military issue for North Carolina to deal with. A man named David Fanning—feared by Whigs, seen as a protector by Tories—was still at large.

Fanning's early life is nearly as vague as Rutherford's. He was born in Virginia, about forty-five miles southwest of Richmond. Depending on the source, it was sometime between 1754 and 1757, the consensus being 1755. His family was "obscure," said a nineteenth-century historian. His father drowned either before he was born, or while his mother was pregnant. His mother died when he was nine, possibly after moving to backcountry North Carolina. He was then indentured or apprenticed to a foster family, from whom he learned carpentry and loom-making, and built a reputation for breaking wild horses.[25]

Fanning's youth was made more difficult because of any of several diseases then called "scald head." It resulted in hair loss, scaling, and pustules that smelled so badly that one account says Fanning didn't eat at a table or sleep in a bed. For the rest of his life, he wore a silk cap under his hat, and "his most intimate friends never saw his head naked."[26]

A Whig historian who interviewed people who met Fanning said, "his powers were developed under the influence of poverty, disease, and neglect, without early instruction or example, and without any moral or religious training." He was "an outcast from genteel society, he never received any favors, or had any kind attentions paid him except from pity on account of his forlorn condition."[27]

Around sixteen or seventeen, Fanning ran away from his foster parents, who he later said were abusive, and settled in South Carolina. He became moderately prosperous, acquired property, farmed it, and traded with Indians. He built a cabin on former Cherokee land, in what is now Laurens County.[28]

He later said his commitment to Britain began in 1775, when, returning from a trading trip, he was robbed by a gang of Whigs. In May, a militia company he served in split into Whig and Loyalist factions. If he had any doubts about staying loyal, they ended when rebels seized a Tory militia colonel, "burnt his feet, tarred and feathered him, and cut off his hair."[29]

Over the next three years, Fanning took part in numerous raids and skirmishes—and he was captured, escaped, or released fourteen times. With each raid, each skirmish, each capture, each escape, his notoriety grew. By 1779, with a $300 price on his head and years spent eluding pursuers, "I looked so much like a rack of nothing but skin and bones, and my wounds had never been dressed, and my clothes all bloody. My misery and situation was beyond explanation, and no friend in the world that I could depend upon."[30]

When South Carolina's Whig governor offered him a conditional pardon, Fanning accepted and agreed to sit out the rest of the war. But in May 1780, the British captured Charlestown, and Fanning began recruiting militia and raiding Whigs, eventually moving his base to Chatham County, North Carolina, about 125 miles upcountry from Wilmington. He was the kind of Loyalist partisan Craig encouraged, popular with his men and disruptive to rebels. In July 1781, Craig commissioned him as a militia colonel.

Over the next year, Fanning and his men, whose numbers varied from a handful to more than one thousand, fought thirty-six skirmishes and battles. "Fanning inflicted more injury on the country, and was more dreaded at the time than any other man," said the Whig historian.[31]

He raided Pittsboro, captured rebel judges and lawyers, and turned them over to Craig. In a letter to the Whig governor, the prisoners said they were being treated with "the greatest civility," unlike the treatment Fanning told them Loyalists had received. "Some [Loyalists] had been unlawfully drafted, others had been whipped and ill-treated without trial, others had their houses burned and all their property plundered, and barbarous and cruel murders had been committed in their neighborhoods." Fanning captured a rebel colonel in his own house. He attacked Campbelton and took more prisoners. He also won a victory over rebels at McFall's Mill.[32]

Then, on September 13, Fanning and other Loyalist militia raided the rebel capital, Hillsboro. They killed fifteen rebels and wounded twenty, released thirty Loyalists, and captured two hundred prisoners—including Governor Thomas Burke. On the road to Wilmington, where they intended to give their prisoners to Craig, the rebels counterattacked. "I received a shot in my left arm which broke the bone in several pieces," Fanning said. "The loss of blood was so great that I was taken off my horse and led to a secret place in the woods." The rebels retreated after a four-hour battle, but both sides had heavy casualties. Craig got his prisoners.[33]

Craig praised Fanning, "who, for spirit and activity," was the best of the Tory militia leaders. In late October, with Rutherford focused on Wilmington and the coast, Craig ordered a now-recovered Fanning to the backcountry "to lay waste the countries from whence his[Rutherford's] men come." Craig added that he trusted Fanning's "good sense, which, though plain, is not deficient in point of thought."[34]

After Craig evacuated Wilmington on November 18, Whigs increased their activities against the remaining Tories—harassed them, plundered them. Fanning retaliated as best he could with his diminishing force, raiding and destroying the homes of rebel leaders.

"I continued acting in the interior parts of North Carolina," he said. Loyalists there "had been induced to brave every danger and difficulty during the late war rather than render any service to the rebels; had their properties real and personal taken to support their enemies; the fatherless and widows stripped; and every manner of support taken from them, their houses and lands and all personal property taken, and no resting place could be found for them. . . .

Stripped of their property, driven from their homes, deprived of their wives and children, robbed of a free and mild government, betrayed and deserted by their friends, what can repay them for the misery?"[35]

Both sides escalated their terrorism, executing enemies, settling old scores. Even in January 1782, when Fanning tried to negotiate a truce that protected Loyalists, the killing continued. When Whigs killed one of Fanning's captains, they "cut him to pieces with their swords." Fanning, in turn, captured two rebels and "hung them, by way of retaliation, both on a limb of one tree." A rebel who had been "distressing the Loyalists": Fanning burned his home and two others. A rebel who was "very assiduous in assisting the rebels": "I killed him," Fanning said. A rebel who failed to moderate his behavior toward Loyalists—"I shot him." After a Whig militia colonel said he'd never agree to a truce, Fanning killed him at his plantation in front of his sister and young daughter as he was trying to escape, and, according to one account, kicked and beat the women. It "put an end to his committing any more ill deeds," Fanning said.[36]

By April, three hundred Whig militia were hunting for Fanning, and Fanning ended his fight. He planned to marry the sixteen-year-old sister of one of his officers on April 23 at a ceremony where two other officers would be married. But a rebel killed one officer on the wedding day. As the rebel tried to escape, Fanning shot him dead. The wedding proceeded. Then Fanning disappeared. He resurfaced on June 17 in Charlestown, and his bride joined him two days later.[37]

Fanning planned to start a new life in East Florida, because North Carolina's postwar pardon of Loyalists specifically excluded him and two others. But the peace treaty gave Florida to Spain, so Fanning and his family went to New Brunswick, Canada, where they arrived in October 1784. There, he farmed; ran a gristmill and sawmill; and, to support his claims for war compensation, wrote an autobiography. He served in the provincial assembly until 1801, when he was expelled after accusations of raping a judge's teenaged daughter. He was convicted, but either because of his popularity or weak evidence, the governor nullified the verdict. Fanning himself believed the jury was biased because of his personality, war record, reputation of brutality, and political ambitions. Guilty or not, Fanning moved to Digby, Nova Scotia, where he spent the rest of his life farming, fishing, and shipbuilding.[38]

9. Georgia: "Making Bricks Without Straw"

AFTER YORKTOWN, WASHINGTON SENT GREENE TWO THOUSAND experienced Continental army troops from Maryland and Pennsylvania. But by the time the troops arrived in early January 1782, illness and enlistment expirations left Greene "little stronger than we were before."[1]

Greene soon found that he had another problem: The generals who led the reinforcements despised each other. The three-month march south exacerbated an "old grudge" between Major General Arthur St. Clair and Brigadier General Anthony Wayne. An officer observed "much warmth" between the two—and he wasn't referring to cordiality.[2]

Greene's solution met several needs. He made St. Clair his second-in-command (fitting his senior rank), with mostly administrative duties. He then moved Wayne, the more aggressive general, away from St. Clair's direct command and into a problem spot: Georgia, a state of about fifty-thousand people, half of whom were slaves.

Like North Carolina before Rutherford's return, the British maintained a strong presence in Georgia, supporting Loyalist militia and encouraging Indian raids against the rebels. The British had held Savannah, Georgia's only city and first settlement, since shortly after Christmas 1778. It was a low-country port, built on a bluff along the Savannah River about sixteen miles inland from the ocean. Unlike most American cities, Savannah was planned: no random alleys or streets carved from cow paths, but symmetrical blocks that framed six squares (today, twenty-four).

In their three years of occupation, the British fortified the city and manned it with 1,300 regular troops, 500 Tory militia, 150 armed African Americans, and assorted armed galleys and brigs plying the river.

The man responsible for the fortifications, for all of Georgia, was Lieutenant Colonel Alured Clarke, 37. He came from a well-to-do family: His father was a lawyer and judge; his namesake uncle was a high-ranking Church of England cleric. George III described Clarke as a man with "much temper and prudence." Unlike Craig in North Carolina, Clarke was "a professional soldier whose modest talents and courteous manner had enabled him to discharge the civil duties of a colonial administrator without either distinguishing or disgracing himself," a biographer said.[3]

He served in Germany and Ireland before his promotion to captain. In 1770, he married the notorious daughter of a member of Parliament. Elizabeth Catherine Hunter—Kitty—had eloped in 1762 with a married earl. The earl reconciled with his wife the next year, several months after Hunter gave birth to his son, who the earl supported financially. Clarke and Hunter never had children.

In 1776, now-Lieutenant Colonel Clarke arrived with his regiment in New York. He was stationed first in Canada, then in the South. He arrived in Savannah as the Georgia commander in May 1780, and found the same civil war that affected its neighboring colony.[4]

"The rage between Whig and Tory ran so high that what was called a 'Georgia parole' and to be shot down were synonymous," a Whig general remembered.

Greene periodically tried to persuade Whig officials in Georgia that mercy was a wise military strategy. "It is always dangerous to push people to a state of desperation, and the satisfaction of revenge has but a momentary existence, and is commonly succeeded by pity and remorse," he wrote the governor. "The practice of plundering, which I am told has been too much indulged with you, is very destructive to the morals and manners of a people."[5] His plea for generosity went unheeded.

In August 1781, with Cornwallis in Virginia, and Greene continuing his war of attrition against the bulk of the southern British army in South Carolina, the Georgia Whig legislature reenergized its resistance.

It created the Georgia Legion, intended as an elite force of two hundred cavalry and two hundred infantry, equipped with arms and supplies bought with promissory notes and proceeds from the sale of confiscated Tory plantations. In reality, British deserters and ex-Loyalists formed much of the legion—"dangerous and untrustworthy," said one historian.[6]

An experienced leader, Lieutenant Colonel James Jackson, 24, led the legion. "He wooed danger," a friend said. "He was steady, persevering, and immovable in the prosecution of his measures . . . He suffered perhaps the impetuosity of his temper to hurry him into extremes, too often and unnecessarily . . . He was impatient under contradictions, and apparently intolerant to his opponents."[7]

Born in England, Jackson had arrived in Georgia recently—1772—apparently to study law under a wealthy friend of his father's. The friend was a politically active Whig, and Jackson volunteered for the militia. By early 1776, Jackson was a captain, and participated in a raid on British ships in the Savannah River. He later saw action near the East Florida border and in late 1778, as a major, helped defend Savannah, fleeing when the British took the city. The next year, he fought in the unsuccessful attempt to retake Savannah.[8]

Jackson was a fighter in and out of the army. He fought at least twenty-three duels, the most notorious being the result of a political feud: He dueled and killed the Whig lieutenant governor in 1780. Before dying, the victim severely wounded Jackson in the knees. He recovered to fight in South Carolina and Georgia battles through spring 1781, when the Whigs retook Augusta, Georgia. In October, the general of the state militia ordered Jackson and his legion to move closer to Savannah and begin raiding British outposts.

Clarke, in Savannah, countered by sending forty-five British regulars to the Augusta area in support of a plot by twenty legionnaires to bayonet Jackson while he slept. The plot was foiled, and three ringleaders were hanged. The assassination attempt didn't deter Jackson. On November 2, his legion fought British troops about fifteen miles southwest of Savannah. Jackson surprised a Tory and British detachment, which was willing to surrender. But one trigger-happy legionnaire shot a British officer. Seeing what had happened, the Tories counterattacked, and Jackson was forced to retreat. He was more successful in skirmishes that afternoon. By day's end, the Whigs reported that while they suffered thirteen casualties, the Tories and British had about fifty. "The slaughter of the enemy was great," Jackson said.[9]

The British account was nearly the opposite. "A few days ago there was an engagement, which we call bush-fighting, between a party of royalists and Americans," said an official. "Twelve or 14 of the royalists fell and about 50 of the rebels, which will prove some check to their bold incursions. Colonel Clarke immediately went out to pursue them, but they had fled too fast to be overtaken."[10]

While Jackson skirmished near Savannah, the main body of state troops intercepted a force of Indians and Tory raiders headed toward Augusta on December 3. The Whigs routed them, killing twelve Tories and twenty Indians. To the British, this was no raiding party. Instead, the rebels "plundered and murdered several traders and Cherokee Indians, not even sparing women and children who were on their way to Savannah."[11]

By mid-December, the British heard reports that the rebels were being reinforced by a "formidable force" of regular army troops led not just by Wayne, but also by Greene, St. Clair, and Lafayette. "We are at this moment in the utmost danger and distress," the royal governor said. "God knows what will become of us."[12]

Clarke ordered his troops to pull back from outlying areas toward Savannah, practicing a scorched-earth policy in their wake. Among the retrenchments was a two-hundred-man garrison in the strategic town of New Ebenezer, on the Savannah River, 25 miles north of Savannah. Founded by a religious sect, New Ebenezer was the site of a rebel arms and supply depot until November 1778. Two months later, Loyalist militia turned the town into a major base, headquarters for 2,300 men. Whig forces regained control in October 1779, but they eventually left. In May 1781, the British moved back in.[13]

Now, with New Ebenezer abandoned again, Jackson made it his headquarters. (In the summer of 1782, the Whig legislature would meet there.) There, he waited for the reinforcements.

The "formidable force" the British feared didn't include Lafayette, who was sailing home to France. Nor did it include Greene or St. Clair, whose priorities were to contain Leslie in Charlestown. Instead, the "formidable force" was one hundred Continentals, three hundred South Carolina militia, and a handful of artillerymen.[14] Only the commander's reputation—well known by the British—was formidable.

Anthony Wayne's nickname, "Mad Anthony," was a misnomer: He was neither insane nor angry. In fact, he had been given the nickname just the previous spring. One of his men, known as Jemy the Rover or the "commodore," was a sometimes-spy for Wayne. Jemy either pretended he was deranged or actually was; no one was sure. Either way, Wayne apparently had a soft spot for Jemy. In spring 1781, the army detained Jemy for disorderly conduct. On his way to the guardhouse, he demanded to know who ordered his arrest. "The general," he was told. Several hours later, Jemy was released, and he asked the sergeant who had helped guard him whether Wayne was angry—"mad"—or playing a joke on him. The sergeant replied that Wayne was displeased, and if Jemy repeated his conduct, he would be whipped. "Then Anthony is mad," Jemy said. "Farewell to you. Clear the coast for the commodore, mad Anthony's friend." The nickname stuck.[15]

Wayne was an aggressive fighter, but methodical in his preparations and training of troops. "An officer," he said, "never ought to hazard a battle, where a defeat would render his situation much worse than a retreat without it (unless numbers and circumstances rendered success almost certain)."[16]

He demanded discipline from his troops, even when it came to appearance. "I have an insuperable prejudice in favor of an elegant uniform and soldierly appearance," he told Washington. "I would rather risk my life and reputation at the head of the same men in an attack, clothed and appointed as I could wish, merely with bayonets and a single charge of ammunition, than to take them as they appear in common with 60 rounds of cartridges," because good uniforms promote "laudable pride . . . which in a soldier is a substitute for almost every other virtue."[17]

Despite being "somewhat addicted to the vaunting style," a captain said, Wayne "could fight as well as brag." Greene said his general had "military ardor, which, no doubt, is heated by the fire of the modern hero"—not a wise quality. Still, Greene said, "He is an excellent officer." Others had a similar assessment. "His excessive courage never destroyed his self-possession, nor obscured the excellent judgment which he possessed," wrote a contemporary.[18]

Wayne's swearing was notorious. Once, he failed to find a sentry at an expected position. "He damned all our souls to hell," said a lieutenant. "[I] shall not forget his damns, which he is very apt to bestow upon people."[19]

Privately, Washington was critical of Wayne's over-the-top personality. After the war, Washington described Wayne as "more active and enterprising than judicious and cautious. No economist it is feared. Open to flattery, vain, easily imposed upon, and liable to be drawn into scrapes. Too indulgent (the effect perhaps of some of the causes just mentioned) to his officers and men. Whether sober or a little addicted to the bottle, I know not." Nonetheless, Washington fed Wayne a stream of important assignments both during the war and while president a decade later.[20]

He was born on New Year's Day 1745. His grandfather had immigrated to Pennsylvania and eventually owned 1,600 acres about twenty-five miles west of Philadelphia. From an early age, Wayne showed a military aptitude. His uncle, who ran a school Wayne attended, complained to Wayne's father: "What he may be best qualified for, I know not, but one thing I am certain of, that he will never make a scholar. He may make a soldier; he has already distracted the brains of two-thirds of the boys under my direction by rehearsals of battles and sieges, etc. . . . Unless Anthony pays more attention to his books, I shall be under the painful necessity of dismissing him from the school."[21]

At eighteen, he became a surveyor, like his future superior, Washington. And, like Washington, he was good at it. Franklin and other Philadelphia speculators hired him in late 1765 to survey land they owned in Nova Scotia and later to be superintendent there. He returned to Pennsylvania the next year.[22]

In 1774, with the dispute between Britain and the colonies heating up, his neighbors elected Wayne to chair the county committee of safety. The committee coordinated local militia efforts, which

Wayne helped organize. When war broke out, he was named a colonel. He was wounded in the leg in mid-1776 at Trois Rivières, Québec, where he had been sent to support retreating troops from the Canadian invasion debacle. Later that year, he commanded the strategic Fort Ticonderoga.

Wayne fought at the Battle of Brandywine in September 1777, and led troops at what became known as—probably more for rebel propaganda reasons than for what happened—the Paoli Massacre. On the night of September 20, the British supposedly bayoneted rebel troops trying to surrender. Massacre or not, Wayne was surprised and routed, then accused of negligence. A court-martial unanimously acquitted him, concluding that Wayne "did everything that could be expected from an active, brave, and vigilant officer, under the orders he then had."[23]

Two weeks after Paoli, Wayne led a nearly successful assault at Germantown. He spent that winter at Valley Forge, where he was named brigadier general and given command of the Pennsylvania line—Continental army regulars from his home state. His troops continued to fight well at the Battle of Monmouth in June 1778.

Washington's respect for Wayne's abilities grew. In June 1779, Washington gave him a special assignment: command of an elite strike force of fifteen hundred men. Unlike the Georgia Legion, it proved its quality: On July 15, Wayne led his corps on a meticulously planned surprise night attack on Stony Point, a British fortification guarding an important ferry crossing on the Hudson River. The attack succeeded.

"I believe that sanguine god is rather thirsty for human gore," Wayne wrote a friend. "The horrid depredations of the enemy to the southward indicate an inundation of it." The British would only capitulate when "the price of much blood" becomes "too great a hazard for Britons to make many purchases."[24]

Wayne became Washington's troubleshooter. After Benedict Arnold's treason was discovered in August 1780, and the rebel stronghold at West Point nearly given to the British, Wayne took command of the fort. Back with his Pennsylvania troops in New Jersey in winter 1780–1781, Wayne faced a mutiny by fifteen hundred men with grievances about recruitment bounties, pay, living conditions, and enlistment length. At least two were killed, and others were wounded. Most mutineers, however, were peaceful. A Congressional delegation worked with Wayne on a settlement: total amnesty, discharge of many of the troops who had served at least three years, back pay, and clothing.

The mutiny settled, Washington sent Wayne with eight hundred men to Virginia, joining Lafayette in his efforts to harass Cornwallis. Wayne reached Lafayette in early June 1781.

On July 6, Lafayette ordered Wayne, with five hundred men (later reinforced by another three hundred), to find the whereabouts of the main British army. Cornwallis set a trap, and Wayne blundered into it. Around sunset, Wayne suddenly found his force being enveloped by five thousand British and Hessian soldiers, the bulk of Cornwallis's army. Instead of immediately retreating, which Wayne believed could turn into a panicked rout, he attacked the main British army, halting its advance. Then, he ordered his men to retreat while Lafayette, viewing the action from a distance, ordered reinforcements to cover Wayne. With darkness setting in, Cornwallis didn't pursue. At the end of the day, 139 of Wayne's men were killed, wounded, or missing—seventeen percent of his force. Seventy-five British soldiers were killed or wounded. A Wayne biographer concluded from the mixed contemporary critiques that peers could "hardly decide after the battle whether to admire Wayne for his brave and impetuous character or to condemn him as a foolhardy adventurer."[25]

Two months later, a friendly sentry accidentally shot Wayne in the leg. That wound kept him from fighting at Yorktown.

In January 1782, Wayne headed to Georgia. Greene's orders: Coordinate all the Whig military efforts; work closely with the Whig government; encourage Loyalist sympathizers to stay out of the fight; give the Georgians "more effectual support" in both offensive and, if necessary, defensive actions. "Try by every means in your power to soften the malignity and deadly resentments subsisting between the Whigs and Tories, and put a stop as much as possible to that cruel custom of putting people to death after they have surrendered themselves prisoners." Try as much as possible to stop the militia's "practice of plunder."[26]

A couple of weeks later, Greene sent a postscript: "Before you left here, I forgot to impress you with an idea of not hazarding too much. . . . Your reputation depends more on avoiding a misfortune than on achieving something very great. Brilliant actions may fade, but a prudent conduct never can."[27]

Wayne crossed the Savannah River from South Carolina into Georgia on January 12, 1782, and rendezvoused with Jackson in New Ebenezer. Other militia would straggle in to join Wayne in coming weeks and months, but Jackson's legion was a constant. It became Greene's advance guard, operating a dozen miles ahead of Wayne, "frequently skirmishing with the enemy, and sustaining all the hardships of want, nakedness, and a desolated country." Jackson would later remember "horrid" conditions—his men often going up to two days without bread, beef, rice, rum, whiskey, or any drink other than "common swamp water."[28]

Wayne complained to Greene about provisions, and he repeatedly pleaded for more men. "For God's sake, reinforce the soonest possible," he wrote in early February. Two weeks later, he told Greene his Virginia dragoons "are almost as naked as nature left them." Jackson had only 130 men, and because they weren't professionals, the burden of guarding against enemy attacks "falls severe upon a few Continental dragoons unsupported by infantry." A week after that, he begged Greene, "Pray send me at least 200 picked infantry."[29]

Even with his small force of about five hundred men with occasional reinforcements, Wayne made progress narrowing Clarke's area of control. "A party of Continental horse[men] have showed themselves at different times and places for two or three days past within eight or 10 miles of Savannah," the royal governor reported on January 23. "Now, all our outposts are broke up and called in." By the 26th, Wayne had "maneuvered the enemy" from three more outposts. In their retreat, the British "set fire to and consumed all the grain and forage," forcing Wayne's men to forage or get supplies from as far away as Augusta and across the border in South Carolina.[30]

Wayne also was concerned about his rear. Most Indians in backcountry Georgia felt their best interests were protected by the British, and some tribal groups participated in raids with Tory or British officers. In late January, Wayne sent a militia detachment to intercept a trading party of thirty Indians and Tories, accompanied by ninety-three packhorses loaded with supplies for Savannah. The force captured twenty-six Creek Indians without a fight.[31]

Encounter followed encounter. Jackson repulsed Tories at a sawmill on February 13. More Indians were intercepted on the 19th, and they were sent back with a plea to remain neutral. Not so lucky was a sole Indian the Whigs captured: They tied him to a tree during an interrogation, then shot him to death and hacked his body to pieces. On the 26th, Jackson made a night raid to burn British provisions on the royal governor's plantation half a mile from Savannah. But a diversionary force of South Carolina Whig militia was ambushed.[32]

In March, an encounter with British and Indians cost one Whig dragoon his life. The man, said a Wayne aide, was "scalped in a most barbarous manner, under the eye and inspection of a British officer, cut off his upper lip and nose, and cut his face, most barbarously, for which the [royal] lieutenant governor gave an entertainment to those wretches a little while after."[33]

More skirmishes in April. In the backcountry, on the Oconee River, four hundred Georgia Whigs attacked a party of Loyalists and Indians, killing a dozen while suffering one death. Closer to Savannah, Jackson fought thirty British, killing their commander. On the Alatamaha River, a Whig major and twenty-eight men captured some Indians, and then were attacked themselves. The major died. In May, a dozen Whigs ambushed fifteen Choctaw scouts, killing five and wounding more. The Whigs retreated as the main Indian body of seventy approached. The Indians were "finding every path leading to their nation shut up and bloody," and resented the British for getting them into the situation, Wayne told Greene.[34]

Wayne achieved what was by Georgia standards a major victory on May 20 and 21. Clarke, in Savannah, had asked his Creek and Cherokee allies for reinforcements, and he sent more than three hundred Tory militia to rendezvous with them and escort them back to Savannah. Wayne, with Jackson as his advance guard, seized control of a crucial causeway through a swamp, and around midnight attacked the British, killing their colonel, killing or wounding forty others, and capturing twenty. Five of Wayne's men were killed and two wounded. "The advantage was gained by the liberal use of the sword and bayonet," said one account.[35]

In June, Wayne felt confident enough to move his army from the well-fortified New Ebenezer to about five miles west of Savannah.

There, in the early morning of June 24, one hundred fifty to three hundred Creek Indians with Tory guides attacked. It was a blunder on both sides. The Indians thought they were attacking a small camp of pickets, not the main body, but Wayne had changed the pickets' location the night before. His army was mostly asleep and surprised. Still, Wayne formed his troops, inspired them with a shout of "Death or victory," and ordered a bayonet charge. The Creek attack was "most furious," Wayne later told Greene. The Indians "met our charge with that ferocity for which they're famous. . . . The bravery of the Indians, fighting hand to hand, gave an opening for the free use of sword and bayonet." He praised the Creek commander, Emistisiguo (spelled in an infinite number of ways in contemporary accounts). "Such was their determined bravery that after mortally wounding one of their chiefs, and charging at the head of the dragoons over his body, he, with his last breath, drew his trigger and killed my horse under me." A different account, by a Whig captain, disputes Wayne's story: The Creek commander, "the largest and bravest of the warriors—six feet three inches—weighing about two hundred twenty pounds . . . after receiving an espontoon [lance] and three bayonets in his body, encouraged his warriors all the while, he retired a few paces, composedly laid himself down, and died without a groan or struggle."[36]

Fourteen Indians were killed and an unknown number wounded, while five Whigs were killed and eight wounded. After sunrise, when it appeared that the enemy would counterattack, Wayne ordered the execution of twelve Creek prisoners, "to free us from encumbrance." Again, the British saw it differently. The British Indian superintendent reported that the Indians "surprised and routed the rebels and with a very trifling loss, the gallant Emistisiguo excepted." Moreover, the majority of Creeks were able to reach Savannah, reinforcing Clarke.[37]

Overall, however, rebel successes caused Clarke problems. The Whig legislature had acceded to Wayne's request to pardon Tory and Hessian mercenary deserters who agreed to fight for him. For the Hessians, the legislature promised two hundred acres, a cow, and two breeding hogs—and they publicized the offer in German-language broadsides. The policy's first major success was the February surrender of Tory militia leader Sir Patrick Houston with a "considerable" number of Hessians. One of Houston's brothers was a Whig leader (and future Georgia governor), but another remained loyal to the Crown.[38]

More desertions followed. "The enemy have filled the swamps round their [defensive] works with Tories, Indians, and armed negroes to prevent [Hessian] desertions. Notwithstanding which, a number of Hessians find the way out," Wayne told Greene. He later joked that his troops consisted of "British, Hessians, new levies, outliers, Tories, crackers, Ethiopians, and Indian allies to the number of thirteen tribes." German-American women helped Wayne in his efforts to encourage desertion. "The women are the best recruiting agents for the rebels," said one Hessian.[39]

It wasn't Whig propaganda. Leslie, in Charlestown, after reading Clarke's reports, said: "I find the Hessian Regiment has been there too long, they desert fast, and I am afraid little dependence is to be put in them. . . . I am sorry to find some leading people of our militia going over to the enemy and persuading others to follow them."[40]

Clarke's increasingly untenable situation resolved itself on May 23 when Guy Carleton, who had succeeded Clinton earlier that month, ordered Savannah's immediate evacuation, pending the arrival of transports. Clarke asked Wayne for a cessation of hostilities. Wayne refused, deferring to the Whig governor, who, in turn, deferred to Congress. Wayne moved his troops to within sight of Savannah, and tried unsuccessfully to lure the British from their fortifications.[41]

Savannah Tories were livid at what they saw as capitulation and abandonment. They wrote Leslie about their "astonishment" that Savannah would be evacuated. Nonetheless, British transports began arriving off Savannah around June 20. Clarke moved his heaviest equipment first to the waterfront at the bottom of Savannah's bluff, then to small boats that ferried the equipment down the river to ships anchored off Tybee Island more than 15 miles east.[42]

Loyalist merchants and militia began to negotiate the terms of the evacuation with Wayne. He was generous: Merchants could stay in Savannah another six months to get their affairs in order and sell any property or inventories. He and the Whig government assured the Tories they would be safe. They also promised amnesty to any Tory soldier who agreed to serve in the Whig army for two years or the duration of the war.

"I think this was an act of justice, tempered [with] mercy," Wayne said.

Wayne also coordinated the evacuation's timing with Clarke, and received assurances that the British would leave the city intact.[43]

The day before the last British troops left, Wayne ordered his men to change into clean clothes and warned them of "the most severe and exemplary punishment," if they or civilians began plundering. Finally, he honored his top commander. "Lieutenant Colonel Jackson, in consideration of his severe and fatiguing service in the advance, is to receive the keys of Savannah, and is allowed to enter at the western gate taking possession thereof."[44]

At noon, July 11, 1782, Jackson's legion entered Savannah. It had been occupied for three years, six months, thirteen days. Ahead of Jackson, Clarke's one thousand-man garrison left for New York, while twenty-five hundred Loyalists, four thousand of their slaves, a small number of free African Americans, and two hundred Creek and Choctaw Indians headed for multiple destinations: New York, England, Jamaica, or St. Augustine.[45]

"Nothing can surpass the sorrow which many of the inhabitants expressed at our departure, especially those ladies whose sweethearts were under necessity of quitting the town at our evacuation," a Loyalist soldier wrote in his diary that day. "Some of the ladies were converted and brought over to the 'faith,' so as to quit as well and follow us."[46]

Clarke also went to New York, where he was promoted to brigadier general and oversaw the return of British prisoners. He later became the peacetime administrator of Jamaica, and served in Canada, Gibraltar, Cape Town, and, in 1798, India, as commander-in-chief. He returned to England in 1801, a wealthy and honored man.

With Savannah evacuated, Greene immediately ordered Wayne to join him in South Carolina—but first, Wayne had cleanup work to do. Toward the end of July, he received reports of a five hundred-man Tory and Indian militia force "skulking" nine miles from Savannah. He sent Jackson and the legion to check them on Skidaway Island, but they were forced to retreat on July 25 in the face of superior force and numbers. The Tories burned a plantation, but eventually either left the state or disappeared into the population. In August, British raiders out of St. Augustine sailed as close as twenty miles from Savannah, burning a plantation, capturing thirty-three slaves, and stealing a valuable store of indigo.[47]

None of this pleased Greene, because it meant his most accomplished general couldn't return to South Carolina. "My motive for withdrawing the troops from Georgia was to have our force collected and avoid, if possible, being defeated in detachments," he wrote Wayne in early August. "Destroy the trunk, and the branches will soon perish. . . . Our line is daily diminishing by deaths and discharges, and is far less than you can imagine. . . . Leslie may have it in his power to give us a more certain and fatal defeat."[48]

About the time Wayne received Greene's letter, he had become confident that state militia could handle any crisis. In fact, the next month, the militia forced the Indians to surrender virtually all of Georgia.[49]

Wayne rejoined Greene's army on August 15. He wasn't modest about his accomplishments. "The duty we have done in Georgia was much more difficult than that of the children of Israel," he said. "They had only to make bricks without straw, but we had provision, forage, and almost every other article of war to provide without money . . . and what is yet more difficult than all, to make Whigs of Tories . . . all of which we have effected, and wrested this state out of the hands of the enemy."[50]

After the war, Wayne and Jackson had a bitter falling out. Jackson was elected to the first U.S. Congress, and became a Jefferson ally, opposing Washington's federalist policies. Wayne defeated his reelection bid. "Jackson's a damned liar," Wayne said. "Let him do his worst, God damn him. I don't care a damn for him." Jackson later resurrected his political career with election as a U.S. senator and governor. His greatest political accomplishment was cleaning up the aftermath of a land-fraud scandal.[51]

10. Leslie's Work

CLINTON LIBERATED CHARLESTOWN FROM THE REBELS IN MAY 1780. For a headquarters, he expropriated "one of the handsomest houses in America." Charlestown's leading slave trader, Miles Brewton II, built the mansion and compound over four years. One guest described the mansion as having "the grandest hall I ever beheld—azure blue satin window curtains, rich blue paper with gilt . . . most elegant pictures, excessive grand and costly looking glasses." The "fine brick house on King Street, with . . . generous doorway and double flight of marble steps" cost Brewton £8,000—about $1.4 million today. The British seized it because Brewton was "an ardent Revolutionist."[1]

But Brewton was already dead. In 1775, he and his family sailed for Philadelphia, and their ship was lost at sea. Brewton's sister, Rebecca Motte, inherited the home, and the British allowed her, her three daughters, and ailing husband to live in part of the house until the husband died in 1781. (The Mottes made their daughters live and eat in the attic to avoid contact with soldiers.) Then the Mottes moved to their plantation.[2]

In late 1781, Leslie commanded Charlestown and worked to address complex problems. The occupation was expensive. His troops were barracked in all or parts of one hundred commercial buildings and private homes, for which the British paid residents more than £5,500 (about $835,000 today). He gave allowances and rations to Loyalist refugees, and bought supplies and services from residents—some of them rebels who smuggled goods for sale across the lines. Money, however, was a minor logistical problem compared to meeting the refugees' other needs. Many lived in hovels. The diseases endemic to the low country and overcrowded conditions felled both refugees and soldiers.[3]

Illness struck Leslie himself, and periodically, he continued to plead in vain with his superiors to be allowed to return to England: "I have been severely attacked with an inflammation in my eyes, which has confined me to a dark room . . . As I have your Excellency's orders to remain here, nothing but the immediate apprehension of my health being in danger can induce me to remove myself to New York, although my physicians have pressed me to it."[4]

When Craig arrived in Charlestown after withdrawing from Wilmington, Leslie assigned the unit to Johns Island, thereby improving the defense of crucial pastureland needed for Charlestown's food supply. Concerned about attacks on Charlestown proper and raids on poorly defended outposts, Leslie began pulling his troops in closer to the city.[5]

When Clinton ordered him to send two thousand men to Jamaica, Leslie protested that removing the troops from Charlestown would jeopardize the city and, ultimately, the South. He eventually sent 1,300 troops to Jamaica under the command of O'Hara, who, by then, had been exchanged. With his army reduced, Leslie contracted his defense perimeters further.

While he had little success conducting an immediate prisoner exchange with the rebels, Leslie was able to exchange prisoners with France's ally, Spain.[6]

Care for refugees. Feed the troops. Defend the city. Protect Loyalists even while reducing areas of control. Maintain troop levels despite disease and desertion. Negotiate prisoner exchanges. Deal with superiors in New York and London. These were the first challenges Leslie faced.

Soon, he would face two more: decisions about slaves, and orders to evacuate.

British law, tradition, and belief supported slavery. British courts had ruled that slavery on British soil was inconsistent with the law, but it wouldn't ban the slave trade for another generation, and wouldn't emancipate slaves in the empire until 1833.

"A horse, a cow, or a sheep is much better protected with us by the law than a poor slave," said an Anglican minister. Most English—and Americans—didn't consider blacks as equal human beings. The minister had to argue that differences between whites and blacks were "accidental or circumstantial," and felt compelled to deny "any essential difference between the European and African mental powers." In fact, "had nature intended Negroes for slavery, she would have endowed them with many qualities which they now want [lack]. Their food would have needed no preparation, their bodies no covering, they would have been born without any sentiment for liberty." Blacks, he concluded, "are capable of learning anything."[7]

Leslie respected that Loyalists needed protection for their property—that is, slaves. Prime field slaves cost about £60 each ($10,000 today) and could be rented for up to £8 a year ($1,400). The owner or renter would incur additional costs for food, shelter, and clothing. The Loyalists couldn't run their plantations without slaves. No plantations, no food, more Charlestown refugees. It also worked the other way: Rebel property—slaves—"flies to us and famine follows," said a British spy.[8]

Leslie's own officers, and sometimes units, owned slaves. The artillery unit owned forty-four black women and children. The horse unit owned six women and children.[9]

But in 1775, Virginia's royal governor, John Murray, Earl of Dunmore, offered freedom to all male slaves owned by rebels if they could escape to British lines and fight for the Crown. Four years later, Clinton expanded Dunmore's offer, promising freedom to escapees from the rebels and "full security to follow . . . any occupation which he shall think proper." African American men and women streamed into British lines. Half-a-million blacks lived in the thirteen colonies—about twenty percent of the population. An estimated 80,000 to 100,000 slaves escaped during the war, despite Whig efforts to stop them. In South Carolina in 1775, slaves comprised sixty percent of the 146,000 residents; up to 59,000 of them escaped during the war from their Loyalist and rebel masters. Many went into the frontier or Spanish territory; many more defected to the British. Some, the British would abandon, as O'Hara did in his retreat to Yorktown.[10]

In Charlestown, Leslie and his predecessors used thousands of African Americans. Often impressed or seized from rebel plantations, sometimes paid or not, sometimes free, sometimes still slaves, they built fortifications; served in the navy; acted as messengers; spied; hauled supplies; emptied latrines; foraged; and plundered. They were carpenters. They were wheelers and smiths, sawyers, and collar-makers. They repaired wagons, boats, bridges, roads, equipment, and arms. The built artillery platforms, barracks, and fascines. Some were prostitutes. Some were raped. And some, the British armed to fight the war as psychological weapons against rebels fearful of slave rebellions.[11]

Dunmore's Ethiopian Regiment, at its peak, had about eight hundred soldiers, fought in Virginia, but was soon devastated by disease, and the survivors were dispersed into other British units, many of them serving in the elite Black Brigade. The Black Pioneers, a company of escaped South Carolina slaves, served in New York, Providence, Philadelphia, and Charlestown. In the Caribbean, a unit of free blacks became the Jamaica Rangers.

In 1782, Leslie created the Black Dragoons regiment, a small unit of about two dozen cavalry, captained by an ex-slave. It would see action against rebel general Francis Marion in late August. More important, from Leslie's perspective, the regiment made almost nightly raids, supplying cattle, sheep, hogs, and horses to Charlestown.[12]

That escaped slaves now carried weapons was, said a Whig general, "sufficient to rouse and fix the resentment and detestation of every American who possesses common feelings." A colleague concurred. "The black dragoons . . . are daily committing the most horrible depredations and murder." In January 1782, for example, a farmer reported that "a party of armed Negroes . . . surrounded the house and endeavored to get me out," leaving after telling the man "that had I not been an invalid they would have fired the house and cut me in pieces." Even a British official reported that the Black Dragoons had committed "indiscriminate outrages" against civilians, thereby tipping white civilians to the rebel side.[13]

Some of the raids failed. On April 21, 1782, about two dozen Whig cavalry skirmished with forty British cavalry, three or four of whom were black. One of them was "cut . . . to pieces" after making "a most gallant defense." At another skirmish, a Whig officer reported, "A party of our men . . . fell in with a party of the British Negro horse [cavalry], consisting of 10 men, of which they killed and wounded all but two men." He described another of the Black Dragoons' assignments: "The British deserters come in now every day, and may be averaged at 30 per week . . . More would come off, but are prevented by the Negro horse, as they are kept constantly patrolling for that purpose."[14]

Although the number of actual Black Dragoons was small, their raids grew into a myth. "The enemy are arming with great industry a large body of Negroes," Greene told Washington. "Not less than 700 are said to be armed and in uniform."[15]

Whether the blacks were armed or worked as laborers, Leslie said, "There are many Negroes who have been very useful . . . and from their loyalty have been promised freedom."[16]

The greatest friction between Leslie and Greene wasn't the arming of slaves, but the stealing of them. When the South Carolina legislature ordered the confiscation of Loyalist property—including slaves—Leslie protested. "I was in hopes [that] humanity, as well as policy," would have prevented the confiscations, he wrote a rebel general. Since that didn't happen, he could "no longer remain the quiet spectator of their [Loyalist] distresses."[17]

He proposed to Greene a suspension of confiscations and creation of a commission "to lessen the devastations of war, and secure, inviolate, the property of individuals." Greene passed on Leslie's proposal to the governor, who refused the proposal because "every species of property, Negroes, plate, household furniture, horses, carriages, cattle, etc., etc., have been indiscriminately torn from their owners by persons under your immediate command . . ."[18]

With the rebels hard-lining, Leslie vowed to continue seizing slaves from rebel plantations so that restitution could be made to Loyalists suffering from the legislature's "oppressive and ruinous" confiscation law. His orders for one of many raids were explicit: "The principal business to prosecute is the collecting of the slaves who belong to those in arms against the British government." He ordered that the slaves be assured the British were "never to return them to their masters, but to take care of them and their families."[19]

In his May 1782 order—to evacuate the South—Carleton told Leslie to "expect a fleet of transports" to carry Loyalists and troops from Savannah and Florida. (Carleton rescinded the Florida orders the next month, so that the colony could be used for refugees.) Evacuation of Charlestown would come later, but "with the utmost dispatch." He warned Leslie to make the evacuation as friendly as possible. "No destruction nor waste to be suffered," he said. "Even the fortifications shall remain uninjured; no plundering nor insults nor incivility shall be offered to those who remain behind. Severe and instant punishment must check the first attempt." His reasoning: "The evacuation is not a matter of choice, but of deplorable necessity in consequence of an unsuccessful war." Although he was mindful of Loyalists' distress in the South, New York's safety came first.[20]

To avoid panic among the refugees, and to keep the rebels from using the information to their advantage, the British kept a lid on the orders; they wouldn't publicly announce them until August. One member of the small circle that knew was New Jersey's royal governor, William Franklin, Benjamin's estranged son. William reflected Loyalist sentiment when he complained that the British army was impotent in the face of a weaker enemy. "In Charlestown, I find 5,000 or 6,000 regulars, besides militia, closely pent up by about 1,200 ragamuffins and suffering every inconvenience for want of fresh provisions and other necessaries, as if actually besieged by a greatly superior force."[21]

Without disclosing the evacuation plans, Leslie wrote to Greene, explaining Parliament's resolution to end offensive operations and noting the peace talks underway in Paris. He then proposed a ceasefire on behalf of "the rights of humanity, the welfare of this country, and the sentiments of the legislature of my own."[22]

Greene refused. He said couldn't act unilaterally without Congressional authorization and the consent of his French ally. Moreover, he was convinced that the reasons for Leslie's ceasefire proposal were to "detach us from our alliance . . . relax our exertions," and unite Britain in "pushing the American war."[23]

Washington agreed. Three months later, even as it became apparent that the British would indeed evacuate Charlestown, he said he still questioned whether the British were engaging in a deception until "they could put their marine and other matters in a more prosperous train for prosecuting the war."[24]

The fighting in South Carolina continued.

11. "Howlings of a
Triple-Headed Monster"

TOO WEAK TO ATTACK CHARLESTOWN, GREENE DISPERSED HIS Continental army and state militia forces around the state. Most units were led by state-appointed generals: John Barnwell in the south; Andrew Pickens, guarding against Indians in the west; Thomas Sumter, and later, William Henderson, in central South Carolina; and the most reliable state general, Francis Marion, northeast of Charlestown. Greene and the Continentals defended the country immediately west and south of Charlestown. His most active general was Marylander Nathaniel Gist. (Wayne rejoined Greene in July 1782, but soon fell seriously ill.)[1]

Greene had several goals: Protect civilians from Tory attacks without themselves resorting to reprisals and terrorism. Isolate and destroy British outposts. Thwart Leslie's ability to forage and feed his army and Tory refugees. Force Leslie to evacuate Charlestown, just as Wayne and Rutherford had done in Savannah and Wilmington. Like Leslie, Greene had to feed his army, keep enough of his men free from illness to be effective, and prevent his army from disappearing as enlistments ended or through desertion. Unlike Leslie, Greene also had to arbitrate additional personality conflicts among his officers.

It was a patchwork of problems. One colonel described the fighting as a campaign of "inconsiderable skirmishes." Wayne wrote a friend about "our little army moldering away to a handful by the baneful effects of short enlistments and the fatal fevers natural to this inhospitable climate." Marion ordered his men to stop the "scandalous and infamous practice" of stealing food from civilians. Desertion was rampant—a "shameful practice . . . prevailing among the troops," Greene said. For emphasis, he executed the ringleader of an attempted mutiny.[2]

Days later, he told Marion: "The enemy threatens us with an attack. We have had no small uneasiness in our camp for want of pay, clothing, and spirits. [Knowledge of] the discontent has reached the enemy, and it is confidently asserted that they are coming out to take advantage of it."[3]

William Seymour, a sergeant major, described the routine as mostly marching in anticipation of what the British and Tories might or might not do. From September 8, 1781, until mid-1782, Seymour's regiment maneuvers were a gazetteer of plantations, villages, and landmarks, two miles march one day, sixteen miles another, five miles, twenty-two miles, twenty miles, five miles, twenty-three miles: Eutaw Spring, Gooden's Mill (where "our men were taken sick with the fever and ague"), Stono Ferry, Stono Church, Parker's Ferry, Drayton's Cowpens, Warren's plantation, McQuin's, Goose Creek, Bacon Bridge, Izard's Plantation, Dorchester, Hatley's Point, Strawberry Ferry, near Quarter House, Gough's plantation, Farre's plantation, Thomas Warren's plantation, all along the Ashley River, and back again.[4]

Then, there were the colonels. Henry "Light-Horse Harry" Lee, who commanded the elite and successful cavalry company, Lee's Legion, retired suddenly in January 1782 because he felt he wasn't appreciated—writing "the indifference with which my efforts to advance the cause of my country is considered by my friends." Two of Marion's colonels, Peter Horry and Hezekiah Maham, feuded over seniority, and even over Marion's command of them. Horry quit when Marion gave Maham command of a cavalry legion.[5]

Then there was Colonel John Laurens, whose influence, accomplishments, and connections gave him gravitas, but whose intensity grated on his superiors.

Laurens's connections began with his father, Henry, a successful Charlestown import-export merchant whose early wealth came from the slave trade. Henry might have been responsible for one-third of all the slaves imported into and sold in Charlestown from 1751 to 1761—more than 7,400 people. With cash from his business, Henry bought land, about twenty thousand acres in six Georgia and South Carolina rice plantations, farmed by five hundred slaves.[6]

In ordering such "merchandise" for resale, Laurens was particular. "Our people like tall slaves best for our business and strong," he wrote a business associate. Yet he was a moralist, and conflicted by the trade. "I abhor slavery," he said. "I am devising means for manumitting many of them and for cutting off the entail of slavery."[7]

Henry was a Whig activist. In 1777, he was elected to the Continental Congress, and that November, succeeded John Hancock as president. Congress then named him a foreign minister with the intent of helping Adams and Franklin in Europe. But on his way there in 1780, the British captured him and made an example of him. They jailed him in the Tower of London. There, his health deteriorated until a conditional release in late 1781. By then, he was "much emaciated, and so heavily afflicted with the gout as to be obliged to make use of crutches," a London newspaper reported.[8]

Henry's son, John, was a different kind of man. In 1771, he turned eighteen, and his father took him to Switzerland to study. John wanted to become a naturalist or doctor. His father wanted him to study law. John studied law in London. While in London, he lived with one of Henry's friends—and got the friend's daughter pregnant. They married in October 1776. "Pity has obliged me to marry," John wrote Henry.[9]

As tensions grew between America and Britain, John grew antsy. "I cannot read with indifference the valiant acts of those whose prudent conduct and admirable bravery have rescued the liberties of their countrymen." He left London and his pregnant wife a couple of months after they married. He would never see his wife again, nor his daughter.[10]

Laurens wanted to fight, and in August 1777, Washington welcomed the son of a congressman to his staff as an aide and lieutenant colonel. One month later, Laurens got his wish at the Battle of Brandywine. "It was not his fault that he was not killed or wounded," said Lafayette, using a double negative. "He did everything that was necessary to procure one or the other."[11]

In October, at Germantown, Laurens did get wounded, nicked in the shoulder and side. At Monmouth, in 1778, during hand-to-hand combat, his horse was shot from beneath him. Laurens and fellow Washington aide Alexander Hamilton "seemed to court death," a companion reported.[12]

Reports of John's recklessness had long since reached his father. John admitted as much. "You have asked me, my dear father, what bounds I have set to my desire of serving my country in the military line. I answer: glorious death or the triumph of the cause in which we are engaged." Henry pleaded with his son to be prudent. "You have had many escapes, but I submit it to your wisdom and philosophy whether it be necessary to tempt the fates or to brave them."[13]

But John couldn't be restrained. Two days before Christmas, he fought a duel with General Charles Lee, who, Laurens said, "publicly abused General Washington in the grossest terms." Laurens, a member of Washington's military family, said he had a right to defend his surrogate father's honor. Laurens grazed Lee, but wasn't hit himself, and the seconds—Hamilton was Laurens's—insisted the duel stop.[14]

Laurens and Hamilton had become more than friends. They used over-the-top, sentimental language in their letters to each other, but historians are divided about whether the words they used were just fashionable among young male friends or were suppressed homoeroticism. When, in 1779, Laurens left Washington's staff to fight in the South, Hamilton's farewell letter was typical of their correspondence: "Cold in my professions, warm in friendships, I wish, my dear Laurens, it might be in my power by action rather than words [to] convince you that I love you. I shall only tell you that till you bade us adieu, I hardly knew the value you had taught my heart to set upon you." Laurens returned the sentiment, telling Hamilton of "many violent struggles I have had between duty and inclination—how much my heart was with you, while I appeared to be most actively employed here."[15]

Laurens's southern assignment was a disaster. The Whigs, under the overall command of General Benjamin Lincoln (who later received O'Hara's sword at Yorktown), attempted to take British-held Savannah. In one engagement, Laurens was ordered to lead a two-hundred-fifty-man militia guard into a rear position. Instead, he attacked. The results were two men killed and seven wounded, including Laurens. His immediate commander, General William Moultrie, was furious because it resulted in militia desertions, and

Moultrie was forced to retreat. Laurens acted "very imprudently," Moultrie said. He had "unnecessarily" exposed his men to British fire. "Col. Laurens was a young man of great merit, and a brave soldier, but an imprudent officer; he was too rash and impetuous."[16]

Laurens was conspicuous in the joint Whig-French siege and assault on Savannah, but the British prevailed. Lincoln and the Whigs retreated to Charlestown where, on May 12, 1780, they surrendered to the British. Laurens was a prisoner of war, soon paroled, but bound by his word not to fight until he was exchanged for a captured British officer of the same rank. He begged Washington to expedite a prisoner exchange: "It is the greatest and most humiliating misfortune of my life to be reduced to a state of inactivity at so important a juncture as the present. . . . An exchange would restore me to life."[17]

Laurens got his exchange about five months later, but Congress had other plans for him than fighting. It needed to send a military man to France to update the ally and to immediately secure more money from them. Laurens, with his European education, fluency in French, closeness to Washington, and experience working with a military ally, was a logical choice. Lafayette tried to set up a friendly welcome for Laurens, telling his wife that "General Washington loves him very much, and of all the Americans you have had the opportunity to see, he is (beyond all comparison) the one I would like to see you receive in the most friendly manner."[18]

But Lafayette and other friends warned him to temper his personality when acting as a diplomat. If the French didn't agree to give the money, Lafayette said, "it will, I believe, be because they won't think themselves able to do better—so . . . don't get angry, and be [assured] that their intentions are good."[19]

Hamilton was blunter. "In the frankness of friendship, allow me to suggest to you one apprehension. It is the honest warmth of your temper. A politician, my dear friend, must be at all times supple—he must often dissemble . . . I suspect the French Ministry will try your temper; but you must not suffer them to provoke it."[20]

Laurens arrived in France on March 9, 1781. He immediately broke protocol, offended sensitivities, demanded money, threatened, stormed, and pestered. "Notwithstanding the great efforts we are making for the United States, Mr. Laurens is not satisfied," Vergennes, the French foreign minister, complained to Lafayette.

Moreover, Laurens "is little familiar with the usages and consideration which are due the ministers of a great power. He has made his
demands not only with unfit importunity, but even employing
threats."[21]

Franklin was equally critical. "He was indefatigable while he
stayed and took true pains, but he *brusqued* the ministers too much,
and I found after he was gone that he had thereby given more
offense than I could have imagined . . . It produced me some mor-
tifications."[22]

The only diplomat who enjoyed Laurens was the equally
undiplomatic John Adams, with whom Vergennes refused to talk,
and about whom Franklin had conceded honesty, patriotism, and
wisdom, "but sometimes and in some things, absolutely out of his
senses." Adams said Laurens "succeeded to a marvel, though Dr.
Franklin says he have great offense. I long since learned that a man
may give offense and yet succeed."[23]

And Laurens did succeed. He returned to America on August 25,
1781, with 2.5 million livres in cash ($10.6 million today), two car-
goes of military supplies, a Dutch loan in the works, and a promise
of French naval reinforcements. Although Franklin had already
arranged for loans and gifts of ten million livres in late 1780,
Laurens's presence probably expedited the payments.[24]

Diplomacy concluded, Laurens rejoined the army, which was
closing in on the British at Yorktown. He served under Hamilton
and helped lead the attack on a crucial fortification. Hamilton
reported to his commander, Lafayette, that Laurens "distinguished
himself by . . . entering the enemy's work with his corps among the
foremost, and making prisoner the commanding officer of the
redoubt."[25]

Laurens represented the Whigs in the surrender negotiations.
Within a month of the British surrender, he headed home to South
Carolina to report to General Greene. Laurens had an ulterior moti-
vation for returning to the South.

As a student in Europe, he had come to oppose slavery. "How
can we . . . reconcile to our spirited assertions of the rights of
mankind the galling abject slavery of our Negroes?" he said. In 1778,
he had proposed a fight-for-freedom plan in which he would recruit
three thousand slaves to fight for the Whigs, and pay their owners
$1,000 each. After the war, the slaves would be emancipated and

given $150 each. Laurens pleaded with his father to give him "a number of your able-bodied men slaves instead of leaving me a fortune."[26]

Henry was skeptical, but Congress endorsed the plan. Southern legislatures despised it. In South Carolina, the legislators "received it with horror," sure that "terrible consequences" would result. "Terrible consequences" had resulted in 1739, when a slave revolt began a dozen miles from Charlestown. At least twenty-one whites were killed and nearly all of the eighty rebellious blacks were killed or executed. This is what would happen if blacks were armed.[27]

Arming free blacks, let alone slaves, was problematic for many in the Whig military as well. When Washington took command of the army in 1775, he refused to allow any blacks, whether free or slave, to remain. Several New England officers with integrated units protested. "We have some Negroes, but I look upon them in general equally serviceable with other men . . . Many of them have proved themselves brave," said Massachusetts general John Thomas. With advice from Congress, Washington compromised and grandfathered into the army freemen. Over time, starved for manpower, he relented on slaves. Over the course of the war, about five thousand blacks fought as rebels—including, at any given time, about six to twelve percent of Washington's army. In 1782, he went further and endorsed Laurens's concept.[28]

Laurens also enlisted Greene's support, then was elected to the South Carolina legislature, and began pushing his fight-for-freedom plan. "That they would make good soldiers, I have not the least doubt," Greene wrote the governor in April 1782.[29]

But, as in 1778, the legislature was appalled. One legislator, a Yorktown veteran, was sure the Laurens plan was part of a northern conspiracy for general emancipation and worse. He told a friend of a mutual acquaintance in Philadelphia who "once mentioned seriously to me that our country would be a fine one if our whites and blacks intermarried. The breed would be a hardy excellent race, he said, fit to bear our climate."[30]

Edward Rutledge, the governor's brother and a Declaration of Independence signer, reported the voting results: "We have had another hard battle on the subject of arming blacks. About 12 or 15 were for it, and about 100 against it. I now hope it will rest forever and a day. But I do assure you I was very much alarmed on the occasion."[31]

The proposal, said a Greene aide, was "annihilated" by "the fears of the people." Greene himself was frustrated. "I was in hopes the southern states, by enlisting blacks, might have enabled me to act offensively," he said.[32]

Laurens took the defeat hard, telling Washington: "The single voice of reason was drowned by the howlings of a triple-headed monster in which prejudice, avarice, and pusillanimity were united." Washington consoled Laurens, telling him that "every selfish passion has taken its place." Americans, he said, can't "boast an exception" to self-interest versus the national interest.[33]

Arming slaves would not happen with South Carolina rebels, but using them in other ways was appropriate. Like the British, the Whigs used them as laborers, even boat pilots. Black women could become mistresses or rape victims; sometimes, white men freed their mistresses and children. About one-third of freed slaves were mixed-race children, and black women comprised three-quarters of free adults. Finally, slaves were a unit of currency. South Carolina authorized the governor to use slaves confiscated from Tories to meet back-pay obligations to its troops. The Whig government and military offered confiscated slaves as a signing bonus to new recruits—one grown black for a private, three grown blacks and one small one for a colonel.[34]

12. The Swamp Fox Meets His Match

So GREENE AND LESLIE FOUGHT A WAR OF SKIRMISH, OF PROBE and thrust, parry and counter-parry, forage, raid, terror, counterterror, retaliation; Greene unwilling to concentrate his skinny forces, Leslie unwilling to dilute his Charlestown base; British regular against Continental regular, Tory militiaman against rebel militiaman, the four in various combinations, and, sometimes, plunderers with no conviction.

Historians have documented nearly two hundred encounters in South Carolina in the fifteen months after Yorktown. There are scores more, piddling incidents, footnotes:

"This day," wrote a Continental officer on April 14, 1782, "a small party of the enemy's cavalry came to Dorchester and took Lieut. Carrington prisoner . . . This night, the soldiers slept with their clothes on and lay on their arms."[1]

An officer sent men to guard ammunition wagons, "lest the Tories, who are very numerous, should take them. The Tories fired on part of the guard who were left with one of the wagons."[2]

Assured that he would be treated as a POW, a Loyalist captain surrendered, but as "he had been so notorious a villain . . . he was immediately put to death before[in front of] his wife and children."[3]

On a foraging expedition, British regulars and Loyalists encountered rebels near Monck's Corner. The rebels holed up in a defensive position, and "a heavy fire from these houses" killed two and wounded five or six others. The British "collected a number of cattle."[4]

Near Ninety-Six, Whigs used dogs to track Tories who had "burnt some houses and committed other irregularities." This tactic, a rebel report noted, "succeeded beyond our most raised expectations."[5]

On the Ashley River, a boat manned by soldiers "in the garb and color of negroes" hauling goods to market, captured the *Alligator*, a British galley. A few British were killed, a few escaped, but Whigs captured the captain and twenty-eight sailors before torching the ship. A month later, in Beaufort, three British privateers flying the rebel flag lured half a dozen rebel boats into a trap, captured the crews, burned supplies, and seized slaves.[6]

Most of these skirmishes were ad-hoc affairs. Greene was more methodical, and in December 1781, what might have been described as a skirmish turned into strategic victory.

Dorchester was a small, prosperous trading community on the Ashley River, twenty miles northwest of Charlestown. It was settled in 1697 by Puritan colonists from its namesake town in Massachusetts. Soon, Anglicans joined the Puritans, and Creeks and Cherokees traded with them both. The town prospered from its pine forests, which provided lumber and pitch; from low-lying areas turned into rice paddies; from its location at the head of river navigation for large ships. Dorchester had a large dock and a shipyard. During the Seven Years' War, the settlers built a fort made from tabby, a mixture of oyster shells, lime, sand, and water, which, when dry, had concrete-type strength. The fort, eight feet tall and two feet thick, commanded the river.[7]

When the revolution began, Whigs turned the town into a military depot. Sometime over the next five years, both the military and civilians abandoned Dorchester; in 1780, a British foraging party reported about forty deserted homes. The British seem to have occupied it shortly thereafter, but they, too, abandoned it. Continental colonel Henry Lee raided the town in July 1781, but found no British. But the British soon returned. By November, four hundred infantry, one hundred fifty cavalry, and an unknown number of Tory militia occupied Dorchester.

An enemy post of that size got Greene's attention. In mid-November, he left his main camp north of Charlestown headed for

Dorchester, leading two hundred cavalry and two hundred infantry. "We appeared before Dorchester the first [December 1] after a most fatiguing, wet, and disagreeable march," Greene said. His advance guard spotted a Tory patrol and immediately charged, killing about ten, wounding up to twenty, and taking several prisoners. British cavalry counterattacked, but were driven back "with such fury as left them no doubt but that our whole force was at hand."[8]

The British concluded they had no choice but to abandon Dorchester. That night, they destroyed supplies, sunk their cannon in the river, and burned as many buildings as they could. Greene entered what was left of the town the next day.

Residents eventually returned and repaired the church and their homes, but the town was dying. The school closed in 1818; the church, in 1820. After an 1886 earthquake, the last residents abandoned Dorchester. Archaeological efforts in the mid-twentieth century brought it back to the public's attention. In 1969, a timber company donated the property to the state. Today, the town site is part of the Colonial Dorchester State Historic Site. The fort walls, made of tabby, and the brick bell tower of the church survive.

General Horatio Gates, who led the Whigs to victory at Saratoga in 1777—their greatest until Yorktown—preceded Greene as southern commander. His leadership was a debacle, resulting in defeat at Camden, South Carolina, in 1780.

Where Greene welcomed local partisans and state militias to supplement his army, Gates had little use for them, including Francis Marion, a middle-aged plantation owner and state brigadier general. After Gates's defeat, it was largely Marion who kept the pressure on the British with incessant hit-and-run guerilla tactics.

The frustrated British lieutenant colonel Banastre Tarleton apocryphally gave Marion his nickname: "As for this damned old fox, the devil himself could not catch him." In truth, "Swamp Fox" was a nineteenth-century creation, and Marion's legend didn't begin until the fictional 1809 biography by Parson Weems, the author of an equally fictional biography of Washington.[9]

Far from being movie-star handsome, Marion was short, walked with a limp, and was in his forties during the war. One of his men said he was "rather below the middle stature of men, lean and swarthy. His body was well set, but his knees and ankles were badly formed; and he still limped upon one leg. He had a countenance remarkably steady; his nose was aquiline; his chin projecting; his forehead was large and high, and his eyes black and piercing. He was now forty-eight years of age [in 1780], but still even at this age, his frame was capable of enduring fatigue and every privation, necessary for a partisan. . . . He was dressed in a close round-bodied crimson jacket, of a coarse texture, and wore a leather cap, part of the uniform of the 2nd Regiment, with a silver crescent in front, inscribed with the words, 'Liberty or death.' "[10]

Marion grew up in Georgetown, a port sixty miles northeast of Charlestown. When he was fifteen or sixteen, he worked as a crewman on a schooner sailing for the West Indies. The ship foundered, possible hit by a whale. The crew drifted in an open boat for a week (so the legend goes), two of the men died, and Marion's career as a sailor ended. In 1761, in a war with the Cherokees, Marion fought as a lieutenant in a light-infantry company. He was, his captain said, "an active, brave, and hardy soldier, and an excellent partisan officer."[11]

Marion was a member of the planters' establishment, and in 1770 was elected to the legislature. As tensions grew between Britain and its colonies, Marion opposed the Crown. When the war began, he was elected a cavalry captain in a regiment commanded by his former captain, now Colonel William Moultrie. (Moultrie later commanded John Laurens at Savannah.) Their first action was to attack British Fort Johnson, which overlooked Charlestown harbor. They found the fort abandoned. Marion participated in Moultrie's defense of Charlestown the next year from a different harbor fort, Fort Moultrie. By 1779, he was a lieutenant colonel, and he fought in an unsuccessful attempt to seize Savannah. The British captured Charlestown in 1780, taking as prisoners Lincoln, Moultrie, Laurens, and six thousand other men.

Marion wasn't one of them. Earlier in the year, in Charlestown, an officer invited Marion to a dinner-and-drinking party. As was the custom, the host locked the doors after dinner. Marion, a light drinker and possibly a nondrinker, wanted to leave quietly. He jumped to the street from a second-floor window and broke his ankle. When the British took Charlestown, he was in the country recuperating.[12]

Gates succeeded Lincoln and exiled Marion to command partisans and state troops closer to Charlestown. Now, Marion missed Gates's defeat at Camden in August 1780. But that month, his men rescued one hundred fifty captured Continentals. Weeks later, with just fifty men, he ambushed two hundred fifty Tory militia; overran a Tory outpost; and fought Tories again toward the end of October. South Carolina promoted him to general.

Greene relieved Gates on December 2, 1780. Two days later, the new commander wrote Marion with conciliatory orders, asking him to keep up the partisan raids and to be the eyes of the army: "I am fully sensible your service is hard and sufferings great, but how great the prize for which we contend! I like your plan of frequently shifting your ground. It frequently prevents a surprise and perhaps a total loss of your party. Until a more permanent army can be collected than is in the field at present, we must endeavor to keep up a partisan war and preserve the tide of sentiment among the people as much as possible in our favor. Spies are the eyes of an army . . . At present, I am badly off for intelligence."[13]

When Greene and Marion met in person, one of Greene's generals described an unimpressive sight: "Marion, a gentleman of South Carolina, had been with the army a few days, attended by a very few followers, distinguished by small black leather caps and the wretchedness of their attire. Their number did not exceed twenty men and boys, some white, some black, and all mounted, but most of them miserably equipped. Their appearance was, in fact, so burlesque that it was with much difficulty [that] the diversion of the regular soldiery was restrained by the officers."[14]

The son of another Continental officer who had known Marion used a similar description.

> General Marion was in stature of the smallest size, thin as well as low. His visage was not pleasing, and his manners not captivating. He was reserved and silent, entering into conversations only when necessary, and then with modesty and good sense. He possessed a strong mind, improved by its own reflection and observation, not by books or travel. His dress was like his address—plain, regarding comfort and decency only. In his meals, he was

abstemious, eating generally of one dish and drinking water mostly. . . . Even the charms of the fair, like the luxuries of the table and the allurements of wealth, seemed to be lost upon him. The procurement of subsistence for his men, and the contrivance of annoyance to his enemy, engrossed his entire mind.[15]

Appearances deceived. Throughout 1781, Marion raided and attacked the enemy with an army that ranged from forty to one thousand men. The British sent out two unsuccessful expeditions to destroy him. Tarleton led the first mission. A lieutenant colonel led the second. Marion surprised him and attacked, killing twenty. The British complained that Marion "would not fight like a gentleman or a Christian."[16]

Cornwallis concurred. "Marion has so wrought the minds of the people, partly by the terror of his threats and cruelty of his punishments, and partly by the promise of plunder, that there was scarcely an inhabitant between the Santee and Peedee [rivers] that was not in arms against us." Tarleton described Marion's tactics. "He collected his adherents at the shortest notice . . . and, after making incursions into the friendly districts, or threatening the communications, to avoid pursuit, he disbanded his followers. The alarms occasioned by these insurrections frequently retarded supplies on their way to the army . . ." Although Marion was "timid and cautious, and would risk nothing," said a Loyalist colonel, he succeeded.[17]

Marion and Greene maintained a strong rapport. Greene had Marion co-lead the first attack line with his nearly four hundred infantry and cavalry at the Battle of Eutaw Springs in September 1781. Greene lost the battle, but so devastated the British that it accelerated their pulling in troops from the countryside, culminating with Leslie's arrival at year's end.

Two months after Eutaw Springs, Greene and Marion became concerned that the British were stealing slaves from residents near Monck's Corner, forty miles north of Charlestown. Marion ordered Colonel Hezekiah Maham to take four hundred dragoons and riflemen to the area to intercept the British and "to recover, if possible, a number of Negroes they were sending to [Charles]town." Maham wasn't able to attack the well-defended enemy redoubt, but forced a nearby hospital in a plantation house to surrender, in hopes of drawing out the main body of enemy soldiers from their fortification. From the hospital, he captured arms and supplies, two doctors, and 80 convalescing soldiers. Finally, he burned the building, destroying arms and supplies he couldn't carry off.[18]

The British protested to Marion. "The burning a hospital and dragging away a number of dying people to expire in swamps is a species of barbarity hitherto unknown in civilized nations—especially when the hospital has been left without a guard for its defense—that could justify an attack upon the defenseless inhabitants." To the contrary, Marion and Maham replied: The convalescing soldiers were able to bear arms, and the amount of arms and supplies at the hospital constituted a military installation.[19]

Around New Year's 1782, Leslie, in Charlestown, learned from spies that parts of Marion's force might be vulnerable about fifteen miles northeast of the city. He ordered Major William Brereton with nearly four hundred cavalry and infantry to try to engage the enemy.

Brereton, like Leslie, came from a military family. He was three when his father was killed at Braddock's defeat in 1755. At seventeen, Brereton joined the army, serving under Leslie as they both were promoted through the ranks. He fought at Brandywine and Germantown in 1777, and participated in raids against New England rebels. In the British redeployment from Philadelphia to New York, he was seriously wounded, and took nearly a year to recover. He returned to the army in 1781, reuniting with Leslie in South Carolina.[20]

On January 2, Brereton rested his men at a plantation, bordered on one side by a swamp crossed by a causeway and the Videau Bridge (possibly named after Joseph Henry Videau, whose daughter married Marion after the war). Inexperienced rebel state troops and militia spotted the British vanguard near the bridge and charged. They had the upper hand—until Brereton's main force counterattacked and overwhelmed them. Leslie praised how Brereton's troops "with great gallantry cut to pieces and took nearly 100 of the rebels," with just one Loyalist killed.[21]

Marion's report to Greene was less believable: His men killed four enemy and wounded fourteen, while only six Whigs were killed and nine wounded, with fifteen missing. Given the power of the counterattack and the victors' ability to see dead bodies, Leslie's account is probably more accurate.[22]

Marion's next major encounter was another debacle. Unlike Brereton, this time, the enemy commander was an amateur, a brilliant amateur. Benjamin Thompson, 29, was born in a farming village eleven miles northwest of Boston. His father died a year later, and his mother married again to a man Thompson remembered as "tyrannical."[23]

When he was thirteen or fourteen, Thompson became apprenticed to a Salem storekeeper, and nearly killed himself from an explosion he created experimenting with fireworks. While working for a dry-goods merchant in Boston in 1769, he spent his spare time attending lectures at Harvard, and learning French and fencing. "I had been destined for trade," he said years later, "but after a short trial, my thirst for knowledge became inextinguishable, and I could not apply myself to anything but my favorite objects of study."[24]

The next year, he studied medicine with a physician, and chemistry and physics on his own. He submitted his first scientific paper to an academic society in 1772, and taught school in Rumford (now Concord), New Hampshire. That year, he married a rich widow, and his world changed. He became a landowner and a friend of the royalist governor. As tensions between the Crown and colonists increased in 1774, the governor commissioned Thompson as a major in the New Hampshire militia. But Whigs accused him correctly of collaborating with the British, and he fled the state for British-occupied Boston. "Nothing short of the most threatening danger could have induced me to leave my friends and family," he wrote a friend.[25]

But his collaboration didn't stop. He became a British spy, at one point telling the Whigs that he wanted a Continental commission, and that the reports from New Hampshire about his loyalty were false. The Whigs jailed him, but released him because of ambiguous evidence. In fall 1775, Thompson's collaboration was exposed, and he fled again to Boston. When the British evacuated Boston, Thompson sailed to London, leaving his wife and daughter in New Hampshire. He became the primary liaison between Tory refugees in London and George Germain, secretary of state for the colonies and a war hawk.

It became a close relationship. One acquaintance talked about his frequent visits to Germain's home, where Thompson "always breakfasts, dines, and sups, so great a favorite is he." Germain put him on the payroll first as the nominal secretary to the colony of Georgia, later as deputy to the inspector general of provincial forces, and finally as an undersecretary for the colonies. That gave him the wherewithal to study naval architecture and conduct ballistics experiments. The Royal Society elected him as a member in 1779.[26]

But Thompson wanted to do more than theorize about fighting. In 1780, Germain arranged for his commission as a lieutenant colonel and commander of a Loyalist cavalry regiment whose men he would have to recruit, the King's American Dragoons. He sailed for New York in late 1781, but bad weather and winds forced him to Charlestown. There, he asked Leslie for an active command. Leslie didn't ignore Germain's friend, even one with little military experience. He gave Thompson two hundred cavalry and five hundred infantry.

For the first couple of months, Thompson led foraging raids, stealing cattle, pigs, sheep, goats, and other supplies. He wrote to Germain that he wasn't impressed by the rebels: "If the prisoners we took the other day . . . are a fair specimen of their cavalry, I would venture to attack the whole with 150 of the dragoons that are under my command. They [the rebels] are absolutely no better than children, and their horses are much too fat, as ours are too lean."[27]

In late February 1782, Leslie and Thompson received more intelligence about Marion's location, and secretly planned an operation; if they were lucky, they would capture Greene himself.

Colonel Peter Horry commanded Marion's brigade in the absence of Marion, who was sitting in the legislature in Jacksonboro, eighty miles to the west. Horry was an experienced fighter. He was also an experienced feuder; he and his fellow colonel, Maham, despised each other, each claiming seniority over the other. Marion complained to Greene that "the dispute between the two colonels is very injurious" to the broader military campaign, and that he had been forced to assign the two and their respective troops to different locations, "which weaken[s] the force."[28]

Horry's men camped near his plantation on Wambaw Creek near the Santee River, northeast of Charlestown. On February 24, Horry's scouts spotted Thompson's men and quickly reported it to Horry's next in command: Horry, ill and staying at his plantation, had temporarily relinquished command to a subordinate colonel, who thought the scouts' report was exaggerated. Near sunset, Thompson attacked, and the rebels retreated. Because the light was waning and the bridge over the creek collapsed, Thompson didn't pursue them, but said his men killed at least thirty rebels. Horry reported just four men killed and six wounded, with seven missing.[29]

In Jacksonboro, Marion had already heard reports that Thompson was advancing, and left to rejoin his men. By the 24th, he had ridden about sixty miles to the plantation home of the Laurenses. There, he picked up reinforcements—dragoons from Maham's detachment—and learned of the fighting at Wambaw Creek. They rode another thirty miles, camping at Hester Tydiman's plantation on the Santee River, a couple of miles from Wambaw.

Thompson found Marion the next morning. Almost simultaneously, the two commanders ordered their troops to charge each other. Marion's panicked. Thompson's didn't.

"We had the good fortune this morning to fall in with a chosen corps under the command of General Marion, in person, which we attacked and totally routed, killing a considerable number of them, taking sixteen prisoners, and driving General Marion and the great part of his army into the Santee, where it is probable a great many of them perished," Thompson told Leslie. Rebels who tried to escape through the swamps were shot or drowned. Thompson also captured most of Marion's arms and supplies, including "General Marion's tent and his canteens full of liquor, which afforded a timely supply to the troops."[30]

Thompson claimed to have killed or captured one hundred rebels. Marion claimed twenty-eight were killed, wounded, or captured. Regardless, "the disgrace was great," Marion told Greene.[31]

In a month, Thompson sailed for New York. Marion retreated across the Santee. The now-reduced Horry and Maham regiments were combined, and Marion chose Maham to lead them. Horry resigned, but Marion appointed him commander at Georgetown, sixty miles from Charlestown.

Despite periodic successes, Leslie's pullback to the Charlestown area stressed the Loyalist militia. In June 1781, Horry had agreed to an armistice with Tory major Micajah Ganey (also spelled Gainey)

in the area between the Great Pee Dee River and the North
Carolina border, including part of what is now called Marion
County. The armistice failed because Whig militia continued to raid
Loyalists, and Ganey felt responsible for defending his people.

After a brief skirmish in June 1782, the two parties reached a new
treaty. The Loyalists would restore plundered Whig property, lay
down their arms, turn over Whig deserters, and sign an oath of alle-
giance. In return, Marion promised that the now-former Loyalists
would be free from persecution.[32]

The only exceptions to the pardon: three notorious Tories,
including David Fanning of North Carolina and a man known as
"Bloody Bill."

13. "Bloody Bill" Cunningham
Raids the Backcountry

WILLIAM CUNNINGHAM "SUFFERED FEARFUL WRONGS, AND fearfully did he avenge them," wrote George Atkinson Ward, a mid-nineteenth-century historian whose own great uncle, a Loyalist, was forced to flee Massachusetts. The sympathetic Ward conceded Cunningham's reputation for blood, but said "not even his greatest enemies have ever alleged that, stern as he was, he was at any time guilty of what was but too common in those times: harshness or cruelty towards women and children."[1]

The Whigs disagreed. "Savage barbarity," said William Moultrie. "Heartless unfeeling monster," others said. "Cold-blooded demon." "Bloody Bill."[2]

His origins are obscure. He probably was born in South Carolina, where Cunninghams had lived for several generations, but he claimed his birthplace was in Ireland. In 1775, he was probably nineteen—but he might have been twenty-seven.[3]

He started as a Whig, a rebel against Britain, and helped raise a militia company. He took part in the capture of a backcountry fort, then agreed to participate in a low-country action near Charlestown with the proviso that he be allowed to resign his commission later. But Cunningham's commander refused his resignation, jailed him for mutiny, and tried him. He was acquitted, and returned home near the inland town of Ninety-Six. Cunningham remained a Whig after the court-martial. In late summer 1776, he campaigned with state militia against the Cherokees who sheltered Tories.

During or after the expedition, Cunningham had second thoughts about fighting Britain. How public he was about this isn't known; there's no record of his activities for the next year and a half, although Ward said "he was hunted more like a wild beast than a man." Sometime during this period, William Ritchie, a Whig captain from the Ninety-Six area, vowed to kill Cunningham for being a traitor. In 1778, Cunningham fled to Savannah. He left the state around the time Ritchie drafted William's lame and epileptic brother, John, into the rebel militia. When John failed to appear at muster, Ritchie and two men went to John's house, whipped him to death, then seized his father and "dragged him over the floor by the hair, and kicked and cuffed him."[4]

Cunningham quickly returned to South Carolina, enlisted a handful of sympathetic friends, went to Ritchie's house, and shot him dead as he climbed over a fence trying to escape. For the next four years, the cycle of revenge and retaliation continued. By late 1781, Cunningham was a commissioned Loyalist major leading anywhere from one hundred fifty to five hundred men.[5] Most of their homes were lost to the rebels; many of their friends and family were dead or living in fear. The British were far away in Charlestown, but Cunningham fought on.[6]

Greene began to receive alarming reports from the backcountry. "The Tories are getting troublesome and insolent in the neighborhood of Orangeburg, in the forks of Edisto, and even up as high as the right toward Ninety-Six," he noted. He considered establishing a post at Orangeburg that could "check the depredation of the Tories, which are more distressing and cruel than all the rest of the British army."[7]

The "depredation," nicknamed the "Bloody Scout," peaked in November after Cunningham escalated his revenge:

> At Cloud's Creek, twenty-four outnumbered men tried to surrender to Cunningham. During surrender negotiations, a rebel who had previously killed a Cunningham acquaintance now shot one of the Tory soldiers. According to Whig accounts, Cunningham's men slaughtered all but two, who escaped.[8] Moreover, a Whig colonel reported, "The captain's head was cut off and one Butler, a man who had been remarkably active, was tortured with more than savage cruelty. Both his hands ware cut off while alive, and it is said many other cruelties committed on him shameful to repeat."[9]

At Hayes Station, the home of Whig colonel Joseph Hayes, Cunningham's men demanded that Hayes and his fourteen men surrender. Hayes refused. Cunningham torched the home. Hayes then surrendered, but Cunningham's men killed them. Cunningham tried to hang Hayes after a "trial" that found him guilty of cruelty to Loyalist women and children by forcing them from their homes. A pole holding the noose broke, so Cunningham hacked him to death with a sword.[10]

Near Hayes Station, Cunningham captured Oliver Toles, a notorious cattle thief who had preyed on Loyalists. Cunningham hanged him.[11]

At Orangeburg, Cunningham defeated one hundred eighty rebel militia, the rebels "being thrown into disorder by a heavy fire from a swamp which the enemy lay in," a Whig officer reported.[12]

At what is now Cross Hill, South Carolina, Cunningham went to the home of his former Whig commander, who greeted him. Cunningham shot him dead in front of his wife, then burned his home.[13]

At Anderson's Mills, Cunningham burned the mill and a militia post, and continued burning and looting buildings down the Saluda River.[14]

At Moore's Plantation, Cunningham killed a bedridden Whig captain and two of his men.[15]

At Lawson's Fork, Cunningham destroyed an ironworks.[16] Near the ironworks, he captured Whig lieutenant governor James Wood, dragged him out of his home, shot and wounded him, and as his wife begged for his life, Cunningham's men hanged him from a dogwood tree.[17]

In the Long Canes region, a detachment from Cunningham's force overran a Whig post, burned and looted homes, and escaped into Cherokee territory with a prisoner, the brother of a rebel partisan general. The men turned the prisoner over to the Cherokee, who tortured him to death.[18]

And so it went. By mid-December, state troops and militia focused their efforts on stopping Cunningham, and under this pressure, the men dispersed, retreating into swamps near Orangeburg. The Whigs captured one of Cunningham's camps on the 20th, and killed twenty Tories.

Cunningham escaped to Charlestown. He appears to have limited his activities to the Charlestown area with a couple of exceptions.

In May, Whig colonel Maham was recuperating from an illness at his home in St. Stephens about fifty miles north of the city. Some of Cunningham's men went to St. Stephens, found Maham unguarded except for a lieutenant, and captured them. But Maham's illness was serious enough that the Tory leader of the detachment immediately paroled him. He was honor-bound to sit out the rest of the war. Maham praised Cunningham's men, "as we expected nothing else than to be tortured in the most horrid manner."[19]

In September, Cunningham returned to the Ninety-Six area, whose defenses had been weakened by diversion of militia to fighting the Cherokees. James Butler, the son of the Whig militia captain whom Cunningham had killed the previous November, collected men to hunt him down. Butler forced a Cunningham relative to lead the group to the Tory camp, which they immediately attacked. The twenty Tories immediately scattered. Cunningham himself mounted his horse, and Butler immediately chased him. But Cunningham's horse was faster, and Butler lost him. Returning to the camp, Butler found that his men had captured a few Tories, but one prisoner was executed. Butler's men justified the execution by saying the Tory had once whipped his mother.[20]

The next month, with the evacuation of Charlestown imminent, Cunningham and five of his men on horseback managed to avoid Whig patrols, and made their way to the safety of British-occupied East Florida.

Few historians agree about what Cunningham did then. One source said he married just before he left, and his bride went to Britain. Another says the Spanish deported him to Cuba after a dispute with neighbors. A third says he rendezvoused with his wife in Britain and lived on the half-pay pension of a British major. A fourth says he died in the Bahamas in 1787, while a final historian says he "lived to a good old age and died quietly in his own bed in the West Indies."[21]

Shortly before Cunningham's last skirmish, Marion fought his last fight. He and his men were camped on a plantation near Monck's Corner on Wadboo Creek. A foraging party of more than one hundred British and Loyalist white and black dragoons under Major Thomas Fraser were also near Monck's Corner, following

Leslie's orders to secure "some fresh meat for the use of the general hospital."[22]

Marion and Fraser apparently learned of each other's presence about the same time on the morning of August 29. The accounts now diverge. Fraser felt the only way he could secure his retreat was to chase away Marion's pickets and threaten an attack. Marion was "deceived by this resolute appearance," said the British report. The rebels "confined themselves within the protection of some buildings" from where they generated a "heavy fire" that killed two Loyalists and wounded five others.[23]

Marion saw the battle differently. Most of his cavalry were out on patrol, so his mobility was limited. His defensive positions were deliberate and well thought-out: in an "avenue of trees," with some of his men "under cover of three small houses," he said. The British "several times endeavored to come round me, but found I changed front and took advantage of the house and fences. They dared not come within reach of our muskets." Fraser charged several times, and his men took casualties. "There must have been a good many men wounded as a great deal of blood was seen along the road they went," Marion said. Marion praised his militia, the largest number of whom were "new-made Whigs"—former Tories led by Major Micajah Ganey, who had signed a treaty with Marion the previous June. Ganey's men "behaved with great spirit. Not one offered to give way, but wished to pursue them in the open field, but that would have given the enemy too great an advantage."[24]

Despite his casualties, Fraser claimed a victory. They captured an ammunition wagon that a panicked rebel had unknowingly driven into the British ranks. He later captured ten of Marion's men. And he delivered one hundred cattle and fifty sheep that helped feed Charlestown.

Marion experienced what many experienced during the war. Both sides plundered his plantation, and the British burned it. Half his slaves ran away. With the war's end, he was destitute, and borrowed money to make repairs. But he continued to represent his neighbors in the South Carolina Senate. There, he supported conciliation with former Tories—an unpopular view—and remained a pro-Washington federalist. His finances improved in 1786 when he married a wealthy woman: his first cousin. She was forty-nine; he was fifty-four. He is buried near what is now called Lake Marion, eleven miles from Francis Marion National Forest.

14. Laurens and His Glory

IF MARION WAS UNDERSTATED, JOHN LAURENS WAS, AS THE FRENCH complained, over-the-top. If Marion was a cautious commander who hid in the swamps when the odds didn't favor him, Laurens was, his superiors complained, reckless.

But with all his faults, he was talented. Laurens and Colonel Henry "Light-Horse Harry" Lee (before his resignation) persuaded Greene to let them attack the British post on Johns Island. Greene was reluctant, but deferred to the colonels, warning them: "I am afraid you are too confident of your strength, and have too much contempt for the enemies. You are to remember the place you are going upon is an island. I hate all island[s] for military operations where we have not the command of the water."[1]

The island is one of the innumerable, flat, near–sea level islands surrounded by interconnected tidal creeks and rivers. At its closest, it's a couple of miles from Charlestown. Its farthest point is more than twenty miles away, only a couple from the ocean. The British used Johns Island (and nearby James Island) for forage and cattle-grazing, "our only hopes of supplies," Leslie told Clinton. Craig, the former British commander in Wilmington, now commanded about five hundred men on the island.[2]

The night of January 12, 1782, during a low tide, Laurens, Lee, and their men attempted to ford New Cut, on the far side of the island. It turned into a failed operation. "Our plan fell through," said an officer. "Daylight appearing and a number of the infantry could not get over the marsh. This was very hard to cross, as it was near the middle deep of mud, and the tide making fast, some of them stuck fast until they were assisted. Those who got over were up to their shoulders in water on their return."3

They tried again on the 14th, this time attempting to cross the Stono River onto the island from the north. They were too late. Leslie had seen Craig's vulnerability to attack and had ordered him to evacuate the night before to James Island, closer to Charlestown and with better defenses.

Lee and Laurens arrived to see the last of the British crossing the Stono River in a schooner, which also prevented the Whigs from landing on the island. The Whigs "fired a dozen of shots, three of which struck her, but the metal was too light to do her much harm. They evacuated the island. A party of our troops at low water went on it and got some small articles, which they, in their hurry, could not take off."4

Greene was disappointed. "A few straggling prisoners were taken, and the enemy's baggage and stores on board a schooner very narrowly escaped. . . . We have got territory, but we missed the great object of the enterprise."5

Lee resigned at the end of the month, and Greene named Laurens to succeed him. On the surface, Laurens was an obvious choice for Greene. He was experienced, and, as a native, he knew the country. Laurens also was a fighter, although Greene admitted that Laurens "wishes to fight much more than I wish he should."6

In practice, the marriage of Laurens with Lee's Legion was a disaster. One officer couldn't contain his sarcasm. "Marched at eight o'clock, and made a halt. . . . Here we lay in the woods without anything to eat or drink, and would not be allowed to cook. In this situation we remained until four o'clock, when Col. Laurens had dined and filled himself with wine. We then took up the line of march and came to Bacon's Bridge, where we lay all night without anything to shelter us from the dew. It was so late we could not provide anything for our comfort. So much for Col. Laurens's wild goose chase."7

Greene himself conceded he had made a mistake, even while explaining to a colleague that Lee's Legion "from long indulgence and from their great reputation made them not unlike the Pretorian guards difficult to govern and impatient of subordination." In June, writing to Lee, Greene said: "I am sorry to inform you that Col. Laurens is by no means popular with the Legion. Some of your particular friends have insinuated that Laurens's appointment was the cause of your leaving the army. Nothing, you know, was more untrue." Later that month, a major and all the legion's captains resigned. Greene needed to address the problem.[8]

He detached Laurens from the legion, assigned him a small guard, and asked him to gather intelligence from a forward-observation post near Charlestown. Laurens complained that his thirteen-man guard was "too feeble," and that the post was "too precarious and dilatory to facilitate matters," but he did the job.[9]

A typical report: "A lady in town heard a British officer say a major in your army transmitted regular intelligence to Charlestown and received sums of specie. Another: He talked with "W.," a Whig spy, who said the Charlestown evacuation is imminent, waiting only transport ships. Tories asked the British for arms with which to defend their city from the rebels—"which they promise to undertake with the aid of Negroes." Laurens believed the Tory plan "resembles the desperate unavailing efforts of a downing man." His sources later told him that "the most outrageous of the [Loyalist] refugees mean to burn the town and commit other acts of vengeance at the moment of an evacuation."[10]

The rumors Laurens heard were based on a public announcement Leslie made on August 7: The British would evacuate Charlestown.

Leslie then made Greene a proposal. The British would end their foraging raids and stay close to Charlestown if the Americans would supply food—for which the British would pay. It would be an agreement of "mutual advantage." The British would get "the supply to our further necessities." The Americans, "security from further depredation and a voluntary compensation for what the force of arms has already given us in possession." He warned Greene, however, that if the Americans turned down the deal, it "will justify the measures I shall be forced to take." If Greene wouldn't sell him food, he would send his army to steal it.[11]

Greene referred the proposal to South Carolina's governing council, which unanimously turned it down. Greene concurred. The proposal was more evidence that the British intended to "seduce and lull the people of this country while they operate with vigor against its allies, and until they can seize a more favorable occasion of gaining possession of the country."[12]

Leslie was incredulous. It was an "unexpected refusal of a proposition so generous on our part and so evidently advantageous to the interest of the opposite party." Now, Leslie acted to feed his troops and the Loyalist refugees in Charlestown. His orders to Fraser resulted in the skirmish with Marion on August 29—and Fraser still delivered a supply of food.[13]

About the same time, Leslie ordered Brereton—who had overwhelmed one of Marion's detachments on January 2—to sail a small armada up the Combahee River, roughly fifty miles to the southwest of Charlestown. For safety from attack, Brereton would go no farther than where a ferry had operated for more than seven decades, thirteen miles from the river's mouth as the bird flies, longer on the twisty, serpentine river.

The river was named after Indians who once lived along it. The settlers spelled it creatively. One variation was phonetic, the way locals today pronounce it: "*cum-bee*." Like many low-country rivers, the Combahee flows with the tides, reversing direction four times each day for many miles. It's an area of pine forests and live oak, rice paddies and swamps, thick brush, tall grass, tough footing. At one point along the river is a rare rise in land, the twenty- to thirty-foot-high Tar Bluff, named after the tar pitch that came from nearby pine trees. By 1782, slaves had turned the swamps into one of the most productive rice-producing areas in the colony.[14]

Leslie knew this, although whether and where there was any rice to be had was a question. He told Brereton that from the plantations that provided "the great abundance of rice and other provisions . . . collect as large a quantity as possible. . . . I must, however, caution you not to remain too long on this river, more especially if you should find the enemy have detached in force . . ."[15]

Brereton left Charlestown on August 21 with eight hundred regulars and Loyalists, transported by about eighteen galleys, schooners, brigs, and other small boats.[16]

Two days later, Greene knew from his spies that Brereton was on his way. He ordered General Mordecai Gist with five hundred men to head for the Combahee, intercept the British, and attack them. "Glory attend you," said Greene's aide-de-camp. "If you succeed, a wreath of laurels shall be presented to you." Gist left at daybreak on August 24.[17]

Gist, 40, was a Baltimore merchant and an early Whig activist. A wealthy man, he named one of his sons "Independence" and another "States Rights." In 1775, he was elected a militia captain. The next year, he was commissioned a Continental army major, and fought in New York, Trenton, and Germantown. In 1779, Congress promoted him to brigadier general. Washington ordered Gist to South Carolina in 1780, where he fought at the Camden defeat. The next year, home in Maryland, he recruited a new force, which fought at Yorktown. He then headed South to join Greene, giving the commander another experienced general.[18]

At his forward post, Laurens didn't hear from his spies about the Brereton expedition until August 24, the day Gist set out for the Combahee. Then, Laurens reported, it was just "vague intelligence." Nonetheless, although he was feverish from a malaria recurrence, he left his bed and abandoned his post to join his immediate superior, Gist, to fight the British.[19]

On the morning of Sunday, August 25, Brereton landed and took control of the Combahee Ferry on the river's south bank. (It was near what is today a boat landing beneath a bridge on U.S. 17 that opened in 2008, named after a future rebel—Harriet Tubman.) His men camped at two plantations on both sides of the river.

That night, Gist arrived nearby on the north bank and learned from his scouts about the British presence. He planned two actions once all his troops caught up with each other. First, he intended to attack the British at the ferry at daybreak on August 27. Second, he would establish an artillery position about twelve miles down the river at Tar Bluff on Chehaw Neck, the triangular piece of land, paddies, and swamp near the junction of the Combahee and Chehaw rivers, about four or five miles from St. Helena Sound and the ocean.

The position would allow his men to "annoy their [British] shipping on their return." In other words, he would attack them at Combahee Ferry, driving them back down the river, and then surprise them with another attack from the artillery position.[20]

On the 26th, before Gist could send his men down Chehaw Neck, Laurens arrived, wanting to fight. He "solicited the direction and command at that post," Gist later told Greene. Laurens left that evening, a "warm and disagreeable" one. Laurens commanded fifty men, who hauled a howitzer and a few pieces of lighter artillery.[21]

Six miles from Tar Bluff, Laurens stopped for dinner at the plantation of Whig captain William Stock. "That night was spent in all the enjoyment of hospitality and female society," an early Whig historian learned from contemporaries. Laurens suggested that the women climb a scaffolding where they could witness from afar the attack on the British the next day.[22]

Around 3 A.M. on the 27th, Laurens left for Tar Bluff. His men weren't the only ones on the move in the early hours. At Combahee Ferry, Brereton had his own intelligence. He learned not only of Gist's imminent attack, but that the rebels were "collecting in force and throwing up works on the heights of [the] Combahee" downriver.[23]

At 2 A.M., the British had returned to their boats and "dropped silently down the river with the tide." It wasn't until 4 A.M. that Gist realized there was no one to attack. But Gist also realized that Laurens now might be headed into an ambush. He immediately sent reinforcements. They were too late. The surviving accounts as to how the fighting began are confusing.[24]

A Whig officer, some of whose colleagues from the Delaware regiment were with Laurens, said Laurens set up his howitzer and began firing on the British. The firing "stopped them in the river," forcing them to land three hundred men to take out Laurens's guns. But Brereton said he attacked because the rebels were pressing the British "on all quarters." He sent two galleys close to shore "to feel for the enemy and draw off their attention," while he landed sixty men.[25]

However, the history of Brereton's regiment says the British landed first and hid in tall grass waiting for Laurens to arrive. The rebels "approached unsuspicious of danger." This agrees with early Whig histories. Brereton's men, said one, "lay in ambuscade, in a place covered with fennel and high grass, and were undiscovered until they rose to fire on the unsuspecting Laurens."[26]

What all the sources agree on is this: Rather than retreat, Laurens charged the larger British force. The fight lasted twenty-seven minutes. Laurens and a corporal died immediately. Nineteen men were wounded. Six were missing, presumably taken prisoner. The British captured the howitzer, and suffered one man killed, seven wounded.[27]

Gist and one hundred fifty reinforcements were just two miles away. "I arrived with the cavalry just in time to cover the retreat of the infantry," he told Greene. Some British retreated to the woods, and Gist ordered his men to attack them. But the going was tough, and "their efforts were rendered ineffectual by a small work of logs and brush in which the enemy threw themselves." The cavalry couldn't ride effectively in the brush, and Gist's infantry was "much dispirited and fatigued." He called off the attack.[28]

Brereton thought Gist's cavalry "behaved exceedingly well," but when they were twenty yards away, "our people then fired with success." Soon, the British returned to their boats and sailed off, continuing to collect "without interruption what rice and corn the country would afford." They returned to Charlestown with cattle, three hundred barrels of rice, and some slaves. Brereton would serve in the army until 1792, rising to lieutenant colonel and serving as lieutenant governor of Jamaica's capital. Throughout his life, he suffered from a wound he received during the war.[29]

Gist, knowing that Laurens's death had significance beyond his rank, sent Greene the news that day. "I shall refresh the troops at Captain Stock's till the afternoon of tomorrow, when the corpse of Col. Laurens shall be interred with every mark of distinction due to his rank and merit." Laurens's father later moved the body to a family plot on a hill overlooking the Cooper River near Monck's Corner. The property, now part of a monastery, is open to the public, as is the small cemetery, which is surrounded by trees that shroud the river view.[30]

Charlestown's Loyalist refugees were distraught by Laurens's death. Many knew the family, but more important, they felt Laurens had treated them fairly. "He constantly condemned every oppressive measure adopted against the Loyalists, and always contended that a steady and disinterested adherence to political tenets, though in opposition to his own, ought to render their possessor an object of esteem rather than of persecution," said the *Royal Gazette*. His only error, the paper continued, was in disavowing the king. "Setting aside this single deviation from the path of rectitude, we know no one trait of his history which can tarnish his reputation as a man of honor, or affect his character as a gentleman. His generosity of temper and liberality of opinion, were as extensive as his abilities. Happy would it be for the distressed families of those persons who are to leave this garrison with his Majesty's troops that another Laurens could be found!"[31]

Laurens's death shook the Whig leadership in an even more personal way.

Greene quickly wrote Washington. "Your Excellency has lost a valuable aide de camp; the Army, a brave officer; and the public, a worthy and patriotic citizen." Washington replied that he considered Laurens's death "a very heavy misfortune, not only as it affects the public at large, but particularly so to his family, and all his private friends and connections, to whom his amiable and useful character had rendered him peculiarly dear."[32]

Soon after the war, Washington presented a more complex portrait of Laurens. "It is my firm belief [that] his merits and worth richly entitle him to the whole picture: No man possessed more of the *amor patriae* [love of country]. In a word, he had not a fault that I ever could discover, unless intrepidity bordering upon rashness could come under that denomination; and to this he was excited by the purest motives."[33]

To Greene, Laurens had no one to blame but himself. "Poor Laurens is fallen in a paltry little skirmish," Greene told one of his generals. "You knew his temper, and I predicted his fate. I wish his fall had been as glorious as his fate is much to be lamented. The love of military glory made him seek it upon occasions unworthy [to] his rank."[34]

Hamilton got the news about his "dear" friend in October. "How strangely are human affairs conducted that so many excellent qualities could not ensure a more happy fate?" he wrote Greene. "The world will feel the loss of a man who has left few like him behind, and America of a citizen whose heart realized that patriotism of which others only talk. I feel the loss of a friend I truly and most tenderly loved, and one of a very small number."[35]

His words didn't fully reflect his feelings. "After the death of John Laurens, Hamilton shut off some compartment of his emotions and never reopened it," said Ron Chernow, Hamilton's twenty-first-century biographer.[36]

Lafayette, back home in France, learned about Laurens from Washington himself. "Poor Laurens is no more," Washington said. "He fell in a trifling skirmish in South Carolina, attempting to prevent the enemy from plundering the country of rice."[37]

It fell to blunt John Adams to deliver the news to John's father, Henry, in London recovering from his imprisonment: "I know not how to mention the melancholy intelligence . . . which affects you so tenderly. I feel for you, more than I can or ought to express. Our country has lost its most promising character in a manner, however, that was worthy of her cause. I can say nothing more to you, but that you have much greater reason to say in this case, 'I would not exchange my son for any living son in the world.' "[38]

"I write with weeping eyes," Henry told his sister-in-law. "My dear son . . . dutiful son, affectionate friend, sensible honest counselor, would have fled across the globe to conduct and serve his father; I was striving to go to him. He loved his country, he bled and died for it. . . . I thought I should have stood the shock with some degree of fortitude, but alas, however strong the man, the father feels and yields. . . . Thank God that I had such a son, who dared to die for his country."[39]

15. At Last, the Evacuation

LESLIE AND GREENE HAD BEGUN NEGOTIATIONS FOR A GENERAL prisoner exchange in February 1782, but Greene was restricted by his civilian government's guidance. North Carolina, for example, insisted on treating Loyalists as traitors, ineligible for exchanges. Greene tried to reason with the governor: "It is much better to effect the relief of our good citizens by considering the Tories prisoners of war than trying them for treason, and leave our best friends in captivity and distress."[1]

All this frustrated Leslie. "I can't get General Greene to make any exchange of prisoners nor do anything. He is a downright lawyer." When Leslie asked for a prisoner accounting, Greene refused, saying the British broke the exchange agreement, "but he won't explain how."[2]

Nine months later, in August 1782, Leslie threatened Greene that if a general prisoner exchange wasn't forthcoming, he would ship the rebel POWs "to distant parts of the continent or elsewhere." Greene immediately agreed to a general exchange—of regular Continental and British army troops. Then, he complained that he held more British prisoners than the British held Whigs, and he wouldn't exchange a regular for a militiaman.[3]

Possibly at Leslie's instigation, Greene now heard from his POWs. They were living on a prison ship in Charlestown harbor, penniless, with worn-out clothes, although donations had allowed them to "cover our nakedness." They pleaded, "Grant us some relief."[4]

The prisoners would have to wait longer. Negotiations dragged on. Finally, on October 22, the generals appointed special representatives to iron out the remaining details. Later that month, they reached a deal, and Washington was able to report that "Greene had effected a universal exchange of all prisoners" in the South. All officers were paroled. Greene sent 1,152 men to Leslie. We don't know how many Whigs were returned.[5]

Leslie told Charlestown on August 7, 1782, that the British would evacuate. "A convoy will be ordered, and every possible assistance given" to Loyalists who wished to leave. He encouraged those who wished to stay to "make their peace" with the state government.[6]

So he could plan the convoys, Leslie created a registration system. Within a week, 4,230 whites and 7,163 blacks, both freemen and slaves, signed the list to leave. And those numbers, a coordinating committee of Loyalists said, were "far from complete due to the short notice allowed."[7]

Leslie worried about the logistics. "The great number of loyal inhabitants who will probably desire to remove their property from this place, which will, I fear, much exceed what the limited quantity of our shipping may enable us to transport," he wrote Carleton. A month later: "Our progress has been very much restrained by the small number of ships in this harbor."[8]

Carleton ordered Leslie to prevent plundering. Further, he told Leslie to treat the rebels "with lenity and generosity." Leslie assured Carleton that he would not only "enforce the strictest obedience to the directions you give," but that he himself had a "natural inclination and a just abhorrence for acts of violence and unnecessary distress." But keeping the lid on angry Loyalists who felt abandoned, or frustrated soldiers in retreat, was difficult. Desertion was common, despite Leslie "having made some necessary examples on the gibbet."[9]

Greene's spies gave him a dire picture of Charlestown. "The mobs and riots which prevail in town give me no small pain for its safety. It is said that General Leslie exerts himself all he can to preserve order, but he is so badly supported that his orders are but indifferently executed," Greene reported. A Whig legislator and merchant heard from acquaintances within Charlestown that "the town is in the greatest confusion. The removal of household furniture, merchandise, pulling down the wooden houses that had been built by people going away, and the lamentations of the poor, going away almost destitute of every comfort of life, altogether composed a most melancholy scene."[10]

As for Leslie himself, "I long for our departure," he wrote Carleton, "for no person can be more unpleasantly situated than myself. I would not undertake the same business again . . . for any earthly consideration."[11]

Prisoners, food, ships, desertion, civil order. Leslie also needed to resolve another issue: what to do with the blacks.

The black Southerners fell into several groups, and Leslie had concerns about them all:

Free men and women.

Slaves who had been promised freedom for serving as soldiers and laborers.

Slaves belonging to British officers. Most had been taken from rebel plantations, and the officers considered them property to be evacuated.

"Sequestered" slaves—those belonging to rebels and captured by British or Loyalist troops. Many were used to compensate Loyalists for loss of their own slaves to the rebels.

Slaves belonging to Loyalists.

Slaves who fled to the British assuming they would be free.[12]

Leaving any behind would result in, at a minimum, their re-enslavement. For those who worked closely with the British, the consequences could be worse. One collaborator who belonged to a Charlestown Loyalist had spied for Leslie. Later captured, the rebels decapitated him and impaled his head on a pole as a warning. Rebel governments reimbursed constables for whipping or branding slaves who had committed offenses. A slave caught committing arson might be burned to death.[13]

Leslie felt a responsibility for many of the blacks. "Those who have voluntarily come in under the faith of our protection cannot in justice be abandoned to the merciless resentment of their former masters," he wrote Carleton.[14]

On the other hand, Carleton had ordered Leslie to respect rebel property—including slaves. So Leslie peppered his commander with questions:

"What will be done with the sequestered negroes?" he asked.

"There are many negroes who have been very useful, both at the siege of Savannah and here. Some have been guides, and from their loyalty have been promised their freedom. . . . Many of the [Loyalist] inhabitants will wish to go to Jamaica with their negroes."[15]

"I wish your Excellency's instructions had been fuller with regard to the sequestered negroes; their number, which is very considerable, renders this a subject of much importance, and I am not a little embarrassed how to dispose of them."[16]

"If an officer takes a Negro belonging to the enemy in action, with his master's horse, is that Negro looked on to be the property of the officer who took him or not?"[17]

Leslie faced a special problem with British officers who had taken black slaves as their own. "Every officer wishes to include his slave" in the evacuation. They pretend them spies, or guides, and, of course, obnoxious [to the rebels], or under promises of freedom from Gen. Prevost, Lord Cornwallis, Lord Rawdon, or some other officer of rank, or free by proclamation." Most slaves wanted to stay with their new, more humane British masters because they were "exceedingly unwilling to return to hard labor and severe punishment from their former masters." Given the large numbers involved, including wives and children, the cost of evacuating them "will amount to a monstrous expense."[18]

Carleton gave Leslie one piece of guidance: "Such as have been promised their freedom must have it." Everything else had either been answered previously (ambiguously, Leslie thought) or it was "left to General Leslie's decision."[19]

Leslie decided to negotiate with John Mathews, 38, the Whig governor, Charlestown native, and a lawyer. They reached an agreement on October 10. Leslie would return to the Whigs all slaves, except those to whom the British had promised freedom and those who were "particularly obnoxious" to the rebels because of their collaboration with the British army. Leslie also promised to compensate the rebels for slaves who weren't returned and allow rebel inspectors to search Charlestown for slaves who were being improperly evacuated. In return for these concessions, the Whigs pledged to allow Loyalists to sue in court to recover their confiscated property, as well as to honor debts to British merchants.[20]

Then, the agreement fell apart. While the British were in the process of returning 136 slaves whom inspectors had found in a Florida-bound ship, the rebels captured three British soldiers, and Leslie refused to continue the slave exchange. Mathews, suspicious that Leslie was trying to evacuate more slaves than he was entitled to, cancelled the entire agreement.

Leslie vented his frustration about the "insolent" rebels to Carleton. "All my good intentions of assisting the Loyalists in returning the enemy their Negroes have proved abortive from the behavior of Mr. Mathews, the rebel governor, and General Greene in insulting the outposts at the very time I was acting with the utmost moderation and forbearance."[21]

The first wave of transports arrived in Charlestown on September 20, and in mid-October, the first group of refugees sailed to British-held St. Augustine: 1,147 Loyalist troops, 1,383 Loyalist civilians, and their 1,681 black slaves.[22]

But the skirmishing continued. West of Charlestown in October, Whig militia broke up a meeting of Tories. Loyalist militia then ambushed the Whigs near Saltketcher Swamp, wounding several. In November, Whigs lured ten black British dragoons out of their positions on the outskirts of Charlestown. Eight were killed or wounded; two were captured.

The last fighting with regular British troops took place on November 14. Colonel Thaddeus Kosciuszko, 36, had been with the Continentals since 1776. A Polish cavalry officer and engineer, Kosciuszko built the Whig defenses at Saratoga and West Point. He went south after Gates's defeat at Camden. Despite some tactical blunders during the campaign against Cornwallis, Greene trusted Kosciuszko. After Laurens died, Greene assigned Kosciuszko many of Laurens's former duties, including intelligence, patrolling near the British, and harassing British foragers.[23]

One of Kosciuszko's officers found that up to one hundred British sailors were landing regularly on James Island, across the harbor from Charlestown, to cut wood. On November 14, Kosciuszko and his men prepared to ambush the sailors. But the

British had their own intelligence, and they ambushed the ambush-ers. Kosciuszko's force of about seventy Continentals found them-selves facing more than three hundred British regulars. Five Whigs died, and another five were wounded. Four bullets pierced Kosciuszko's coat and another bullet shattered a lance he held, but he and most of his men escaped.

In October, wrote a Whig captain, "It was now pretty well known that the enemy would soon evacuate the city. Many poor devils had taken protection and followed the British in; provisions scarce in town, and those people sick of their situation. They were anxious to get back to their old places of abode in the country. Some very mis-erable objects came out—whole families, battered and starving."[24]

Leslie wanted his troops to depart without being molested. Greene wanted to inherit a Charlestown that was neither looted nor torched. He assigned Wayne to negotiate the handover with Leslie. Wayne, who had negotiated the British evacuation of Savannah, was now recovered from a long illness.

They concluded their agreement on December 13. "The preser-vation of Charlestown, and the lives and property of its inhabitants being of much greater consequence than striking or capturing a rear guard of a retiring enemy, I agreed to the enclosed propositions from General Leslie," Wayne reported.[25]

As the British pulled back from their positions, Wayne's advance guard would move in, keeping a buffer of two hundred yards. "During the whole of this, it is to be understood that no hostility is to take place until our troops have got on board their transports," Leslie said. If Wayne attacked the British, Leslie would order the city destroyed.[26]

At daybreak, Saturday, December 14, 1782, the last British troops left their fortifications, and Wayne's cavalry and light infantry fol-lowed them through the city. Occasionally, the British asked Wayne to leave more distance between them. Wayne complied. As he moved into the city, Wayne stationed guards "at proper places." Small groups of soldiers patrolled the streets.[27]

Royal lieutenant governor William Bull recalled that "the rebel cavalry were at hand and came to town that morning, but General Leslie sent to them to forbid their approaching the waterside of the town until his troops were totally gone. A few straggling sailors had remained in town who were kindly treated by the American cavalry and permitted to return quietly to their ships."[28]

A Continental captain "saw the last of the enemy embark in their boats . . . An immense fleet lay in sight all day. Found the city very quiet—houses all shut up." He saw no residents until the next day, when some shops also opened.[29]

It was a "melancholy scene," a British soldier said, because of what was happening to the "poor, unhappy Loyalists," who were now "left victims to their merciless enemies, or . . . to suffer every species of indigence and want in a strange land." Charlestown's streets, "formerly crowded and cheerful to the view, now presented one mournful scene of the most complicated wretchedness." As the Loyalists passed by the homes of friends who were staying, "they silently, with grief unutterable, bowed their last farewell. This melancholy salute was returned with feelings that could only be expressed by tears and sobs. A gloomy despair sat on every countenance, and all was wretchedness and woe." [30]

Some blacks, abandoned by the British, grabbed the sides of shuttle boats as sailors rowed them to the transports anchored in the harbor.[31]

The Continentals treated the remaining white Charlestown Loyalists "with civility, and permitted them to carry on business as usual," a Tory paper reported.[32]

With favorable tides, the 126 transports, divided into five fleets sailing to different locations, crossed Charlestown bar on December 18. The smaller of the fleets carried two hundred black soldiers to St. Lucia, in the Caribbean; twenty boats headed for Jamaica; another twenty to England; and eight to East Florida. The remaining, larger fleet, with the army, sailed to New York. Bull estimated that the transports evacuated more than nine thousand civilians from South Carolina.[33]

General Marion dismissed his men on December 15. He told them that "he will always consider them with the affection of a brother."[34]

Greene gave the president of Congress the "agreeable information of the evacuation of Charlestown." To Washington, he added a caution. He was "afraid" of complacency—that southern Whigs "will turn their attention too much to private repose for the public safety."[35]

A friend didn't share Greene's contemplation. "There are very few persons, my dear friend, to whom Providence has given the power to think justly," wrote Congressman Gouverneur Morris. "It is not, therefore, a matter of astonishment to me that you were obliged to perform wonders."[36]

The British army was gone, but there remained unfinished business.

Through at least March 1783, attacks continued on rebel merchant ships off the Carolina coast. Primary sources are inconsistent as to the dates and whether there was one or multiple incidents, but it's clear that one action involved a rebel ship, the *Eliza*, carrying a cargo from Havana of sugar, rum, and possibly specie. On March 30 or 31, a British frigate or Loyalist privateer ran the *Eliza* aground on Bull Island, twenty-five miles northeast of Charlestown. One side or the other burned the ship to keep the enemy from either the cargo or the ship itself. There might have been a skirmish.[37]

Into the mid-1790s, local troops and vigilantes fought fugitive Loyalists, bands of escaped slaves, and gangs of bandits who continued to raid civilians. In September 1783, for example, they tracked down one of the renegade Tories, chased him, and, after they shot him in the leg and he fell from his horse, executed him. In May 1786, Catawba Indian, South Carolina, and Georgia troops destroyed a remote, fortified village of three hundred ex-slaves-turned-raiders. Some of the ex-slaves, who called themselves "The King of England's Soldiers," escaped and continued their raiding.[38]

Despite Greene's reconciliation efforts, Whig civilians wanted revenge. Gangs tarred and feathered some former Loyalists. Anti-Tory mobs appeared around the state. Their worst riot was in July 1783. The South Carolina legislature ordered ex-Loyalists to leave the state in 1784.[39]

Charlestown put symbolic distance between it and Britain. On August 13, 1783, it incorporated as a city and changed its name to something that sounded more American: Charleston.

For Greene, until a peace treaty was signed, he had to maintain what remained of his Continental army. His men were unpaid and anxious to leave. He dealt with some small mutinies. His men were ill; it had been "one of the sickliest seasons known this 30 years,"

Greene said. "I have been unwell with a fever but have got quite over it. . . . We have buried upwards of 200 of our fine fellows." And Greene's troops were hungry. "If the year continues as it has begun," he wrote on New Year's Day 1783, "we shall end badly as we have nothing to eat for man or beast."[40]

On June 21, 1783, Greene told his men they could go home. Speaking in the third person, he said, "The General joined this army when it was in affliction, when its spirits were low, and its prospects gloomy. . . . We have trod the paths of adversity together, and have felt the sunshine of better fortune. . . . It has been the General's good fortune to point the way, but you had the honor to accomplish the work. . . . The General cannot take leave of this subject without adding his strongest assurances to the army that he is fully persuaded their country will do them justice, if not consider their merit with liberality."[41]

After the war, Greene was hounded by creditors, his debts largely incurred by his guarantees related to the purchase of clothing for his troops. In 1785, he, Caty, their five children, and a tutor, moved to a rice plantation outside of Savannah. Confiscated from a former Loyalist official, it was a gift from the Georgia government. Greene was now a slaveholder and farmer. One of his neighbors was Anthony Wayne, also a gift recipient.

Greene died in 1786, at forty-three, possibly from a heat stroke. His neighbor, Wayne, wrote a friend: "Pardon this scrawl. My feelings are but too much affected, because I have seen a great and good man die." Washington also was moved: "He was a good man, indeed." The general proposed to Caty that he raise her namesake son, George Washington Greene, as his own.[42]

Some time after her husband died, four men began flirting with Caty. Three were married, and one was Wayne, estranged from his wife. Once, when Caty went north for a visit, Wayne wrote of his difficulty to "restrain every tender emotion" as she sailed away. "I experienced a sensation more forcibly felt than I had power to describe."[43]

But Caty married her children's tutor, Phineas Miller, who now managed the plantation. When a new tutor, Eli Whitney, invented a cotton gin to separate fibers from their seeds, the Millers financed the invention, and Caty suggested an enhancement. But they lost money on that investment, and lost even more on a land speculation. In 1800, they auctioned off the plantation to pay debts, and moved to a property Nathanael had bought on a Georgia coastal island. The new plantation succeeded. Caty and Phineas are buried there, and the cemetery and the ruins of their house are now part of Cumberland Island National Seashore.[44]

Nathanael was buried in a Savannah cemetery, but in the ensuing years, his grave became lost to memory. Nonetheless, Savannah erected a monument to him in Johnson Square, surrounded today by office buildings and businesses. In 1901, Savannah found his body and reinterred him in Johnson Square. Rhode Island chose Greene to be one of its two state heroes with statues in the U.S. Capitol. Seventeen states named counties after Greene; nearly two dozen cities honor him in their name.

Wayne's plantation was a financial disaster. His political life was more successful. In 1791, he defeated the incumbent congressman— his former subordinate, James Jackson. After Indians routed two American armies in Ohio, President Washington, in 1792, brought Wayne out of retirement. He defeated the Indians in 1794 at the Battle of Fallen Timbers. Two years later, he died near Erie, Pennsylvania. Despite a precarious personal life, the public honored Wayne. Towns, cities, and counties in seventeen states are named after him, including Fort Wayne, Indiana. Books ranging from *The Catcher in the Rye* to *Tender is the Night* allude to him. And he is the ancestor of fictional Bruce Wayne, the alter ego of comic book hero Batman.[45]

Moultrie, who commanded John Laurens and Francis Marion earlier in the war, was, in his day, more prominent than either Greene or Wayne. When his military career ended, his political career began, and he served as governor. In 1802, he published his memoirs, an important record. He was buried on his plantation, seventeen miles northwest of Charleston. It is now a subdivision. His gravesite was forgotten until 1977, when archaeologists found it. He was reburied near the visitors' center at Fort Moultrie, now part of Fort Sumter National Monument.

Leslie returned to Scotland, where he was second-in-command of the army forces stationed there. In 1794, soldiers mutinied in Glasgow, and Leslie ordered five arrested ringleaders to be transported to Edinburgh. When the transfer began, other soldiers freed the prisoners without resistance from the guards. Later, a mob attacked two officers of that guard: an adjutant and a *Major* Leslie. Whether the major was related to the general is unknown. But starting with an account published in 1842, historians distorted or poorly summarized what really happened. One 2013 scholarly history incorrectly said General Leslie died "attempting to suppress a riot outside of Edinburgh." In fact, even the Major Leslie who was attacked "received no material injury except a slight cut over the temple," reported a contemporary newspaper.[46]

General Leslie did die ten days after the riot, on December 27, at his home near Edinburgh "after a few days illness." His obituary said Leslie caught the illness "at Glasgow in the service of quelling the late riots there," but from the perspective of modern medicine, we'll never know where or how he caught his illness.[47]

PART THREE

The Frontier

16. Indians

FROM THE START, INDIANS AND WHITES INTERACTED IN THE SAME kinds of complex, changing ways that the English did among themselves, with the Scottish and Irish, and with allies and enemies on the European continent: Alliances shifted, factions disagreed, wars started and ended, trade ebbed and flowed, rebels were suppressed or supported.

Fifteen days after their 1620 landfall in Massachusetts, Pilgrims looted Indian homes, food storage pits, and graves. Nine days later, Indians attacked a Pilgrim landing party. The same Pilgrims soon formed a military alliance with a different Indian group.[1]

By the Revolution, Indians and whites were co-dependent. Indians needed modern weapons and agricultural tools; Anglos sought military manpower (for many years, used against the French and their Indian allies) and profitable furs and skins. They lived in each other's communities and sometimes intermarried. In winter 1772–1773, for example, about twenty whites lived in the Shawnee town of Chillicothe on the Ohio River. In the South, three hundred lived with the Creeks. Mohawks in upstate New York not only lived as neighbors to Sir William Johnson, the British Indian superintendent, but Johnson had a common-law marriage and nine children with Molly Brant (Gonwatsijayenni), a prominent Mohawk woman who later received a British pension. Indians were a familiar presence in most colonial towns and cities.

The frontier was porous, fuzzy, dynamic, a "cultural cacophony, a country of mixed and mixing peoples."[2]

Here, Scotch-Irish immigrants fought—sometimes violently—with landed English aristocracy; small-time land speculators competed against big-time speculators like Washington; Christian Indians aligned themselves with whites, but refused to cut ties with their tribes, which themselves were divided between neutrality or alignment with the French (before the Revolution) or the British or the Whigs; Loyalist whites fought rebel whites, and both pressured neutral whites; the Spanish lurked along the Mississippi, suspicious of both the British and their land-hungry rebels; traders from old French Canada balanced relationships between Indians and warring whites; misfits and drunks of all races triggered tipping points large and small; Anglicans, Presbyterians, Congregationalists, and Moravians undermined each other; rebel leaders, in hopes of an alliance, warned Bostonians to temper their virulent anti-Catholicism; and the governments and agents of Pennsylvania and Virginia—more sovereign nations than united colonies—fought over frontier lands.

Clashes and disputes between whites and Indians were as frequent as unions and accommodations, but ever-increasing numbers of settlers moving into Indian territory led to ever-increasing tension, cultural misunderstanding, and racism.

In 1773, Johnson updated New York's governor on the situation. The Indians closest to him, the Mohawks, "having at different times been prevailed on to dispose of their lands and suffered many indispositions . . . have very little property remaining." Fighting for Britain during the Seven Years' War, "they suffered great losses," and all that was left of them was about four hundred people. Among all the six Iroquois nations, ten thousand people remained, of whom two thousand were able to fight. Johnson estimated that all the native nations in the northern colonies east of the Mississippi had 130,000 people, of whom about one in five could bear arms. But many of them lived far from white settlements.[3]

A Kentucky settler estimated in 1784 that the twenty-eight major tribes east of the Mississippi, from the Iroquois in the North to the Creeks in the South, were composed of about twenty thousand people, with four- to five-thousand fighting men.[4]

The pressures on their land were immense. Reading, Pennsylvania, for example, in 1750, had one white home. Two years later, there were 130. By 1775, an estimated fifty thousand whites lived west of the Appalachian Mountains. That year, about two thousand whites and 8,500 Cherokees lived in the southern Appalachians, while three hundred whites and two thousand Shawnees lived in what's now West Virginia, Kentucky, and Tennessee. Fifteen years later, more than twenty-six thousand whites lived in Cherokee country, and sixty-seven thousand lived in Shawnee country. The total Indian population: fewer than ten thousand. In Kentucky alone, twenty thousand whites moved onto Shawnee lands in 1779 and 1780.[5]

Frederick Jackson Turner, who wrote in the early twentieth century about the impact of the frontier on the American character, described the white invasion:

> In the course of the seventeenth century, the frontier was advanced up the Atlantic courses, just beyond the "fall line," and the tidewater region became the settled area. . . . The end of the first quarter of the [eighteenth] century saw the advance of the Scotch-Irish and the Palatine Germans up the Shenandoah Valley into the western part of Virginia, and along the Piedmont region of the Carolinas. The Germans in New York pushed the frontier of settlement up the Mohawk to German Flats. In Pennsylvania, the town of Bedford indicates the line of settlement. Settlements soon began on the New River, or the Great Kanawha, and on the sources of the Yadkin and French Broad. The King attempted to arrest the advance by . . . forbidding settlements beyond the sources of the rivers flowing into the Atlantic; but in vain. In the period of the Revolution the frontier crossed the Alleghenies into Kentucky and Tennessee, and the upper waters of the Ohio were settled.[6]

Indians protested the incursions to white authorities. "Take these people off from our land . . . that we may not be at the trouble to drive them off," petitioned the Delawares to Pennsylvania's governor. "[We] cannot enjoy our birthright in peace and quietness, but we are abused as if we were enemies and not friends." Forty years later, a missionary translated another protest: "I admit that there are good white men, but they bear no proportion to the bad; the bad must be strongest, for they rule. . . . There is no faith to be placed in their words. . . . They will say to an Indian: 'My friend, my brother.' They will take him by the hand, and at the same moment, destroy him."[7]

Treaties that granted land to whites in exchange for food, supplies, and firm borders were often made under duress—by "consent in a context of coercion"—or by unauthorized individuals. The Iroquois, for example, ceded Shawnee, Mingo, and Delaware land, without the owners' agreement, to whites in a 1768 treaty in exchange for more than £10,000 in goods ($1.9 million today). The Iroquois themselves, under Johnson's threats, were forced to cede land, and three Indian towns became enclaves within white territory.[8]

In 1763, the British tried to ease tensions—and save money required for fighting Indian wars—by prohibiting white settlements west of the Appalachians. The prohibition was unenforceable. "I am fully convinced that the boundary lines never will be observed," said the British commander. "The frontier people are too numerous, too lawless, and licentious ever to be restrained."[9]

One of those frontier people was Washington. He wrote his land agent that he could never consider the boundary between Indians and whites as anything but "a temporary expedient to quiet the minds of the Indians" before they were coerced into more land cessions. He ordered his agent to continue to scout future acquisitions, and to mark the land "in order to keep others from settling them."[10]

Washington's assumptions were correct: In 1774, a Virginia captain murdered thirteen unarmed Indians west of Pittsburgh, triggering what became known as Lord Dunmore's War. The result was an Indian defeat and further land cessions. Johnson, trying to keep Dunmore's War from becoming widespread, complained that while the Senecas made restitution for one of their men murdering a white, Ohio Valley settlers "trepanned and murdered" forty Indians. "I have daily to combat with thousands who, by their avarice, cruelty, or indiscretion, are constantly counteracting all judicious measures with the Indians."[11]

Johnson's counterpart in the south gave London a similar warning: "I know of nothing so likely to interrupt and disturb our tranquility with the Indians as the incessant attempts to defraud them of their land by clandestine purchase."[12]

After the revolution, Franklin concluded that "almost every war between the Indians and whites has been occasioned by some injustice of the latter toward the former." Arthur St. Clair, one of Washington's generals who was later defeated in a campaign against

Indians, nonetheless took their side: "It has long been a disgrace to the people of all the states bordering upon the Indians, both as men and as Christians, that while they [whites] loudly complained of every injury or wrong received from them [Indians], and imperiously demanded satisfaction, they were daily offering to them injustices and wrongs of the most provoking character, for which I have never heard that any person was ever brought to due justice and punishment, and all proceeding from the false principle that because they [Indians] had not received the light of the gospel, they might be abused, cheated, robbed, plundered, and murdered at pleasure."[13]

Virginia governor Francis Fauquier was frustrated trying to prevent fighting between whites and Indians. "I have found by experience it is impossible to bring anybody to justice for the murder of an Indian who takes shelter among our back [frontier] inhabitants. It is among these people looked on as a meritorious action, and they are sure of being protected."[14]

Each incident, each fight, each war, compounded its impact on both sides and polarized perceptions. "Having lost so many relatives by the Indians," wrote a minister who grew up on the Pennsylvania frontier, "they became subjects of that indiscriminating thirst for revenge which is such a prominent feature in the savage character, and having had a taste of blood and plunder, without risk or loss on their part, they resolved to go on and kill every Indian they could find, whether friend or foe."[15]

The nature of Indian warfare offended white standards. Indians terrorized civilians, often picking off isolated farmers and carrying away women and children, sometimes killing them. Burning prisoners at the stake, torturing them, and even eating their hearts were all part of a religious ritual. For some tribes, taking scalps was a sacrificial offering; for other tribes, they were trophies and incentivized an enemy's surrender.[16]

Far more frequently, tribes adopted prisoners. "It is but seldom that prisoners are put to death by burning and torturing," wrote a missionary. "It hardly ever takes place except when a nation has suffered great losses in war, and it is thought necessary to revenge the death of their warriors slain in battle, or when willful and deliberate murders have been committed of an enemy of their innocent women and children."[17]

Given real atrocities and lack of security, frontier Whigs embellished their accounts "of ferocity and blood as might best serve to keep live the strongest feelings of indignation," wrote an early historian whose father fought in the revolution. "The crude, verbal reports of the day—tales of hearsay, colored by fancy and aggravated by fear—not only found their way into the newspapers, but into the journals of military officers." Fear bred fear until whites *knew* that Indians were "monsters . . . of unparalleled and unapproachable barbarity."[18]

Early in the war, John Adams predicted the British would bring "eternal infamy" on themselves if they allied themselves with Indians. "To let loose these bloodhounds to scalp men, and to butcher women and children is horrid." Washington routinely referred to them as "savages," although he conceded "excellent use" could be made of them. Virginia governor Thomas Jefferson described Indian warfare as "cruel and cowardly," distinguished by "the indiscriminate murder of men, women, and children with the usual circumstances of barbarity."[19]

The belief that Indians were less than human began long before the revolution. To many whites, they were "barbarous, inhuman monsters"—"a savage multitude who are cruel and have no mercy," who made the "brains, hearts, and bowels [of their victims] swim in streams of gore."[20]

Hugh Henry Brackenridge, who moved to the Pennsylvania frontier in 1781, contributed to the common wisdom: "They have the shapes of men and may be of the human species, but certainly in their present state, they approach nearer the character of devils. . . . Are not the whole Indian nations murderers?"[21]

When, in 1775, William Johnson's son and successor, John, tried to mobilize Indians for the British, he invited them to "feast on a Bostonian, and to drink his blood." The Indians understood that Johnson was talking about a roasted ox and wine. Many Whigs believed it literally.[22]

Incidents involved Loyalists who often participated in Indian raids and added their own style to warfare. One Tory, on a raid with Mohawks in 1780, grabbed an eight-year-old boy, slit his throat from ear to ear, then scalped him. Another Tory raider, said a Whig history, was "revengeful and cruel in his disposition, inflexible in his purposes, his bosom cold as the marble to the impulses of humanity." Another was "cruel . . . one of the greatest scourges . . . of a morose temperament, possessing strong passions, and of a vindictive disposition."[23]

One anonymous writer blamed Loyalists for Indian atrocities: "Who prevailed on the savages of the wilderness to join the standard of the enemy? The Tories! Who have assisted the Indians in taking the scalp from the aged matron, the blooming fair one, the helpless infant, and the dying hero? The Tories! Who advised and assisted in burning your towns, ravaging your country, and violating the chastity of your women? The Tories!"[24]

In 1776, the Whigs enshrined their fear of Indian atrocities into the Declaration of Independence. George III, the declaration said, "has endeavored to bring on the inhabitants of our frontiers, the merciless Indian savages, whose known rule of warfare, is an undistinguished destruction of all ages, sexes, and conditions." From Indian and British perspectives, the rebels were hypocrites.

As early as the 1637 Pequot War, whites had responded to isolated incidents with mass murder. After Indians killed captains of trading boats in Connecticut, whites responded with a massacre of four hundred Indian men, women, and children, who were shot if they tried to escape from a burning fort. "It was a fearful sight to see them thus frying in the fire, and the streams of blood quenching the same, and horrible was the stink and scent thereof; but the victory seemed a sweet sacrifice, and they gave the praise thereof to God," wrote a participant. In Virginia, Captain John Smith tortured at least one Indian on the rack.[25]

While Indians didn't usually kill women and children, it was the Whigs' standard practice to kill Indian women and children. A British general saw the rebels as "a treacherous and cruel enemy, resolved to destroy the Indians at all events. When any of the King's troops are taken, they are treated as prisoners of war, but when Indians were taken, they were immediately put to death."[26]

Where Indians rarely, if ever, raped women, it was common for rebels to do so. "Bad as the savages are, they never violate the chastity of any women, their prisoners," said a Whig general as he warned against his own men's conduct. "Yet these rebels call themselves Christians," said an Onondaga warrior after women in his village were raped and killed.[27]

Scalping started as an Indian practice, but was soon adopted by Whigs and encouraged by most of their governments in the form of bounties. The Loyalist chief justice of Massachusetts talked in 1781 about that colony's bounties, which had been used for a century: "I have seen a vessel enter the harbor of Boston with a long string of hairy Indian scalps strung to the rigging and waving in the wind."[28]

Much of the anti-Indian violence was against neutrals and even allies; as in Vietnam and Afghanistan generations later, whites often couldn't or didn't distinguish between native friend and native foe. In 1778, Whigs destroyed an Iroquois town—home to both friendly and enemy Indians—on the Susquehanna River. After the war, a Whig veteran recalled fellow soldiers finding several small children hiding, then boasted about "running them through with bayonets and holding them up to see how they would twist and turn."[29]

A missionary told of "white men flaying or taking off the skin of Indians who had fallen into their hands, then tanning those skins, or cutting them into pieces, making them up into razor-straps or exposing those for sale."[30]

Nor was the brutality only directed against Indians. Rebel mobs tarred and feathered Loyalists and officials. The British reported that after the battles of Lexington and Concord, the rebels "scalped and cut off the ears of some of the wounded that fell into their hands."[31]

A British agent who tried to suppress torture practice by Indian allies said in 1783 that the rebels were "reviving the old savage custom of putting their prisoners to death which with much pains and expense we had weaned the Indians from in this neighborhood."[32]

If Indians had a way to tell "the world the many acts of treachery and cruelty committed by them on our women and children," said a Seneca chief, "it would appear that the title of savages would with much greater justice be applied to them than to us."[33]

As the war began, most Indian nations wanted to take the course that would best preserve their lands, and provide them food, arms, and supplies. Each nation had a different response—and sometimes multiple ones that reflected internal differences of opinion. The Mohawks, influenced by Johnson (who died in 1774) and his native wife, Molly Brant, quickly aligned with the British. Most tribes tried to stay neutral, remembering the ill fortune of those that had allied with the French during the Seven Years' War. The Oneidas, for example, told the Whig Connecticut governor: "We are unwilling to join on either side of such a contest, for we love you both—old England and new. Should the great King of England apply to us for aid, we shall deny him, and should the colonies apply, we shall refuse."[34]

But neutrality became increasingly difficult. The Indians, as a Wyandot chief said, sat between "two powerful angry gods."[35]

Washington urged Congress to help persuade tribes to fight for the Whigs. "It will be impossible to keep them in a state of neutrality," he said in early 1776. "They must, and no doubt will, take an active part either for us or against us. I submit to Congress whether it will not be better to immediately engage them on our side." Massachusetts urged a Whig missionary working among the Iroquois to "whet their hatchet and be prepared with us to defend our liberties and lives." In the Ohio Valley, a Whig general warned Indians against neutrality, saying, "Bystanders must take care lest the splinters should scar their face." Soon after Lexington and Concord, Ethan Allen, a Vermont militia colonel, urged tribes to attack the British. "I want your warriors to join with me and my warriors like brothers and ambush the regulars," he said. "If you will, I will give you money, blankets, tomahawks, knives, and paint and the like as much as you say, because they first killed our men when it was peace time."[36]

But the British also pressured the tribes, and with few exceptions—the Oneidas and a few smaller nations—they succeeded. The British had made good-faith efforts to stop white theft of Indian lands. "The Indians well know that in all their landed disputes, the Crown has always been their friend," a British commander said. A Loyalist ranger chastised Iroquois who had signed a friendship treaty with the rebels, warning: "They mean to cheat you, and should you be so silly as to take their advice, and they should conquer the King's Army, their intention is to take all your lands from you and destroy your people."[37]

Unlike the rebels, Britain had a government that could levy taxes that paid for Indian "gifts"—what's now called foreign aid. As war and land thefts devastated Indian farm lands and hunting territories, the British also provided food and safe havens in their strongholds of Detroit, Niagara, and Oswego, at the eastern end of Lake Ontario.

Finally, the rebels alienated Ohio Valley tribes when, in late 1777, six Pennsylvania militiamen murdered a Shawnee leader, Cornstalk (Hokoleskwa), his son, and two others. Cornstalk, a moderate, had gone to Fort Randolph (in what is now West Virginia) under a truce flag. The rebel commander detained the entire party as hostages. Militia broke in and killed them in retaliation for the death of a white near the fort. Despite apologies from Congress and the governors of Pennsylvania and Virginia, "the Indians are not to be pacified," a British officer said. The next year, settlers murdered White Eyes (Koquethagechton), a pro-Whig Delaware leader.[38]

The frontier war heated up. Indians often worked in joint operations with Loyalist rangers and British officers. They frequently raided New York, Pennsylvania, and Ohio Valley settlements and with disastrous results for the rebels. The Whigs retaliated with their own raids, culminating in a 1779 expedition through Iroquois country led by Continental general John Sullivan. Sullivan's strategy was to starve the Indians to death by destroying their food supplies, including 160,000 bushels of corn, and burning their forty towns.

The strategy was effective. Three years before, North Carolina's Rutherford had destroyed thirty-six Cherokee towns, along with their crops and livestock. It was one of many such expeditions. After one, a Shawnee man reported, "Our women and children ... are left now destitute of shelter in the woods or food to subsist on."[39]

Charles Stedman, a British officer, described the frontier war. "Mutual incursions were made, and ruin and devastation followed on the steps of the ruthless invaders. Whole families were butchered, their houses burnt, the growing corn cut up, and entire plantations laid waste."[40]

News of the Yorktown surrender reached the frontier in late 1781 and early 1782. In upstate New York, the British and Indians began what would be their final expedition against the rebels. But in the Ohio Valley, the war escalated.

17. The Death of Captain Butler

S CHENECTADY, NEW YORK, HAD BEEN A FRONTIER TOWN SINCE 1661, when Dutch settlers traded wampum currency and goods to Mohawks for land along their namesake river. The settlers thrived by illegally trading with the Mohawks for furs that would otherwise have gone to Albany, eighteen miles to the southeast. It was an astute location for a town; Schenectady's name itself was derived from an Indian word meaning "end of the pine plains," a reference to its location as the terminus of a portage between the Mohawk and Hudson rivers.[1]

Three years after Schenectady's founding, the British seized the Dutch territory and renamed the colony New York. When the centuries-long dispute between the British and French spilled into North America, Schenectady became vulnerable. In early February 1690, a French force from Québec with Indian allies attacked Schenectady. They burned seventy-eight of the town's eighty houses, killed sixty people, and took twenty-seven prisoners. A resident, Symon Schermerhorn, though wounded, escaped on a horse and warned residents along the road to Albany.

By the Revolution, about 43,000 whites lived throughout the region. Schenectady had grown to at least three hundred homes, and Albany had five thousand residents. Whites by the hundreds encroached on Iroquois land, making game scarce and people hungry. Many, probably most, settlers became Whigs, if only because the British tried to enforce the Indian treaties. The Iroquois declared neutrality in late 1774 because, its council said, "it was contrary to their custom to interfere between parents [British] and children [Whigs]." But just as there was no place for neutrality among the white "parents and children," the unity of the six Iroquois nations fractured. The Oneidas and some Tuscaroras, influenced by a Whig missionary, became Whig allies. The other Iroquois nations turned to the British. They were pushed by the Mohawks, who, being the easternmost tribe, already had lost most of their land to whites. The rebels also prevented the Mohawks from trading with Canada, and it was the Mohawks who were most influenced by Johnson and Johnson's family, including Molly Brant.[2]

In July 1775, the Johnson family, along with 220 Iroquois and other Loyalists, fled the Mohawk Valley to British-controlled territory on Lake Ontario. Two years later, one British army and their Indian allies invaded the Mohawk Valley from the west, while another army moved toward Albany from the north. The rebels, with Oneidas serving as scouts, stopped both armies. Another wave of Iroquois then fled to Canada for safety. Rebels and Oneidas looted Molly Brant's home along the Mohawk River. By May 1777, about 2,700 Iroquois refugees were living around the British fort at Niagara. Two years later, 3,700 lived there.[3]

Although the threat of a British invasion ended with the British defeat at Saratoga in 1777, British and Indian raids against Mohawk Valley settlers escalated. Molly Brant's young brother, Captain Joseph Brant (Thayendanegea), 35, became the most active of the raiders, leading both Indian and white Loyalist troops. Brant was an experienced diplomat and commander who fought alongside William Johnson, his common-law brother-in-law, and even traveled to London. He was a freemason, and pious; he translated the Gospel of Mark into Mohawk. As a fighter, he became notorious among Whigs who blamed him for atrocities whether or not he was anywhere near the site of the raid.

A 1778 raid against the Cherry Valley settlement became a Whig propaganda tool. Brant and Walter Butler, his Loyalist counterpart, led the raid with 321 Indians and one hundred fifty Tory rangers. But Brant and Butler despised each other. About ninety white Loyalists prevailed on Brant to stay for the raid because they also despised Butler. During the raid, the two leaders lost control of most of the Indians, who plundered and killed settlers indiscriminately. Both Butler and Brant tried to save victims, but a massacre ensued.

One Indian leader later said his men acted in retaliation for the destruction of their town by Whigs.

To stop the raids, Washington ordered Major General John Sullivan in 1779 to attack the Iroquois. The goal, Washington said, would be "the total destruction and devastation of their settlements," including their food supplies. This would force the Indians to retreat away from Whig settlements to distant British strongholds at Niagara and Detroit. "It will be essential to ruin their crops now in the ground and prevent their planting more."[4]

Despite the expedition's success, the raids continued. In 1780 and 1781, Brant and other Indian and Loyalist rangers attacked Ohio and upper Mohawk Valley settlements almost at will. In one raid, Brant destroyed the Oneida and Tuscarora towns. Because their residents had been warned ahead of time, they were able to flee to Schenectady for safety.[5]

"Schenectady," said Governor George Clinton, "may now be said to become the limits of our western frontier." The Oneidas in 1777 had shared their corn surplus to help feed Washington's troops at their winter camp of Valley Forge. Now, they were refugees, more than four hundred mostly women and children—most of their men were with the Whig army. They lived in lean-tos outside Schenectady, suffered from smallpox, and starved. General Philip Schuyler pleaded with Congress to give the Oneidas clothing and blankets. He spent his own money to buy them food. White soldiers harassed the Oneidas, assaulted them, and "barbarously murdered" one. The situation was "an affecting spectacle of distress," Schuyler said.[6]

A French military traveler described the Indian camp as "nothing but an assemblage of miserable huts in the wood along the road." He guessed that Schenectady as a whole, including white refugees, sheltered about four thousand people behind its palisade. Others estimated that two-thirds of Mohawk Valley whites were refugees, of which 380 had become widows, and 2,000 children were now orphans.[7]

Governor Clinton had to stabilize the frontier. With few resources at hand, he enlisted the help of Colonel Marinus Willett.

Willett, 41, was the second of thirteen children born to a Quaker farmer and his wife in the rural Long Island community of Jamaica. During the Seven Years' War, he raised a militia company, fought in upstate New York, and participated in an expedition against Fort Frontenac (now Kingston) on the Canadian shore of Lake Ontario. He became familiar with settlements in the Mohawk Valley, and after the war, may have worked there as a cabinetmaker before settling in New York City.[8]

In New York, he became a leader of the Sons of Liberty, anti-Crown agitators who, after the revolution began, stole arms from a British arsenal. He joined the Continental army's New York regiment and took part in the disastrous invasion of Canada. When the British invaded New York in 1776, Willett, now a lieutenant colonel, led the militia on Long Island before joining the general retreat.

His next commands were all in upstate New York: He defended Peekskill against a British raid. He served as second-in-command at Fort Stanwix. There, in 1777, while under siege, he led a diversionary raid that burned the British camp and took its supplies, while the enemy fought and stopped a Whig relief force at Oriskany six miles away. When the British demanded the fort's surrender, threatening to let their Indian allies murder women and children, Willett refused, saying before he would surrender, "I would suffer my body to be filled with splinters, and set on fire, as you know has at times been practiced by such hordes of women and children killers as belong to your army." Relief came in the form of a force led by the then-Whig general Benedict Arnold, hero of the Battle of Saratoga weeks earlier.[9]

Leaving Stanwix in 1778 for New Jersey, Willett fought at Monmouth, then returned the next year with the Sullivan expedition against the Iroquois. He wintered with the main army at Morristown, New Jersey, while conducting foraging and harassing raids against British positions on Staten Island.

Willett had earned a reputation for competence, and Washington praised his "care, attention, and foresight." But after a reorganization of the New York regiment at the end of 1780, Willett retired from Continental service. That was when Governor Clinton asked Willett to assume command of state troops, militia, and levies (draftees)— troops scattered throughout the New York frontier. Clinton ordered him to fight not just Indians, but Tories as well: "cruel monsters worse than savages." Willett chose as his headquarters Canajoharie, the former Mohawk town where Molly Brant once lived. But headquarters was more a theory; in practice, Willett turned his troops into a "flying" squad, mobile, and always on the move.[10]

Willett probably knew of Washington's interest in land speculation, and in a July 1781 letter, Willett described the Iroquois lands west of Schenectady in detail. "Exceeding rich . . . of the first quality," he said. "In such a country blessed with so fine a soil lying along a delightful river, which afforded an easy transportation of the produce to a valuable market, with a climate exceeded by none, it might have been expected a greater population would have taken place."

Then, Willett addressed military business. Indian raids had reduced local militia from 2,500 militia at the start of the war to eight hundred men available for active duty. He estimated one-third of the militia were killed or taken prisoner, another third left the frontier, and the final third deserted. The remaining settlers huddled near twenty-four forts, ranging in population from ten to fifty families. To protect the settlements, Willett had about two hundred fifty men, excluding the militia and about one hundred twenty levies. "But be the force larger or smaller," Willett concluded, "I can only promise to do everything in my power for the relief of a people of whom I had some knowledge in their prosperous days, and am now acquainted with in the time of their great distress."[11]

The challenge would come soon. In September, rumors panicked both Schenectady and Albany that the British and Indians would attack.[12]

Yorktown was more than a month away when the British governor of Canada, General Frederick Haldimand, ordered a major raid against rebel settlements in the Mohawk Valley. "Destroy all kinds of grain and forage, mills, etc., cattle, and all articles which can contribute to the support of the enemy," he told Major John Ross. "Avoid the destruction of women and children, and every species of cruelty."[13]

Ross was "enterprising and resourceful," his superiors said. He fought in 1762 against the Spanish in Cuba, another battle area of the Seven Years' War. After the war, he travelled the Mississippi

River north from Louisiana; he became the first British officer to enter the Indian country of what is now Illinois following the French defeat. Five years later, he was stationed in Ireland, and then was posted to Canada in 1776 after the ill-fated rebel invasion. There, he raised a Loyalist battalion, and he commanded one of several forts on eastern Lake Ontario.[14]

Ross and his men left Oswego, a British stronghold on the New York shore of eastern Lake Ontario, on October 11, 1781, and rendezvoused with Indian allies and other Loyalist rangers from Niagara. All told, he commanded more than six hundred whites and one hundred thirty Indians.[15]

His second-in-command was, in Haldimand's words, "a very zealous, enterprising, and promising officer," captain Walter Butler, 29— the same Butler who had alienated Mohawk Captain Joseph Brant and other Loyalist rangers. Once, when Haldimand referred to Butler favorably in the presence of Loyalist brigadier general John Johnson, one of William's sons, Johnson was appalled. "I took the opportunity to give my opinion of him pretty freely," Johnson wrote a friend. Haldimand himself acknowledged to Butler's father that Walter's ego outran his experience: "He rates his services very high and is a little inconsiderate in his expectations and request [for promotion]. . . . I cannot in justice to the service, promote him over the heads of so many officers of merit and long service."[16]

Butler's reputation among Whigs was worse. He was a devil who practiced "diabolical cruelties," was a "murderer of little children," and had "damned his soul for all eternity."[17]

He was born and raised in relative wealth in the Mohawk Valley. His grandfather, also named Walter, commanded British forts in the valley. His father, John, campaigned in the Seven Years' War with William Johnson, and received large land grants as a result of his service. John, a lieutenant colonel and deputy Indian superintendent, recruited and led a large Loyalist unit during the revolution, Butler's Rangers, which fought with Indian allies throughout the frontier, from New York to Virginia, Michigan to Kentucky.

At sixteen, Walter served in his father's militia regiment. In his late teens and early twenties, he studied and practiced law in Albany. There's a record of him interceding with authorities on behalf of an imprisoned debtor in 1775. He was, said an Albany judge, "a youth of spirit, sense, and ability." Another Albany resident described him as a "pretty able young lawyer."[18]

When the war began, the Butlers, Johnsons, and other Loyalists were rewarded with a forced flight to Canada to escape rebel jails. Butler's mother and John Johnson's wife weren't as lucky. Rebel militia took them hostage hoping to prevent the Butlers and Johnsons from fighting.

It didn't work. Now a lieutenant, Walter Butler was second-in-command of 125 Loyalist rangers and Indians, who captured the rebel leader Ethan Allen near Montréal in September 1775. The next year, he skirmished with more rebels along the Saint Lawrence River. He and his father wintered at Fort Niagara, where Walter was promoted to captain. "He seems a promising young man," said General Guy Carleton.[19]

He fought at Oriskany in 1777, where the British, Loyalist rangers, and Indians stopped a rebel relief column. (Willett, at the time, was raiding the British camp.) After the battle, and while the siege against Stanwix continued, Butler volunteered to lead a small group to valley settlements to proclaim amnesty to rebels who joined the besieged. At a midnight meeting, the advance guard of another rebel relief force captured him, and charged him with being a "traitor and spy." Willett, who had left Stanwix, served as the judge in Butler's court-martial, which convicted him. Whig general Benedict Arnold, bringing relief to Stanwix, ordered Butler hanged.[20]

Some of Arnold's officers had known Butler before the war, and they protested the sentence. Arnold listened, and instead of being hanged, Butler was sent to Albany in chains. There, he remained manacled. Butler protested and asked "in the most pathetic terms" to be paroled, according to the Whig commander. Butler's mother, still detained as a hostage, petitioned to be allowed to visit her son. After six months in jail, the Whigs paroled Butler with the requirement that he be confined to a guarded home in Albany. He escaped Albany in mid-April 1778, riding a horse provided by a friend.[21]

The November 1778 raid against Cherry Valley in which Butler and Brant lost control of their men became Whig propaganda. Publicly, the Whigs pilloried Butler alone. However, internal British letters noted that Butler tried to stop the massacre. "Men, women, and children all promiscuously butchered by the savages, nor could Capt. Butler or other officers keep any restraint on them," one eyewitness said. Butler himself admitted that he had "much to lament" because he couldn't prevent some of the women and children from "falling unhappily to the fury of the savages."[22]

Nonetheless, Butler took as hostages a small group of women and children to use as trade bait for his still-imprisoned mother and other Loyalist women. Then, he threatened to use Indians against the Whigs. "If you persevere in detaining my father's family with you . . . we shall no longer take the same pains to restrain the Indians from prisoners, women, or children that we have hitherto done," he wrote the Whig commander. And he defended the Indians at Cherry Valley by saying they were merely retaliating for the Whigs "burning of one of their villages, then inhabited only by a few families—your friends—who imagined they might remain in peace and friendship with you, till assured, a few hours before the arrival of your troops, that they should not even receive quarter." He added that when he was manacled in Albany, "I experienced no humanity, or even common justice, during my imprisonment among you." The Whigs agreed to the prisoner exchange, but it didn't occur until 1780.[23]

Butler continued to fight with joint ranger-Indian forces. In 1779, they failed to stop Sullivan in central New York, near what is now Elmira. For the rest of the year and through 1780, Butler traveled throughout the west, from the Ohio Valley to Montréal, providing intelligence and seeking supplies for Butler's Rangers.

There would be one final battle—one final encounter with Marinus Willett.

Ross, Butler, and their rangers and Indians arrived on October 24 at their first target, Currytown, a settlement eight miles east of Canajoharie. They had come 130 miles through "the brooks and rivers, the hills and mountains, the deep and gloomy marshes."[24]

Currytown offered no resistance, but Ross's new prisoners warned that two thousand Whig troops were in Schenectady and other neighboring towns. It was raining, and roads were becoming impassable. Ross decided to cut a path of destruction as close to Schenectady as he could.

Before dawn the next morning, Ross reached Warrensbush (now Florida, Montgomery County), twenty miles west of Schenectady. The settlement was "a nest of rebels." Ross's men torched its buildings. They continued to destroy settlements on the road to Schenectady, coming as close as twelve miles to the town. Guessing that the rebels by then were assembling their forces to respond, Ross turned sharply away from Schenectady and headed to Johnstown—former home of Johnson and Molly Brant—all the while destroying what he could.[25]

Later, the Whigs estimated that Ross destroyed at least twenty-two homes, twenty-eight barns, a grist mill; 1,500 bushels of wheat, 105 of rye, 957 of peas, 1,875 of oats, and 964 of corn; 109 tons of hay; about thirty-five horses, eighty cattle, thirty-one sheep, and sixty-four hogs. The British said they destroyed one hundred farms, three grist mills, a large granary, and "cattle and stock of all kinds."[26]

Ross's guess that rebel defenders were on his tail was correct. When Ross attacked Warrensbush, Willett, with four hundred state and Continental troops, was about twenty-five miles away. He put out a call for militia and levies, and then, with a force that grew to more than 1,200 men, began to chase Ross.

They met in the mid-afternoon twenty-five miles northwest of Schenectady at Johnstown, where Ross was seizing provisions and destroying Whig food supplies. Ross charged the rebels, many of whom, Willett conceded, "turned and fled without any apparent cause." But Ross was unable to follow up the initial rout; his allies failed to cooperate. "I then lamented the want of a good body of Indians," Ross said. If they had, he could have "crushed the spirit of the rebels." As night fell, Ross retreated beyond Johnstown. Each side lost fourty to fifty men, either captured or killed.[27]

Ross now headed for British territory at the head of the Saint Lawrence River. It was a slow retreat, hampered by snow and sleet, as well as "excessive fatigue and hunger, the party now living entire-ly upon horses they had taken." At one point, most of the Indians left to return to Niagara.[28]

Willett, with about five hundred men including sixty Oneidas, followed Ross's trail. "We pursued them as closely and warmly as possible," he said. "Their flight was performed in an Indian file upon a constant trot, and one man's being knocked in the head or falling off into the woods never stopped the progress of his neighbor."[29]

Ross's rear guard, led by Butler, tried letting the main body put some distance between themselves and the rebels. On a foggy October 30, after fording West Canada Creek, eighty-five miles northwest of Schenectady and more than one hundred miles from the British fort and safety, Butler made a stand. "Creek" is a misnomer for the seventy-six-mile-long river—the Mohawk's major tributary. This was a cold river, and fording it was "difficult."[30]

Butler and the rear guard stood on one bank, Willett on the opposite, with some Whigs trying to cross. The enemies fired their guns. Butler was hit, and the rangers retreated so quickly that they left him on the ground.

"He was not dead when found by one of our Indians, who finished his business for him and got a considerable booty," Willett said of the scalping, although other reports say Butler was already dead. "I am certain the loss of the enemy must be great. It is, however, out of my power to ascertain it. . . . Their killed is by no means trifling and many, very many, must be scattered about the wilderness almost sure of perishing there."[31]

Then, with his own provisions "quite exhausted," Willett ended the chase.

The British and Loyalists mourned Butler's death. Haldimand told Ross: "I read with much concern the fate of Capt. Butler. He was a very active, promising officer, and one of those whose loss at all times, but particularly in the present, is much to be lamented."[32]

For New York Whigs, Butler's death was a cause for celebration. "They say the Oneida Indians have scalped him," wrote an Albany official. "This is certain: that he is killed and that part of his clothes and ornaments have already been sold at Schenectady. . . . It gives me pleasure to see the mortification of those miscreants [Tories] whose souls are black as hell and whose minds are as dark as the midnight shades."[33]

Willett's son later wrote that Butler's death caused more joy among settlers than the Yorktown surrender, "such was the terror in which he [Butler] was held by the inhabitants of the frontiers, so cruel a scourge had he been to them."[34]

Ross probably left Butler's scalpless corpse to wolves and rot; John Butler later offered an unclaimed reward for his son's body. One unlikely legend persisted—that he was secretly buried in a Schenectady church, where a minister wrote:

Beneath the pew in which you sit
They say that Walter Butler's buried.

In such a fix, across the Styx
I wonder who his soul has ferried.[35]

After the raid, Ross was promoted to major. In what is now Kingston, Ontario, he provided for Loyalist refugees and served as a magistrate. In late 1784, he received permission to return to England to care for his elderly father. Ross returned to Kingston in 1786, where he was arrested and exonerated in connection with charges brought by his second-in-command. He and his regiment returned to England in 1787. Two years later, he retired. Historians don't know about his life after that, although he might have married the sister of Captain John McDonell, who had fought with William Caldwell, Brant, and John Butler and later became a Canadian politician.[36]

In November 1781, two dozen Indians led by a Loyalist ranger attacked Schoharie, twenty-five miles west of Schenectady. They killed one civilian and five militiamen. In spring 1782, Indians destroyed a gristmill at Little Falls and took prisoners. "The Indians are committing ravages in most parts of this county . . . ," Willett wrote Washington. "They are not deficient in art to improve the many advantages they have over us."[37]

Hearing reports that Schenectady or Albany or both would be attacked, Washington paid a morale visit to the Mohawk Valley in June 1782. In Schenectady, the town honored him at a banquet, and he wrote an open letter of support, saying: "May you, and the good people of this town . . . be protected from every insidious and open foe . . ." He also urged the Oneidas to raid Loyalist and pro-British Indian strongholds and capture as many prisoners as they could.[38]

Willett intended to help by seizing Oswego, on the New York shore of Lake Ontario, 160 miles from Schenectady. In spring 1782, Ross and four hundred rangers had strengthened and garrisoned the fort; it became a safe haven for Indians and a base for future raids. To Whigs, the garrison was dangerous. "While the enemy remain posted in force at Oswego," wrote one politician, "we have nothing to expect but total desolation of the scattered remains of that once flourishing district."[39]

Washington blessed Willett's proposal to attack in early February 1783. Such an attack "appears very practicable in my eyes, provided the troops for the enterprise can be properly accommodated." He would provide Willett woolens for the winter raid, but Willett would have to find his own sleds, moccasins, and snow shoes. Finally, Washington recommended that Willett seize British or Loyalist deserters who were acquainted with Oswego and use them as guides.[40]

Willett used a trusted Oneida man as a guide. He was the wrong choice. The guide, "who has a commission from Congress [and] whose behavior has been uniform and upright," got lost and led Willett's four hundred men in circles just a few miles from Oswego. With his men becoming hypothermic and frostbitten, Willett abandoned the raid. "It is no small mortification to me," he wrote Washington. "Great fatigue got the better of the spirits of the soldiers, and . . . we could have no right to hope to remain undiscovered through the day." Two men, including a slave whose freedom was promised for his military service, "got frozed to death."[41]

Washington tried to ease Willett's "mortification." "No imputation or reflection can justly reach your character," he wrote Willett. "The failure, it seems, must be attributed to some of those unaccountable events which are not within the control of human means; and which, though they often occur in military life, yet require, not only the fortitude of the soldier, but the calm reflection of the philosopher, to bear."[42]

British governor Haldimand had no sympathy. "Fortunately for Mr. Willett," Haldimand had discouraged Indians from wintering at Oswego. "Otherwise, it is probable that not a man of his detachment would have escaped."[43]

Willett was also fortunate after the war. Voters elected him to a number of political positions: the state assembly, New York City sheriff, and mayor. He died in 1830.

18. Massacre and Revenge

THE INDIANS NEVER FOUGHT *FOR* THE BRITISH; THEY FOUGHT *with* them in a calculated, self-interested way that would best protect native property rights, while maximizing economic gain. In this war, in this place, the ally just happened to be the British.

Most Iroquois in New York, Shawnees in the Ohio Valley, Cherokees and Creeks in the South, and the affiliated, allied, and kinship-related nations in between—Mingoes, Delawares, Chickasaws, Wyandots, and others—united against the rebels. More often than not, they combined their military forces and, sometimes, their diplomatic efforts.

The anti-Indian incidents that William Johnson and other sympathetic whites complained about before the war escalated during the war. They culminated in the mass murder of neutral, pacifist Christian Indians.

The Reverend David Zeisberger, 61, was a modest, religious man, said an acolyte. "He was of a humble, meek spirit, and always thought lowly of himself. . . . His words were few, and never known to be wasted at random or in an unprofitable manner." Short, even by eighteenth-century standards, he had "a cool, active, intrepid spirit, not appalled by any danger or difficulties, and a sound judgment to discern the best means of meeting and overcoming them."[1]

At seventeen, he immigrated to Georgia to join his parents, who were part of a community of fellow German-speaking immigrants from Moravia (now part of the Czech Republic). The community was a religious one founded by members of the evangelical, pacifist Moravian Church, formally known as the United Brethren. Zeisberger immediately began participating in missionary work with Creek Indians.[2]

He and his parents left Georgia two years later to help establish a mission in eastern Pennsylvania. In the early 1740s, Zeisberger prepared for his personal mission among the Iroquois. He learned their language, as well as Delaware, Mohigan, and Ojibway dialects, and became a prolific author of Indian grammars and dictionaries. Starting in his twenties, Zeisberger traveled widely, frequently lived with Indians, converted many of them, and helped found settlements for Christian Indians forced off their land by whites.

Three of the settlements, begun in 1770, were strung along the Tuscarawas River in Ohio country about ninety miles west of Fort Pitt (Pittsburgh). Since the Tuscarawas feeds into the Muskingum River, whites referred to the region as the Muskingum. The largest Moravian Indian settlement was Gnadenhütten ("huts of grace"). Schoenbrunn ("beautiful spring") was ten miles upriver; Salem, six miles downriver.

Both the British and their Indian allies, as well as the Whigs and white settlers, suspected the Moravian Indians of colluding with the enemy. Part of the perception was caused by Zeisberger's efforts to appease both sides. On one hand, he and the villagers provided intelligence to the Whigs; at the same time, they offered supplies and hospitality to anyone who passed through, regardless of who was fighting whom.[3]

It was a lose-lose situation for the Moravians. In fall 1781, with most of the cornfields ready to be harvested, the British and Indian allies forcibly removed the Moravians from the three villages. They relocated them about 125 miles west, with the intention of moving them closer to the British stronghold at Detroit. Any collaboration with the enemy would be much harder.

Without adequate food, the Moravians nearly starved that winter. "Many of the brethren went to the Shawnee towns to see for corn, for here in this neighborhood no more is to be had, and what there is, is enormously dear," Zeisberger wrote in January 1782. "So some went also to the Muskingum to harvest yet something from our plantations." The trickle of the Moravian Indians back to their homes continued the next month, and Zeisberger despaired. "The hunger among our people . . . is so great that for some time already they have had to live upon dead cattle, cows, and horses. Never in their lives have they felt such want. . . . Why, then, does the Savior let all this come upon us?" In mid-February, Zeisberger wrote that "yet more brethren have gone to the Muskingum. Indeed, they would prefer to move there than here to suffer want and hunger."[4]

The country the Moravians returned to was a tinderbox. Indians had continued to raid Whig settlements throughout the winter. "The country talks of nothing but killing Indians, and taking possession of their lands," said Whig colonel William Croghan. After one raid near Fort Pitt, the Wyandot and Delaware warriors, with their prisoners, stopped in Gnadenhütten for food. They warned the Moravians to leave; Whig pursuers were probably near. In fact, one Whig prisoner escaped, returned to Fort Pitt, and reported that many Moravian Indians had returned, and had fed the raiding party.[5]

Without the knowledge of Fort Pitt's commander, one hundred fifty to two hundred militia met and voted to ride to Gnadenhütten.

As leader, they elected Colonel David Williamson, 30, of the Washington County, Pennsylvania, militia. Continental army lieutenant John Rose, who accompanied Williamson on a later expedition, described him as "brave as Caesar and active, but divested of conduct. Fond of thrusting himself into danger, he leaves everything else to chance. . . . He knows too well how high he is in the opinion of the people in general, and among these, he takes upon himself the airs of a man of consequence. However, he is open to advice and instructions. His oratory is suited to the taste of the people his countrymen, and their bigoted notions stand him in lieu of arguments."[6]

What happened after the militia left Fort Pitt is based largely on the accounts of two Moravian Indian eyewitnesses who escaped, with confirmation by Continental officers; most of the militia didn't talk. "There seems to have been some difference amongst themselves about that business, yet they will say nothing," a newspaper reported two months later.[7]

The militia approached Gnadenhütten on March 7, 1782. They saw a young man in a field—one account says he was a white Moravian who had married a native woman. They killed him, scalped him, and then peacefully entered the village. There, they warned the Moravian Indians of dangers they faced and offered to escort them back to Fort Pitt and safety. The Indians agreed, and they sent a messenger to the Salem settlement, telling the people there to rendezvous in Gnadenhütten.

Over night, most of the militia became convinced that the furs, clothes, axes, pewter utensils, horses, and other evidence of wealth they saw in Gnadenhütten were proof that the Moravians had plundered whites. The militia even saw what they believed to be the dress of a white woman killed in a raid. They voted to execute the Indians. A handful of men dissented.

In the morning, the militia isolated the Indians in two homes, bound them, bludgeoned them to death with a mallet or tomahawk, and then scalped many. When the Indians from Salem arrived, the militia did the same to them. Some militia went to Schoenbrunn, which had been abandoned thanks to someone finding the scalped body of the white Moravian outside Gnadenhütten and alerting the others. In all, more than ninety men, women, and children were murdered.[8]

But the militia weren't done. They returned to Fort Pitt with eighty horseloads of confiscated Indian property. Then, on March 24, they attacked friendly Indians living on an island in the Ohio River near Fort Pitt, the day before Continental brigadier general William Irvine arrived to take command. The Indians "were not only under our protection, but several actually had commissions in our service," Irvine said. The militia also imprisoned the island's guard of Continental troops, and sent the acting Fort Pitt commander a message that "they would also scalp him . . . [because they] imagine that he has an attachment to Indians in general." The acting commander had been adopted by Indians, and his common-law wife was Indian.[9]

The newly arrived Irvine quickly learned about Gnadenhütten. "My Dearest Love," he wrote his wife. The militia had attacked the Moravian Indians "while they were singing hymns and killed the whole. Many children were killed in their wretched mothers' arms. Whether this was right or wrong, I do not pretend to determine. . . . People who have had fathers, mothers, brothers, or children butchered, tortured, scalped by the savages reason very differently on the subject of killing the Moravians to what people who live in the interior part of the country in perfect safety do."

Another Continental officer, Major William Croghan, was livid: "Instead of going against the enemies of the country, they [the militia] turned their thoughts on a robbing, plundering, murdering scheme on our well-known friends, the Moravian Indians." Rose later inspected the remains of Gnadenhütten and found that "the ruins of the lowest house in town were mixed with the calcined [ashy] bones of the burnt bodies of Indians."[10]

The first word Zeisberger received of the murders was March 14, the day before he and the remaining Moravians left under guard for Detroit. A messenger said that most of the Indians were sent to Fort Pitt, and a few were "bound and some killed, but all of this we could not believe." Nine days later, Zeisberger learned what really happened. "Our Indians were mostly on the plantations and saw the militia come, but no one thought of fleeing, for they suspected no ill," he wrote in his diary. "They prayed and sang until the tomahawks struck into their heads." (Zeisberger and the remaining Indians, after moving several times, ended up back in Ohio, where Zeisberger died in 1808.)[11]

The massacre shocked many: all Indians, regardless of whom they fought with; the British; and Whigs as far away as Franklin in Paris, who wrote "the abominable murders . . . has given me infinite pain and vexation."[12]

But the Whig frontier was ready to continue the fight, and Indians continued to attack, this time with revenge in mind.

Irvine, commanding Fort Pitt, felt he was in a weak position, undermanned and beset by both the enemy and the friendly militia. "The present strength of the garrison at Fort Pitt is 230, with at least thirty of these are unfit for field duty, and several [for] even garrison duty," he told Washington. All along the frontier, the situation was similar. "The inhabitants are dispirited, and talk much of making their escape early in the spring to the east side of the mountain[s], unless they see a prospect of support." He was worried about what the British commander in Detroit had in store for them—possibly an attack on Pitt itself. "There is no magazine of provision laid in at any of our posts to hold out a siege. Ammunition exhausted, no craft to transport materials for repairing the fort, or to keep up a communication with Fort McIntosh or Wheeling—or to supply these posts with provision or stores in case of exigency." Irvine concluded that he wanted to go on the offensive to take the pressure off Whig settlements, but he had no wherewithal to do so.[13]

His own men complained in a petition. "Your honor . . . saw when you first arrived here in what a deplorable condition we were, for want of clothing, almost naked, several days wanting provisions, in cold, open barracks with little fuel or fire." Irvine ended a May mutiny by whipping and executing two soldiers.[14]

As for Pittsburgh, the settlement around Fort Pitt, the residents "live in paltry houses and are as dirty as in the north of Ireland or even in Scotland," said a traveler. "There is a good deal of small trade carried on. . . . There are in the town four attorneys, two doctors, and not a priest of any persuasion, nor church nor chapel, so they are likely to be damned without the benefit of clergy. . . . The place, I believe, will never be very considerable."[15]

Meanwhile, the British and Indian attacks continued. On March 22, Indians killed seven Whigs near Mt. Sterling, Kentucky. March 31: Two killed at Miller's blockhouse. April 6: Two killed, two taken prisoners near Fort McIntosh. April 7: One farmer killed and a sixteen-year-old girl tomahawked and scalped outside Waldhauer's blockhouse. April 15: Tory rangers destroyed the Bald Eagle Creek blockhouse. May 12: A woman, her husband, and five children attacked near Garard's Fort; two daughters and their father survived, the girls recovering from scalping.

"The Indians are murdering frequently," said a militia colonel and Cumberland County official. "Last Friday night, two men were killed on the frontiers of this county, and about a week before I got home, 14 people were killed and captured in different parts, and last week some mischief was done near Hannastown."[16]

The county militias had to act, and on May 14, they asked Irvine's permission to assemble a volunteer force. Remembering what happened at Gnadenhütten, Irvine consented but with some "express" conditions: "That they did not mean to extend their settlements nor had anything in view but to harass the enemy with an intention to protect the frontier; and that any conquests they might make should be in behalf and for the United States; that they would be governed by military law as militia; that they must collect such numbers as might probably be successful; and last, that they would equip themselves, and victual at their own expense."[17]

In exchange for this agreement, Irvine gave them "a few flints and a small supply of powder." To further rein in excesses, Irvine asked that two Continental officers—all he could spare—accompany the group: The first was his aide, Lieutenant John Rose, "a very vigilant, active, brave young gentleman well acquainted with service." Rose had fled his native Russia after killing a man in a duel. He served at Valley Forge, and rose through the Continental ranks. When the war ended, he would return to Russia, but maintain a correspondence with Irvine and his family until he died. The other officer was a Scottish-born surgeon's mate, Dr. John Knight, who also served with Washington's army.[18]

To command the force, Irvine took "some pains" to ensure the militia would elect as their leader former Continental colonel William Crawford. The militia took the hint. Crawford would command. But they also elected as second in command the popular militia colonel who had led them to Gnadenhütten, David Williamson.[19]

Crawford was not only Washington's peer—they were both 50—but also Washington's friend and land agent. They had known each other for more than thirty years through their mutual profession as surveyors. Like Washington, he fought in the Virginia regiment during the Seven Years' War, but his military career was far less spectacular; it was Washington who, as the Virginia army commander, had promoted Crawford to captain in 1758.

After serving in frontier posts, Crawford left the army and moved to Pennsylvania, about forty-five miles south of Fort Pitt. He homesteaded, traded with Indians, served as a justice of the peace, did surveying work, and served as Washington's agent in land speculating. They traveled together on land-scouting missions.

From 1757 to 1781, Crawford wrote at least twenty-eight letters to Washington; Washington reciprocated with at least thirteen. Most of Crawford's letters were reports related to Washington's requests. He bought land for Washington ("Agreeable to your desire, I have bought the Great Meadows from Mr. Harreson . . ."). He kicked out squatters ("I turned six men off in the first of March who had built houses . . ."). He commanded troops who fought against the Cherokee in 1774, and kept Washington informed about the war ("I am now setting out to Fort Pitt at the head of 100 men . . . where we shall watch the motions of the Indians and shall act accordingly").[20]

Washington respected Crawford and told him so. "I shall ever hold in grateful recollection your friendly endeavors to serve me," he wrote four months before Yorktown. Then Washington returned to business. "Can you tell me how matters stand with respect to my Raccoon Tract? Are the people who live on it still unconvinced of my having a patent for it? . . . I pray you also to be so kind as to let me know how Simpson employs his time—his force—and my mill; he has not that I can hear of rendered any account or paid one far-thing for the profits of my mill or share of the plantation since he has been on the land, which is poor encouragement for me to lease my property in his hands."[21]

Irvine's aide, Rose, had a nuanced view. Crawford, Rose said, was an experienced Indian fighter, "blessed with a constitution that may be called robust" and "inured to fatigue." In his private life, he was "*exceedingly* affectionate." Although "cool in danger" and "personally brave and patient of hardships," he was "too cautious and frightened of appearances, always calculating the chances against. . . . He want-ed to be all in all: By trusting everything to the performance of his own abilities only, everything was but half done, and everybody was disgusted. . . . At a council, he speaks incoherent, proposes matters confusedly, and is incapable of persuading people into his opinion or making use of their weak sides for his purposes. He is somewhat capricious, yet easily and indiscriminately led by people who have once gained an ascendancy over him."[22]

Crawford sided with the Whigs from the start, raising a regiment for Virginia, and commanding Virginian troops as a Continental colonel. He fought in Long Island and crossed the Delaware River with Washington for the battles at Trenton and Princeton. In 1777, Crawford left the Continental army to settle the affairs of two broth-ers who had recently died. He apologized to Washington, who reluctantly let him go. "I can assure you that it goes much against my inclination to part with a good officer," Washington said. However, "I regret exceedingly the loss of your two brothers . . ."[23]

After attending to family needs, Crawford rejoined and com-manded Virginia state troops stationed in the Fort Pitt area in 1778. There, he helped fortify the frontier and skirmished with Indians. After learning of Yorktown, he retired from military service until Irvine persuaded him to lead the expedition against the Indians.

The Indian towns around Upper Sandusky, Ohio, were about two hundred miles west of Fort Pitt. Most residents were Wyandots (also called Hurons), but the alliances with other nations—Delawares, Shawnees, Mingos—meant the towns were cosmopolitan.

The 480 militia took about nine days to travel from their assembly point forty-five miles west of Fort Pitt to the towns. Their horses "tired under their heavy loads in those enormous hills and swamps we had to cross," Rose said.[24]

Two days after they left, Indian scouts spotted them. Reports of the expedition already had reached the British commander 125 miles away in Detroit, Major Arent Schuyler DePeyster. He sent reinforcements under Loyalist captain William Caldwell. Caldwell's seventy rangers and forty-four Indians joined about one hundred fifty Wyandots to await Crawford.[25]

On Tuesday, June 4, 1782, Crawford reached the Upper Sandusky region, but because the villages had changed location over time, they had trouble locating the main town. "We continued our march about five miles farther on through an almost continued glade, and halted in the skirts of a piece of woods," Rose said. There, most militia voted to call off the mission, being "discouraged by the scarcity of their provisions, and that there was not the least sign of any cultivation or habitation, nor of cattle or horses."[26]

In the early afternoon, Caldwell, the rangers, and Indians attacked. Caldwell's second in command, Lieutenant John Tierney (also spelled Turney), later described the rebel army taking cover in trees where they "had every advantage of us as to situation of ground. . . . The battle was very hot till night, which put a stop to firing. Both parties kept their ground all night." Rose's account was similar. "A hot firing was kept up until sunset. . . . We were very much distressed on this ground for the want of water, and discovered at last a puddle of rainwater at the foot of an old turned-up tree." A militiaman said the fighting was "the play of human destruction. . . . A number of our men got wounded, some badly, and some fell to rise no more." By day's end, the Whigs had lost five men, one of them scalped, and sixteen were wounded. Only two enemy Indian scalps were taken, Rose said.[27]

The next day, "firing began at sunrise and continued all day at long. The enemy's intention was, evidently, to cause us to waste our ammunition," Rose said. The British believed they had the rebels pinned down. "At daybreak, we again commenced firing which we kept up pretty briskly till we found the enemy did not wish to oppose us again," Tierney said. "However, we kept firing at them whenever they dared show themselves. They made two attempts to sally but were repulsed with loss." More important for the British and Indians were the arrival of one hundred forty Shawnee reinforcements during the day.[28]

That night, Crawford's council of war agreed their situation was dire. They would try to slip through the enemy lines and retreat. By daybreak, three hundred of the original four hundred eighty militia had escaped across the Sandusky River. Many had been killed. Others were missing. Tierney was frustrated. His men "had got the enemy surrounded, but through some mistake of the Indians, there was one pass left unguarded through which they made their escape." Worse, he and Caldwell didn't learn of the escape until the morning.

Caldwell ordered a pursuit. "The enemy was mostly on horseback. Some of the Indians who had horses followed and overtook them, killed a number, and it was owing to nothing but the country's being very clear that any of them escaped," Tierney said. During the Chase, Caldwell was wounded in both legs. He left the field.

Among the missing Whigs: Crawford. The new commander, Williamson, reported the news to Irvine: "We were reduced to the necessity of making a forced march through their [enemy's] lines in the night, much in disorder . . ." As for Crawford, "we can give no account of since the night of the retreat." (After the war, Williamson was elected county sheriff, but his business investments were generally unsuccessful, and he died a pauper.)[29]

Rose elaborated. "We proceeded with as much speed as possible through the plains, wanting to gain the woods, fearful of the enemy's horse." Once in the woods, "a good many deserted us, who mostly lost themselves in the woods. . . . We marched unremittingly through a severe rain," not stopping until about 1 A.M. on June 7, "when we found it absolutely impossible to keep or find so narrow a path in these thickets." The chase continued at dawn. Those who had stayed with Williamson and Rose soon heard the Indians and found they had "scalped a boy of ours who, with two others, remained behind to bake bread." It was their last encounter with the enemy, but the way back to Fort Pitt would be difficult. The nights were frosty, and there was rain. "The men were kept together with the utmost difficulty and began to break off in small parties pushing ahead." They crossed the Ohio River to relative safety on June 12 and 13.[30]

But where were Crawford, and Irvine's surgeon, John Knight?

Separated from the main militia body during the chaotic break-out, they and six others escaped the encirclement. But instead of catching up with their companions, Delaware Indians caught up with them on June 7. Crawford knew immediately that they were in danger: The Delawares were kin of the Gnadenhütten Moravians.[31]

A Delaware chief who had known Crawford before the war told him that he would have to suffer for Williamson's actions at Gnadenhütten. "You have placed yourself in a situation which puts it out of my power and that of others of your friends to do anything for you . . . by joining yourself to that execrable man, Williamson, and his party."[32]

The narrative of what happened in the ensuing days comes large-ly from an account Knight later dictated to a lawyer from a sick bed. The lawyer, Hugh H. Brackenridge, embellished the narrative and distorted facts. In 1987, a historian compared it with other eyewit-ness accounts and concluded that Brackenridge "rewrote history."[33] But Brackenridge published his version of Knight's account in 1783. It framed American perception of the events for two centuries.

The Indians took their prisoners—additional ones having been captured—to various Delaware and Shawnee towns, separating them, bringing them together again, sometimes forcing them to run gauntlets, sometimes killing and scalping them. Eleven prisoners, including Crawford and Knight, found themselves back in one of the Upper Sandusky towns on June 10.

At this point, Crawford "was very desirous to see a certain Simon Girty, 41, who lived with the Indians," Knight's narrative said. Crawford hoped that Girty, a Loyalist he had fought with during Dunmore's War in 1774, would be able to intervene.[34]

Frontier propaganda and American historians portrayed Girty in much the same way they portrayed Walter Butler:

"Simon Girty acts wickedly. . . . As brutal, depraved, and wicked a wretch as ever lived"—Moravian missionary, 1779.[35]

"He was a monster. No famished tiger ever sought the blood of a victim with more unrelenting rapacity than Girty sought the blood of a white man"—Kentucky governor, 1840.[36]

"The horrors attributed to Girty, or immediately associated with his name, exceed the horrors of even savage barbarity. To his bloody imagination the tomahawk and scalping knife were both the toys of war, and the slaughter of captives, without distinction of age and sex, the merest matter of course. His delight was in the prolonged torture of the sufferer, and the frenzied cruelty of the Indians, whom he knew only too well how to excite. . . . He seemed marked from his infancy to be the scourge of the frontier"—historian, 1882.[37]

"The white savage . . . the deaths head of the frontier. The mention of his name alone created terror in any household; in every pioneer's cabin, it made the children cry out in fear and paled the cheeks of the stoutest-hearted wife"—novelist, 1903.[38]

Girty's reputation for cruelty grew from his being a traitor, not just to his country but also, in Whig perception, to his race. He was born in central Pennsylvania. His father, Simon Sr., was a packhorse driver and Indian trader who had been killed in a drunken brawl with an Indian named Fish (according to nineteenth-century accounts) or in a drunken duel with a bondservant (a late-twentieth-century account and family tradition). Simon Jr.'s mother remarried in 1753 to John Turner. During the Seven Years' War, Delaware Indians captured the Girty family—the two parents and their five sons. Assuming that Turner was responsible for their friend Simon Sr.'s death, the Indians tortured him, then burned him at the stake. Justice satisfied, the Indians adopted the family—Simon Jr. by the Senecas in the Iroquois nation, other brothers by Shawnees and Delawares. Pursuers rescued one brother. The Girtys lived with the Indians for three to five years, when they were reunited after the war ended.[39]

The family lived near Fort Pitt. Girty, knowing Iroquois, Delaware, and Shawnee dialects by then, worked as an interpreter and Indian trader. At one point, he was indicted for a misdemeanor related to a Pennsylvania–Virginia border dispute—he supported Virginia's claims. During Dunmore's War, he enlisted in the Virginia army as a scout and interpreter, and likely first met Crawford then. When the revolution began, he again enlisted with Virginia and was commissioned as a 2nd lieutenant in the rebel army. His first mission was diplomatic: He served as a guide and interpreter in Virginia's efforts to keep Ohio Valley Indians neutral. He continued to serve the Whigs in other negotiations.

Girty hoped to be commissioned as a captain in the Continental army. To further that, he recruited men in the Fort Pitt area in early 1777. The Whigs rewarded him only with another 2nd lieutenancy; he resigned from the army in August. Suspected of disloyalty, the Whigs arrested him, but he was acquitted after a hearing. The army held no grudge, and used Girty as a messenger to Senecas living in Pennsylvania. He returned from the mission to warn the Fort Pitt commander that the Senecas were on a war footing; they wouldn't be neutral. In early 1778, Girty guided a Whig expedition into Indian country; the so-called "Squaw War" resulted in the deaths of just one Indian man, three women, and one boy.[40]

About this time, Girty signed over land he owned in western Pennsylvania to his half-brother, John Turner Jr. Then, Girty and six others changed sides. (Turner and brother Thomas Girty remained Whigs, while the other brothers, George and James, fought for the British, sometimes with Simon.) For the rest of the war, Girty served as a British liaison to Indians, often living with them, interpreting at conferences, participating in raids, and serving as a scout and guide for rangers. If he commanded troops, it was rare; British officers led most joint Indian-Loyalist raids.[41]

At times, Girty seemed to be omnipresent, and from the settlers' perspective mythologically evil, condoning, if not conducting, torture and executions. In southwest Pennsylvania, northwest Virginia, and throughout Kentucky, Girty's name became a "household word of terror." The raids were violent, but the Indians respected Girty enough to accept his intervention on behalf of many prisoners. Some Whigs defended him. One captured acquaintance recalled: "He flung his arms around me and cried like a child. . . . He made a speech to the Indians—he could speak the Indian tongue, and knew how to speak—and told them if they meant to do him a favor, they must do it now and save my life." In 1780, he was with Indians who captured two Kentucky forts and took three hundred captives; he helped save their lives. William K. Beall, an American taken prisoner in the War of 1812, said he talked with many people who knew Girty personally: "People here say that Simon Girty was beneficial to Americans prisoners during the Indian wars; that he often gave all he had to get them their liberty and frequently risked his life to save them from the Indians inhuman tortures; and that there are many Americans in Canada to attest the truth of it." Some historians speculate that many of the cruelties attributed to Simon Girty were actually committed by his Loyalist "savage brothers."[42]

He was, however, a frontiersman, "deeply bronzed by exposure," shaped by harsh conditions, and often harsh himself. "He was cruel as were most of the backwoodsmen of his time; but he was not wantonly cruel," a Canadian historian concluded. Those who knew Girty said he had large or piercing black eyes, and despite a heavy frame, was agile and strong. A British captain said in 1779 that Girty was "one of the most useful, disinterested friends in this department that the government has." The next year, the same captain said he was "useless." Missionaries said he plied Indians, even Moravian Indians, with alcohol. In Native American oral tradition, far from being renegade and traitor to his race, he was a hero, a clever and kind man who fought "settler terrorism." Yet he could have violent disagreements. In August 1781, while on a raid with Mohawk captain Joseph Brant, Girty said Brant's exploits were exaggerated, and Brant lied about them. The two were reportedly drunk, and Brant slashed at Girty's forehead with a sword. Girty took nearly six months to recover.[43]

Knight's account of the Crawford-Girty conversation—as distorted by Brackenridge—made Girty infamous.[44]

"I asked the colonel [Crawford] if he had seen Mr. Girty. He told me he had, and that Girty had promised to do everything in his power for him, but that the Indians were very much enraged against the prisoners." Soon after, according to the narrative, the Delawares tomahawked and scalped four other prisoners. While Crawford and Knight watched, Indian women and boys tomahawked another five.

They severed one dead man's head, "and the Indians kicked it about upon the ground."

Now, it was just the two of them on a forced march, finally stopping by a campfire. "When we were come to the fire, the colonel was stripped naked, ordered to sit down by the fire, and then they beat him with sticks and their fists. Presently after, I was treated in the same manner. They then tied a rope to the foot of a post about fifteen feet high, bound the colonel's hands behind his back and fastened the rope to the ligature between his wrists. . . . The colonel then called to Girty and asked if they intended to burn him. Girty answered, yes. The colonel said he would take it all patiently."

Knight watched Crawford's ensuing torture: punctured with burning sticks, hot coals rubbed in his wounds, forced to walk on fire. "In the midst of these extreme tortures, he called Simon Girty and begged of him to shoot him, but Girty making no answer, he called to him again. Girty, then, by way of derision, told the colonel he had no gun, at the same time turning about to an Indian who was behind him, laughed heartily, and by all his gestures seemed delighted at the horrid scene." The torture, including scalping alive, lasted another two hours. At one point, Girty, according to the narrative, approached Knight and told him he would suffer the same fate, but in a Shawnee town.

Both British and Whig accounts agree that the Knight-Brackenridge account of Crawford's torture was accurate. Caldwell, although not on the scene, reported to DePeyster in Detroit that the rebel officers "have suffered much," and that Crawford "died like a hero, and never changed countenance."[45]

Where the accounts disagree is Girty's role. Other prisoners who escaped or were released, agents and rangers, Indian oral tradition, and Girty himself differ with Knight-Brackenridge.

DePeyster said an Indian agent on the scene—presumably Girty—used "every means" to save his life. Irvine told Washington that Girty ignored Crawford's plea to put him out of his misery, but he made no mention of Girty gloating or laughing. Another Whig officer said Girty didn't have a gun with him.[46] A female prisoner and eyewitness told her son years later that "Girty really did everything that a mortal man could to save Crawford," offering Indians his black slave, horse, rifle, and wampum in exchange for his life. "Girty shed tears while witnessing Crawford's agonies at the stake and ever after always spoke of Crawford in the tenderest terms as a particular friend," the woman said. Another eyewitness, a thirteen-year-old boy, confirmed in 1849 that Girty tried to buy Crawford's life, but was threatened with his own life if he didn't stop trying. "Say one more word, and I will make another stake to burn you," another account quoted the chief. When the torture began, and Crawford asked Girty to shoot him, Girty replied that he dare not, and he left the scene rather than watch. Indian tradition says that a chief responded to Girty's pleas by saying "if Crawford had been his own father, he could not have saved him." In his later years, Girty himself said he tried to intercede, and he remained in friendly contact with Crawford's son, John.[47]

Two days after Crawford's death, on June 13, Knight was able to strike an escort to a Shawnee town and escape. Another prisoner, the guide John Stover, escaped by freeing himself from buffalo-hide ropes and stealing a horse.

Crawford wasn't the first person who was tortured to death—on both sides—but both British and Whigs reacted strongly. DePeyster, who had been trying to suppress torture among his Indian allies, told an Indian agent to threaten the chiefs that if they persisted, "I shall be under the necessity of recalling the [British and Loyalist] troops." He told his superior, General Frederick Haldimand, that he had worked hard to cool the Indian reaction to Gnadenhütten, but it didn't help when the rebels declared they intended to "exterminate the whole Wyandot tribe, not by words only, but even by exposing effigies left hanging by the heels in every encampment." Haldimand, in turn, told Carleton that he regretted the cruelty not only on a personal level, but because "it awakens in the Indians that barbarity to prisoners which the unwearied efforts of his Majesty's ministers had totally extinguished."[48]

Notwithstanding his superiors' concern about torture, Caldwell put his army's accomplishment into perspective. As near as he could determine, two hundred fifty enemy soldiers were killed or wounded. "Our loss is very inconsiderable": one white man killed, one wounded (Caldwell himself); four Indians killed, eight wounded.[49]

On the other side, Washington wrote Irvine, "I cannot but regret the misfortune and, more especially, for the loss of Col. Crawford, for whom I had a very great regard."[50]

Irvine told Benjamin Lincoln—now secretary of war—that the settlers and militia "think their only safety depends on the total destruction of all the Indian settlements within 200 miles; this, it is true, they are taught by dear-bought experience." Less than a year later, Irvine proposed a final solution: "Nothing short of a total extirpation of all the western tribes of Indians, or at least driving them over the Mississippi and the lakes, will ensure peace."[51]

Before the Whigs could bring the war back to the enemy, the Indians struck again, this time, thirty-five miles east of Fort Pitt. Hannastown (or Hanna's Town) was a relatively new settlement, founded in 1773, but it had become a county seat. (Now reconstructed as a county park, it is just north of Greensburg, Pennsylvania, named in 1785 after Nathanael Greene.) At the settlement's hub was a fort, well built and considered a safe shelter from attacks.[52]

A little more than a month after Crawford's defeat, a passerby saw about one hundred Indians and warned the settlers working in the fields. "The whole reaping party ran for the town, each one intent upon his own safety," an eyewitness said. "Fathers seeking for their wives and children, and children calling for their parents and friends, and all hurrying in a state of consternation to the fort."[53]

The Indians—Senecas led by Kayashuta—and Loyalist rangers arrived in mid-afternoon on July 13, found the homes deserted, and started looting and burning the buildings—as Whig expeditions had done to Indian towns. Then, they attacked the fort, commanded by Captain Michael Huffnagle.

"If you consider our situation, with only 20 of the inhabitants, 17 guns, and very little ammunition to stand the attack in the manner we did, you will say that the people behaved bravely," Huffnagle told Irvine. The attack was "very severe until after dark when they left us. The inhabitants here are in a very distressed situation having lost all their property but what clothing they had on." As for Huffnagle himself, "I have lost what little property I had here," but he saved the county records, which had been moved to the fort. Two settlers were wounded, but throughout the area, the Indians killed or captured twenty, took a large number of horses, and killed about one hundred livestock, "burning and destroying as they went along."[54]

19. Ambush at Blue Licks

LOYALIST CALDWELL, WOUNDED IN BOTH LEGS AT CRAWFORD'S defeat, recovered quickly. By August 1782, he was "determined to pay the enemy a visit with as many Indians as would follow me."[1]

Caldwell was born in northern Ireland in the 1750s. As a teenager or in his early twenties, he immigrated to Virginia, and soon after joined the Virginia army to fight in Dunmore's War; Indians wounded him near Fort Pitt. When the revolution started, he stayed loyal to the Crown, and was wounded again in fighting around Norfolk, Virginia, in 1776. When their position proved indefensible, the Loyalists evacuated. By early 1777, Caldwell was at Fort Niagara, where he was named a captain in the Loyalist rangers led by John Butler, Walter's father.[2]

In the ensuing years, Caldwell was "a very active partisan," Niagara's commander said. On the Pennsylvania frontier in July 1778, a joint Indian-ranger force he helped command attacked Wyoming Valley, where six thousand mostly Whig settlers had encroached on Indian lands and harassed Tory settlers. Whig historians called it a "massacre." They said about three hundred militia and Continentals were killed, and rebel propaganda told of Tories refusing to give quarter, and Indians burning prisoners alive and killing babies. John Butler, however, reported that no civilians were killed: "Not a single person was hurt except such as were in arms. To these, in truth, the Indians gave no quarter." Caldwell did order the execution of two rangers who had snuck away to visit their families; he considered this desertion, and it put the rest of the rangers at risk of discovery by the enemy.[3]

On the New York frontier two months later, Caldwell reported he attacked several settlements, destroying rebel grain, burning their buildings, and driving off "a great many cows and oxen, horses and mares. The oxen were all large New England cattle, kept on the flats for the use of the Continental troops."4

During these years, Caldwell led his men on missions throughout the frontier, from near Schenectady to Detroit. He even went on a spy mission to Philadelphia. Now, in August 1782, he wanted to strike a blow at the rebels where they had formed a "white wedge in the heart of Indian America"—Kentucky.5

The whites came to fertile, rolling green country south of the Ohio River, west of Virginia, past the Appalachians. They came on the promise of a 1768 treaty between the Iroquois and British, in which the Iroquois ceded to the land they didn't own: Shawnee and Cherokee land.

A land agent and speculator named Daniel Boone and a party of hunters crossed into Shawnee territory in 1769. The Shawnees caught them, confiscated their furs and weapons, and sent them home. Again and again, Boone returned, first with his own family, then with more settlers. The Shawnees called them "crazy people [who] want to shove us off our land entirely." They complained to the British that their land was "covered with white people." William Johnson, in turn, reported to London that the settlers "generally set out with a general prejudice against all Indians, and the young Indian warriors or hunters are too often inclined to retaliate."6

Boone was one of many easterners who explored and settled Kentucky, then a Virginia county. He had been a twenty-one-year-old teamster on the disastrous Braddock expedition against the French and Indian allies in 1755. When the revolution began twenty years later, he was an agent for a land-speculation company that bought wilderness from the Cherokees and sold it to settlers. It was a disputed sale: The Cherokees disavowed it, saying company officials lied to them about the nature of the sale. Johnson's counterpart in the southern colonies, John Stuart, suggested the title might be fraudulent—a common practice, he said.7

Boone became a legendary figure, largely because of a best-selling book, the 1784 ghostwritten autobiography whose author interviewed Boone but took liberties with and romanticized the details. Lord Byron memorialized him in *Don Juan* in 1822 as the "backwoodsman of Kentucky." He was probably an inspiration for James Fenimore Cooper's *Last of the Mohicans* and other Leatherstocking tales. In the mid-twentieth century, his legend inspired a six-year, 165-episode run of a television show called *Daniel Boone*, which continues in reruns in the twenty-first century.

The legends were based on an eventful life. Boone found a way to Kentucky through the Appalachians by discovering the Cumberland Gap, and helped build the Wilderness Road through the mountains. Indians killed his brother, two of his sons, and captured one of his daughters. The Shawnees captured Boone himself and adopted him; he later escaped to fight them. In 1781, the British captured and released him. He served as a militia lieutenant colonel, legislator, sheriff, government surveyor, tavern owner, land speculator, and bear hunter. He was court-martialed for collaborating with the British, but acquitted. At one point, he was one of the wealthiest men in Kentucky, but he lost his money and his land. Boone would continue to fight Indians after the war, make peace with them, and work for prisoner releases. He would flee creditors for Missouri, and die in 1820 in his son's home.

One contemporary described Boone as understated: "He was solid in mind as well as in body, never frivolous, thoughtless, or agitated, but was always quiet, meditative, and impressive, unpretentious, kind, and friendly in his manner." Nathan Boone, one of his sons, said he was about five feet eight with "moderately" black hair, blue eyes, and fair skin. The self-description in his autobiography talked about his hard life. "Many dark and sleepless nights have I spent, separated from the cheerful society of men, scorched by the summer's sun, and pinched by the winter's cold, an instrument ordained to settle the wilderness."[8]

Indians, supported by and sometimes accompanied by the British and Loyalist rangers, unrelentingly attacked Kentucky settlements.

Major Hugh McGary, chairman of the committee that governed Kentucky County, pleaded with Virginia governor Patrick Henry in 1777 for military help: "We are surrounded with enemies on every side; every day increases their numbers. To retreat from the place where our all is centered would be little preferable to death. Our fort is already filled with widows and orphans; their necessities call upon us daily for supplies."[9]

By June 1782, the Indians and British had conducted successful raids for nearly a year and a half, with feeble response from the Whig settlers. From the falls of the Ohio—Louisville—a militia colonel pleaded for help. "The savages . . . are constantly ravaging the most interior parts of the county, which makes it impossible for any one settlement to assist another. . . . Your exertions on this occasion may possibly save our families from the hands of merciless savages."[10]

After an attack on a small fort one hundred miles from Louisville, Boone said the situation was "more and more alarming; several stations [forts] which had lately been erected in the county were continually infested with savages, stealing their horses and killing men at every opportunity." Moreover, Simon Girty and other Tories were inciting Indians to "execute every diabolical scheme."[11]

On August 15, Caldwell would begin to make matters worse. He had assembled an army of three hundred men—thirty to sixty rangers, including the brothers Simon and George Girty, two Indian agents, and Indians from Wyandot, Cherokee, Shawnee, Delaware, and other nations. Their goal was the destruction of Bryan's Station, a fort near what is now Lexington. They didn't arrive undetected, however, and when Caldwell appeared before the fort, the settlers had already taken refuge behind the palisade.

Seeing this, Caldwell tried to "draw them out by sending up a small party to try to take a prisoner and show themselves." Girty led the small party, but the Indians "were in too great a hurry," and the bulk of the attack force appeared, reinforcing the garrison's decision to stay behind their walls. The Whigs killed five attackers and wounded two, Caldwell reported. Boone's autobiography said otherwise: The enemy "furiously assaulted the garrison, which was happily prepared to oppose them," resulting in thirty rangers and Indians killed, while the settlers lost four men.[12]

Knowing rebel reinforcements were on the way, Caldwell called off the siege the next day. Wind prevented him from burning more than three adjacent homes as he retreated, but his army did "considerable damage," destroying three hundred hogs, one hundred fifty cattle, sheep, potatoes, corn, and hemp. They camped about twenty miles north. There, about one hundred Indians left.

Caldwell reached a more defensible position on August 17. It was near a spring and salt lick—the Blue Lick—forty-five miles northwest of Bryan's Station, surrounded by water on three sides on a loop of the middle fork of the Licking River—a "remarkable bend" of the river, as Boone described it.[13]

There, Caldwell laid a trap. "We encamped near an advantageous hill," said a British Indian agent, "and expecting the enemy would pursue, determined here to wait for them."[14]

The enemy had every intention of pursuing. More than one hundred eighty militia from Boone's Station (Boonesborough), Harrodsburg, and Lexington joined the Bryan's Station men to plan their action. They debated whether to wait for several hundred reinforcements known to be on the way, but decided they couldn't wait, and started their chase on the eighteenth. They divided into three divisions led by Colonel John Todd as overall commander, Boone, and Colonel Stephen Trigg. McGary—who had asked the governor for more troops in 1777—was part of the officers' council of war.

McGary, 38, had emigrated with his family from Ireland as a youth. During the Seven Years' War, he worked as a teamster. After the war, he settled on the North Carolina frontier near Boone. With Boone and other settlers, he brought his family to Kentucky in 1775. Two years later, he was elected chairman of Kentucky County. As the frontier war intensified, he led militia raids against Indians, and was commissioned a major in the state militia in 1781.[15]

About 7:30 A.M. on the 19th, Caldwell learned from scouts that the enemy was approaching. From across the river, the Whigs saw several Indians on a hill. What happened next is unclear. Some reports say Boone urged the militia to wait for reinforcements, but McGary yelled for all non-cowards to attack, and led a chaotic charge across the river. "The conduct of our officers is by some censured and charged with want of prudence in attacking at any rate," Colonel Todd's brother and participant, Levi, said. Another officer complained about "the vain and seditious expressions of a Major McGary. How much more harm than good can one fool do?" The rumors about his rashness were so pervasive that after the battle, McGary demanded a formal hearing for which no record survives.[16]

The official accounts by Boone and others don't mention McGary, other than that he led the center column. Regardless of McGary's role, the battle was a Whig disaster, and the militia were in "the utmost confusion, each viewing the other with that consternation foreboding destruction."[17]

Boone described the chaos: "The savages, observing us, gave way, and we, being ignorant of their numbers, passed the river. . . . An exceedingly fierce battle immediately began, for about 15 minutes, when we, being overpowered by numbers, were obliged to retreat . . . When we gave way, they pursued us with the utmost eagerness, and in every quarter spread destruction. The river was difficult to cross, and many were killed in the flight, some just entering the river, some in the water, others after crossing, in ascending the cliffs. . . . Many widows were now made."[18]

Levi Todd concurred. "The enemy put us wholly to the rout."[19]

Caldwell praised his defeated enemy, which bore up to Indian and ranger attack "very well for some time, 'til we rushed in upon them, when they broke immediately." As for the Indians, they behaved "extremely well." The rebels killed only one white man, an interpreter, who "died like a warrior fighting arm to arm." Only six Indians were killed.[20]

While Caldwell reported 146 militia killed or captured, Boone said seventy-seven men were killed, with twelve wounded. Among the victims: Todd, the commander; Trigg, a division commander; and Boone's twenty-three-year-old son, Israel. Years later, a militiaman remembered Boone's reaction: He "wept bitterly."[21]

The battle lost, Boone, Levi Todd, and other officers and civilian leaders again pleaded with the governor: "We sensibly feel and deem our situation truly alarming. We can scarcely behold a spot of earth but what reminds us of the fall of some fellow adventurer massacred by savage hands. Our number of militia decreases. Our widows and orphans are numerous. . . . If something is not speedily done, we [don't] doubt will wholly be depopulated."[22]

After the war, McGary continued to be controversial. He was convicted of illegal gambling, which didn't prevent him from serving as a county judge. Fighting against the Shawnees continued, and in 1786, now-Lieutenant Colonel McGary murdered an elderly chief he believed was present at Blue Licks. He split open the man's head with a hatchet and chopped off three fingers of the chief's wife before he was restrained. Found guilty of murder, his punishment was the loss of his militia commission for a year. Then, McGary became involved in a bigamy case involving future president

Andrew Jackson, with whom he had traveled. Jackson's wife was accused of bigamy, and McGary testified in support of the accusations. Jackson supporters accused him of perjury because of an argument they said McGary once had with Jackson. McGary and his family moved to southwest Indiana in 1804, where he died. His son helped found Evansville.[23]

Caldwell led an equally controversial postwar life. He settled on land grants in Amherstburg, Ontario, with other refugees, and married a white woman. His half-Indian son, Billy, and Billy's mother lived with the Mohawks along the Grand River, about one hundred eighty miles to the east. Caldwell's trading post business failed, but a government career was more successful: He was county deputy lieutenant. During the War of 1812, Caldwell commanded rangers and fought alongside Billy in skirmishes and battles. After the war, the British named him Indian superintendent. Billy, a captain, was his assistant. Caldwell's tenure was difficult. Some accused him of incompetence; ultimately, the British disliked his belligerence and fired him after a year. Billy replaced him. Caldwell spent his aging years restoring his property damaged by the Americans during the war, and arguing with the government about his pension. He donated land to both Anglican and Catholic churches. Billy Caldwell surpassed his father in fame. He became a Chicago resident, U.S. citizen, fur trader, justice of the peace, and diplomat, and Congress rewarded him with a pension. Chicago named North Caldwell Avenue after him.[24]

20. Final Fights on the Ohio

THE NEXT MAJOR BRITISH-INDIAN RAID WAS NINETY MILES downstream from Fort Pitt along the Ohio River.

The first official white claim to the land that became the settlement of Wheeling (now in West Virginia) was in 1769 by Ebenezer Zane, 22, and his two brothers, Jonathan and Silas. They weren't the first whites at the hilly, forested junction of Wheeling Creek and the Ohio River; the name first appeared on a map in 1755. It was a transliterated Delaware Indian phrase for "place of the skull," where Delawares had earlier beheaded trespassing whites and placed their heads on poles as a warning to other whites who might think of settling there.[1]

For Ebenezer Zane, however, Wheeling was "like a vision of Paradise." Of Danish descent, Zane was born on the northwestern Virginia frontier. Friends remembered him as a short but athletic man with dark skin, piercing black eyes, large brows, and a big nose. He was "quick, impetuous, and hard to restrain when excited." He built a cabin at Wheeling in 1770 and brought his extended family and friends there a year or two later. About the time Zane built his cabin, Washington and Crawford passed through the country on a land-scouting trip. "On this creek is the appearance of good land a distance up on it," Washington wrote. (Jonathan Zane would accompany Crawford on his doomed expedition.)[2]

Far from a paradise, Wheeling was, to whites, dangerous. During Dunmore's War in 1774, the Virginia government, represented by then-Major Crawford, built a fort in Wheeling, and named it Fort Fincastle, after one of Governor Dunmore's titles, Viscount

Fincastle. About this time, Zane served as a dispersing officer for the state militia; he was a colonel, although the rank might have been honorary.

The next year, the fort named after a royal governor was renamed after Whig governor Patrick Henry. Fort Henry was by the river, at the foot of a sharply rising hill, near two dozen log homes. Its palisade, shaped like a parallelogram with towers in each corner, had eight to seventeen-foot-high white oak pickets. They enclosed about three-quarters of an acre. Just outside the fort: a spring. Inside the fort: a well. The fort's only cannon dated to the Seven Years' War; it had been recovered from the Monongahela River near Fort Pitt.[3]

Several attacks against area settlers during 1777 culminated in the late summer with an attack on Fort Henry itself. About four hundred Indians and Loyalists besieged the fort for a day, killing twenty-three of the forty-two defenders. The Indians, who lost forty or fifty men, called off the siege after militia reinforcements arrived.

Five years later, in July 1782, settlers began seeing increasing numbers of Indians in the area. Zane concluded, "We may shortly expect an attack." He asked Irvine at Fort Pitt for extra gunpowder and reinforcements. The only defenders other than settlers were five militiamen. "We mean to support the place or perish in the attempt," Zane said.[4]

The next month, an expedition of forty Loyalist rangers and about two hundred forty Indians left Detroit headed for Fort Henry. After they left, Detroit commander DePeyster learned that Parliament, anticipating peace, ordered an end to offensive operations, but it was too late to stop the expedition.[5]

The expedition was led by a Schenectady-born Loyalist whose roots in New York went back to at least the mid-seventeenth century. Andries Bradt, 27—he went by Andrew—was a farmer's son and a nephew of John Butler, the rangers' top commander. Like many families, the extended Bradt family split their loyalties; some fought against British general John Burgoyne in 1777. Bradt began fighting with the British in 1778, first as a lieutenant in the Indian Department, then in the rangers. John Butler promoted Bradt to captain in 1780, and Bradt led various raids against the Ohio Valley settlers.[6]

His raid on Fort Henry would be the final expedition the British would make against Whig settlers on the northwest frontier.

As with Caldwell's expedition against Bryan's Station in midsummer, the settlers learned ahead of time that Bradt was approaching. When Bradt arrived at Fort Henry around sundown on September 11, about eighteen men and forty women and children were behind the fort's palisade; another nine people were in Zane's fortified home, a two-story blockhouse that's been described as anywhere from sixty feet to sixty yards from the fort.

Bradt acted immediately. According to Zane, the enemy "immediately formed into lines around the garrison, paraded British colors, and demanded the fort to be surrendered, which was refused." Three times that night, Bradt's men tried to storm the palisades, but the settlers and militia repulsed them. Throughout the next day, the rangers and Indians "kept a continual fire." Around 10 P.M., they stormed the fort again, and again were turned back. By the morning of September 13, Bradt, anticipating Whig reinforcements, retreated, killing livestock and burning homes.[7]

Zane, one of his slaves, three or four other men, and a few family members had remained in his blockhouse—possibly to provide a crossfire, possibly because he wanted to protect the home from being torched. Regardless, it led to a legend.

An 1802 account of Fort Henry's defense told the story of Zane's teenaged sister, Betty. The story said that on September 12, during the "continual fire," the fort's defenders were running out of gunpowder. Betty volunteered to run to her brother's cabin and return with more. Bradt's men were so surprised to see a young woman running out of the fort that they didn't fire at her. Depending on the account, on her return run, Betty carried a gunpowder keg held in an apron or a tablecloth, tied around her waist or slung over her shoulder; the enemy fired at her and either missed or shot off a lock of her hair.[8]

Zane Grey, Ebenezer Zane's great-grandson who was a prolific and best-selling early twentieth-century author, contributed to the legend with his first novel, a fictional account of Betty. "Her eyes shone with a fateful resolve; her white and eager face was surpassingly beautiful with its light of hope, of prayer, of heroism. 'Let me go, brother. You know I can run, and oh! I will fly today. Every moment is precious. . . . You cannot *spare* a man. Let me go.' . . . 'God, what a woman!' he said between his teeth, as he thrust the rifle forward."[9]

Whether this happened is unknown. In 1849, an aging eyewitness swore that it was another woman who made the gunpowder run, and said Betty wasn't even at the fort. The woman's account was contradicted by her grandson, who said that when she was younger, she had credited Betty.[10]

Few documented facts exist about Betty's later life other than she married twice and is buried in the same plot as her brother, in Martins Ferry, Ohio. The Navy named a World War II liberty ship, used for transport, in her honor. As for Ebenezer Zane, his investment in Wheeling paid off, and he made money selling lots. A son-in-law named Zanesville, Ohio, after him.[11]

Another disputed legend is Girty's role in the attack. Some accounts say that he, not Bradt, commanded; others say he was there, but in a lesser role; another says it was Simon's brother, George, who participated.[12]

Legends aside, after the failed assault, Bradt's force split up. He, his rangers, and most of the Indians recrossed the Ohio and went to the Sandusky Indian towns two hundred miles to the northwest. About sixty to seventy Indians headed to the northeast, where, sixteen miles away, they intended to attack a smaller fort, Rice's, near what is now Bethany, West Virginia. As with Fort Henry, the families in the area learned about the coming attack and retreated behind their palisade, which was defended by six men. The Indians besieged the fort for about twelve hours (some accounts say four hours), killing one defender while he was looking through a loophole, and another two who were riding to help in the fort's defense. The Indians lost two or four men, but before they left, they killed livestock, and burned a barn with its stores of grain and hay.[13]

Around mid-month, Bradt and his men joined forces with Caldwell. By the time they returned to Detroit, they were starving and sick. DePeyster described them as "walking spectres." Bradt eventually settled in the Niagara area, where the British rewarded him with a land grant.[14]

Successfully defended or not, the British and Indian attacks were constant, and so was the pressure on Irvine in Fort Pitt and Governor Harrison in Virginia to do something.

Irvine was skeptical that any offensive would work given the lack of men and supplies. He told Washington, "I never could see any great advantages gained by excursions of this kind; at least, they have not been lasting." The only way to stop the raids was to capture and destroy the British strongholds at Detroit and Niagara, and that was unlikely to happen. Irvine said his priority in summer 1782 was to repair Fort Pitt.[15]

Governor Harrison told his military men that the government could do little because Virginia was broke: "Money matters" were "wretched," he said. Nonetheless, Harrison and other Virginia officials began urging, then ordering, action from a former frontier military hero, a general of the state militia, George Rogers Clark, 27, who seemed to be immobilized at his base at the Falls of the Ohio—Louisville.[16]

Clark believed the only way to defeat Indians was "to excel them in barbarity." Once, trying to encourage the surrender of an enemy post, he ordered bound Indian prisoners to be tomahawked in plain view.[17]

The tall, reddish-haired, Virginia-born Clark had little formal education. He learned surveying, which was helpful in his land-speculating activities. Like Boone, he and his family settled in Kentucky in the early 1770s, and he served as a state militia officer in Dunmore's War. Then-Governor Patrick Henry promoted him in 1775 to major, with responsibility for Kentucky's defense. Clark called for and co-led a delegation that demanded more military support from the government. Virginia responded by formally annexing Kentucky as a county, and giving Clark five hundred pounds of gunpowder. In 1777, Virginia promoted him to lieutenant colonel.

Clark made his reputation in 1778 and 1779 by recruiting an army of 180 men in Pittsburgh; establishing a base five hundred miles down the Ohio River at the Falls of the Ohio; taking the British post at Vincennes (now in Indiana) 115 miles farther west; then traveling another two hundred miles to capture Kaskaskia (now in Illinois) on the Mississippi River. While Clark marched, the British, led by the Detroit commander Colonel Henry Hamilton, had retaken Vincennes. With the help of residents of French ancestry who had remained in the region after the Seven Years' War, Rogers led a difficult, winter expedition, surprised the British, retook Vincennes, and captured Hamilton. (DePeyster succeeded him.)

Promoted to general, Clark led a 1780 expedition against the Shawnees at their stronghold at Chillicothe, nearly halfway between

Louisville and Fort Pitt. (The town was near present-day Xenia, Ohio, and is known as Oldtown and Old Chillicothe. Modern Chillicothe is sixty-three miles to the southwest.) The Shawnees avoided a major engagement with the better-armed Clark, but he burned eight hundred acres of crops. The next year, Clark led an expedition to capture Detroit; he turned back after learning that reinforcements from Fort Pitt were defeated by rangers and Indians led by Mohawk captain Joseph Brant.[18]

By the end of 1781, Clark and Virginia officials were frustrated with each other.

Clark had tried to raise men and money for supplies to mount another expedition against Detroit, but instead, "I find myself enclosed with few troops, in a trifling fort, and shortly expect to bear the insults of those who have for several years been in continued dread of me." He despaired. "My chain appears to have run out." After Virginia officials questioned his integrity regarding procurements, he resigned in early 1782 as Kentucky commander to devote his time to his land holdings—an "unprecedented quantity of the finest lands in the western world." Virginia refused his resignation. In the spring, using some of his own money, he tried to build four armed galleys to patrol the Ohio; desertion thwarted his efforts.[19]

Other militia leaders sent a stream of complaints to Virginia about Clark's inability to protect Kentucky. Boone and others said that by staying close to his base in Louisville—"a town without inhabitants"—Clark left the frontier "open and unguarded." Another colonel said Clark "has lost the confidence of the people, and it is said become a sot, perhaps something worse." Harrison heard a different report about Clark's drinking, that there was a common belief "of his being so addicted to liquor as to be incapable of attending to his duty." To other Kentucky militia commanders, Harrison complained that Clark failed to obey orders to set up forts at key locations. "I am apt to think if he had obeyed his orders, this disaster [Blue Licks] would not have happened."[20]

Clark replied that he was "at a loss" to understand the criticism. His critics were "enemies to the state" who didn't understand the military necessity of reinforcing Louisville.[21]

Creditors also pressured Clark, who had promised repayments for supplies. "I have already taken every step in my power to get the creditors of the state paid [but] to no effect," he said. "If I was worth the money, I would most cheerfully pay it myself and trust the state, but can assure you with truth: I am entirely reduced myself."[22]

He had defenders. One of his colonels wrote to Harrison that Clark didn't deserve censure. "His greatest misfortune and loss of useful operations of the campaign was the want of men, although the general strained every nerve in this power to raise a sufficient number to penetrate into the heart of the enemy's country."[23]

In September and October 1782, Clark and Irvine planned a two-pronged expedition into Indian country; it would be the expedition the frontier wanted, designed to cripple the ability of Indians to raid. Irvine would lead 1,200 Continentals and militia from Fort Pitt against Delawares and other Indians in Upper Sandusky, while Clark would collect one thousand men in Louisville against Shawnees in Chillicothe. In preparation, Clark traded 3,200 acres of his own land for provisions, and left Louisville on November 4. Meanwhile, Irvine learned of the provisional peace treaty, and received orders to stop his participation. However, he condoned Clark's intention to proceed against the Shawnees. To help Clark, Irvine would try to draw off some of the Indians by starting a rumor that the Sandusky attack was still on. Creating the rumor was "the only strategem left me to make use of in your favor."[24]

Clark's army included militia led by Kentucky veterans, including Boone and McGary. It took six days to reach Chillicothe and other Shawnee villages. There, he found most Shawnees had retreated before him. His efforts to bring about a general action were "fruitless," he reported. "We might probably have got many more scalps and prisoners could we have known in time whether or not we were discovered." Still, his men killed and scalped ten Shawnees, and took seven prisoners. They freed two imprisoned whites. More important, he left the Shawnees without food or shelter as winter approached. "In a few hours, two-thirds of their towns were laid in ashes, and everything they were possessed of destroyed. . . . The quantity of provisions burned far surpassed any idea we had of their stores of that kind."[25]

Clark was a hero. The U.S. honored him with a stamp in 1929 and a postal card in 1979. Streets, colleges, and counties are named after him. Pursued by creditors for much of his later life, he died in 1818 in his sister's home near Louisville. But Clark's younger brother, William, achieved greater fame: He was second in command of the eponymous Lewis and Clark Expedition.

The Shawnees were discouraged by the Whig invasions and the British inability to stop them. "We see ourselves weak and our arms feeble to the force of the enemy," a Shawnee chief said. " 'Tis now upwards of twenty years since we have been alone engaged against the Virginians."[26]

None of the Indians were pleased with their ally. With peace near, the British not only discouraged raids, but refused to support them. "Your Father can take no part" in such raids, DePeyster told the Shawnees.[27]

Still, the attacks continued.

In early 1783, some forty people were killed or captured on the Pennsylvania frontier alone. "The inhabitants of the frontiers seem more discouraged this spring than they have been, having flattered themselves with the most sanguine hopes of peace, which hopes they now think are frustrated," said a militia lieutenant.[28]

Attacks in Kentucky also continued. One Indian ambush near Louisville in April killed a prominent militia leader, Colonel [James] John Floyd. Floyd was a veteran of Dunmore's War, Blue Licks, and Clark's expedition the year before.[29]

In May, Simon Girty and some Indians raided settlers near Nine-Mile Run, a creek about five miles east of Fort Pitt, now part of Pittsburgh's Squirrel Hill neighborhood. Girty's mother and Whig half-brother, John Turner, lived in the area, and it's possible Girty visited them while on the raid. Girty and Turner were close, they might have secretly visited each other after the war, and Turner's will included Girty's children.[30]

Before Girty left Nine-Mile Run to return to Detroit, he captured a boy, John Burkhart. An aging contemporary said years later that as Girty left, he heard cannon firing from Fort Pitt. He asked Burkhart if he knew what the firing was for. Burkhart said the fort was celebrating the peace treaty. Girty didn't believe him, and kept him as a prisoner, bringing him to Detroit, where DePeyster returned him in the care of another traveler.[31]

After the war, Girty was persona non grata in the U.S., where, if captured, he likely would have been executed, if not lynched, for perceived atrocities. He made his home in Amherstburg, Ontario, and fell in love with a nineteen-year-old woman who had been captured in 1780 and adopted by the Shawnees. Girty had four surviving children with her and many grandchildren. The British rewarded him, giving him a half-pay pension, while he continued to work as an agent and interpreter. He remained in touch with his family, giving title of his Pennsylvania lands to his American half-brother, and having a reunion with his mother in Detroit. Around 1796, Girty became depressed and began drinking heavily; his wife left him. His physical health failed: By the time he was seventy, he was lame and nearly blind. After the War of 1812, his wife rejoined him when he gave up drinking. The British honored him at his funeral with a color guard.[32]

21. Sevier Hunts for Dragging Canoe

B Y THE TIME OF CORNWALLIS'S YORKTOWN SURRENDER, THE
Cherokees in the South already had lost much of their land—
a catastrophe for people who lived in more than sixty small towns
with communal farms, raising crops and keeping livestock.[1]

Between 1759 and 1761, their war against white incursions was
quashed by three expeditions whose members included Francis
Marion and Henry Laurens. In 1776, Loyalists and Cherokees
attacked settlements all along the southern frontier. "I hope that the
Cherokees will now be driven beyond the Mississippi," said Thomas
Jefferson, then in Congress. "Our contest with Britain is too serious
and too great to permit any possibility of avocation from the
Indians."[2]

Jefferson's wish wouldn't be fulfilled for half a century. Instead,
the result of several expeditions sent into Cherokee country (one of
which was led by North Carolina's general Griffith Rutherford)
were two 1776 treaties that forced the Cherokees to cede all their
land east of the Blue Ridge Mountains.

But what angered many Cherokees more than military defeats
was the sale of land by other Cherokees to whites. In March 1775,
land speculators, including Boone, had met with Cherokees at
Sycamore Shoals in the western foothills of the Blue Ridge
Mountains. There, two chiefs representing two groups of Cherokees
sold 27,000 square miles of land, including Shawnee land—most of
Kentucky and part of Tennessee—for ten wagons of goods, liquor,
and arms.

Dragging Canoe (Tsi'yugunsi'ny), a dissenting chief in his 30s, was livid. He warned the speculators that the sale meant "a black cloud hung over the country," and "it was the bloody ground, and would be dark, and difficult to settle it." He later explained to the brother of a British Indian agent that the chiefs were "too old to hunt," and "by their poverty, had been induced to sell their land." Clearly, said Dragging Canoe, "it seemed the intention of the white people to destroy them [the Cherokees] from being a people."[3]

Dragging Canoe was born in the Nippising nation in Canada around 1738, but Cherokees captured him as an infant and adopted him. He survived smallpox, and his face, like many whites and Indians of the day, was pockmarked. He earned his name as a boy when he singlehandedly dragged a canoe across a portage to accompany a war party. A British official said he was "the only young warrior of note" among the Overhill Cherokees, those who lived in and near the mountains. "He was a man of consequence in his country," a fellow chief said.[4]

After Sycamore Shoals, Dragging Canoe participated in the 1776 Cherokee war against settlers, and during one battle was wounded in both legs. When most Cherokees signed the peace treaties, he led his followers to the Chickamauga Creek area, near present-day Chattanooga, and planned to resist. (He sarcastically called Cherokees who didn't continue to fight "Virginians.") He encouraged like-minded Indians to join him, Cherokee or not. What became known as the Chickamaugas was a multiethnic tribe, with an army of about one thousand Cherokees, Shawnees from the Ohio country, Creeks from Georgia, and even whites who had become persona non grata among the Whigs because of loyalties or criminal acts.[5]

The Chickamaugas, with British support, began raiding rebels in 1778. In response, the Whigs raided Cherokee and Chickamauga country in 1779, 1780, and 1781, burning farms and towns, including those of peaceful Cherokees. Two expeditions alone had burned fifty thousand bushels of corn and one thousand homes. "Our families were almost destroyed by famine this spring," said one Cherokee.[6]

"The towns of the Cherokees are too much exposed to the incursions of the rebels from the frontiers of Pennsylvania, Virginia, and the Carolinas," a British official reported in January 1782. He said the rebels were trying to persuade Cherokees and Creeks to turn against the British. "The rebels and Spaniards spare no pains to excite the Indians to abandon us and take up the hatchet against us." Four months later, he described a desperate situation: "The wanton bloody outrages therein mentioned, committed by the rebels on such unfortunate Indian women and children as have fallen during the course of the war into their hands, have been truly barbarous and more than savage."[7]

Neutral Cherokees complained to Whig North Carolina governor Alexander Martin. "We are a poor, distressed people, in great trouble," said Chief Old Tassel (Utsi'dsata). "Your people . . . are daily pushing us out of our lands. We have no place to hunt. Your people have built houses within one day's walk of our towns. . . . We are the first people that ever lived on this land. It is ours, and why will our elder brother take it from us?" Martin also heard from a sympathetic Virginia governor Harrison: "Indians have their rights, and our justice is called on to support them. Whilst we are nobly contending for liberty, will it not be an eternal blot on our national character if we deprive others of it who ought to be as free as ourselves?"[8]

In February 1782, Martin ordered his leading frontier militia colonel to stop white invasions into the territory of peaceful Cherokees. "I am distressed with the repeated complaints of the Indians respecting the daily incursions of our people on their lands . . . I beg you, sir, to prevent the injuries these savages justly complain of, who are constantly imploring the protection of the State, and appealing to its justice in vain." If the colonel was unable to persuade the settlers to leave voluntarily, he was authorized to raze their cabins and drive them off.[9]

The colonel was John Sevier. Driving away illegal settlers wasn't in John Sevier's plans.

The Over Mountain men—frontier settlers like Sevier who lived beyond the Appalachians, beyond the Virginia, Carolina, and Georgia low country—were far from the aristocratic plantation owners in geography, demeanor, background, religion, and wealth. Charles Woodmason, a Charlestown planter, merchant, and Anglican evangelist traveled the region in 1768. He described the settlers with contempt:

"Their ignorance and impudence is so very high, as to be past bearing. Very few can read; fewer write. . . . They delight in their present low, lazy, sluttish, heathenish, hellish life, and seem not desirous of changing it. . . . Hence their many vices—their gross licentiousness, wantonness, lasciviousness, rudeness, lewdness, and profligacy—they will commit the grossest enormities before my face, and laugh at all admonition.

"They were as rude in their manners as the common savages, and hardly a degree removed from them. Their dresses almost as loose and naked as the Indians, and differing in nothing save complexion."[10]

Colonel Isaac Shelby, a future Kentucky governor who led Over Mountain men in battle, had a different perspective: "These mountaineers were poor men who lived by keeping stock on the range beyond the mountains; they were volunteers and neither expected or received any compensation except liquidated certificates worth two shillings in the pound."[11]

With the revolution, most Over Mountain men opposed the British, if only because the British tried to enforce the 1763 boundary between whites and Indians. Their most important war contribution was to defeat—in some cases, executing prisoners—an army of British and Loyalists at Kings Mountain, South Carolina, in 1780. The victory gave Greene time to rebuild the Continental army in the South. Shelby was one of the militia commanders; the other was Colonel John Sevier, 38.

Sevier's son remembered his father as about five feet nine, one hundred ninety pounds with a "long face, small deep blue eyes, aquiline nose, fair complexion, fair hair." He wasn't religious, but once donated land for a Baptist church; hired Presbyterian ministers to teach his children; attended a Catholic church at least twelve times; and even tolerated Quakers. He was "with all people an object of attention and a depository of their confidence." Moreover, said a trader who knew him, "John Sevier was a very handsome man, probably the handsomest in the state. He had a noble bearing, really military, although very conciliating, without haughtiness. . . . He knew how to get along with people better than any man I knew."[12]

As a military man, Sevier was "the best Indian fighter on the border," said Theodore Roosevelt, a historian before he became president. Sevier had a far better record than Clark of killing more Indians and Tories with fewer losses. "He moved with extreme rapidity and attacked with instantaneous suddenness, using ambushes and surprises wherever practicable," Roosevelt said. "Still, he never struck a crushing blow, nor conquered a permanent peace." Nonetheless, he ended up fighting thirty-five battles during his lifetime, all of them victories.[13]

Sevier was born in the hills of western Virginia. As a boy, he worked as a clerk in his father's general store, and he married at seventeen. He supported his family by farming, buying and selling land, and running a store. Around 1770, he moved to the western side of the mountains, on Cherokee land, and was a captain during Dunmore's War. In the revolution's early years, he defended against Indian attacks and participated in an invasion of Indian country. Recognizing his growing influence among the settlers, he was named a county clerk and district judge, and in 1778, was elected colonel of his county militia. During the war's middle years, he and the militia were active in intimidating Tories.

Soon after King's Mountain, Sevier led a month-long campaign against the Cherokees, defeating them in battle and burning their towns. In negotiating peace terms, he told the Cherokees, "I never hated you as a people, nor warred with you on that account. I own I fought with you, but it was for our own safety, and not from any delight I had in hurting you."[14]

At Greene's request, Sevier crossed the mountains in September 1781 with about five hundred mounted riflemen and joined forces with Marion. In South Carolina, they persuaded a British garrison to surrender without a shot by threatening that any resistance would result in another King's Mountain. By the start of 1782, Sevier and his men were back on the frontier.

With the Chickamaugas and others continuing to attack settlements—"they committed many murders that season with impunity"—and with his own pro-settler sentiments, Sevier ignored Governor Martin's orders to stop white incursions on Indian land. In mid-summer, however, the state authorized Sevier to act against the Indians. The frontier militia attacked in September. From the south, militia general Andrew Pickens with three hundred South Carolina and one hundred Georgia troops burned Indian towns and crops in the Chattahoochee River Valley in northern Georgia. An ensuing treaty resulted in more land cessions. Sevier aimed his attack at Dragging Canoe and the Chickamaugas over the protest of Virginia general and Indian agent Joseph Martin. The Chickamauguas, Martin said, had returned all but three of the prisoners they held. "I believe that never were people more desirous of peace than the Cherokees, but I hear the forces from this state are now starting. I shall set off this evening to see Colonel Sevier."[15]

It was too late. With about two hundred fifty men, Sevier invaded Chickamauga country. The Chickamaugas had time to abandon their towns, but Sevier destroyed their homes and recently harvested food supplies—"all their stock, corn, and provisions of every kind," Sevier's son James, a major, said. "The Indians eluded our march and kept out of the way in general, although a few men and women and children were surprised and taken." Some Cherokees, but not Dragging Canoe, agreed in October to peace and a prisoner release. "Thus ended the war of 1782. We all set out for our homes without the loss of a single man."[16]

Dragging Canoe abandoned the former town sites and moved the Chickamaugas twenty miles west, where they established a new home, Running Water Town, near present-day Jasper, Tennessee. The revolution ended soon, but Chickamauga resistance continued. With Spanish supplies, he began raiding settlements again in 1784. When, in 1788, settlers murdered a Cherokee chief who was under a flag of truce, more Indians joined the Chickamauguas, who defeated a militia army. In 1791, Dragging Canoe commanded seven hundred Chickamaugas, three hundred fifty Creeks, and one hundred Shawnees, who joined northern Indians to defeat an invading American army in Indiana. He continued to build alliances. In 1792, after an all-night celebration of a new alliance and successful raid against settlers, he suddenly died. Two years later, the Chickamaugas, finally defeated by a militia army, agreed to peace with the whites in exchange for permission to continue living in their villages.[17]

Sevier turned his military career into a political one. After the war, the Over Mountain settlers became increasingly hostile to North Carolina. They seceded from North Carolina in 1784, formed their own state, Franklin, and elected Sevier its first governor. To North Carolina, this was treason; its militia arrested Sevier and seized his slaves. With friends' help, Sevier escaped. Franklin was doomed, but North Carolina ceded the territory to the federal government. It became the state of Tennessee in 1796. Sevier was its first governor, serving six two-year terms. Like Hugh McGary, Sevier had a run-in with future president Andrew Jackson. Jackson perceived a Sevier comment as a slur on his wife, and challenged him to a duel. Mutual friends intervened to separate the two. After serving as governor, Tennesseans elected Sevier to Congress. While serving as a commissioner to determine the Georgia–Creek Nation boundary, he contracted a fever and died near Fort Decatur, Arkansas. He is buried on the grounds of the Old Knox County Courthouse, in downtown Knoxville.

22. Arkansas Post and the Spanish Frontier

L IKE THE MOHAWKS IN THE NORTH, THE CHICKASAW NATION east of the Mississippi River opposite Arkansas had long aligned their self-interests with the British. They fought Spanish explorers as early as 1540, then the French and their Choctaw allies in the Seven Years' War in 1763. During Dunmore's War, the Chickasaws stayed neutral, to British approval.[1]

The British, in turn, supplied the Chickasaws with modern firearms. The Chickasaws used the arms to raid other tribes—often, the French-allied Quapaws across the Mississippi and along the Arkansas River. They adopted Quapaw captives as their own, and supplied them to the British as slaves. At the end of the Seven Years' War, the Chickasaws reached an accommodation, if not a military and trade alliance, with the Quapaws.[2]

It was astute diplomacy, because the European peace treaty superimposed a new power on Indian land in the Mississippi Valley to replace the French: Spain. From St. Louis to New Orleans, nearly seven hundred miles, the Spanish now manned scattered posts along the western side of the river. Spain governed gently. Many of the mostly French, French Creoles, and French-Canadian settlers joined the Spanish army, and some served as high-ranking officers.

Despite the treaty, relations between Spain and Britain remained edgy. Spain's traditional enemy, Britain, had posts on the Mississippi's eastern bank, from Natchez, south to Baton Rouge, east to West Florida and its capital, Pensacola, and to East Florida and its capital, St. Augustine. In the South Atlantic, the two almost went to war in 1770 over the Falkland Islands. (Britain and Argentina went to war over the islands in 1982.) On the Spanish mainland, the British occupation of Gibraltar since 1704 was a constant irritation, friction that still flares up. In North America, Spain and Britain, as well as individual traders, competed against and tried to undermine each other for favorable position with the Chickasaws and other Indians. Sometimes, the enemies fought: Officially still at peace in 1777, the British plundered Spanish posts along the Mississippi and seized a Spanish ship. Spain retaliated by seizing eleven British boats and encouraged French Canadians to settle in Spanish territory as a counterbalance.[3]

Spain also secretly armed and traded with the American rebels. Its goal: Undermine British influence in the Gulf of Mexico and, ultimately, regain Gibraltar. The rebels encouraged this. In 1776, Continental general Charles Lee urged Louisiana's Spanish governor to send guns, blankets, and quinine. In 1777 and 1778, Governor Henry of Virginia reinforced the benefits of trade in three letters to a new Spanish governor. Governor Bernardo de Gálvez, 31, kept New Orleans open to Whig commerce, and ignored British demands to surrender the Whig business agent. In 1778, a rebel force raided British posts from Natchez to Baton Rouge; Gálvez gave the raiders sanctuary in New Orleans.[4]

The Chickasaws, Quapaws, and other Indians took advantage of the situation, playing the British and Spanish against each other. One chief said neutrality might preserve the Chickasaw nation as a "people to ourselves." This neutrality angered the warring parties. At a 1777 conference with the Indians, the British warned that a rebel victory would make the Chickasaws "a lost people." Virginia told the Chickasaws they had a choice of friendship or destruction. Tensions with the Spanish also rose. Chickasaw visitors to a Spanish trading post were harassed, and Chicksaws began raiding Spanish boats on the Mississippi—careful to avoid attacking any Quapaws who might accompany the boats.[5]

At the revolution's start, the Chickasaw population was about 2,300, including four hundred fifty warriors. Just as they had adopted captive Quapaws in the past to replenish population lost to war and smallpox, the Chickasaws attracted and welcomed escaped slaves, Loyalist refugees, and others.[6]

James Logan Colbert was one of the "others." Information about his early years is contradictory. He was probably born in Scotland around 1720 or 1721, although Colbert, writing in the third person, claimed America as his birth country. An aging Chickasaw interpreter interviewed in 1841 said Colbert was a Carolinian. Some reports say he immigrated to Georgia from Scotland in the winter of 1735–1736.[7]

Sometime in the mid-to-late 1730s, perhaps as late as 1740, he made his way inland and chose to live with the Chickasaws, who adopted him. He married into the tribe three times, outliving at least his first two wives, who were full-blooded Chickasaws. His third wife was of mixed race. Between them, Colbert had eight children. Because of his family connections, his fighting ability, and his wealth, he had "considerable influence" in his adopted nation, an official said. He was a successful trader, and he owned both a "fine house" and about one hundred fifty African slaves, according to a Franco-Spanish merchant. His sons were "very important chiefs in that [Chickasaw] nation," the merchant said. He added that Colbert was virulently anti-Spanish, therefore "one of the greatest enemies of our nation, against which he is so angered." Colbert was "insolent, ironic, and contemptuous," with a "violent temper," and, despite being in his sixties, was able to endure "the greatest hardships."[8]

Whether his motivation was hatred of the Spanish or preference for the British, when war came, Colbert led a pro-British Chickasaw faction.

The war was late in coming to the lower Mississippi because Spain was late in coming to the war. The American rebels and the French agreed to an alliance in February 1778. Despite French pressure to join the fight, Spain's chief minister, José Moñino, Conde de Floridablanca, resisted. Britain threatened Spanish possessions around the world, including the Caribbean and America, but Floridablanca was wary about American Whigs growing too strong and populous, overwhelming the Spanish territory west of the Mississippi. "A sort of equality of enmity . . . makes it difficult to prefer either" Britain or the Whigs, he said.[9] Lafayette was blunter. The

Spanish, he said, "fear the loss of their colonies, and the success of our revolution appears to be an encouragement to this fear. . . . They labor under fits of occasional madness." To persuade Spain to enter the war, France secretly agreed in April 1779 to help Spain recover British-held Gibraltar and Minorca in Europe, Central American posts, and West Florida. Spain declared war on Britain the next month.[10]

Even then, it refused to recognize American independence or formally ally with the Whigs, despite John Jay's two years of lobbying Floridablanca. (Jay described Floridablanca as a "little man" in stature, but one with "more than a common share of understanding.") Fellow Whig diplomat John Adams said he wasn't surprised that "Spain has been cool to us." This would be a relationship of co-belligerents, not allies, with cooperation based on self-interest. For example, trade between the Whigs and Spain increased, with the Americans sending flour to Spanish Havana, and the Spanish continuing to arm and supply the Whigs. Congressman and financier Robert Morris described the impact on Philadelphia in 1782: "Our port is filled . . . with many, many Spanish dollars."[11]

Those Spanish dollars helped defeat the British at Yorktown. The British navy posed a danger to French trans-Atlantic convoys that might carry money to America, so France and Spain skirted the problem: The Spanish, with their Bolivian silver mines, transferred silver to the French in the Caribbean. The silver found its way north to subsidize the insolvent Continental army prior to Yorktown, and to pay for French expenses in Virginia. France repaid Spain with a reverse transfer in Europe.[12]

News of war reached Governor Gálvez in New Orleans in August 1779. On September 7, he began an offensive with Spanish regulars, Indians, and white and black militia. It resulted in British surrender throughout the Mississippi Valley and West Florida: Fort Bute, Baton Rouge, Manchac, Natchez, Mobile, and, in May 1781, Pensacola. In St. Louis, a Spanish commander repelled a British-led expedition of mostly Indians, and later, in January 1782, made a quick, prophylactic raid against British Fort St. Joseph (now Niles, Michigan).

While Gálvez besieged Pensacola in April 1781, the British commander, General John Campbell, prepared for the worst. Chickasaws, led by Colbert, and Choctaws, traveled to Pensacola to help defend it. When the British failed to supply them adequately, they returned home, but Campbell commissioned Colbert as a British captain and "leader and conductor of such volunteer inhabitants and Chickasaws, Choctaw, Creek, or other Indians as shall join you for the purpose of annoying, distressing, attacking, or repelling the King's enemies." Gálvez refused to treat Colbert as anything but a pirate, because the defeated Campbell, despite his orders to Colbert, suspended (probably under duress) *all* military operations in West Florida and the lower Mississippi. "By no means consider James Colbert a captain," Gálvez told his officers.[13]

Before he surrendered, Campbell also commissioned Loyalists in Spanish-occupied Natchez as British officers with a duty to rebel. This, they did, violating their oath to the Spanish to remain peaceful. The Spanish garrison surrendered to the Loyalists in May 1781. Spain retook the town in June. Most Loyalists fled to refuge among the Chickasaws and Choctaws. A few made it to Georgia. But Spain arrested the rebellion's leaders and sent them to New Orleans for trial.[14]

One of Colbert's goals in the coming months would be to force the Spanish to release the Loyalist prisoners.

Without British regulars present in the lower Mississippi, thanks to Gálvez, Colbert became the de facto leader of Loyalist resistance to Spain. His band never numbered more than one hundred forty men—white Loyalists, mixed-race warriors (many of them relatives), blacks, Indians, and escaped or wanted criminals.

Similar, smaller bands had less altruistic motivation. They were in it for the goods they could capture. Spain couldn't differentiate between them: "The great part of these vagabonds, dregs of Europe and America, are men abandoned to all vices and capable of committing any crime. These are the ones who have devastated this district with their continual thefts of horses, mules, and Negroes," a Spanish official said. "The Chickasaw and Choctaw nations, because of a humane spirit common in almost all the Indians, receive and shelter these vagabonds, sharing with them the little they have to eat, and thereby give them the means and facilities to come [to Spanish settlements] and steal."[15]

A Whig captain who traveled the area in 1771 and 1772 described the Chickasaws as "the most fierce, cruel, insolent, and haughty people" among the southern tribes. Despite their small population, "they are very intrepid in the[ir] wars." The white traders who lived with the Chickasaws were "monsters in human form, the very scum and outcast of the earth . . . more prone to savage barbarity than the savages themselves." The captain had no use for Chickasaw morals, either, saying that they were "more corrupt than those of any of their neighbors."[16]

Despite Spanish and Whig perceptions, most Chickasaw chiefs tried to put some distance between themselves and Colbert's fighters. In the years Colbert was active, they maintained contact with both Spanish and Whig leaders, saying they neither supported nor condoned him. Their statements weren't entirely honest: Colbert shared the supplies he looted, and the tribe never betrayed his location.[17]

Colbert's first post-Pensacola operation was in the northern part of Chickasaw territory, in Kentucky, just south of what is now Cairo, Illinois. In 1780, George Rogers Clark built Fort Jefferson there without the Chickasaws' permission. The Chickasaws harassed and attacked the fort from the start, but the one hundred-man garrison held. In summer 1781, Colbert led a force to end the rebel presence, raiding settlements along the way. During a short siege, Colbert was wounded in his arm, and his force retreated, burning rebel crops and homes. The Whigs, with little to eat and fearing the Chickasaws' return, abandoned the fort soon after.

In January 1782, Colbert's wound was healed, and he faced a new opponent. Gálvez had gone to Spain, and later sailed to Hispaniola to plan an invasion of Jamaica. He left an acting governor—his top aide, Colonel Esteban Rodríguez Miró, 38. Miró joined the army as a teenaged cadet in 1760. He fought in a campaign in Portugal two years later, and afterward was transferred to Mexico. When the revolution began, Miró was in Algiers. During the years when France was trying to persuade Spain to join the war, Miró was assigned to the Spanish military academy. He arrived in Louisiana in 1778 as the highest-ranking officer after Gálvez. Louisiana agreed with him: He married a prominent French Creole woman from New Orleans. They had one child, a daughter, who died young.[18]

Miró immediately faced a surge in Tory activity. In April 1782, a Loyalist named John Turner, with about fifteen Natchez men, captured a large Spanish barge and took the crew prisoner. A few hours later, the prisoners surprised the Loyalists, bludgeoning them with the oars, and killing all but six who were able to swim ashore. Colbert himself was more successful, capturing two small Spanish flotillas that month. Those cargo boats were just the start.[19]

On May 2, Colbert and a multiethnic band of about forty men captured a boat headed from New Orleans to St. Louis with rum, gunpowder, other supplies, a large sum of cash to pay for army necessities—and Doña Anicanova Ramos de Cruzat, 27, the wife of the St. Louis commander, along with her four small sons and four black slaves. Colbert immediately tried to put Doña Cruzat at ease. He said he would "respect her person and her sons," according to a Spanish merchant who was captured with her. "They should not receive the slightest offence, and . . . he would have her conducted in safety" back to New Orleans.[20]

But first, Colbert ensured the safety of his own men, taking them and his captives back to their camp near present-day Memphis, Tennessee. The camp, Cruzat remembered, consisted of eighteen huts covered with skins or oilcloth. All of Colbert's men were armed with one or two carbines and assorted clubs and knives. Four days later, they moved up Wolf River to a more secure location, where they built new huts. There, Cruzat said, Colbert's men were "continually drunk," and they spent much time divvying up plunder and auctioning slaves. Colbert told Cruzat that some of their actions were in response to Spanish commanders overcharging for goods and demanding bribes. "These are the grievances which oblige them to decide to abandon themselves to this kind of living," he said. In all, Colbert had about fifty Spanish and Franco-Spanish prisoners.[21]

Colbert was as good as his word. On May 22, he paroled Cruzat, her sons, a black female slave, and nine whites. Through them, he sent a message to Miró that the prisoner release was conditioned on Miró's good faith that he would parole the nine jailed Natchez rebellion leaders.

Cruzat's husband, meanwhile, had learned (probably from friendly Indians) of his wife's capture and sent thirty men to hunt Colbert down. They found and burned the first camp, but then returned to St. Louis.

Cruzat reached New Orleans and Miró on May 30. After debriefing her, he wrote Gálvez, updating him on the situation and asking the commander to endorse his course of action: No parole of the Natchez prisoners, and reinforcement of the Natchez garrison.

"I have some doubt as to how I ought to consider the case of James Colbert," Miró told Gálvez. "He has never been a prisoner, he was defending Mobile and Pensacola, but always retired at the time when these cities surrendered." Campbell commissioned him as a captain, but apparently without higher approval. Therefore, Miró said, he would deal with Colbert as a criminal associated with the Natchez uprising, rather than a military peer. Miró also told Gálvez of his frustration in trying to capture Colbert and his band of "fugitives of Natchez and of roving traders who have remained among the Indian nations." The criminals were far from New Orleans. "It is almost impossible to attack them, to capture or slay them, as they do not wait for our attack. . . . The forests of the interior of the lands are close by, and there, they may easily hide themselves." As for Natchez, beyond reinforcing it, "I shall attempt to tranquilize those inhabitants with a kind treatment."[22]

Gálvez praised Miró's game plan. Colbert's proposal to parole the Natchez prisoners was "entirely out of season." Moreover, he advised against any general prisoner exchange: Holding Loyalists was the only way the Spanish could ensure good treatment of Colbert's prisoners. Overall, Gálvez was "disgusted by the numerous revolts in this province."[23]

To his superiors in Spain, Gálvez summarized the situation. "The navigation on the Mississippi is interrupted from Arkansas to Illinois." He had no budget with which to buy off the Indians. Besides, the Chickasaws condoned the raids. Without their support, "the rebellious fugitives of Natchez, with the other insignificant union with rovers or vagrants . . . could not have accomplished anything."[24]

By fall, Colbert learned about Miró's decision. He responded with a half-threatening, half-conciliatory letter. "I would have you to know that I have as much authority to distress my King's enemies as you have to maintain Natchez or any other place in behalf of your King," Colbert said. "I have prevailed with my Indians to make peace both with you and the Americans and with all the world, as it is proper that no Indians ought to interfere with what concerns none but white[s]." But unless Spain released the Natchez prisoners, he would continue to keep his prisoners. He ended with a request: "If you should have any occasion to write anymore to me, please to write in English or send an interpreter with it, having none here."[25]

Colbert continued to raid Spanish and Whig boats. The Spanish, who estimated Colbert's band as having 30 men, stepped up the pressure on the mainstream Chickasaws to betray Colbert. They incentivized the Kickapoos, a traditional enemy, to raid Chickasaw villages. The Kickapoos stopped their raids after the Chickasaws pledged to refuse refuge to Colbert's men and protect any Spanish prisoners who escaped from him. By the end of 1782, Miró felt confident that the Chickasaws had stopped abetting Colbert. "The Chickasaws are poor, and there are no other white people except the Spaniards who can supply their necessities," he said. The Chickasaws also worked the other side of the mountains. They sent peace feelers to the Whigs, who demanded land cessions, which the Chickasaws refused.[26]

In January 1783, Colbert seized a Whig boat. Its crew joined Colbert's band. Then, they successfully attacked a Spanish boat. More attacks ensued in February and March. An escaped Spanish prisoner reported that Colbert intended to increase shipping raids, and expected his thirty men to be augmented by one hundred more Loyalists and two hundred Chickasaws.[27]

But Colbert wanted to do more than act the role of a pirate. He wanted to hit the Spanish head on. He planned to do this at a settlement called Arkansas Post, guarded by Fort Carlos III, named after the Spanish king.

The French founded Arkansas Post in the late 1680s as a station half way between New Orleans to the south, and St. Louis to the north. Although it was moved over the years due to floods, it remained near the junction of the Mississippi and Arkansas rivers, and was continuously manned after 1732. It was an important location, not only because of the St. Louis–New Orleans link, but because the nearly one thousand five hundred-mile-long Arkansas River was a major portal into the interior for trappers and traders.

Its permanent population was under one hundred. In 1766, eight white families totaling forty-four people with nineteen slaves lived there. By 1778, it had fifty whites, eleven slaves, and a twenty-man Spanish garrison called Fort Carlos III. Scores of hunters and traders might be at the post at any given time.[28]

Fort Carlos III was thirty-five miles upstream from the Mississippi "in the middle of a hill that overlooks the Arkansas River, which may be forty-five feet in height when the river is low and six feet when it overflows," a postwar American captain said. Beyond the clearing around the fort was a forest of oak, hickory, elm, and elder trees. Corn and wheat fields surrounded the dozen civilian homes outside the fort.[29]

This was Quapaw land. They lived in three nearby villages with a population of about seven hundred led by their chief, Angaska. Like the Chickasaws—their former enemy-turned-ally—the Quapaws preserved their national integrity with a diplomatic balancing act. They cooperated with the Spanish around them, serving as scouts, but refused to undermine their relationship with the Chickasaws, as the Spanish would learn.

As a trading center and military base, Arkansas Post offered entertainment beyond what its permanent population could support. In 1770, two licensed—and an unknown number of unlicensed—cantinas served residents and traders. A decade later, merchants tried to shut down a billiards room because, they said, hunters lost their money there and couldn't pay their bills. The fort itself had thirteen-foot-high stockades, each pole with a diameter of ten to sixteen inches. It was, its commander said, "a solid post capable of resisting anything which may come to attack it without cannon."[30]

A later commander disagreed. As part of the efforts to improve security, Miró reinforced the garrison and ordered Captain Jacobo Dubreuil Saint-Cyr to take charge. Dubreuil arrived in January 1783. He found that the carriages of three of the fort's four cannons had rotted. The stockade was solid, but it had been built without embrasures—slits in the wall for firing guns. The garrison's provisions were low, and Dubreuil ordered many of his now sixty-seven soldiers to go game hunting. He told Miró that he had been forced to spend money to repair the fort: "I hope that it shall be the shelter from the insults of a rabble without discipline . . . and that the expense will merit your approval."[31]

Dubreuil was probably in his mid-thirties when he took command of Arkansas Post. He first appeared in army records in 1767 as a sub-lieutenant. By 1780, he was a captain. During the early 1780s, he provided a military escort for a supply convoy to St. Louis, and later commanded Ste. Genevieve, a Franco-Spanish village south of St. Louis. At Arkansas Post, he lived with his wife, Inez, and their two children. Dubreuil was more than the post's military commander; he was its civil administrator and judge for the District of Arkansas.[32]

In January 1783, civil duties weren't Dubreuil's priority. He heard reports that the enemy was in the vicinity. He sent Angaska and his Quapaws on a scouting mission, but they reported no signs of British Loyalists. In fact, Colbert was still planning an attack. It wasn't until mid-April that he and his force—sixty-four Americans (mostly Loyalists, but a few Whigs), a Frenchman, five African Americans, and eleven mixed-race Chickasaws (many of them Colbert's relations)—crossed the Mississippi in a small flotilla and headed up the Arkansas River to Arkansas Post.

Their first challenge was to get by a Quapaw village either undetected or by agreement. This they did, using muffled oars, in the early hours of the morning of April 17. Around 2:30 A.M., they landed south of the fort, and immediately attacked the village outside. A ten-man guard tried to defend the homes, but they were overwhelmed. Two were killed (one of them scalped), a slave and a soldier wounded, the rest taken prisoner. One escaped to the fort because, he said, he "ran like a rabbit." Colbert's men also captured seven families, including that of Dubreuil's second-in-command, Lieutenant Luis de Villars; they had moved outside the fort's walls when their home blew down during a "violent wind."[33]

By 3 A.M., Colbert was at the gates of Fort Carlos III, and for the next six hours, the two sides kept up steady, but inconclusive, firing. Dubreuil's cannons shot over the heads of the attackers, who were entrenched in a gully, while Colbert's small arms were useless against the stockade. The bullets, Dubreuil said, were "piercing like a sieve" into the wood, but failed to penetrate through.

Around 9 A.M., the two leaders simultaneously changed tactics. Colbert released Villars's wife, sending her as a messenger with a white flag to the fort with a surrender demand: "M. Le Capitaine Colbert is sent by his superiors to take the post of the Arkansas, and by this power, sir, he demands that you capitulate. It is his plan to take it with all his forces, having already taken all the inhabitants."

Colbert told Mrs. Villars to give Dubreuil an additional message: If the fort didn't surrender, he would return at noon with both Loyalist and five hundred Chickasaw reinforcements. "You can judge my fury. . . . If the commandant of the fort doesn't surrender before the given time, if he doesn't wish to be vanquished, as no doubt he will be unless I restrain my men, and if he arouses the Arkansas [Quapaws] against us, I shall certainly kill all the prisoners."

As Mrs. Villars approached the fort, Dubreuil sent ten Spanish soldiers and four Quapaw warriors out the gate to attack. "Our sally was not stopped by the white flag," Dubreuil said. Instead, the Quapaws' cries spooked Colbert's men, who retreated, fearing other Spanish soldiers would encircle them. Dubreuil heard Colbert's men shout, "Let's go! Let's go! The Indians are upon us."

Once Colbert reached his boats, he released his captured women and children, taking the male prisoners with him. One of Colbert's men had been killed, and another wounded.[34]

At the fort, Colbert's noon deadline passed, but instead of the enemy with five hundred reinforcements returning, Angaska appeared with one hundred Quapaws. Dubreuil berated him. "I blamed [him] roundly for having allowed the enemy to enter this river without giving me the usual notice," he told Miró. Angaska's excuse was that the Quapaws themselves had been deceived because they hadn't heard or seen Colbert the night before. As for failing to immediately come to Dubreuil's aid, Angaska said his men were "scattered in the mountains, some hunting, others seeking rations to sustain their families which had no other hope of provisions, for the harvest had failed entirely the past year." (Support of Quapaw's modest cooperation with the Spanish wasn't universally popular among the Quapaws. One chief refused any involvement with either side because, he said, he was "not obligated to help the whites make war.")[35]

Dubreuil let the matter drop because he wanted to use the Quapaws to track the enemy, negotiate for the release of prisoners, and then attack them. To ensure Angaska would follow orders, Dubreuil sent a Spanish lieutenant and twenty soldiers—"which were my pride"—to accompany the Quapaws.

About a week later, the Quapaw-Spanish force caught up with Colbert on the Mississippi, about ten miles below the mouth of the Arkansas. Given the Quapaw-Chickasaw alliance, Angaska wasn't about to attack Colbert. Instead, according to the Spanish account (the only extant account), Angaska hid most of his men, and told Colbert that he had two hundred fifty, not the one hundred twenty he really had. Given this supposedly overwhelming force, Colbert released all but eight prisoners: four Spanish soldiers, three slaves, and a boy. Colbert paroled Lieutenant Villars on the condition that five Loyalist Natchez leaders be released. If not, Villars must pay Colbert a ransom.[36]

Dubreuil wasn't pleased with the agreement. He told Miró that because Colbert retained hostages, his plan "to destroy the unworthy dogs of pirates" wasn't executed.

Neither Colbert nor Dubreuil knew that the preliminary peace treaty had been signed, and that at the request of a British diplomat in Jamaica, Gálvez ordered the parole of the Natchez prisoners, on condition they never return to Natchez. The prisoners agreed, and they were released from their New Orleans jail several days after the Angaska-Colbert negotiations. Soon, the now-parolees were on a British ship headed to Jamaica.[37]

But word of peace had yet to reach the lower Mississippi. Colbert continued to raid Spanish boats. On May 11, a Spanish convoy spotted signs of Colbert's band near the mouth of the St. Francis River about ninety miles northeast of Arkansas Post. About one hundred white and two dozen Quapaw volunteers pursued them. They caught up with some stragglers, including Colbert's second-in-command, who was killed. One man drowned, another broke his arm, but the others got away, allowing three of their Spanish prisoners to be liberated.

In mid-May, Miró ordered Dubreuil to contact Colbert to inform him of the peace. He sent Dubreuil a Jamaica newspaper that announced the treaty, as well as a copy of the treaty translated into English. Dubreuil wrote a personal letter to Colbert, addressing him as a "subject of His British Majesty, Chickasaw Nation." The newspaper and the treaty translation proved that "you can see without doubt that I am authorized to reclaim the prisoners," including slaves. He also asked Colbert to reimburse the Spanish for the supplies he took from Arkansas Post.[38]

Colbert received the letter nearly four months later. He told Dubreuil he would immediately release his remaining prisoners, but asked about Chickasaw prisoners still held in St. Louis. As for reimbursements, "I am persuaded by the articles of the peace that I am within my rights in not paying, although the price is cheap. . . . You seem very much interested in charging me for too many articles far more than they are worth." He told Dubreuil that he intended to seek guidance from the British governor in St. Augustine. His war, however, was over.[39]

Even as Dubreuil was trying to reach Colbert, the main body of Chickasaws made peace with Spain. Their self-interest lay in disassociating themselves from their adopted son. "A party of Chickasaw came to ratify the peace," Dubreuil told Miró in August 1783. "They assured me that with the exception of the Colbert family, all the Chickasaws are well contented with the new friendship which they have agreed upon, and they see clearly that all the promises of Colbert's have been nothing more than falsehoods. And, notwithstanding that they paid very little attention to him, he threatened them that he would not live in peace in the Spanish possessions. To keep from being ill-treated or suffering the consequences, he tells them [it] is only a matter of playing the cards right. He tries to make them believe that the war which has been carried on with the Americans is nothing more than a sham, and that the Treaty of Peace which closed it between Spain and Great Britain will last only a short time on the part of the English, and so on. Forty thousand lies to prejudice them!"[40]

After the war, Colbert continued to work on the Chickasaws' behalf, trying to position the tribe between the Spanish and Americans. Depending on the account, he either went to St. Augustine in 1784 to consult with the British, or to Georgia to consult with the Creeks. En route home, somewhere in Alabama, he either was thrown from his horse and died, or his black slave, Cesar, murdered him.[41]

Despite his anger with Angaska, Dubreuil was sympathetic to the Quapaws. He pleaded with Miró for supplies, ammunition, and food for the Quapaws. Dubreuil allowed their women and children to stay by the fort due to "the sad plight of these poor people in sustaining their families."[42]

Promoted to lieutenant colonel, Dubreuil stayed at Arkansas Post until 1787, approving marriages, wills, and land grants, regulating trade, advertising for escaped slaves, managing Indian relations, and regulating liquor sales. In 1802, as commander of San Marcos

Apalachie, in West Florida, he outlasted a siege by a group of Creeks, Seminoles, and assorted blacks and whites led by an adventurer and idealist trying to establish an independent Indian state. A Spanish relief fleet broke the siege. Dubreuil died in 1804.[43]

Under the peace treaty, Spain took possession of East Florida, and in 1785, the last British exiles in St. Augustine left: 3,400 whites and 6,500 free and enslaved blacks.[44]

Spain and the U.S. settled a border dispute in 1795, and Spain opened the lower Mississippi and New Orleans to American traders. Five years later, the Spanish and French agreed to a swap: the Louisiana Territory for an Italian duchy. The French, in turn, flipped the territory to the Americans in 1803. In January 1804, the commander of Fort Carlos III transferred the post to an American representative. Arkansas Post became a thriving town of 3,500 people, and, until 1821, the Arkansas Territory capital. During the Civil War, U.S. troops seized the town after a two-day battle. After the war, Arkansas Post faded, and its residents moved elsewhere. It became a state park in 1929, and a unit of the National Park Service in 1960. The site of Fort Carlos III is now under water.

23. Between Two Hells

Parliament's February 1782 order to end offensive military operations in North America reached the British commanders at Niagara, Detroit, and Charlestown that spring. That summer, field commanders passed the word to their Indian allies: No more raids, no more arms supplies—just a reassurance that the British wouldn't forget their allies once a final peace treaty was signed.

In the South, Leslie ordered that "that no offensive operations be carried on by the Indians against the frontiers," said Lieutenant Colonel Thomas Brown, the British Indian superintendent. Brown directed his agents to "prevent the Indians from acting offensively without special orders and recommend to them to pursue their hunting within the limits of their respective territories in order to divert their thoughts from war." He told his superiors in London about his concern for the Cherokees. "From the exposed situation of their towns, they have twice been laid in ashes and their plantations laid waste by the rebels from the frontiers of Pennsylvania, Virginia, and the Carolinas. Numbers of their women and children have been butchered in cold blood or burned alive; yet no species of rebel barbarity or the loss of their towns, provisions, families, or friends have induced them to abandon His Majesty's service."[1]

Even a Whig colonel acknowledged the Cherokees' plight: "The miseries of those people, from what I see and hear, seem to exceed description. Here are men, women, and children almost naked. . . . But this is not the greatest of their evils: Their crops this year have been worse than was ever known, so that their corn and potatoes, it is supposed, will be all done [eaten] before April. And many are already out, particularly widows and fatherless children."2

Other Indians were furious at what they felt was a British betrayal. "The English put the bloody tomahawk into our hands," a Chickasaw chief said. They "have done their utmost and left us in our adversity. We find them full of deceit and dissimulation."3

Joseph Brant, the Mohawk and Loyalist captain, vented to his cousin, the British northern Indian superintendent, Brigadier General John Johnson, son of Sir William. He said "the white savages, the Virginians" had mistreated Shawnee prisoners. He mocked the British suggestion that Indians return to their traditional pursuits. "I beg of you, don't tell us to go hunt deer . . . because we shall soon forget the war, for we are gone too far that way already against the rebels to be doing other things." He tried to shame the British into supporting a new offensive against the rebels in spring 1783. "Let us not hang our heads between our knees and be looking there." Although he was "as much forward to go to war as I ever did," he was "not so well contented as I used to be formerly, because the warriors are in want. They are treated worse instead of better."

Brant predicted that "the rebels will ruin us at last if we go on as we do, one year after another, doing nothing" except using up supplies, with the British "crying out all the while for the great expenses. So we are, as it were, between two hells."4

The end of British support for Indian raids meant a corresponding increase in Whig efforts to take Indian land and push the Indians farther west—or kill them. If the British wouldn't stop Indian resistance, said one newspaper in late 1782, the settlers "will cry aloud from the valleys to Congress—RETALIATE—the hills will resound RETALIATE—and the sound will reverberate . . . from mountain to mountain, with increasing repetitions RETALIATE, RETALIATE, RETALIATE!"5

Irvine, at Fort Pitt, told the secretary of war that the settlers were moving quickly. "The people are in great numbers flocking over the Ohio into what has hitherto been called the Indian country and are busy taking up and improving lands."6

More than a century later, Theodore Roosevelt—no friend to Indians—described the unabated seizure of their lands during this period. "The whites were now, in their turn, the aggressors, the trouble being, as usual, that they encroached on lands secured to the red men by solemn treaty. . . . The rage for land speculation, however, which had continued even in the stormiest days of the Revolution, grew tenfold in strength after Yorktown."[7]

In January 1783, more than two thousand Creek, Choctaw, and Cherokee fighters showed up in British-controlled St. Augustine, Florida, asking for aid to fight the rebels. They didn't get it.[8]

Not a single one of the Paris peace treaty's two thousand words referred to Indians. Instead, the British ceded all land east of the Mississippi to the Americans, ignoring that Indians had a legal claim to much of the land. The Indians and sympathetic British were astounded:

> After nine years of service to the British, we "find ourselves and country betrayed to our enemies." The betrayal is "cruel and ungenerous"—Alexander McGillivray (Hoboi-Hili-Miko), Creek chief.[9]
>
> Giving Indian country "to the Americans without their consent or consulting them . . . [is] an act of cruelty and injustice that Christians *only* were capable of doing." The Indians "were a free people subject to no power upon earth . . . faithful allies of the King of England, but not his subjects"—Captain Aaron Hill (Kanonraron), Mohawk war chief.[10]
>
> "The peacemakers and our enemies have talked away our lands at a rum drinking"—Little Turkey, Cherokee chief.[11]
>
> "These Indians have great merit and sufferings to plead in the cause of Great Britain. It will be a difficult task after what has happened to convince them of our good faith. They seem peculiarly hurt that no mention is made of them in the treaty"—Canadian governor Frederick Haldimand.[12]
>
> The King "had no right whatever to grant away to the states of America their rights or properties"—Iroquois reaction reported by General Allan MacLean, the Niagara commander.[13]
>
> "The minds of these people appear as much agitated as those of the unhappy Loyalists . . . and however chimerical it may appear to us, they have very seriously proposed to abandon their country and accompany us, having made all the world their enemies by their attachment to us"—Brigadier General Archibald McArthur in St. Augustine.[14]

In Parliament, Thomas de Grey, the 2nd Baron Walsingham, attacked the government for abandoning its allies. "All faith was broken with the Indians," he said. The "cruelty and perfidy" of the abandonment was beyond Walsingham's "feeble power of description." The Iroquois "engaged in all our wars. In the present contest, they were invited by the most flattering and deductive professions. . . . They refused the offers made them by America. They served us well." Their reward was that "they were driven completely from their country" and were now living in Niagara at great expense to Britain.

But it wasn't just cruelty, perfidy, and expense that made the abandonment wrong. "We were peculiarly bound to protect them by the good faith and the obligation of our own treaties with them," not just with the Iroquois in the North, but with the Choctaws, Chickasaws, Creeks, and Cherokees in the South. "Our treaties with them were solemn and ought to have been binding on our honor," Walsingham said.

The prime minister, Shelburne, spun his government's action with two rationales. First, the Americans would be better able to tame the Indians' "savage natures." Second: "The Indian nations were not abandoned to their enemies; they were remitted to the care of neighbors whose interest it was as much as ours to cultivate friendship with them, and who were certainly the best qualified for softening and humanizing their hearts."[15]

John Marshall, former Continental captain, Valley Forge veteran, and future American secretary of state and chief justice, was more honest. In 1832, he said the Indians were "divided into separate nations, independent of each other and of the rest of the world, having institutions of their own, and governing themselves by their own laws." The idea that other nations "could have rightful original claims of dominion over the inhabitants of the other, or over the lands they occupied" was "difficult to comprehend." Nevertheless, "power, war, conquest, give rights which, after possession, are conceded by the world."[16]

For every Indian nation east of the Mississippi, regardless of where their self-interest led them, the revolution was a disaster.

The Cherokees signed forty treaties over three hundred years, first with the British, then with the Americans. Most resulted in a loss of land. In the 1830s, the American government forced most members of the southern tribes—Cherokees, Creeks, Choctaws,

Chickasaws, and Seminoles—to leave their homelands in the 1830s, despite many of their assimilation as English-speaking farmers. This ethnic cleansing became known as the Trail of Tears.[17]

A year after the peace treaty, in 1784, nearly sixty thousand whites with their twelve thousand slaves had settled on traditionally Shawnee land in Kentucky. "You are drawing so close to us that we can almost hear the noise of your axes felling our trees and settling our country," a Shawnee chief told American officials in 1785. That year, the confederacy of Ohio Valley Indians escalated the fight. In 1790 and 1791, they routed two American army expeditions. President Washington then put General Anthony Wayne in charge. Wayne defeated the Indian alliance in 1794. The Indians signed a treaty that ceded most of Ohio, and parts of Illinois and Michigan, for goods and supplies. Tensions rose again in 1811 when another Indian confederacy led by a Shawnee chief, Tecumseh, resisted the Americans. During the War of 1812, Tecumseh allied himself with the British, but the Americans killed him in battle the next year. The confederacy disintegrated.[18]

In New York, the revolution destroyed Iroquois power, turned neighbor against neighbor, decimated their population, and forced most to become refugees. The British responded to Joseph Brant's pleas by buying land from Canadian Mississauga Indians along the Grand River west of Niagara and giving it to the Mohawks. Brant, in turn, welcomed other Indian refugees. Brant and others received military pensions, and the British continued as late as 1792 to supply provisions. He devoted many years to lobbying the British and Americans on behalf of his people's welfare and land claims. He also translated the Bible into Mohawk. In 1786, he visited England for a second time, and in 1792, met President Washington. Brantford, Ontario, has its roots as part of the land grant. Brant's sister, Molly, settled in what is now Kingston, Ontario, and received the highest British pension of any Indian.

In 1784, the remaining Iroquois signed a treaty with the U.S. in which they ceded most of their land. There was one exception: The Oneidas and Tuscaroras, American allies during the war, would keep their land. Later, the Americans gave individual rewards for service, and grants to build churches, sawmills, and gristmills. From there, the Oneidas' relationship with the U.S. deteriorated. The land grants were mostly wetlands. Veterans' pension claims were denied.

Officials pressured the increasingly poor Oneidas to sell their land. Starting in 1823, most Oneidas left New York for Wisconsin and Canada. Two hundred Oneidas remained in 1845 on a small reservation. In 2013, the Oneidas—about one thousand, of whom half lived in central New York—earned money from a resort and casino. That year, the state announced a comprehensive settlement of multiple, longstanding disputes with the Oneidas that had begun in 1795 regarding taxing power, land, and reservation issues. In exchange for a regional monopoly on casino gambling, the Oneidas were given certain taxing rights, with the revenue to be shared with the state. "Today, sovereign governments came together," an Oneida spokesman said.[19]

PART FOUR

The Carribean

24. Riches

Charles O'Hara's parole ended in February 1782, four months after his Yorktown surrender: He was exchanged for a rebel general, Lachlan McIntosh, who had been captured when the British took Charlestown in 1780. Now, O'Hara rejoined the war.[1]

Clinton ordered him to the Caribbean, where French and Spanish forces threatened the British stronghold of Jamaica. But first, O'Hara stopped in Charlestown to pick up two thousand troops that Clinton ordered Leslie to provide. Leslie reluctantly gave O'Hara 1,200. But when O'Hara and his troops arrived in the West Indies in late June, the British commander there assured him that Jamaica was in "perfect security." O'Hara's troops went to other islands. By fall, O'Hara was back in New York.[2]

Promoted to major general, O'Hara returned to England in late 1782. He began gambling—poorly—and spending money. In 1784, he fled England to escape creditors. In Italy, he met an author, Mary Berry, and the two fell in love. Berry described him as "the most perfect specimen of a soldier and a courtier of the past age." While they corresponded for the rest of their lives, they never married; Berry turned down his proposal because she didn't want to be a military wife traveling from post to post.[3]

In 1785, with Cornwallis's help, O'Hara repaired his finances and returned to England. He spent two years in Jamaica, and then in 1792 was named Gibraltar's lieutenant governor. While he was captive in France, one of his former commanders, Henry Clinton, became Gibraltar's governor. But Clinton died before taking his post. By then, O'Hara had been exchanged, and he succeeded Clinton and an interim governor.

Contemporaries described Governor O'Hara as anachronistic, wearing mid-eighteenth-century uniforms. While some praised his hospitality and popularity with rank-and-file troops, others complained of his rigid discipline and "fits of ill-humor which he was at no pains to conceal." His nickname, "Old Cock of the Rock," was affectionate—or sarcastic. His last months were "excruciating tortures" from old wounds. He died on February 21, 1802, leaving a brother and two mistresses, each with two of his children. "He died very rich," an obituary said, rich enough to leave his "two ladies" and four children annuities from a £70,000 trust fund ($8.2 million today). He willed his black servant, who may have been a slave, about £7,000 pounds worth of china, silverware, linen, and cash, as well as his name.[4]

He left Gibraltar a permanent legacy. Atop Gibraltar's highest point, he built an observation tower. While the tower didn't survive a session of naval target practice in 1888, the point was later fortified, and today, O'Hara's Battery is a tourist attraction.

What happened in the West Indies between February and May that turned a situation so threatening as to require major reinforcements into one of "perfect security"?

The West Indies is vast. The distance from one end—New Providence Island in the Bahamas—to the other—Berbice (now part of Guyana), the war's southernmost disputed post within the Caribbean theater—is nearly 1,850 miles. It's greater than the distance from Savannah to Newfoundland, greater than Boston to Jamaica. Those are air distances. For eighteenth-century ships, dependent on winds and currents, sailors measured distance in days and weeks. Because of those winds and currents, it was often faster to sail the 4,700 miles from Jamaica to England than the 1,200 miles from Jamaica to Barbados.[5]

Travel in the West Indies during hurricane season—from late summer through late fall—was limited. European navies, trading ships, and convoys that frequented the Caribbean colonies at other times of the year, sailed elsewhere to avoid potential destruction. Even Whig privateers preyed in other waters. Staying behind or returning too early could be dangerous: three thousand sailors drowned during an October 1780 hurricane and a September 1782 tropical storm.[6]

In the minds of whites, it wasn't healthy to stay long in the Caribbean anyway. One naval doctor listed a litany of diseases and injuries that befell crews in a West Indies fleet in one month of 1782: fevers, fluxes, scurvy, ulcers, smallpox, pectoral complaints, venereal complaints, colds, rheumatism, angina, gravel, dropsy, ophthalmia, leprosy, fistules, hernias, abscesses, fractures, and "various slight accidents as bruises, cuts, scalds, etc." He concluded, "Disease was still more destructive than the sword."[7]

Beyond disease and the elements, people faced deadly animals and insects. A British admiral in 1782, for example, was "bit by a centipede on the temple, which afterwards worked itself into his ear, and continued to wound him, 'til oil, poured in, destroyed it. A deafness and insensibility affects that side of the head so much attended with frequent twitches that he finds himself incapable of performing."[8]

Whites believed that African blacks—that is, slaves—were better adapted to the Caribbean. Adam Smith, the Scottish economist, reflected in 1776 the European consensus: "The constitution of those who have been born in the temperate climate of Europe could not, it is supposed, support the labor of digging the ground under the burning sun of the West Indies." The truth was that slaves died at the same, if not higher, rates as whites.[9]

And yet, despite the dangers and the cost of constantly replenishing slaves, the ships would always return. The West Indies made empires possible.

Settlers took years to discover that rice was an ideal crop for the Carolinas and Georgia. The Caribbean experience was different. Columbus brought nonindigenous sugar cane there on his second voyage in 1493. He expected it to grow well, and it did. By 1506, sugar had become an industry, and Spain built its first sugar-refining mill. Within a decade, Spain used African slaves in the mills and fields.[10]

The West Indies attracted other Europeans, first pirates, then settlers and traders. For three centuries, they raided or invaded each other's islands, ceded them at the end of wars, then reinvaded when new wars began. When France entered the American war in 1778, the West Indies was a checkerboard of nations. Britain, France, and Spain owned the best sugar-growing islands; the Dutch and Danes turned their less productive islands into trading centers. Despite Spanish dominance and anger, British and Dutch settlers formed villages on the coastal mainlands of Central and northern South America. Although Britain could do only minor ship repairs in Jamaica, the French had four ports capable of major refitting, while Spain owned Havana, which had shipbuilding yards.[11]

None of these countries could resist sugar's lure, nor its by-products, molasses and rum. In 1698, the British imported 207 gallons of rum; by 1775, it was two million. Europeans used sugar in everything from tea and coffee to jam, and the British used sugar more than anyone. The French, with a lesser sweet tooth, captured the sugar market on the European continent.[12]

The sugar colonies meant wealth for the largely absentee plantation owners who grew it and for the governments that taxed it. "The sugar colonies possessed by the European nations in the West Indies, may be compared to those precious vineyards," Adam Smith wrote. Another contemporary described Jamaica as the source of "prodigious riches." In fact, Jamaica was the wealthiest British colony in the Western Hemisphere.[13]

The French made even more money from their Caribbean colonies. In negotiations to end the Seven Years' War in 1763, France didn't hesitate to trade all of Canada (minus a fishing village off the Newfoundland coast) for Martinique, Guadeloupe, and St. Lucia. Spain swapped Florida and nearly all territory east of the Mississippi for Cuba. The final treaty caused an uproar in London; most British felt they got the short straw.[14]

France knew what it was doing. The Caribbean trade accounted for thirty percent of its imports and, because none of its islands were self-sufficient, thirty-five percent of its exports. Its Saint-Domingue colony (now Haiti) was the most valuable land on earth. It produced more and cheaper sugar than all British Caribbean islands combined. Saint-Domingue's trade was greater than that of the British North American colonies combined. The West Indies accounted for one-third of all French trade overseas.[15]

"The profits of a sugar plantation in any of our West Indian colonies are generally much greater than those of any other cultivation that is known either in Europe or America," Adam Smith said.[16]

George III was blunt: "If we lose our sugar islands, it will be impossible to raise money to continue the war."[17]

The West Indies was important to Americans, as well. Before the war, America had supplied lumber, corn, flour, rice, fish, and other food and provisions to the sugar colonies. Americans also traded illegally (under British law) with French islands that produced sugar at significantly cheaper prices.

Once the war began, the French and Dutch colonies (and to a lesser degree, Danish and Spanish) were centers for international arms smuggling, and safe havens for state and Continental Whig navies and privateers. In the early years, about ninety percent of the Whig gunpowder was transferred in the West Indies from European ships to small, fast rebel ships that outsailed British pursuers.[18]

American pirates—or privateers from the Whig perspective—hurt British trade. By early 1777, they had captured two hundred fifty British ships and seized cargo worth more than £10 million ($1.8 billion today)—enough to cause four English merchant companies to fail.[19]

British West Indians also participated in smuggling and fencing. In fact, few West Indian merchants and plantation owners had loyalty to any country. By the mid-1700s, civilians almost never resisted invaders or helped the typically small garrisons that defended their islands. Their property was too valuable to risk destruction. "The genius of all West Indians without distinction seems turned to piracy and freebooting," said Grenada's governor. One British admiral complained that he was "laboring to protect men who wished not to be protected." His complaint could have applied to any Caribbean nationality.[20]

The long-time resident whites the admiral referred to—many of whom were born in the West Indies—developed their own society. Europeans often criticized the so-called "creoles." A French naval officer said, "the creole women are all ugly, with the yellow complexion of the country. They are, too, very ill-mannered. Accustomed to speak to their slaves, they have a certain tone which they can never drop."[21]

Then there were the Jews—one thousand in Jamaica alone. They settled in Martinique in the 1620s, only to be expelled after Jesuits pressured the French government. Most found havens in the Dutch colonies. In St. Eustatius, for example, three hundred fifty prospered. Janet Schaw, a Scottish traveler visiting there in the mid-1770s, described her shock and revulsion when Jews talked with her on landing. "I could not look on the wretches without shuddering," she said. She later learned that two of the Jews she met had been tortured by the French and Spanish inquisitions, examples, she said, of "Christian cruelty."[22]

Free black and mixed-race people—about two percent of the population—lived on all the inhabited islands. Some were the children of black mistresses who had been freed by their masters. Others were freed blacks who had served in Loyalist militias, fled from America, and now, in the West Indies, continued to serve in Loyalist units. Others, like the Maroons, were descendants of escaped slaves. In Jamaica, they fought the British to a draw from 1700 to 1739, when the two sides agreed to a treaty that recognized Maroon freedom and land in exchange for their service as a militia, available for suppressing slave revolts or catching runaways. The French used free black and mixed-race men similarly, and the Spanish had black militia officers.[23]

Finally, the slaves. "In all European colonies," Adam Smith said, "the culture of the sugar-cane is carried on by Negro slaves." He advised his readers to treat their property well. "Gentle usage renders the slave not only more faithful, but more intelligent, and therefore, upon a double account, more useful." But he conceded that "in the good management of their slaves, the French planters—I think it is generally allowed—are superior to the English." An Anglican minister who spent twenty years in the Caribbean concurred. "In the French colonies, the public pays an immediate attention to the treatment and instruction of slaves. . . . The power of the master is restrained to the whip and chain; he may not wound or mutilate his slave." A modern scholar concluded that the "English sugar planters created one of the harshest systems of servitude in Western history." Most planters, however, would have agreed with Janet Schaw. "When one comes to be better acquainted with the nature of the Negroes, the horror of it must wear off," she said.[24]

Planters and the government needed slaves. Without slaves, there could be no sugar cultivation. And planters needed hundreds of thousands of them. "It is as great a bondage for us to cultivate our plantations without Negroes as for the Egyptians to make bricks without straws," explained the St. Kitts council in 1680.[25]

No slaves, no sugar. No sugar, no revenue. A British admiral said abolition of the slave trade would "deprive the state of one of the most valuable branches of the national commerce . . . a sort of suicide against the trade of their country and its navigation." Besides, "the Negroes in the many [Caribbean] plantations I have seen never appeared to me to be in a desponding state, but rather satisfied with their condition."[26]

By 1700, the British alone had brought 250,000 Africans to the West Indies. On the eve of the war, French Martinique had more than 71,000 slaves, compared to 12,000 whites. Jamaica had nearly 193,000 slaves to 13,000 whites. In the 1780s, the French West Indies had 64,000 whites, 13,000 free blacks—and nearly 438,000 slaves. By the 1790s, British islands had 65,000 whites and 456,000 blacks, most of them slaves.[27]

The Africans and their descendants refused to accept their enslavement. The first documented slave rebellion in the West Indies was in 1522, against the Spanish on Hispaniola. It was not the last. Revolts were frequent—often every several years—and they occurred in nearly every major British, French, Spanish, and Dutch colony. Shortly before the war began, for example, white Jamaicans demanded greater protection from "massacre and desolation from an internal enemy." They were "on our constant apprehension of the revolt of our slaves." In 1776, skilled Jamaican slaves including millwrights and distillers, desperate because the war restricted food imports, rebelled; seventeen were eventually executed, some burned alive or gibbeted. Across the Caribbean, just thirteen years before, in Dutch Berbice, slaves formed an army of four thousand men that fought for a year before it was put down. Just 116 of 286 white civilians survived the war. A little more than half of the blacks survived, many dying from disease. Nearly 1,700 were tortured to death. Eight years after the American war ended, slaves revolted in French Saint-Domingue. Hundreds of thousands of blacks died; estimates of the French dead range from the tens of thousands to one hundred thousand.[28]

Once France and Spain joined the war, the fighting inevitably moved to the West Indies, and Yorktown accelerated the pace of fighting already taking place there. Spain intended to recover its former colonies of the Bahamas and Jamaica. France wanted to expand its profitable possessions. Both France and Britain needed the Caribbean cash flow to survive. Americans—both Loyalists, assuming they won, and Whigs—needed a friendly West Indies for trade. "The West Indies will become the principal theater of war," a British cabinet member predicted in early 1780.[29]

25. The Golden Rock

FRANCE AND BRITAIN BEGAN SEIZING EACH OTHER'S ISLANDS within months of the Franco-American alliance's formation in mid-1778. Major naval battles, as well as hundreds of minor encounters, shipping seizures, and chases ensued; they would continue for the rest of the war. In early 1780, after Spain entered the war, Britain invaded Spanish territory in Central America—what is now Nicaragua.

The only safe harbors belonged to the neutral Dutch and Danish colonies. For Holland—officially, the United Provinces—that would soon change in the worst way.

Holland's lifeblood was international commerce, and as a neutral, it wished to continue its lucrative trade with America and its Europeans neighbors, France and Spain. No Dutch colony was more central to commerce—and to the rebel war effort—than St. Eustatius (Sint Eustatius), Statia for short.

It's a small, hilly, volcanic island, less than five miles long, three miles wide, roughly two hundred miles east of Puerto Rico, forty miles south of St. Martin (Sint Maarten). The tallest point on its tallest volcano crater is 1,975 feet—forty percent higher than the Rock of Gibraltar. Statia, said an early geographer, is "small and inconveniently laid out by nature." Edmund Burke, a British MP, described the island as "different from all others. It seemed to have been shot up from the ocean by some convulsion: the chimney of a volcano, rocky and barren. It had no produce." He called it a freak of nature, "hastily framed, neither shapen nor organized, and differing in qualities from all other."[1]

An early seventeenth-century attempt by the French to settle there failed due to lack of water. The Dutch arrived soon after; they made it habitable by building cisterns to catch rain; they made it profitable by turning it into what Burke called "an emporium for all the world." When, in 1756, the Dutch made Statia a free port and eliminated custom duties, it became the "Golden Rock," the "general market and magazine to all nations."[2]

Janet Schaw said its "whole riches . . . consist in its merchandise. . . . The town consists of one street a mile long, but very narrow and most disagreeable, as every one smokes tobacco, and the whiffs are constantly blown in your face. But never did I meet with such variety; here was a merchant vending his goods in Dutch, another in French, a third in Spanish, etc., etc. . . . Here hang rich embroideries, painted silks, flowered muslins, with all the manufactures of the Indies. Just by hang sailor's jackets, trousers, shoes, hats, etc. Next stall contains most exquisite silver plate, the most beautiful indeed I ever saw, and close by these iron-pots, kettles, and shovels. Perhaps the next presents you with French and English millinery wares."[3]

Schaw didn't mention the arms trade. As early as March 1776, a rebel agent was sending arms north. That November, the Dutch returned the ritual salute of a gun-buying Continental navy ship—the "first salute" to officials of the new nation. In 1780, forty percent of all ships entering Philadelphia and Baltimore came from Statia. It wasn't just the Whigs that neutral Statia helped. France sent an armed convoy there every other week for supplies for its colonies. Even merchants from British Caribbean colonies used Statia warehouses as a hedge against French attack. An English historian complained, "The Dutch settlers waxed fat, and a discreditable feature of this free-trading was the number of British subjects engaged in the traffic." By 1779, up to ten ships a day were unloading goods at Statia. A Dutch rear-admiral reported 3,182 ships sailing from Statia over a thirteenth-month period.[4]

For Britain, Statia's so-called neutrality was notorious. The password for British troops at the Battle of Saratoga was "St. Eustatius." A British admiral complained that "the piratical rebels" pointed their guns at his ships from the safety of Statia harbor. "The Dutch governor took no notice of this insult."[5]

The situation became untenable in late 1780, when Holland joined a loose alliance with Russia, Sweden, Denmark, and others that vowed to resist any seizures of their "neutral" cargo ships. A month later, Britain declared war on Holland. It outlined a list of warlike Dutch acts, from failing to come to Britain's aid in violation of a 1678 mutual defense treaty to secret negotiations with the rebels for an alliance. Moreover, "at St. Eustatius, every protection and assistance has been given to our rebellious subjects. Their privateers are openly received into the Dutch harbors, allowed to refit there, supplied with arms and ammunition, their crews recruited, their prizes brought in and sold."[6]

The same day it declared war, London ordered its top admiral and general in the West Indies to seize Statia and other Dutch colonies. Three days after receiving their orders, Admiral George Bridges Rodney, his second-in-command Rear Admiral Samuel Hood, and Major General John Vaughan, sailed for Statia with fifteen warships and three thousand troops. Six days later, on February 3, 1781, they demanded that Statia's governor surrender the town within one hour. The Dutch were shocked: They hadn't gotten the word that they were at war. Their "surprise and astonishment was scarce to be conceived." The governor surrendered, asking Rodney and Vaughan to give the town's inhabitants "clemency and mercy." Clemency and mercy—that is, allowing civilians to keep their property—had been the West Indian norm for peaceful capitulations for the previous two centuries.[7]

Rodney refused.

Rodney's life revolved around his men, family, and money. His men liked him for his success in capturing enemy ships—prizes whose eventual proceeds were shared with them. They considered him humane. He advocated for his men and supported innovations that led to healthier onboard living conditions. To his son-in-law, Rodney was "generous, friendly, full of humanity, the tenderest and most indulgent of parents, a kind and affectionate husband, and a faithful friend." Virtually every letter he wrote to his wife expressed love for her and his children.[8]

But he needed money. Born around 1718, he was raised by wealthy relatives because his father, a marine captain, had lost everything speculating. Like most career officers, Rodney began young. By fifteen, he was an able seaman on a guardship. He spent many of the ensuing years in the Mediterranean and off Newfoundland. By 1743, he was a captain. For about eighteen months, Samuel Hood, a young midshipman, served under him— the same Hood who later joined him in Statia.

During these years, Rodney captured rich prizes. At the end of one war, he was promoted to commodore and governor of Newfoundland, and elected to Parliament. As governor, he worked with Boston merchants whose republican impulses "gave me such disgust." After a tour of duty in Portugal, he returned to England in 1752, exhausted and ailing, a pattern that would repeat. In the Seven Years' War, Rodney gained fame by successfully blockading the French navy off Le Havre. He was promoted to rear admiral, and later helped take four French Caribbean islands.[9]

With peace, his debts mounted despite a well-paying job as governor of Greenwich Hospital. His campaigns for re-election to Parliament, gambling debts, and expenses forced him to borrow money from an early-day version of a loan shark. By 1770, he was faced with ruin. To escape his debts, he accepted the post as commander-in-chief in Jamaica. There, wrote a friend, "He does, and must, save money." Four years later, he returned to England where he found his pay frozen because of unauthorized expenses. A navy official later described him as a "vulture," ready to steal public money. He fled to Paris to avoid debtors' prison.[10]

When France entered the American war in 1778, Rodney was still in Paris, and had run up debts there. A friend described him as in a "forlorn, unfriended state, with nothing but exclusion and despair before his eyes." But a French acquaintance paid some of his debts, and he returned to England. He was sixty-one.[11]

The navy named him commander-in-chief of the Leeward Islands squadron (those islands other than Jamaica). On his way to the West Indies in late 1779, he destroyed a Spanish fleet and brought supplies to the besieged Gibraltar. In the West Indies in 1780, he fought three inconclusive battles with the French, then spent hurricane season in New York, where he alienated its commander in a dispute over prize money, men, and supplies. London admonished him not to seize other admirals' prizes and resources again.[12]

To Rodney, Statia residents deserved no clemency, no mercy. "What terms did perjury, treason, rebels, traitors deserve? None. And none they had," he said. "This island has long been an asylum for men guilty of every crime, and a receptacle for the outcast of every nation."[13]

He confiscated and began selling all the property and goods he found, even that of British merchants. "The riches of St. Eustatius are beyond all comprehension," he wrote his wife. To London, he reported, "The capture is immense and amounts to more than I can venture to say." The seizures came to £3–£5 million ($527–$878 million today)—of which Rodney was entitled to one-sixteenth.[14]

He allowed some civilians to stay, albeit minus their property. Others, he either made prisoners of war or deported. He singled out Jews—even Jews who had escaped persecution in America for their loyalty to Britain. He confiscated Jewish property, and separated the men from their families, deporting them to unstated destinations.[15]

Soon, British merchants raised hell in London. Burke, in an unsuccessful demand for an investigation, said Rodney confiscated "all the property found upon the island, public and private, Dutch and British, without discrimination, without regard to friend or foe . . . the wealth of the opulent, the goods of the merchant, the utensils of the artisan, the necessaries of the poor . . ." It was "a most unjustifiable, outrageous, and unprincipled violation of the law of nations." Ironically, Rodney's auction of confiscated goods allowed neutral and British traders to buy them cheap, and sell them back at below-market prices to the American rebels, the French, and the Spanish. Another politician quipped, "Admiral Rodney has a little over-gilt his own statue."[16]

Hood, Rodney's second-in-command, secretly protested to influential friends in government for a different reason: Rodney had hurt the war effort. He was so distracted by the money that he refused to authorize an expedition to seize Dutch Curaçao, and failed to try to intercept the French fleet that eventually helped defeat Cornwallis at Yorktown.[17]

During his four-month stay in Statia, Rodney made a personal enemy of a French general. François-Claude-Amour, the Marquis de Bouillé, governor of all French West Indian islands other than

Saint-Domingue, protested to Rodney that the British were treating Statia's French civilians poorly. Rodney replied with acid: "Perfidious people, wearing the mask of friendship, traitors to their country, and rebels to their king deserve no consideration or favor, and none shall they ever meet with at my hands."[18]

An angry Bouillé got in the last word: "Your excellency, no doubt, forgot that you were writing to a French general, who, from the events of the war, has been for some time in the habit of despising insolence." Bouillé said he would refuse to engage in any prisoner exchanges or any further communication with Rodney: "In the future, the interpreters of our sentiments shall be our cannon."[19]

Bouillé, 42, was twenty-one years younger than Rodney. His mother died giving him birth; his father died several days later. An uncle, a royal court official, raised him. He began the Seven Years' War as a captain, fought in Germany, and was wounded several times. By war's end, he was a colonel, had been captured, and then exchanged. He first visited the West Indies immediately after the war. He returned in 1768 as governor of Guadeloupe.[20]

His new bride joined him there, already pregnant with their first son. Years later, the son would spend the first eleven pages of his autobiography describing what he felt to be his mother's cruelty. As much as he detested his mother, he loved his father: "He was my idol as well as my model. I gained insight into his examples that showed me not only encouragement, but large obligations to fulfill."[21]

Bouillé returned to France in 1771, not returning to the Caribbean until 1777, when he was named military governor and "maréchal" (equivalent of a major general). With war the next year, he showed himself to be an aggressive general, even creating his own small fleet when the French navy was in North America or Europe for hurricane season. "Wherever the enemy appeared," a contemporary said, "he found Bouillé, and Bouillé alone was worth an army because of the confidence he inspired in each island's garrison, and by the fear that his name caused to the enemy."[22]

He also showed grace. When a British frigate shipwrecked off Martinique, he released its crew, explaining he would have treated them as prisoners if he had captured them in battle, but he "scorned to profit by the misfortunates of an enemy." Burke contrasted Bouillé with Rodney. "Bouillé, by his spirit and activity, had wrested from us many of our possessions, but he treated the conquered with tenderness and humanity."[23]

Rodney left Statia at the end of May 1781, and before hurricane season began he returned to England. No one carried out his orders to keep the 670-man garrison on high alert and defended with three frigates. Unhappy Statia residents informed the French.[24]

In the early hours of November 26, Bouillé, with a fleet of small ships carrying one thousand five hundred men, made a quiet but difficult landing on a remote part of the island. His men "underwent very great toil in ascending a steep craggy mountain before they could reach a path by which they could proceed to attack the garrison." Near the fort, they captured Lieutenant Colonel James Cockburn, the British commander who was out on morning exercises with some of his men. Approaching the fort, other British soldiers mistook the red uniforms worn by some of Bouillé's men for their own. When the British recognized their error, it was too late. The garrison surrendered. It was a "clever affair," Lafayette said. "I never read of a prettier *coup de main* [surprise attack]."[25]

That evening, Bouillé restored Dutch law, named some of the remaining Dutch residents to civilian posts, and began returning about £250,000 of goods to their owners. Within the two days, Bouillé also recaptured St. Martin, Saba, and St. Bartholomew, which Rodney had taken earlier.[26]

Rodney got the news about Statia in late February or early March 1782. He reacted angrily. "The surprise of St. Eustatius is the most disgraceful affair that ever happened to a nation," he said. He echoed widespread condemnation of Cockburn. One account concluded that "nothing but the most culpable negligence in the British commandant can account for his [Bouillé's] success. With him lay all the blame, for he had a garrison of such strength and spirit that if he had done his duty as a good officer, he must have made the French to smart for their temerity." The general opinion was that Cockburn had accepted French bribes.[27]

Cockburn, though, was experienced and trusted. He had served thirty-six years in the army, been wounded several times during the Seven Years' War, and fought at Bunker Hill and White Plains. At his May 1783 court-martial, his character witnesses included a stellar list of generals—Thomas Gage, Jeffrey Amherst, William Howe. General Vaughan, who, with Rodney, had captured Statia ten months before, said Cockburn was "an exceedingly good officer who perfectly understood his duty." Cockburn defended himself by saying other officers had been surprised in war, but none were persecuted like him. "My reputation as a soldier in every rank was unblemished till this unfortunate accident, which I shall ever look upon as the greatest misfortune of my life." The court found him guilty of "culpable neglect," and cashiered him. He apparently retired to an estate, possibly owned by his Irish heiress wife. One source says he died shortly after. A family genealogy, however, says he inherited a baronetcy in 1800, and died in 1809.[28]

26. More British Humiliations

SPAIN CONTROLLED MOST OF CENTRAL AND NORTHERN SOUTH America, but here and there, Dutch, French, and British adventurers, traders, and plantation owners created other scattered settlements. Three of them clustered along rivers in Guiana (now Guyana), four hundred fifty miles south of Barbados, a British Caribbean stronghold.

Once ships navigated past shoals and sandbars where the rivers met the ocean, they could sail several hundred miles upriver. This opened land to coffee growing, lumber cutting, and, like the West Indies, sugar plantations. Guiana's climate was as difficult as the Caribbean's. Coastal settlements got up to one hundred thirty inches of rain a year, and before the settlers' slaves could plant sugar, they had to clear "dense, luxuriant, and magnificent vegetation," while avoiding deadly insects, reptiles, snakes, wild boars, and big cats.[1]

By the 1590s, the Dutch had established a strong base: Fort Kijkoveral on the Essequibo River, fifty miles from its mouth. Despite Spanish harassment, other colonies followed. Like Fort Kijkoveral, they were identified by the names of their rivers. The colony on the Berbice River began in 1627, about sixty miles to the southeast of Essequibo, and sixty miles from the coast. Closer to Essequibo, a trading post on the Demerara River opened in 1691, ten miles from the ocean. By 1775, Demerera was the region's largest town, in part because the Dutch welcomed prosperous British planters.[2]

The South American colonies frequently changed ownership. The British unsuccessfully attacked Berbice in the mid-1660s, but they succeeded in taking Essequibo and a colony north of it that had been settled by Portuguese Jews from Brazil. The French later plundered Essequibo, but the Dutch retook it. The French held Berbice from 1712 to 1714, when the Dutch bought it back. The Spanish raided Dutch outposts in 1758 and 1769.

Slave rebellions also threatened the colonies, and, as a counterbalance, the Dutch tried to stay on good terms with the native Arawak and Caribs. The policy didn't prevent slaves from taking control of Berbice in 1763 for eleven months; a joint Dutch-Indian army finally suppressed the rebellion, and the Dutch executed its leaders, mostly by roasting them alive. Another slave rebellion in 1772 brought Demerara to "the brink of total destruction," the governor said.[3]

In early 1781, the Dutch governor of Demerara sent word to his British counterpart on Barbados that he would be willing to surrender to British regulars because his colony was threatened by privateers—"adventurers" who jeopardized the colony's physical safety. He was right. Four or five British privateers, in late February 1781, looted the town, and captured thirteen Dutch ships "laden with sugar, coffee, cotton, flour, and lumber." Several weeks later, they did the same to Essequibo.[4]

Help was on the way. On March 17, the Dutch surrendered Demerara and Essequibo to the British navy, which offered generous terms. Berbice followed in April.

Now, the French planned an attack. Armand Guy Simon de Coëtnempren, Comte de Kersaint, 40, was the son of a navy captain. As a teenager, he had served as an ensign on his father's ship. In early 1782, he was a captain leading a squadron of frigates and smaller ships against the enemy.[5]

On the night of January 29, 1782, his squadron arrived off the coast of Demerara. Despite British attempts to slow the attackers by destroying a navigation landmark and flooding a road, Kersaint landed troops and took the town on January 31. British navy captain William Tahourdin escaped upriver with his small squadron and 376 men. Three days later, Kersaint caught the British.

Outgunned, Tahourdin surrendered. Kersaint captured half a dozen small armed ships and thirteen merchant ships. He sent Tahourdin to Barbados on parole. On the 5th, Kersaint took Essequibo; several days later, Berbice.[6]

Again, Rodney was beside himself. The Admiralty "may easily imagine my surprise and astonishment at this event," he wrote. Tahourdin, "who seems to have taken the lead in this capitulation," would be court-martialed. "So many frigates being given up to the enemy is of great detriment to His Majesty's service." Tahourdin's court-martial apparently ended in acquittal: Navy records in 1783 list him as a captain, and when he died on May 1, 1804, the navy approved his widow's application for a pension. His will provided modest gifts to his siblings, nephews, and nieces, including a gold watch, twenty-volume Shakespeare set, and a print of Isaac Newton.[7]

Although the French returned the colonies to Holland in 1784, they were active interim rulers. Kersaint built a new capital at the mouth of the Demerara (now Georgetown, Guyana's capital). To help collect taxes, he conducted a census, finding nearly thirty thousand slaves in the colonies who worked on 387 plantations and two hundred fifty smaller estates. He concluded there was widespread rum-tax evasion, and he enforced the capitation tax against British residents, but exempted the Dutch and American allies to encourage their trade. At year's end, a new governor replaced Kersaint.[8]

After the war, Kersaint was sympathetic to the French Revolution. He wanted to reorganize the navy based on competence, not nobility, and supported demands for Louis XVI to abdicate. However, because he opposed the king's execution and the revolution's violent excesses, he was arrested in 1793 and then executed.

Bouillé's naval counterpart was an architect of the Yorktown victory, Admiral François Joseph Paul, Marquis de Tilly, Comte de Grasse. In August 1781, Grasse and his fleet eluded Rodney and spent part of hurricane season repulsing the New York–based British fleet that tried to rescue Cornwallis from Yorktown.

Washington's first meeting with Grasse was memorable, according to family tradition. Grasse greeted the prim-and-proper general with a hug, kissed him on both cheeks, and called the fellow six-footer, "my dear little general." Washington's staff hid their laughter, except for Major General Henry Knox (the future secretary of war) who, "heedless of all rules, laughed, and that aloud, till his fat sides shook again."[9]

Grasse, 60, was "reckoned as one of the handsomest men of the age" when he was younger. He was born a noble with a family history of military service. But his advance through the navy "has been more slow and gradual than might naturally be expected from his rank and interest."[10]

His ability, however, was respected. "He was the best skilled captain in the squadron," said an admiral who commanded him. "Although his vessel was very inferior in quality, he nevertheless gave to the evolutions all the precision and brilliance possible." In hindsight, a mid-nineteenth-century French naval historian gave a more critical assessment: "He brought to command a biting arrogance and a disposition that never stooped to conciliate. . . . He was capable of sacrificing a whole plan of operations to a single detail. Brave and good as captain of a ship, the count de Grasse was an embarrassing commodore and a still more ill-starred admiral."[11]

He spent much of his career in the Mediterranean working for the Knights of Malta, which protected convoys against pirates. An ensign in the French navy in 1747, the British captured him in a battle in which he received a severe head wound. In the next British war, he served in the East Indies and captained his first ships. After the war, he returned to the Mediterranean where he again fought pirates. Later, he was based on Saint-Domingue. After the French entered the American war, he fought in an indecisive battle off the Normandy coast in 1778, saw more action in the unsuccessful attempt to stop the British from taking Savannah, and spent two years fighting inconclusive Caribbean battles. Ill, and with hurricane season approaching, Grasse left for France in August 1780.

His final promotion, to rear admiral, and final assignment, commanding the West Indian fleet, came in March 1781. With Rodney preoccupied at Statia, Grasse arrived in Martinique with twenty-three warships and a convoy of one hundred fifty supply ships, having fought off Hood's interception attempts.

Grasse tried unsuccessfully to take strongly defended St. Lucia, but settled instead for capturing Tobago in June. The next month, he was in Saint-Domingue, where he received Rochambeau's plea to rendezvous in Virginia. He agreed that with hurricane season approaching the plan made sense, but promised his Spanish allies to return for a joint spring campaign against the British. His gamble of bringing the entire fleet with him led to the Yorktown victory.

Before leaving Yorktown to return to the Caribbean, Grasse excused himself from a final meeting with Rochambeau and Washington. "My sickness grows worse every day, and I do not know how it will end," he said. "The longer I live, the more I am convinced that a man 60 years old is not fit to direct a fleet such as this."[12]

He would have one final victory, at an island called St. Kitts—formally, St. Christopher. Columbus, in 1493, "was so pleased with its appearance that he honored it with his own Christian name." Janet Schaw, the traveler, described it as "crowned with wood-covered mountains," the highest being the 3,800-foot Mount Misery (now Liamuiga). "The people in town live very well . . . The stores are full of European commodities, and many of the merchants very rich. . . . There is, however, a great want of shade, as every acre is under sugar." A Swedish sailor couldn't believe the island's "most beautiful imaginable" view. "It resembles a large, well-equipped plantation, which rises in an amphitheater on the high mouldy [overgrown] hills clear up to the clouds, in a continuous variation of extensive fields, alternating with groves of trees and beautiful estates."[13]

Starting in 1623, British and French settlers shared the island when they weren't attacking each other during wars, or being attacked by the Spanish. A 1713 treaty gave Britain sole possession; most French residents moved to Saint-Domingue.

Grasse arrived in Martinique from Yorktown in November 1781. He tried to go on the offensive, but contrary winds and storms thwarted two December expeditions against Barbados and another two against St. Lucia. He switched his target to the more-distant (two hundred twenty miles) St. Kitts, less than ten miles from Statia. Seven hundred fifty British regulars and three hundred militia garrisoned St. Kitts, defending five thousand white civilians and their thirty thousand black slaves. Bouillé and eight thousand ground troops accompanied Grasse.[14]

They arrived on January 9, 1782. Assured by civilian leaders that they wouldn't oppose him in return for humane treatment, Bouillé landed his troops without resistance. But the British garrison at St. Kitts retreated to the heavily fortified, 765-foot-high Brimstone Hill—"considered impregnable," said a French officer. They were led by Brigadier General Thomas Fraser—it was probably a local rank; army records show him as a colonel—and Governor Thomas Shirley, son of a Clinton and Carleton predecessor and brother of two soldiers who died in Pennsylvania and New York during the Seven Years' War. The attack became a siege, and a relief expedition came in the person of Samuel Hood.[15]

Hood, 58, was the son of a country vicar, and his family had no navy connection. Family tradition says Hood's father befriended a captain passing through the town whose carriage had broken. The captain repaid the favor by mentoring the son in a navy career. As a midshipman, he served on two ships commanded by then-Captain Rodney. Three years later, he was a lieutenant fighting the French off Scotland, and in the North Sea and the Channel; during one fight, he was wounded in his hand. He married in 1749 into a family with political connections, which helped his advancement. As a captain during the Seven Years' War, he again saw action off Britain, but also served in American waters, and toward the war's end, the Mediterranean. He distinguished himself in all the theaters of war.

After the war, the Admiralty promoted him to commodore and naval commander-in-chief in North America, based in Halifax. He visited Boston often as colonial unrest increased. When rebellion began in 1775, Hood was in England, overseeing the Portsmouth shipyard and governing the Naval Academy. France entered the war in 1778; Hood's prime job was to ready the fleet.

But the Admiralty had a problem: It couldn't find a suitable second-in-command with whom Rodney could get along. "It has been difficult to find out proper flag officers to serve under you," it wrote Rodney. "Some are rendered unfit through their factious connections, others from infirmity or insufficiency." Hood was the solution. The government promoted him to rear admiral, and in late 1780, he left England for Rodney and the West Indies. For his part, Rodney reacted, apocryphally, by likening Hood to "an old apple-woman."[16]

Being second-in-command didn't mean silence. Hood obeyed Rodney's orders, but when he disagreed with them, which was often, he challenged them to Rodney's face and behind his back. His pushback to Rodney's face could be long and convoluted. When he disagreed on positioning ships after the Statia capture, he wrote Rodney: "I most humbly beg leave to suggest, with all due submission to your better and more enlightened judgment, whether it would not be more advisable when the whole of the very respectable force you have done me the honor to commit to my charge are watered, stored, victualed, and collected together and was stationed to the windward."[17]

Behind Rodney's back, Hood was blunt. He complained constantly to Charles Middleton, the navy's controller, and George Jackson, the Admiralty's deputy secretary, about Rodney:

"Sir George Rodney requires a monitor perpetually at his elbow, as much as a froward child. . . . There is, I am sorry to say it, no great reliance to be placed in a man who is so much governed by whim and caprice."

Referring to Rodney's account of a battle, and alluding to his debts: "Lord Rodney has not lived in France for nothing, for I defy any Frenchman living to have written a more gasconade [boasting] account.

"How Sir George Rodney could bring himself to keep his whole force to guard one path . . . to leave another . . . without any guard at all, is a matter of utmost astonishment to me."[18]

He complained about both Rodney and General Vaughan after Statia: "The commanders-in-chief could not bear the thought of leaving the money behind them . . . They will find it difficult to convince the world that they have not proved themselves wickedly rapacious." He complained about Rodney's flagship captain: "Sir Charles Douglas is so weak and irresolute. He is no more fit for the station he fills than I am to be an archbishop." He complained about Admiral Robert Digby in New York, when Digby failed to loan him ships: "I endeavored all I could to prevail upon Admiral Digby . . ." He complained about Admiral Hugh Pigot: "Very unequal to the very important duty."[19]

But Hood praised himself often. "I am not a little proud of my own conduct while in sight of the enemy's fleet," he wrote Middleton. After one naval action, he told Jackson: "I am perfectly conscious of no one omission in the whole of my conduct and of having done everything that was in my power for the support of the honor of the British flag."[20]

And yet, his self-praise wasn't undeserved. He mentored Horatio Nelson, the epitome of British admirals, who described Hood as "the greatest sea officer I ever knew." Another admiral said Hood "took me by the hand soon after I entered the profession and never quitted his hold. . . . I never saw an officer of more intrepid courage or warmer zeal. . . . Without the least disposition to severity, there was a something about him, nevertheless, which made his inferior officers stand in awe of him."[21]

At St. Kitts, Hood proved himself worthy of the praise.

Bouillé and Grasse had besieged Brimstone Hill for two weeks when, on January 23, Hood arrived with a relief expedition of twenty-two ships. Hood hoped to surprise Grasse, but two of his ships collided, and Grasse, with his twenty-six ships, left their anchorage to engage the British. They fought the next afternoon and continued on the 25th.[22]

Then, in what a British captain called "the most masterly maneuver I ever saw," Hood seized Grasse's former anchorage and positioned his ships defensively so that Grasse was unable to continue the attack without severe losses. By the next day, Hood counted seventy-two dead and 244 wounded, while Grasse had 107 dead and 207 wounded. Grasse now changed his strategy: He would blockade Hood in the harbor. On the 28th, Hood sent a small force ashore. Bouillé drove it off.[23]

Hood and Grasse now were at a standstill, but Bouillé on shore continued to tighten his noose, bombarding Brimstone Hill without stopping. He was helped by abandoned British guns and ammunition that civilians hadn't retrieved. Then, on February 12, Grasse's men "saw a white flag raised on the breach of the redoubt. We could scarcely believe our eyes, for the toil and hardship that de Bouillé's army had to undergo are incredible, and men must love a commander to suffer the severe duty imposed on 7,000 men doing that of 21,000."[24]

Fraser explained his surrender after the five-week siege. "The fortifications were very old, and in a ruinous state . . . The fire from the enemy increased daily on us, new batteries frequently opening, and for the last three weeks, they were constantly night and day, bombarding and cannonading the garrison." He had few provisions left, little ammunition. His men had been killed, wounded, took sick, or deserted. "I would be wanting in humanity to have risked the lives of the small body of gallant soldiers."[25]

Hood was now in trouble. Reinforcements had reached Grasse during the siege, and the French had 50 ships. They took Montserrat, sixty miles away, without difficulty. Hood himself watched Grasse take Nevis, two miles off St. Kitts's southeastern tip, without firing a shot. (Alexander Hamilton had been born there twenty-seven years before.)[26]

Hood needed an escape plan. On February 14, he met with his captains and lieutenants to synchronize watches. That night, Hood's squadron quietly cut their anchor cables at 11 P.M. and slipped past Grasse. By the time the French realized Hood had run the blockade, it was too late.[27]

Rodney privately criticized Hood for quietly slipping away—what he deemed a "very unofficer-like action, and tending to discourage the fleet in general." But future generations said this was Hood's finest hour: The leading nineteenth-century naval historian, Alfred Thayer Mahan, said Hood's maneuvers—taking the enemy's anchorage, fighting Grasse to a standoff, and then escaping the blockade—were "brilliant." If Hood had been in command off the shores of Yorktown, "Cornwallis might have been saved."[28]

Hood and Rodney collected their ships at St. Lucia at the end of the month. Grasse returned to Martinique. The only British possessions left in the West Indies were St. Lucia, Antigua, Barbados, and Jamaica. Grasse wanted to remove Jamaica from the list.

27. Battle of the Saintes

THE FRENCH HAD WON VICTORIES AT YORKTOWN, ST. KITTS, Nevis, Montserrat, Demerara, Essequibo, and Berbice. "At home, general despondency or apathy pervaded the country," a British politician wrote. "Disasters more severe than any that we had yet experienced were predicted or anticipated."[1]

By March 1782, the British knew from their scouts and spies that Grasse intended to rendezvous with their Spanish allies on Hispaniola—probably the French port of Cap Français (now Cap Haïtien).[2]

The invasion of Jamaica would include seven thousand Spanish troops and up to twelve Spanish warships, ten thousand French regulars, six thousand black or mixed-race French militia, all of Grasse's fleet, and a contingent of Bouillé's men. All Grasse was waiting for before leaving Martinique was the arrival of reinforcements and a supply convoy.

Rodney and Hood on nearby St. Lucia needed to stop them. They failed. French reinforcements arrived March 20. Hood, as usual, blamed Rodney for poor deployment of the fleet, "as I feared, foretold, and labored to prevent." Rodney didn't cast blame, least of all on himself: "Notwithstanding all our vigilance . . . the enemy's convoy consisting of two line-of-battle ships and three frigates with sixty transports with six thousand troops are arrived at Martinique."[3]

Rodney and Hood had thirty-six warships. Accounts are contradictory, but Grasse's fleet had thirty-three to thirty-six warships. The convoy had 150 to 270 ships, "the richest which had ever sailed from Martinique." Once Grasse joined the Spanish at Cap Français, the odds against the British would be overwhelming. Rodney had to intercept Grasse and his convoy; Grasse had to ignore Rodney, ensure the convoy's safety, and make it to the rendezvous.[4]

Grasse's flagship, the *Ville de Paris*, with 110 cannon, was (with a companion ship) France's largest warship. His second-in-command, Louis-Philippe de Rigaud, the Marquis de Vaudreuil, was competent and experienced. Vaudreuil's grandfather had served twenty-one years as governor of Canada; his father was a commodore; his brother, a captain. Vaudreuil had fought battles from Africa to Savannah, Europe to Martinique.[5]

Louis-Antoine, Comte de Bougainville, commanded Grasse's third division. Like Vaudreuil, he was experienced, and had sailed around the world on a scientific expedition. (A large island of Papua New Guinea is named after him, as is the shrub, Bougainvillea.)

The French, warships and convoy, left Martinique early on April 8 for their rendezvous with the Spanish. Rodney was prepared, and he immediately began the chase. By evening, the two fleets were in sight of each other. The next day, instead of staying ahead of the British and continuing to Cap Français, Grasse signaled the convoy to take shelter off Guadeloupe, while Vaudreuil's squadron protected two straggling warships from Hood's squadron, which was sailing ahead of Rodney's main fleet. Hood later said that if Grasse's entire fleet attacked him at this moment, "he might have cut us up by pouring a succession of fresh ships upon us as long as he pleased." Instead, after about four hours' fighting, Vaudreuil withdrew his squadron as Rodney's ships caught up with Hood. But Vaudreuil's action damaged Hood's squadron so badly that Rodney was forced to send it to the fleet's rear.[6]

That night, two of Grasse's ships collided with each other; it began the erosion of Grasse's fleet. By morning, Grasse put fifteen miles between him and Rodney. Rodney continued the chase.

The night of April 11 was "unusually dark and horrible," a French officer later remembered. "The very weather seemed to forbode something unusual. The wind was so strong that several ships had to reef the topsails. The channel was so narrow that we had to go about two or three times during the watch. Besides, [we were] pursued by a superior enemy." Around 2 A.M. on the 12th, one of the ships involved in the earlier collision now collided with the *Ville de Paris* itself. The flagship was fine, but the other ship needed to be towed to Guadeloupe, reducing Grasse's fleet again.[7]

By sunrise, Rodney again caught up with Grasse. They were near the Saintes, nine small islands in the channel between Guadeloupe and Dominica, named by Columbus in 1493 shortly after All Saints' Day.

Until the sixteenth century, warships were galleys with weapons in front and oars out the sides. Sails meant that cannon could be mounted where oars once were. Because mounted cannon couldn't pivot to any great degree, ships fought battles in parallel lines firing broadsides at each other. Keeping warships in a close formation within the line was the classic defensive position; it meant fleets of equal size fought bloody, but usually inconclusive, battles. (A warship—one with at least sixty-four cannon—equivalent to the twentieth-century's battleship, derived from "line-of-battle ship." Other armed ships fought heated battles, but not necessarily in the main line.) The common wisdom was to fight defensively and by attrition unless you had overwhelming superiority. "The desire to distinguish oneself should never induce a captain to break formation to look for a glorious adventure, no matter what appearance of success it may have," said one training manual.[8]

Neither Grasse nor Rodney had any history of changing the rules.

The Battle of the Saintes began around 8 A.M. on April 12. From the beginning, Grasse was undergunned; he had thirty warships to Rodney's thirty-six. When Grasse ordered his fleet repositioned to set up the appropriate line of battle, Vaudreuil and Bougainville either didn't get the signal, were unable to comply, or refused. An hour later, the winds changed, and Grasse's position was disrupted even more.

Around noon, Rodney did the unexpected: He broke his own line and, with winds in his favor, sailed into the loose French line, splitting Grasse's ships into three groups. It turned the battle into a French rout because Rodney was able to pick off French ships and concentrate his fire. Whether it was Rodney's idea or his flagship captain's, whether it was premeditated or ad-libbed, became hotly disputed.[9]

Despite the new development, the fighting continued unabated. "All was now in a scene of disorder and confusion throughout the enemy's fleet, from end to end," a British captain said. In midafternoon, Bougainville had had enough and sailed away. In the late afternoon, Vaudreuil saw the crippled *Ville de Paris* surrounded by enemy ships. He signaled Grasse, offering a tow. It was an implausible offer. Grasse signaled back that Vaudreuil was to save himself and his squadron.[10]

By 6 P.M., Hood's ship was part of the pack surrounding Grasse, and when he saw the *Ville de Paris* edge toward him, "I concluded de Grasse had a mind to be my prisoner." He sailed toward Grasse and "as soon as I got within random shot, he began to fire upon me, which I totally disregarded" until he was close enough to fire point blank, using a new type of destructive weapon, the carronade—the "smasher"—because of its short-range power. "I opened such a tremendous fire as he [Grasse] could not stand for more than 10 minutes, when he struck. This was at sunset."[11]

Vaudreuil, now in command of what remained of the French fleet, ordered retreat. His ship alone had incurred more casualties than all the British ships together.[12]

On the *Ville de Paris*, Grasse was one of only three unwounded men on the main deck. "Stripped of all her rigging, rerigged under enemy fire, constantly unrigged, her masts pierced and tottering, her sails torn to shred, yards cut, her crew without food from early morning to night fall, the *Ville de Paris* surrendered without shame and without reproach," Grasse said. "I would have been willing to defend her longer, but . . . my cartridges were exhausted. I finally had to charge my guns by the spoonful and only by the glimmer of lanterns in the midst of smoke and great confusion. Then, not being able to fire a single shot nor to use musketry, I was compelled to surrender."[13]

The British captain who took charge of Grasse's ship found himself "over his buckles in blood." The quarterdeck was "covered with dead and wounded." Grasse, having been "for so many hours exposed to a destructive fire which swept away almost all his officers," still stood, "a tall, robust and martial figure presenting, in that moment, an object of respect, no less than of concern and sympathy."[14]

A physician called another captured French ship a "scene of horror. The numbers killed were so great that the surviving, either from want of leisure or through dismay, had not thrown the bodies of the killed overboard, so that the decks were covered with the blood and mangled limbs of the dead, as well as the wounded and dying, now forlorn and helpless in their sufferings."[15]

Rodney's fleet lost 355 men to mortal wounds; another 722 recovered. Nineteen of his thirty-six ships were damaged. No precise accounting of French casualties exists, but the twenty-three warships, plus frigates, that reassembled at Cap Français had suffered 539 dead. A week after the battle, Hood found five straggling ships. He captured four of them. The one that got away carried Bouillé.[16]

Bouillé would return to France in May 1783 honored by his country, and respected by Britain. He was "in the vigor of life and possessed of an ample fortune." But he found France "greatly changed." A royalist, he worked to suppress the revolution, and tried to help Louis XVI escape execution. Bouillé himself fled to England, "carrying with me nothing but the consciousness of an honorable conduct." He died in London at age sixty-two. His name survives in the French national anthem, but not as a hero. *La Marseillaise's* fifth verse says there will be no mercy for "bloodthirsty despots, these accomplices of Bouillé."[17]

Grasse's humiliation was more immediate. He spent four months as a prisoner—and making the rounds of British society. The British released him to carry peace proposals to Paris. There, he found himself a scapegoat for the Saintes and excoriated for his behavior in London. "There is at present among the people, much censure of Comte de Grasse's conduct," Benjamin Franklin said. Grasse defended himself with a memoir that criticized most of his captains. An inquiry exonerated them. Grasse's reputation was destroyed, and the king declared him persona non grata. He was restored to the king's graces in 1786, but Grasse had less than two years to live. His death, Washington wrote, "is not, perhaps, so much to be deplored, as his latter days were to be pitied. . . . His frailties should now be buried in his grave with him, while his name will be long deservedly dear to this country."[18]

Despite Rodney's success, Hood complained bitterly that his commander hadn't ordered a chase immediately after the battle. "Surely there never was an instance before of a great fleet being so completely beaten and routed and not pursued. So soon as the *Ville de Paris* had struck, Sir George's faculties seem to have been benumbed." Rodney defended his decision, saying his ships were crippled, and a chase at night was dangerous. "We have done very handsomely," he told Hood. To London, Rodney said God gave the country "a most complete victory." He also praised Hood with "my warmest encomiums."[19]

Ironically, Rodney's victory embarrassed the government. A new Admiralty lord, concerned about the Statia fiasco, had recalled Rodney before news of the victory reached London. Rodney was now a national hero: celebrated in paintings, songs, and the news media. His victory, said MP Nathaniel Wraxall, "constituted a sort of compensation to Great Britain for so many years of disgrace, for so great an expenditure of blood and treasure, and even for the loss of America itself." All but his creditors forgave his Statia actions. Even Edmund Burke said the Saintes "obliterated his errors."[20]

The government made an about-face, honored him, and gave him a large pension. Despite the many court judgments against him, he lived a comfortable life with the help of his son and friends. In 1788, Rodney helped defeat an anti-slavery bill. Ending the trade, he said, would be "an act of suicide" for commerce; besides, West Indian slaves lived better than most poor English whites. Even in his last year, Rodney continued to buy lottery tickets and gamble. He died at his son's home.[21]

Hood lived a long and honored life. He was elected to Parliament, and received a steady salary as a shipyard commander and Admiralty Board member. When war broke out in 1793 with revolutionary France, he commanded the Mediterranean fleet, and worked briefly with General O'Hara at Toulon. Promoted to full admiral in 1794, he returned to England, but retired (or was fired) the next year after a dispute with the Admiralty. He spent his final years as governor of Greenwich Hospital with a large pension.[22]

John Adams believed the Saintes would prolong the war. "England is so giddy, with Rodney's late success in the West Indies, that I think she will renounce her ideas of peace for the present."[23]

The Saintes forced Vaudreuil and the Spanish to postpone their joint Jamaica expedition until late 1782. "We talked for a long time about this calamity, which appeared to cut short all our plans," a Spanish leader said. The Spanish returned to Cuba. Vaudreuil sailed his fleet to Boston for refitting during the hurricane season.[24]

In Charlestown, Greene predicted that Rodney's "confounded thump of the back" would "totally change the face of matters in the West Indies and the plan of operations in the United States. [British commander] Clinton, finding himself secure from the cooperation of the French, will most undoubtedly push the Southern war."[25]

At Versailles, Louis XVI reacted to the Saintes much like George III had reacted to Yorktown: "My enemies are mistaken if they rely on this success to rise in their demands."[26]

28. Flip-flops in Central America

B RITISH LOGGERS, TRADERS, PLANTERS, AND PIRATES HAD LIVED IN scattered settlements along Central America's Caribbean coast and nearby islands since the mid-seventeenth century. Its thousand-mile coastline runs from Bluefields (now in Nicaragua), north along the Miskito Coast (sometimes spelled "Mosquito," but named after native people, not insects), to the cape, Gracias à Dios, where it turns west to Omoa on the Bay of Honduras. Soon after, it takes a right turn north past Roatán, the bay's largest island, up to the Hondo River (the Belize–Mexico border).

As with Guiana, the bay and Miskito Coast settlements were a constant irritant to the Spanish, who made regular efforts to oust the British settlers. All the settlements traded in contraband, and, in war, they served as staging areas for attacks. The settlement at the mouth of the Black River (now Río Sico) was to the Spanish what Statia was to the British.[1]

A 1797 writer described Black River as the place that was, "for more than sixty years, the refuge of the logwood cutters when the Spaniards drove them from the forests . . . The coast is sandy, low, and swampy; higher up near the rivers and lagoons, which are full of fish, the soil is more fertile . . . the forests are full of deer, Mexican swine, and game. The shores abound with turtles, and the woods with mahogany . . . Indeed, the whole settlement flourishes sponta-neously without cultivation." In 1759, nearly eight thousand people lived in the Black River area. They usually were able to resist the Spanish, in part because of an alliance with the Miskitos and mixed-race Zambo people, who also helped suppress slave rebellions.[2]

The war reached the coast and bay in fall 1779, when the Spanish attacked British logwood cutters on the Hondo River, defeated a British attack at Omoa, and then gave up both settlements to British reinforcements, who themselves abandoned Omoa when more Spanish arrived.

The next year, in April, the British sent a joint navy-army expedition to seize Lake Nicaragua and take the cities of Granada and Léon, splitting Spanish America in half. It was a disaster. The Spanish resisted, and disease killed many. In August, an officer described the scene: "The sick in a miserable, shocking condition, without anyone to attend them or even to bury the dead who lay on the beach shocking to behold. The same mortality raging among the poor soldiers on board ship where accumulated filth had made all air putrid." The navy commander, Captain Horatio Nelson (a future national hero), was desperately sick, but made it out alive; 190 of his two hundred-man crew died. When the British finally withdrew to the coast, 1,420 men of the expedition's original 1,800 were dead.[3]

Spain attacked and burned Black River in April 1781. The British governor in Jamaica responded—with a threatening letter. "Be assured that for every house you burn, a village shall submit to our flame. For every village, a town. And for every town, if you have sufficient, a city." Despite the damage, residents returned and rebuilt Black River.[4]

But the Spanish weren't done. The general who had defeated the Nicaraguan expedition wanted to reassert the Spanish naval presence.

Matías de Gálvez, 65, came from a high-achieving family. His brothers were, respectively, a diplomat, field marshal, and minister of the Indies, in charge of Spain's American empire. His son, Bernardo, conducted the successful campaign against the British in the Mississippi Valley and West Florida in 1779; he would have been Bouillé's counterpart had the Jamaican invasion not been postponed after the Saintes.

Matías, while competent, hadn't experienced the kind of success that his son had. He rose slowly through the ranks. In 1775, he was military commander and governor of the Canary Islands. With the help of his brother, the Indies minister, he became governor of Guatemala in 1778. There, he rebuilt the capital, which an earthquake had leveled. He also reformed the military in Guatemala and built a fourteen thousand-man army.[5]

On December 21, 1781, Gálvez and several thousand troops left Guatemala City on a four hundred fifty-mile journey to Trujillo, a coastal town between Black River and Omoa. There, in early March 1782, he joined with the navy and began to attack British settlements. Roatán Island fell in mid-March; Black River, in late March. He then returned to Guatemala, leaving garrisons to defend the settlements.[6]

The Jamaican governor ordered a new offensive. "From everything I can learn," he wrote Rodney, "those [Spanish] vessels are still upon that coast, and mean to prosecute their intentions of extirpating the settlers from the shore." He told the commander at Gracias à Dios, Major James Lawrie, to put another major, Robert Hodgson, in charge of the offensive. Lawrie replied that Hodgson had angered both Indians and settlers, who refused to fight under him.[7]

But Lawrie had a solution. Lieutenant Colonel Edward Marcus Despard, 31, arrived in Gracias à Dios on personal business in early August 1782. Four of his five brothers served in the army; one became a general. Despard owned a reputation as a competent military engineer. He had served in the Nicaraguan campaign scouting, making maps, situating artillery, and overseeing the building of fortifications. Lawrie named him commander of the new offensive. His army included white settlers, black and mixed-race freemen, Miskitos, British regulars, Jamaican militia, American rebel POWs, and American Loyalists recruited in New York—one thousand men, eleven ships.

Despard split that force. First, on August 23, a detachment of mostly Miskito soldiers commanded by a few British officers seized the thirty-three-man garrison at Fort Quepriva (called Fort Dalling by the British) on the outskirts of Black River. They massacred all but one man, who escaped. On the 26th, Despard and his main force anchored at Black River and demanded the surrender of the town's key fort, Immaculada Concepcíon de Honduras. He hinted that the Miskitos were impatient. The one hundred forty-man garrison, weakened by disease and running short of supplies, complied. Despard sent them to Spanish Omoa on parole.[8]

London rewarded Despard by promoting him to colonel and superintendent of the Central-American settlements, which the peace treaty reduced in size to what is now Belize. He married a black West Indian woman shortly after the war, and they had a son. As superintendent, he was caught between factions, and his fair treatment of blacks and mixed-race people became an issue. The government relieved Despard in 1790, but not before eighty-one percent of the eligible voters elected him a magistrate. The government cleared him of all charges, but then eliminated his job. In his ensuing London years, he worked to democratize British society and government. In 1802, authorities arrested him and charged him with treason, including a plot to kill the king. He denied the charge. To help prove his loyalty, Despard presented an elite list of character witnesses, including Horatio Nelson. Nonetheless, the jury found Despard and five co-conspirators guilty. They were sentenced to be disemboweled alive, then beheaded and quartered. Public sentiment stopped the disembowelment, but on February 21, 1803, Despard was hanged and then beheaded. His wife apparently received a pension from supporters in Parliament.

Spain promoted Gálvez in 1783 to viceroy of New Spain—Mexico and the Central-American colonies. He focused on civic improvements: plans for a new government palace, better streets, preservation of canals and bridges, creation of a bank, and permission for a banned newspaper to start publishing again. His tenure was a short one: He died less than nine months after taking office.[9]

Whig diplomats John Jay (left) and Benjamin Franklin (center) exchanged the final peace treaty documents with British diplomat David Hartley (right), a member of Parliament and one of Franklin's scientific colleagues. They made the exchange at Franklin's residence in a Paris suburb more than two-and-a-half years after the British surrendered at Yorktown, Virginia. (*Jay, 1786 portrait by Joseph Wright, New-York Historical Society; Franklin, 1780 French print, Library of Congress; Hartley, after a 1783 painting by George Romney, New York Public Library*)

A whimsical 1781 French copper engraving showing the victorious American and French armies surrounding the British at Yorktown, with French admiral de Grasse's naval blockade in place. (*Anne S. K. Brown Collection, Brown University Library*)

British generals Charles O'Hara (left) and Charles Cornwallis (center) were defeated at Yorktown by a combined French and American army under Washington and French general Jean-Baptiste Donatien de Vimeur, comte de Rochambeau (right). O'Hara represented Cornwallis at the surrender ceremonies, saying his commander was ill. This is O'Hara's only known portrait. (*O'Hara, as colonel, 74th Regiment of Foot, ca. 1791–1795, private collection; Cornwallis, after a 1783 portrait by Thomas Gainsborough, National Portrait Gallery; Rochambeau, by Charles Willson Peale, 1782, National Park Service*)

"View of Charles Town, the capital of South Carolina," after a 1774 painting by Thomas Leitch. The city was the fourth largest in British North America and the financial and trading center of the South. After the war, it was renamed Charleston. (*Library of Congress*)

The opposing southern commanders were the British Alexander Leslie (left) and rebel American Nathanael Greene (right). The only thing the men agreed on was the need to reduce the savage, brutal nature of the revolution in the South. (*Leslie, as major general ca. 1783–1787, by Thomas Gainsborough, private collection in Scotland; Greene as he looked during the war, miniature by fellow officer John Trumbull, 1792, Yale University Art Gallery*)

Rebel general "Mad" Anthony Wayne (left) fought British lieutenant colonel Alured Clarke (right) in Georgia. (*Wayne, after a portrait by Charles Willson Peale, ca. 1783, Library of Congress; Clarke, as major-general in 1794, after a portrait by William Beechey, Library and Archives Canada*)

Three southern commanders. British lieutenant colonel James Henry Craig (left) resisted the rebel insurgents from North Carolina. General Francis Marion (center), nicknamed long after the war the "Swamp Fox," kept the rebellion alive after two disastrous defeats. Rebel colonel John Laurens (right) was Washington's aide, a diplomat, Alexander Hamilton's close friend, and a reckless soldier with a death wish. (*Craig, ca. 1810–1811, as captain-general of Canada, by Gerrit Schipper, Library and Archives Canada; Marion, a fanciful portrait from the 1876 book,* The Centennial Book of American Biography, *James Dabney McCabe; Laurens, unknown artist, only known portrait, National Portrait Gallery, Smithsonian Institution*)

The 1782 British evacuation of Charleston by Howard Pyle, 1898. (*Delaware Art Museum/Bridgeman*)

Shawnee man (left), French engraving. (*Darlington Digital Library, University of Pittsburgh*) Right, Simon Girty. Fanciful drawing of "Girty, the Renegade" from an 1896 Ohio history textbook. (*W. H. Venable*, Tales from Ohio History for Home and School)

Joseph Brant (Thayendanegea) (left) was a Mohawk leader and in-law of a British Indian superintendent. Colonel Marinus Willett (center) defended the Mohawk Valley in upstate New York from Indian, British, and Loyalist raids. John Sevier (right) fought Indians, British, and Loyalists in the Carolinas and what is now Tennessee. (*Brant, probably painted by Charles Bird King for* History of the Indian Tribes of North America, *and based on an 1806 portrait from life by Ezra Ames, Library and Archives Canada; Willett, ca. 1800, unknown artist, Albany Institute of History & Art; Sevier, Charles Willson Peale portrait, 1791, detail, Tennessee State Museum*)

"David Zeisberger preaching to the Indians," after an 1862 painting by Christian Schussele. Zeisberger was the spiritual leader of the pacifist Moravian Indians, the victims of a massacre by insurgent Americans. (*ca. 1864 print, Library of Congress*)

British attack on St. Eustatius, 1781. Dutch-owned Statia, as the West Indian island is known, was an international haven for British enemies. Outraged, Admiral George Rodney took the island, and his brutal treatment of residents and overt anti-Semitism outraged many in Britain. (*French print, Library of Congress*)

British admiral George Brydges Rodney (left) and his subordinate, Admiral Samuel Hood (center), won a game-changing victory over the French in the Caribbean. The French general, François Claude Amour, Marquis de Bouillé (right), successfully opposed British land forces. (*Rodney, ca. 1789, after a portrait by Joshua Reynolds, Library and Archives Canada; Hood, 1784, after a portrait by James Northcote, New York Public Library; Bouillé, ca. 1797, after a portrait by Henri Grévedon, New York Public Library*)

Off the Islands of the Saintes, in the Caribbean, French admiral François Joseph Paul de Grasse, comte de Grasse (left) lost a disastrous 1782 battle to the British and was captured. (*Nineteenth-century print from the original 1842 portrait by Jean Baptiste Mauzaisse*) At right is an imagined scene of de Grasse surrendering to Rodney. In reality, Hood was the British admiral closest to de Grasse's *Ville de Paris*, and whether de Grasse handed over his sword is speculative. British print ca. 1785 from *A New, Universal, and Impartial History of England*, George Frederick Raymond. (*Library of Congress*)

Battle of the Saintes, "Combat naval 12 avril 1782," a turning point that might have preserved the British presence in the Caribbean, and allowed the British to negoti-ate from strength after a string of losing battles. A 1793 gouache by Swiss artist François Aimé Louis Dumoulin, who lived in the West Indies during the war. (*Musée historique de Vevey; photo by Rama, Wikimedia Commons, Cc-by-sa-2.0-fr*)

Johannes de Graaff (left), the Dutch governor of St. Eustatius who surrendered to Rodney. Jean François Galaup, comte de Lapérouse (center), successfully raided and destroyed two remote and lucrative trading posts on Hudson Bay. The leader of one of the posts was Samuel Hearne (right), a trader and explorer who was the first European to reach the Arctic Ocean by land. (*Graaff, portrait by A. L. Brockman, 1834, after an earlier [unlocated] portrait, New Hampshire State House; Lapérouse, unknown artist and date, Library and Archives Canada; Hearne, posthumous portrait, 1796, unknown artist, Darlington Digital Library, University of Pittsburgh*)

Bernardo de Gálvez (left) wrested the Mississippi River Valley and West Florida from the British, and was the Spanish commander of an invasion of Jamaica, called off after the French defeat at the Saintes. His father, Matías de Gálvez (right), defeated the British in Central American campaigns. (*Bernardo, 2014 Carlos Monserrate copy of 1783 portrait by Mariano Salvador Maella, copy in Senate Foreign Relations Committee; Matías, ca. 1783-1784, by Andrés López, Museo Nacional de Historia, Mexico City*)

The final naval battle involving Continental ships was on March 10, 1783, off the Atlantic coast of Florida. The *Alliance*, left, under John Barry, engages the British *Sybil*, commanded by James Vashon. Both sides claimed victory. (*Naval History and Heritage Command*)

British admiral Richard Kempenfelt (left) prevented the bulk of a French convoy from reaching the Caribbean and reinforcing de Grasse's fleet in late 1781. The convoy was led by Admiral Luc Urbain de Bouëxic, comte de Guichen (right). (*Kempenfelt, posthumous engraving by J. Fielding, 1785, Library of Congress; Guichen by lithographer Antoine Maurin in* Biographie Maritime . . . *by Joseph François Gabriel Hennequin, 1837*)

Kempenfelt's flagship, the *Royal George,* sank suddenly during repairs in August 1782, killing him and 800 other sailors and civilians. The poet William Cowper wrote "The Loss of the Royal George" in his honor. (*From* A Narrative of the Loss of the Royal George *by Julian Slight, Samuel Horsey publisher, 1840 second edition*)

View of a sortie made by British soldiers at Gibraltar against Spanish lines on November 27, 1781. The view looks north toward the Spanish mainland. (*1792 engraving by Italian-born London resident Antonio Cesare De Poggi, gallica.bnf.fr, Bibliothèque nationale de France*)

Commanders at Gibraltar. French-born Spanish general Louis des Balbes de Berton de Crillon, duc de Crillon (left), his opposing general George Augustus Eliott (middle), and the French engineer who created the floating batteries, Colonel Jean-Claude-Éléonore Michaud d'Arçon (right). (*Crillon, unknown date and artist, Österreichische Nationalbibliothek; Eliott, 1788 engraving by F. Bartolozzi after Antonio Cesare De Poggi, in* The Gallant Defence of Gibraltar, Ellis & Elvey Publisher, ca. 1898; *d'Arçon, 1769, after a portrait by Jean (Johann Melchir) Wyrsch, Bibliothèque nationale de France, département Estampes et photographie, N-2*)

British general Eyre Coote (left) swapped victories and defeats with Mysorean troops. Admiral Edward Hughes (middle) and French admiral Pierre-André de Suffren (right) fought five major naval battles against each other; in the last, Hughes was forced to withdraw, and the Mysorean and French allies might have taken southern India had they not received news of the peace treaty. (*Coote, 1782, after a painting by William Lawranson, published by William Faden, Österreichische Nationalbibliothek; Hughes, 1786-1787, by Joshua Reynolds, Budapest Museum of Fine Arts; Suffren, posthumous image, 1789, engraved by Marie Louise Suzanne Champion de Cernel, Bibliothèque nationale de France*)

Coote's nemesis was the innovative Mysorean leader Hyder Ali (left). Both Coote and Hyder died unexpectedly. Suffren and Hyder respected each other and spent several days together in face-to-face strategy sessions (right). The picture of Hyder at left by a contemporary is more accurate since he had no facial hair. (*Hyder, unknown date, in Maistre de la Tour's* History of Hyder Shah, *revised in 1855; meeting, Jean-Baptiste Morret after Antoine-François Sergent, Bibliothèque nationale de France*)

Negroes Names.	Age	Description		Remarks.
Paul Coffin...	29	Stout Labourer...		Property of Major Coffin purchased from Mr. ?
Harry...	23	Ditto... Ditto...		Ditto...
Phebe...	21	Stout Wench...		Ditto...
Fortune...	35	Stout Man...		Certificate from Genl. Birch, formerly the p...
Letitia...	26	Stout Wench...		Ditto... held by Mr. Dea...
Peter...	10	Stout boy...		Ditto... Ditto...
William...	22	Stout Man...		Ditto... free born in Vir...
Ceasor & a boy 4 yrs...	38	Do.		Property of Peter Ryerson with whom he is go...

To determine which African Americans would evacuate from New York with the Loyalists, the British created a register of Loyalist slaves, freed blacks, blacks promised freedom for service, and escaped slaves who would not be repatriated to the Americans. "The removal of the Negroes . . . is certainly an act of justice due to them from us," Lord North said. These are details from one page of the register, the *Book of Negroes*. (*Nova Scotia Archives*)

Reception of American Loyalists in England, 1783, by Benjamin West. Destitute Indian, black, and white Loyalists are welcomed to England. Many rebel leaders pleaded with their countrymen for tolerance for their fellow Americans, but they were largely ignored. Most Native Americans who fought against the rebels to protect their land from speculators like George Washington and Daniel Boone were forced into exile, if not killed. The British kept most of their pledges to liberate African Americans who fought with them, and evacuated thousands of them. West's original painting is lost, but he reproduced it in the background of an 1812 portrait of John Eardley Wilmot, the Loyalist Claims Commission's chief commissioner. (*Yale Center for British Art, Paul Mellon Collection*)

British commander-in-chief Sir Guy Carleton (left), who conducted the final evacuation from New York in December 1783. British and Loyalists evacuating New York City (right) as imagined by Polish-German artist Daniel Chodowiecki, 1784. (*Carleton, unknown artist, Library and Archives Canada; Library of Congress*)

A British cartoon published in 1783. From left to right, an Englishman, Dutchman, and Indian (representing the US), Spaniard, and Frenchman—all combatants. The Englishman says, "Say what they will, I call this an honourable P–." The American: "I call this a free and Independent P–." The Frenchman: "Jack English, we confess your exceeding good nature, tho' we have wrangled you out of America you freely make P– with us." (*Library of Congress*)

29. A Future Hero

THREE FRENCH SHIPS COMMANDED BY GRASSE'S NEPHEW, Marquis de Grasse-Briançon, captured Turks Island without a shot on February 12, 1783. The island was "low, sandy, and barren, without a drop of fresh water," but it was a major source of salt, used to preserve fish. Grasse-Briançon left a strong garrison there before leaving in search of more prizes.[1]

Three weeks later, on March 2, the British captured him after a short battle, and learned from their prisoners that Turks was now French. A day or two later, a small squadron commanded by Horatio Nelson—the same Nelson who led the naval support in the 1780 Nicaraguan debacle—met up with their colleagues. He explained his next move in a letter to Hood. "I determined to look what situation the French were in, and if possible, retake it [Turks]."[2]

Nelson, 25, had joined the navy when he was twelve, and traveled the world, from the Arctic to the East Indies, Canada and Europe to the West Indies. He had been a captain for five years, and now commanded the *Abermarle*. "Captain Nelson . . . appeared to be the merest boy of a captain I ever beheld," said the future King William IV, then a midshipman on Hood's flagship. "His lank, unpowdered hair was tied in a stiff Hessian tail of an extraordinary length. The old-fashioned flaps of his waistcoat added to the general quaintness of his figure. . . . There was something irresistibly pleasing in his address and conversation, and an enthusiasm, when speaking on professional subjects, that showed he was no common being."[3]

Nelson was a naval wunderkind, but his March expedition to Turks failed. He demanded that the 530-man garrison surrender; landed 167 sailors and marines who met with stiff resistance resulting in eight wounded men; bombarded the island overnight; re-embarked the shore party; and, on March 9, sailed away. He was surprised by the French artillery, and, "with such a force, and their strong situation, I did not think anything farther could be attempted," he said.[4]

One of Nelson's ship commanders privately mocked his captain, whose fool's mission distracted him from the taking and sale of prizes: "The ridiculous expedition against Turk's Island, undertaken by a young man merely from the hope of seeing his name in the papers, ill-depicted at first, carried on without a plan afterwards, attempted to be carried into execution rashly, because without intelligence and hastily abandoned at last for the same reason that it ought not to have been undertaken at all, spoilt all."[5]

Nelson's next assignment was an order from his mentor, Hood: Find French Admiral Vaudreuil's fleet. Vaudreuil had spent the 1782 hurricane season refitting his ships in Boston. He left Boston in December heading to a new staging area for a Jamaica invasion. Puerto Cabello (in today's Venezuela) was closer to Jamaica than Martinique, and British ships were less likely to infest its waters.[6]

It "resembles a small village, although toward the sea, defended by tremendous batteries and on the land side by fortified heights," an officer wrote. "The repair wharf is the best in nearly the entire West Indies. . . . When the thunder rumbles on the roadstead, one hears a most unpleasant music of tigers, bears, and birds of prey, whose hideous noises are always multiplied through the echo in the overhanging mountain cliffs."[7]

Vaudreuil was still waiting for the Spanish fleet to arrive when, on March 29, 1783, an unknown ship entered the harbor to scout the French fleet. "At its ease, it examined and counted the ships of the squadron," a French historian said. "You could see his insolent presence." Vaudreuil ordered chase, but it was too late. Nelson and the *Albermarle* escaped to continue the scouting mission. When he returned to Jamaica on April 7, the peace treaty had ended hostilities.[8]

With peace, Vaudreuil returned to France and was elected to the
assembly, but he opposed the French Revolution, and was forced to
flee to Britain in 1791. When Napoleon seized power, Vaudreuil
returned home.

Nelson became a national hero during the wars with revolutionary and, later, Napoleonic France. In 1805, during a decisive victory
over a Franco-Spanish fleet off the coast of Cape Trafalgar, Spain, a
sniper shot him. He died the next day.[9]

The Bahamas' New Providence Island was a strategic location,
the closest British island to the North American mainland, 535 miles
to Savannah, and the gateway to the Caribbean. Protected by Forts
Nassau and Montague, the British held the Bahamas for more than
a century, despite pirate raids and war-related attacks (with one
brief occupation by the Spanish and French).

The revolution brought a new martial player into the Bahamas:
American rebels and Loyalists. The rebels first raided New
Providence in 1776, when Continental marines landed and faced
token resistance before capturing the governor and an important
cache of munitions. Two years later, rebel raiders returned, freeing
prisoners, seizing more arms, and taking five ships as prizes.

In January 1782, Spanish commander Bernardo Gálvez authorized an invasion. The expedition was promoted and led by Juan
Manuel de Cagigal y Montserrat, governor of Havana, captain general of his native Cuba, Gálvez's second-in-command in the West
Florida offensive, and a facilitator of money that supported French
and rebel operations in North America. But the Spanish navy was
uncooperative, reluctant to sail into unfamiliar waters and preferring
to wait for the Jamaica invasion.[10]

Cagigal could assemble transports for his troops, but couldn't
proceed without naval support. Then, he got lucky: The South
Carolina Whig fleet had arrived in Havana earlier that month.

Most states sponsored navies, although the British viewed them
as illegal privateers. The South Carolina navy was led by
Commodore Alexander Gillon, 41, a wealthy, Dutch-born
Charlestown merchant. He was pro-independence from the start,
active in politics and the militia, and founder of the Marine Anti-
Brittanic Society, known for harassing Tories. He owned a tavern, a

shipping business, and a pier at the foot of what is still called Gillon Street. Tradition says he captured three British ships in Charlestown harbor without a shot by hiding marines in a disguised merchant ship until they boarded the enemy vessels.[11]

The legislature named Gillon its first commodore in 1778, and said the money to fund the ships would need to come from export sales and future prizes. This was a problem. Gillon spent about eighteen months in Europe trying to get the French government to supply ships. It wasn't until May 1780 that he reached an agreement to lease a large frigate in exchange for consigning in France all enemy ships he captured; a quarter of the prize money would go to the lender. If he lost the ship to storms or in battle, the state would compensate the lender. Gillon renamed the frigate *South Carolina.*

Gillon's sailing was delayed by weather, winds, gathering a crew, and finding money to pay for provisions. He finally left port in August 1781 carrying American dignitaries, including the sons of Connecticut's governor and John Adams. But instead of sailing west to America, he went north, then south, to capture British prizes. In November, after alienating his passengers and creating an incident in Spain smoothed over by Whig diplomat John Jay, Gillon sailed for home. He arrived outside Charlestown at year's end only to find the British there. He then changed course for Havana, where he arrived on January 13, 1782. With the ships Gillon captured on the way, the South Carolina navy now had three frigates, six smaller armed ships, and twelve transports.

Gillon's arrival was Cagigal's fortune. Cagigal contracted with Gillon to accompany his expedition against New Providence. The *South Carolina's* "armament is superior to all other vessels in her class," Cagigal said.[12]

After the British victory at the Saintes in mid-April, Gálvez cancelled Cagigal's expedition. The orders, however, either crossed in transit, or Cagigal ignored them. Using the *South Carolina* as his flagship, Cagigal left Havana on April 22 with Gillon, the nine-ship South Carolina navy, and fifty-seven transports and privateers carrying 1,500 sailors and 2,500 Spanish troops and militia.

Two weeks later, on May 8, New Providence's "invalid garrison of 170 fit for duty" surrendered without resistance. Cagigal captured more than six hundred soldiers, along with twelve ships, and he promised no confiscation of private property.[13]

Gillon now had had enough. His relations with the Spanish already had deteriorated. Cagigal's no-confiscation promise meant no prizes, and a British relief expedition was rumored to be on its way. Cagigal scraped up a partial payment for leasing Gillon's fleet, and the Whigs sailed away. Gillon's French creditors would pursue him for years, but he kept his plantation and continued political pursuits. He supported ratification of the U.S. Constitution at his state convention, and tradition says that when another delegate gave a speech in Latin, Gillon sarcastically replied in his native Dutch. He served in the South Carolina legislature, and was elected to Congress twice.

Cagigal left a small garrison in New Providence while he and the rest of his army sailed back to Havana in small boats, arriving piecemeal. There, he met an unexpected reception: Gálvez charged him with ignoring orders to cancel the expedition, failing to punish a subordinate, and consorting with the enemy. (When he was Havana governor, he gave a tour of the city to a captured British general.) Cagigal soon left Cuba to face a court-martial in Spain, where he was found guilty. He spent four years in jail before being cleared and given back his rank and privileges. He served in the army until 1795. Cagigal was replaced as Havana governor by Gálvez's brother-in-law.[14]

The man Cagigal left in charge at New Providence was Captain Antonio Claraco y Sanz. Tensions escalated between the Spanish and British residents so quickly that by May 1782, Claraco complained that New Providence was "one of the miserable spots of the universe." He feared the British residents wouldn't stay neutral. Scouts and informers warned him frequently about imminent British invasions. He arrested privateers and traders he believed preyed on Spanish ships, and he confiscated their goods.[15]

In early April 1783, he received word of the ceasefire and peace treaty. The treaty returned the Bahamas to the British, and Havana ordered Claraco to surrender it to the first British officials. Accordingly, he opened the harbor and moved most soldiers from the outlying Fort Montague to the more central Fort Nassau.

Four hundred miles away, in British-held St. Augustine, Florida, news about the ceasefire and treaty were widely known, but not officially confirmed. A Loyalist militia officer who fled South Carolina when the British left, Colonel Andrew Deveaux, 25, took advantage of the ambiguity. Like many refugee families, his had been wealthy plantation owners. The war split the Deveaux family. He and his father remained loyal; their relatives opposed British rule. Deveaux spent most of the war years fighting rebels, supplying intelligence to the British, and raiding plantations. Unlike other Tory and rebel militiamen, Deveaux didn't condone atrocities. Nonetheless, he earned a reputation as "that young rascal." From Deveaux's perspective, "I am an American, a Loyalist who has sacrificed a considerable fortune in South Carolina for my attachment to the crown." In St. Augustine, he ignored the peace rumors, claiming he had no confirmation, assembled an expedition at his own expense, and on April 1, 1783, his ten-ship flotilla sailed toward New Providence "to restore the inhabitants of it, with those of the adjacent islands, to the blessing of a free government."[16]

He had recruited sixty-five veteran militiamen (including Creek and Seminole sharpshooters) by promising prizes or land. After about ten days sailing, the invasion force anchored off an outer island, and there, recruited another 170 whites, free blacks, and slaves; they let the ninety slaves carry swords and clubs, but not guns. The Bahamans told him about the ceasefire, but Deveaux ignored the information. Adding fifty fishing boats to his fleet and wearing British uniforms to fool the Spanish into thinking his force was larger than they were, Deveaux first attacked the outer fort, Montague, on the morning of April 14. The twenty-nine-man garrison tried to escape, but were captured.[17]

Deveaux then moved on Fort Nassau. Under a truce flag, Claraco sent Deveaux a letter showing him proof of the ceasefire. Deveaux ignored it and then broke a temporary truce by firing on the fort, claiming the Spanish broke the truce. By the 16th, Claraco's situation was untenable. Deveaux occupied hilly positions overlooking the fort, the Spanish were running out of water, and several fires broke out.[18]

Claraco surrendered on the eighteenth. The Caribbean war was over.

Deveaux went to England after the war. His family lost their South Carolina land, but built a mansion on Cat Island in the Bahamas, which today is a ruin. Deveaux married a New York woman, and they eventually moved to her native Hudson River Valley.

Claraco wasn't as fortunate. He remained a hostage pending a prisoner exchange. But Spanish officials ignored him, possibly because he was associated with the disgraced Cagigal. By 1784, Claraco was destitute and living on charity; eventually, the British governor gave him a captain's salary and then billed Havana for it. Claraco escaped, or was allowed to escape, in August 1784. In Havana, authorities arrested him for alleged financial mismanagement. Nine years later, in Spain, a court-martial acquitted him, recommended that he be promoted and given back wages. He soon left the army around 1795 and spent ten years representing the U.S. in Spain as vice-consul.[19]

PART FIVE

The Sea and the Raiders

30. Britannia Doesn't Rule the Waves

After Friday, February 6, 1778, when Whig diplomats and their French counterparts signed a treaty of alliance, Britain no longer could assume nearly unchallenged control of American waters. Nor could Britain focus its military efforts in America alone: The British navy would be stretched, guarding the homeland and English Channel from French invasion and rebel privateers, prosecuting the war in the Caribbean, the Atlantic Ocean, the Indian, and, to their surprise, nearly the Arctic. "Britannia rule the waves," the lyrics of a popular eighteenth-century song, was no longer a given.

The French and, later, Spanish navies, said a British politician, "annually insulted us in the Channel, intercepted out mercantile convoys, blocked our harbors, and threatened our coasts." It was a new war. Whoever controlled the sea would control the war's outcome.[1]

Upwards of 250,000 men served in the British navy. In the war's first four years alone, it recruited 176,000. Of these, more than one in ten died, all but 1,200 from illness. Another 42,000 deserted, some to privateers, some to the enemy. Rebel privateers would cause maritime insurance rates to rise twenty-eight percent.[2]

Britain wasn't alone. In 1782 and 1783, some forty-one British navy ships were taken, destroyed, burnt, foundered, or wrecked. But the Whig, French, Spanish, and Dutch navies lost forty-five. Of the thirteen ships that were part of the American Continental navy during the war, only two remained in service by 1783.[3]

Conditions on British ships were bad, but those on French ships were worse. Filthy water accumulated in the lower decks. "There is a great defect in every point of cleanliness and order," said an appalled British fleet surgeon looking at a captured French ship. "The blood, the mangled limbs, and even whole bodies of men were cast into the orlop, or hold, and lay there putrefying for some time." Although the use of lemons and limes was known to prevent scurvy, their use wasn't mandatory—if they were available. At one point, Rodney's Caribbean fleet had 1,555 men on the sick list for "fevers, fluxes, scurvy," and smallpox.[4]

Even without disease, sailing was dangerous. An example: British crewmen going ashore to find water overturned in the high surf. "Several men had their limbs broken, and some lost their lives by being crushed or drowned," the doctor reported.[5]

The ships themselves often were no healthier, needing constant maintenance. After the Battle of the Saintes, one officer listed twenty-one defects, including "the port timbers of the 13th port (from fore) appears to be boring rotten and decayed 11 inches in from outside of the plank" and "the knuckle timber at the heel, bores rotten, and the upper part defective and sprung at the knuckle." The British navy attached copper sheathing on many ship hulls to make them sail faster; however, the copper would corrode, "entirely destroying everything made of iron that may be near it," an officer said. Moreover, "the sheets of copper conceal defects in the wood."[6]

Luck often separated a successful admiral or captain who retired to a pension from one headed to a court-martial and disgrace. Making a naval strategy work depended on which enemy had the prevailing wind as much as which was outgunned. Because communication between ships was difficult during a battle, captains misconstrued, failed to see, or ignored signals. With few exceptions—Rodney at the Saintes being one—the enemies chose defensive formations.[7]

Even finding the enemy in the ocean, let alone knowing how strong it was, was a crapshoot, as the British found when Grasse first sailed undetected to Yorktown and then prevented the British fleet from relieving Cornwallis. The more ships and guns you had in the water, the better the chance that you'd find and defeat the enemy.[8]

The American rebels had several "navies." Before Congress created the Continental navy, Washington assembled his own fleet of armed ships to support army maneuvers (called "Washington's navy" by historians). All but two of the colonies had their own navies to protect local trade and seaports. (Gillon's *South Carolina* odyssey was an exception.)[9]

The enemies complemented their navies with privateers.

Seven months after Lexington and Concord, Massachusetts became the first Whig government to authorize privateers—legal pirates. Congress followed in March 1776. To operate legally, privateers agreed to play by the rules: Prey only on enemy ships or ships carrying contraband. Don't ransom, murder, or torture prisoners. Sell captured ships and their goods (prizes) only in friendly ports under the oversight of special admiralty courts. Split the proceeds from prizes according to a formula that owners and crews agree to before sailing. Post a bond to ensure good behavior.[10]

Privateering needed startup capital, and wealthy men usually fronted the costs for the high-risk, high-reward work. Like gold rushes, it attracted thousands of men, of whom a large proportion were captured or died, and few made their fortunes. At their peak numbers, in 1781, 449 rebel privateers were asea, employing an estimated three thousand men at any given time. Many more sailed during the course of the war: The British captured about eight hundred rebel ships, most privateers, and took sixteen thousand prisoners, many of whom died aboard hellish prison ships.[11]

New Englanders alone contributed at least ten thousand privateer sailors, a contemporary account said. Half of those were from Salem, the town from where then-Colonel Leslie retreated in 1775. Privateering became Salem's principal industry, despite one-third of its privateers captured or destroyed. Nearby Gloucester lost all twenty-four of its privateers during the war.[12]

When they succeeded, privateering paid well. Unlike the Continental and British navies, privateer owners and crews kept a much larger percentage of the prize money. Because of this, sailors preferred to join them, and many deserted navy ships to do so. The inability to attract navy crews was a common refrain. "It was this division of spoils, rather than the wages that induced many of our best seamen to enter this peculiarly dangerous service," a nineteenth-century naval historian said.[13]

The need for crews modified racial attitudes: Integrated crews were common. Two or three black sailors might work on a typical privateer. All the navies employed black men. Some were freemen, some slaves hired out by owners or promised freedom, some impressed into service, some runaways. Although many worked in lesser positions such as "gunpowder boys," others were pilots, seamen, carpenters, and marines. Many were experienced, having worked on fishing boats and merchant ships before the war.[14]

As the war went on, the rebel privateers' impact grew. In 1776, a typical privateer might have, at most, ten guns and a crew of up to sixty men. By 1783, their armament doubled, and their crews could reach two hundred men. Although Tory privateers never matched the rebels' quantity, they maintained a dangerous (to the rebels) and productive (to Loyalists) presence in the years after Yorktown. In the war's first years, Britain only reluctantly authorized New York Loyalist privateers, but the greater their success, the less the reluctance.[15]

Four of the thousands of privateering incidents show the dangers crews faced and the profits, if successful:[16]

Off Salem in May 1782, a British navy frigate captured a rebel privateer heading toward France with spars and masts. Taking the frigate back to Halifax with the rebel captain and some of its crew prisoners, the ship ran aground on an uninhabited island. Two more rebel privateers saw the ship, investigated, found the large British crew and its prisoners, and negotiated an agreement: The rebels brought the British crew to the mainland, and the British freed their prisoners.

Off Bermuda in September 1782, a large rebel privateer attacked two smaller British ships carrying rum and sugar. They fought for an hour before surrendering to the rebel ship. The rebels sailed both their prizes to Connecticut.

Off Virginia in September 1782, a British navy squadron attacked a French navy ship escorting ten rebel privateers. After the battle, and in the ensuing days, the British captured all but one or two of the privateers.

On the New Jersey coast in October 1782, Loyalists attacked a rebel privateer crew that was unloading cargo from a grounded British merchant ship, which in turn had once been a rebel ship. The Loyalists killed twenty-five rebels before being driven off.

The Whig privateers, with their allied navies, did more than make money if they weren't captured or sunk. They disrupted British trade and forced the British to spread thin their own fleet. Instead of concentrating solely on fighting the French and Spanish, the British had to assign naval detachments to escort trading and supply convoys.[17]

The allies had similar challenges—epitomized by their own convoy, which met the British off an island called Ushant.

31. French Disaster, British Tragedy

USHANT (OUESSANT, IN FRENCH) IS TWELVE MILES OFF THE westernmost point of mainland France, twenty-five miles as the bird flies from the French naval base at Brest. It's a rocky, claw-shaped island: five miles long, two miles wide. About 1,500 people lived there as the eighteenth century ended—mostly sailors, shepherds, and their families. One traveler described it as "Storm Island . . . austere and windswept. . . . The name alone evokes dread. . . . It is one of the ocean's notorious places, the treacherous leeward shore at the entrance to the English Channel, a deadly outcrop of rocks among strong tidal currents."[1]

On December 10, 1781, French admiral Luc Urbain de Bouëxic, Comte de Guichen, left Brest with nineteen warships and seven frigates escorting a one hundred fifty-ship convoy. His plan was to protect the convoy from any coast-hugging enemy ships, then separate his charges in mid-ocean: Two of the warships and some of the convoy would reinforce French positions in the Indian Ocean. Vaudreuil, Grasse's future second-in-command at the Saintes, would take seven warships and the bulk of the convoy to the Caribbean. Guichen would sail the remaining ten warships to join an allied fleet in Spain.[2]

Guichen, 69, earned a reputation for being the French navy's best defensive tactician and for his ability to move fleets efficiently. He also probably had more scientific knowledge than any of his British counterparts. Guichen had fought his first battles against the British in the 1740s, but he wasn't rusty. In 1778, he was part of the fleet that embarrassed the British in an inconclusive naval battle one hundred miles off Ushant. Two years later, as commander of the French West Indian fleet, he fought defensively and inconclusively three times against Rodney.[3]

Preparing Guichen's convoy for sailing was a secret the French couldn't keep. By mid-October, British spies reported convoy preparations, and on November 22, London ordered one of its admirals "to use your utmost efforts to take or destroy it."[4]

If Guichen was a tactician, British rear admiral Richard Kempenfelt, 63, built his reputation as a brilliant naval jack-of-all-trades and reformer. The navy controller described him as "not merely a sea officer, but a man of deep knowledge in most professions." After promoting him above other senior officers to fleet captain (a fleet admiral's chief of staff), George III referred to his political abilities: "Much respected by all parties and one well-qualified to heal all the little breaches." At one point, Kempenfelt published a book of poetry.[5]

He sent regular letters to the Admiralty suggesting reforms, innovations, improved strategies and tactics, some philosophical, others practical. He offered a detailed proposal for a signaling protocol, suggestions for more efficient rope-making, and a way to bring more discipline to crews: "Our seamen are more licentious than those of other nations. The reason is, they have less religion." (His appearance was puritanical as well. He wore plain clothes and was once mistaken for a clerk on his own flagship.)[6]

He could be blunt. Complaining about a superior, Kempenfelt said: "An admiral who commands in chief should have the esteem, the respect, and the confidence of his officers, but our admiral fails in all these. He never associates with any of them; though good-natured, his manners are rude; his impatience is such that when an officer comes, he almost shoves him out of the ship; he never invites any to dine with him." What's worse, the admiral didn't keep his ships in sailing readiness. "It seems very extraordinary to me that we keep vessels as cruisers in the service who can't sail. 'Tis really throwing so much money away."[7]

About one hundred eighty miles southwest of Ushant, one of Kempenfelt's scouting frigates reported that it had found Guichen and the convoy. On the morning of December 12, 1781, Kempenfelt and his squadron of twelve warships and seven frigates caught up with the French.

There, the British saw something unusual: Guichen's warships were not only separated from the convoy, but they were downwind of it. Kempenfelt took advantage. "Having a prospect of passing between the enemy's ships of war and a great part of their convoy, I continued a pressed sail with a view of cutting them off, and succeeded in part," he said.[8]

The British captured nine of the convoy ships that day, and another five stragglers in ensuing days. They took as prisoners about 1,000 soldiers and 330 sailors. The cargo they seized from one of the ships was typical: 230 barrels of wine, 100 barrels of beef and pork, 20 tons of balls, 150 muskets, and 20 tons of lead, power, and tents.[9]

Most of the convoy scattered when Kempenfelt began the attack, but Guichen stayed in the area, albeit helpless to engage. The next morning, both enemies prepared to fight. "I formed a line," Kempenfelt said, "but perceiving their force so much superior to my squadron, I did not think it advisable to hazard an action." He returned to England with his prizes. If he had had a larger squadron, then Guichen would have been "within an ace of suffering a most ridiculous disgrace—that of having all his convoy taken from him before his face."[10]

What Kempenfelt couldn't finish, the weather did. Guichen tried to reassemble the convoy, but a storm scattered the ships again and damaged many of his warships. Most returned to France. Only Vaudreuil, another warship, and five convoy ships made it to the West Indies. Historians speculate that Grasse might have won at the Saintes if the planned complement had reached him.[11] Washington later said the battle and storm was a "disaster" that gave the British "fresh spirits."[12] Franklin, in France, saw the practical impact: "We have great quantities of supplies of all kinds ready here to be sent over, and which would have been on their way before this time, if the unlucky loss of the transports that were under Mr. de Guichen . . . had not created a difficulty."[13]

Kempenfelt's next major assignment was to command the three-deck, 100-gun *Royal George*, which, when it launched in 1756, was the world's largest warship. On August 29, 1782, it floated in the dockyards being readied for sailing to the Mediterranean. Because of a leak below its waterline, workers tilted it slightly to one side for repair. Suddenly, there was a loud noise, the keel's bottom gave way, and it quickly sank. At least eight hundred people on board drowned, including tradesmen, women and children, sailors, and Kempenfelt, who was in his cabin.

"Brave Kempenfelt is gone," wrote poet William Cowper.

"His last sea fight is fought.

His work of glory done."[14]

Four months after Guichen's disaster, a smaller French convoy met its fate eighty miles off Ushant. Guarded by three warships, the eighteen-ship convoy was "laden with stores, provisions, and ammunition" headed to the Indian Ocean. This time, the British squadron of twelve warships wasn't outgunned.[15]

On the morning of April 20, 1782, after heavy night fighting, the French armed transport ship *Pégase* surrendered. About eighty of its seven hundred-man crew were killed, and the *Pégase* itself suffered massive damage. The British had five casualties. The *Pégase* was overmatched: It was built in haste, its captain had assumed command just a week before, and its crew was inexperienced landsmen, since the French couldn't find enough sailors. In addition to the *Pégase*, the British captured twelve convoy ships.[16]

32. Secret Mission to the Arctic

O NE OF VAUDREUIL'S CAPTAINS HAD BEEN PLANNING A SECRET mission since 1780. At first, storms delayed him. Then, other assignments. In early 1782, his participation in the St. Kitts attack diverted him. In April, it was the Saintes, where he missed the fighting because his ship was towing a disabled one to safety.[1]

Jean-François de Galaup, Comte de Lapérouse, 41, was the only surviving son of a minor aristocrat. He joined the navy at fifteen, was wounded twice and captured once in the Seven Years' War, and, like most career officers, served across the globe, from Newfoundland south to the West Indies, east to the Indian Ocean, and off the shores of Europe. When war broke out in 1778, and before the year was over, he helped capture twelve prizes in the North Sea. Later, he fought successfully in the West Indies, and off South Carolina and Spain.

The navy gave him a special assignment in late 1780: He sailed to Boston as captain of a new frigate, the *Astrée*, named for the heroine of a popular seventeenth century novel. What made his mission special was his cargo: 1.5 million livres (conservatively, $315,000 today) needed for payrolls, supplies, and for supporting France's American allies. Mission accomplished, he sailed to the West Indies.

After the Saintes, Lapérouse eluded the British and reached Cap Français. There, Vaudreuil named him captain of a warship, the 74-gun *Sceptre*, and put under his command the *Astrée* and another frigate, the *Engageant*. The secret mission was on. Lapérouse's squadron would destroy a source of British wealth: Fur-trading posts on Hudson Bay, then Canada's northernmost settlements.

The fur trade—in the eighteenth century, it meant mostly beaver pelts—grew as the European hat and felt industries grew. The highest-quality pelts came from Hudson Bay's huge drainage basin where Hudson's Bay Company (HBC) maintained trading posts. Its most important was York Factory, opened in 1684 on the bay's southwestern shore.[2]

About one hundred fifty miles by water to the northwest was Fort Prince of Wales, built in 1717 as both a trading post and fort to protect against French raids. "The strength of the fort itself was such as would have resisted the attacks of a more considerable force," wrote Edward Umfreville, York Factory's second-in-command in 1782. (His 1790 book was the angry result of a salary dispute with HBC.) "It was built of the strongest materials, its walls were of great thickness and very durable, it having been 40 years in building . . ." But, Umfreville said, HBC, "in their consummate wisdom," failed to man it adequately. "What folly." The fort also had no drinking-water source, no moat, poor masonry, and a low elevation.[3]

Given their Atlantic and Caribbean priorities, Britain let the posts' isolation be their best defense. Only one supply ship arrived each year, in August or early September, when the bay's ice, as well as the sea channels, were melted. Ships that stayed too long would be iced in for another ten months. "In the summer, such as it is . . . myriads of tormenting mosquitoes" arrive, an HBC employee wrote in 1784. "From the end of October to the end of April every step we walk is in snow shoes. . . . All our movements more, or less, were for self-preservation. . . . The cold is so intense, that everything in a manner is shivered by it." Umfreville was more graphic: Rum and brandy can freeze "to the consistency of honey. . . . [Native] women have been found frozen to death with a young infant likewise froze, clasping its arms round the mother's neck."[4]

HBC's leader at Prince of Wales since 1776 was Samuel Hearne, 37, "a handsome man of six feet in height, of a ruddy complexion and remarkably well made, enjoying good health." A native Londoner, Hearne joined the navy and saw action in the Seven Years' War. After the war, he joined the crew of an HBC trading boat out of Prince of Wales. Later, he led the first of three HBC exploring expeditions into the interior, and took copious notes about the Indians, flora, and fauna. On July 17, 1777, he became the first European to reach the Arctic Ocean by land, the first to see and cross Great Slave Lake, and the first to conclude that Hudson Bay didn't connect to a northwest passage to the Pacific.[5]

Lapérouse left Cap Français on May 31, 1782, his destination a secret to his two captains, crews, and nearly three hundred soldiers until they reached New England. In mid-July, they reached Hudson Strait, the passage from the Atlantic to the bay. There, they traded with natives for warmer clothes. Another two weeks, and they entered the bay. Eight days later, on the early evening of August 8, they arrived off Prince of Wales. "The sight of such unexpected visitors did not fail to engage the attention of the Factory [post] people, who were not used to see so many strangers in these seas," Umfreville said.[6]

Around 3 A.M. on August 9—summer sunlight is extended at higher latitudes—they landed troops, and two officers met with Hearne. They demanded his surrender. With just thirty-eight white men at the post, Hearne had no choice. He surrendered without a shot. "The British flag was lowered, and a table cloth from the Governor's table hoisted in its stead." That day and the next, the French demolished the stone fort as best they could, loaded their ships with HBC furs and goods, and burned the wooden buildings.[7]

On the 11th, with the *Severn*, Hearne's small ship, as a prize, Lapérouse began sailing toward York Factory. In the distance, they saw a ship, presumably a British supply ship, headed for the Churchill River. One of the French ships chased it, but it escaped.

They arrived on August 20 at York Factory, where Hearne's colleague, Humphrey Marten, had been dealing with a smallpox epidemic that devastated the nearby Cree and Ojibwa Indian communities. Just the day before, Marten wrote in his journal: "The Surgeon visited the sick. Another boy dead. A few out of danger; some dubious." His next entry recorded more trouble: "Three masted ships were seen in the offing. . . . Loaded our guns to make the best defense we can." On the 21st: "The ships were of force and an enemy." Two days later: "We are now assured the French are landed in great force." Lapérouse delivered his surrender demand on August 24, "offering us our lives and private property, but threatening the utmost fury should we resist." Like Hearne, Marten surrendered. With hindsight, Umfreville was indignant at Marten's "tepid stupefaction." York Factory "was most ingloriously given up in about ten minutes . . . to a half-starved wretched group of Frenchmen." As with Prince of Wales, the French burned the post, but in a humane gesture, possibly at Marten's request, they left some food and supplies on shore for traders returning from the interior and the ill, starving Indians.[8]

With the weather and season turning harsh, the now-four French ships left York Factory on September 2. By the 10th, they reached Resolution Island at the mouth of Hudson Strait. There, Lapérouse allowed Hearne and the thirty-two prisoners to proceed on parole in the *Severn* to Britain. The *Astrée* sailed for France, while Lapérouse's *Sceptre* and *Engageante* headed for the allied naval base in Cadiz, Spain. All arrived at their destinations, but the crews of the *Sceptre* and the *Engageante* suffered. Of the *Sceptre*'s 536 sailors and soldiers, seventy died, most from scurvy, and another four hundred were so ill they couldn't work. The *Engageante*'s crew was proportionately decimated.[9]

Lapérouse had destroyed or seized furs and supplies worth seven to 11 million livres (at least $1.5 million today). He wrote his mother: "I must tell you that I had neither a chart nor a pilot. Not a single Frenchman in the last hundred years had come within three hundred leagues of this bay."[10]

He impressed his British prisoners. He allowed Hearne to keep his journal of exploration and suggested he publish it. Lapérouse's "politeness, humanity, and goodness, secured him the affection of all the company's officers, and on parting at the mouth of Hudson Straits, they felt the same sensation which the dearest friends feel in an interview preceding a long separation," said Umfreville.[11]

Hearne returned to Hudson Bay in late summer 1783. There, still employed by HBC, he built a new trading post across the Churchill River from the destroyed Prince of Wales fort. By 1787, his health began to fail, and he left Churchill that summer, retiring to London. There, he mixed with scientists and naturalists, and wrote a book about his experiences. It was published posthumously. Canada honored Hearne in a 1971 postage stamp, and Charles Darwin cited his nature observations three times in *The Origin of Species*. The ruins of Fort Prince of Wales is a national park, and Hearne's final settlement, Churchill, attracts tourists from around the world to view polar bears.[12]

Lapérouse married the daughter of a Mauritius merchant. "I fell madly in love with a very beautiful and charming girl" in 1775, he wrote, but didn't marry her then because she had no money, and his father disapproved. The war over, Lapérouse married her anyway in 1783, but he didn't spend much time with her. Two years later, he began his career as an explorer, leading a two-ship royal expedition. It sailed throughout the Pacific, from Cape Horn to the Gulf of Alaska; to Kamchatka, Japan, China, and the Philippines; to Samoa; to Australia—and then, the record ends. His ships apparently foundered in a hurricane. Lapérouse's wreck was found in 1826 near the Solomon Islands. Several geographic landmarks were named after him, including the town of La Perouse, near Sydney, and Lapérouse Bay off Maui.[13]

33. Coastal War: Halifax to Boston

H ALIFAX, NOVA SCOTIA, WAS A NEW TOWN, EVEN FOR THE NEW
World. Its first settlers arrived in 1749, part of a plan to build
a strong naval base to counter the French and to protect British
interests in the cod fishery. Its protected harbor is ice-free year
round, and it is four hundred miles closer to London than Boston.
When the rebel army forced the British to evacuate Boston in 1776,
Loyalists took refuge in Halifax.

If Halifax was a British stronghold, Boston harbored the rebels.
Settled in 1630, it is four hundred fifty miles southwest of Halifax by
sea.

Between Halifax and Boston, thousands of islands lie off the
Atlantic coast—more than 3,100 alone in what is now Maine (a
Massachusetts district until 1820, just as New Brunswick was part of
Nova Scotia until 1784). On shore, the Maine and Nova Scotia
coastlines are broken comb teeth. Their coastlines extend 8,100
miles, including bays, inlets, and fiords. It's the equivalent of sailing
from Halifax to London and back, and back to London again. These
are rocky shores, but beyond the rocks are dense woods. Even
today, they cover ninety percent of Maine and eighty percent of
Nova Scotia.

This was frontier. As late as 1779, Micmac Indians attacked
British settlers two hundred fifty miles north of Halifax. British
marines fought the Micmacs, took sixteen prisoners, and forced
them to sign a peace treaty. The last Indian attack in Maine
occurred in August 1781, when natives from Québec plundered a
remote settlement and took two prisoners.[1]

Along the coast, rebel privateers and the British navy harassed each other for the war's duration. One settlement, near the mouth of the Penobscot River and almost equidistant between Halifax and Boston, became a center of conflict for two hundred years. Pilgrim traders founded the Penobscot post (near current Castine, Maine) in 1629. The French and British fought over Penobscot in nearly all of their ensuing wars. In 1673, Flemish pirates attacked and kidnapped the governor. Two years later, settlers drove off a Dutch attack.

In the revolution, both sides saw Penobscot's strategic value. Its trees turned into ship masts and lumber. Its harbor provided a base for rebel privateers—or British navy ships. A Boston legislator told Washington he was concerned about Penobscot. If the British controlled it, they could "furnish themselves with masts, necessary for the repairs of their ships in America and every species of lumber for the supply of their West India islands; as well as effectually prevent the inhabitants of Boston, and all our other seaports, from receiving that supply of wood and lumber, which seemed necessary to their existence."[2]

In February 1779, Henry Clinton, in New York, ordered troops from Halifax to fortify Penobscot. By mid-July, more than six hundred men, accompanied by five ships, had nearly completed the fort. Massachusetts responded by sending to Penobscot a fleet of twenty armed ships and seventeen transports carrying 800 marines and 1,200 militia. But unlike Grasse and Bouillé at St. Kitts, the rebel naval and army leaders didn't coordinate their efforts, and different militia companies had their own ideas. They landed troops on July 25, and besieged the British fort.[3]

Two weeks later, a British relief squadron of seven ships arrived. For the Boston men, Penobscot became a catastrophe. Their ships either surrendered, ran aground upriver, or were destroyed. The British killed nearly five hundred men. "The remains of their army and sailors are now exploring their way through thick woods and desert wastes, where probably many of them will perish with hunger," the British captain George Collier reported.[4]

Abigail Adams spoke of the ensuing recriminations. Boston is "groaning under disgrace, disappointment and the heaviest debt incurred by this state since the commencement of the war." For the rest of the war, Penobscot ate away at Boston, its presence interfering with fishing and timber businesses, and threatening privateers.[5]

A Maine county pleaded for help in a 1782 petition to the legislature: "Nearly all our coasting vessels and fishing boats have fell into their [enemy] hands . . . Many of our houses they have robbed or burned and carried off much of the stocks of cattle and sheep. . . . The enemy has kept the people under constant fears, frequent alarms, and expensive watching. . . . Large quantities of lumber decaying on the landings—coasting vessels and fishing boats nearly all taken or destroyed—and the enemy holding a strong post in the heart of the county."[6]

When they could, the residents fought back. On August 8, 1782, near what is now Kennebunkport, two Loyalist or British ships burned a boat and seized another. About forty rebel militia fought back, and they killed sixteen or seventeen of the one hundred fifty British. The only militia casualty was its captain, killed "with a musket ball through his breast, which brought on instant death." Later that month, a Massachusetts state navy vessel attacked a Loyalist ship anchored in Penobscot Bay, seized it, and sailed it back to Boston as a prize.[7]

Still, Penobscot remained "very troublesome," French general Rochambeau told Vaudreuil, who, in late July, was with his fleet in Boston. Massachusetts was "very anxious" to retake the post. Vaudreuil had heard it firsthand and made Washington an offer: "I would wish to attack Penobscot with the troops of land which I have on board." Washington declined. He thought Massachusetts would sacrifice the French fleet for Penobscot, when he had more important priorities. "The object is by no means equal to the risk that will attend the attempt," he told Vaudreuil. "Your fleet will be placed in the great hazard of being totally destroyed."[8]

But raids continued, and Massachusetts kept the pressure on Washington. In March 1783, Washington pushed back again. "Penobscot is a secondary object," he said. Attacking it would "waste time for an unnecessary purpose."[9]

Massachusetts wouldn't take Penobscot during the war—territorial disputes in Maine weren't resolved until an 1842 treaty—but preying on Nova Scotia ports and ships never stopped.

"The lawless plunderers have lately done us much mischief and been so great a terror to the inhabitants," said Captain Andrew

Snape Hamond, Nova Scotia's governor. The rebels intended to "annoy the coasts of the Bay of Fundy during the ensuing summer by small vessels as may elude the vigilance of his Majesty's ships by keeping in creeks and shallow places."[10]

Despite some successes—British ships captured two privateers in May 1782, and another in June after a battle that killed or wounded half the rebel crew—the navy couldn't be everywhere. From spring 1782 to the war's end, rebel privateers experienced their greatest success. Small squadrons not only took larger ships, but also picked off fishing boats and, contrary to the rules, held prisoners for ransom.[11]

Captain Noah Stoddard, commander of the *Scammel*, was one of those Massachusetts privateers. Sometime in June, Stoddard and four other captains planned what they hoped would be a lucrative raid on Lunenburg, Nova Scotia. Lunenburg was even younger than Halifax. In the early 1750s, then-Governor Edward Cornwallis (the Yorktown general's uncle) complained to London that English immigrants to Nova Scotia were "lazy and worthless." London obliged by recruiting German protestants. By 1753, some 2,700 of the immigrants arrived in Halifax. The government resettled two-thirds of them in other parts of the colony. Their incentive was 50 acres, free from taxes or rent for a decade. Several hundred of the immigrants lived in Lunenburg's forty or fifty homes at the base of its hilly peninsula sixty miles west of Halifax. Perhaps 1,500 people, half of them children, lived in the area.[12]

On July 1, 1782, of the town proper's sixty men, twenty were away, and twenty more were sick, infirm, or lame. Stoddard's squadron landed ninety men about two miles from town, intending a surprise. A farmer's wife saw them, and her husband ran into town to warn the militia. When the raiders arrived, militia colonel John Creighton and five men already were in a blockhouse, and they fired at their enemy, wounding three.[13]

English-born Creighton, 61, a British cavalry veteran, was one of Lunenburg's original settlers. He helped lay out the town, assign plots, and led the militia. In the 1760s and early 1770s, he served as a judge and assemblyman, and had amassed a fortune by Nova Scotia standards. He was, said a former governor, "a man of good character and understanding, in easy circumstances."[14]

Around 7 A.M., the privateer ships entered the harbor. Caught between the ships' cannon and the ground force, Creighton surrendered. By 11 A.M., after a house-to-house search, the raiders secured the town. "The rebels . . . spiked the guns, broke everything, turned the guns and balls down to the water. Some remained at Mr. Creighton's, spoilt and burned his house," a militia officer reported. "They carried the colonel, with the others, prisoners on board their vessels. . . . Now they fell a-plundering the chief houses and the shops . . . We are at present almost without arms, ammunition, provision, and merchandise. Besides, I hear they have carried off from some houses money—gold and silver."[15]

A militia relief force arrived in the early afternoon. Under a truce flag, the raiders threatened to torch the town if the militia attacked. The militia refrained. The raiders got a bonus from their threat: Merchants and other residents ransomed Lunenburg's safety by giving the rebels a £1,000 promissory note.

Stoddard sailed away in the early evening, arriving in Boston two weeks later. (Creighton was eventually repatriated, and died in 1807 at eighty-six.) The attack outraged the British and their colonists. Bostonians praised the raiders' moderation: "The strictest decorum was observed toward the inhabitants, their wearing apparel and household furniture being inviolably preserved for their use."[16]

34. Coastal War: Delaware to Chesapeake

CHESAPEAKE BAY IS TWO HUNDRED MILES LONG, BUT ITS indentations create a shoreline of almost twelve thousand miles—fifty percent longer than Maine's and Nova Scotia's combined. To Chesapeake's north is Delaware Bay, sixty miles long, with as smooth a shoreline as Chesapeake's is complex.

Who controlled Chesapeake and Delaware bays directly affected the government and economy. Near the head of Chesapeake was Baltimore; in 1791, with 13,500 people, it was the nation's fourth largest city and a major port. Delaware Bay was even more important: At its head, Philadelphia was not only the English-speaking world's third largest city in 1775 (after London and Edinburgh) with almost forty thousand people; it was the Whig capital.[1]

When the British abandoned Philadelphia in 1778 after a nine-month occupation, the bays continued to shelter Loyalist enclaves, and Loyalist and British ships preyed on rebel shipping and settlements. "The barges and small vessels of the enemy . . . can pass up and down any of our rivers with impunity, to the great disquiet of the inhabitants," a Maryland militia colonel complained. One Virginia man told a friend, "The business of horrid nightly depredation proceeds now, as before, in the same relentless and cruel manner."[2]

The Continental navy was incapable of protecting the bays' merchant ships: From 1775 through 1783, Congress built, bought, or borrowed fifty-seven ships. By 1782, all but two were inactive, the rest being captured, burned, lost at sea, wrecked, or sold. Congress bought a third active ship in late 1782.[3]

The state navies also were thin. French ships helped when they could.

In Philadelphia, merchants paid to convert a trading ship to a 16-gun armed escort for duty in Delaware Bay. They named the ship *Hyder Ally*, after a native leader fighting the British in India. To lead the ship and 110-man crew, they hired an unemployed Continental navy captain who arrived in Philadelphia three days before, on March 21, 1782, after escaping from a British prison.[4]

Captain Joshua Barney, 23, had already made a name for himself. He was a Baltimore man, one of fourteen children of a prosperous family. His parents apprenticed him to a counting-house at age ten; he insisted on a maritime career. By fourteen, he had made several voyages to Europe, and was a second mate on his brother-in-law's merchant ship. In 1775, his brother-in-law died one month into a nine-month trip. Barney assumed command, conducted his European business with the help of a British commercial agent, was arrested in a dispute and then released with diplomatic help, participated in a European attack on North African pirates, and, arriving back in Chesapeake Bay, was boarded by the British navy, inspected for contraband, and informed of the fighting in Massachusetts.[5]

That same month, October 1775, Barney enlisted in the Continental navy. He served on three ships. As a lieutenant, he sailed to Statia in the same ship the Dutch saluted; it was the incident that infuriated Rodney. Later that year, while commanding a captured Tory privateer, he surrendered to a larger British ship. It was the first of three times the British would capture him in coming years serving on both privateers and Continental ships.[6]

He escaped from a British prison in May 1781, after impersonating a British officer, connecting with rebel sympathizers, and making his way to Amsterdam. There, he boarded Alexander Gillon's *South Carolina*, supposedly headed to America. When the *South Carolina* arrived in Spain after Gillon's circuitous prize-hunting detour, Barney and other passengers debarked for more reliable passage home. The passengers believed Barney saved their lives during a storm that Gillon had been unequal to. "The ship became unmanageable," one said, "the officers lost their self-possession, and the crew all confidence in them, while for a few minutes, all was confusion and dismay. Happily for us, Commodore Barney was among the passengers. . . . He flew upon deck, saw the danger, assumed the command, the men obeyed, and he soon had her again under control."[7]

On April 7, 1782, Barney began his first assignment as the *Hyder Ally* captain: He escorted seven merchant ships to the mouth of the bay. There, they anchored, waiting for the right winds and tides to enter the Atlantic. The next morning, two British navy ships cruising off the bay saw the eight anchored rebel ships. A Loyalist privateer, the *Fair American*, joined the British *Quebec* and *General Monk*.

Barney's *Hyder Ally* headed for the British ships in hopes the convoy would scatter and escape. One convoy ship ran aground, and its crew deserted. The British captured another. The *Fair American*, the Tory privateer, then either ran aground or took the disabled rebel ship. (The accounts are confusing.) The *Quebec*, a frigate and larger than the others, stayed outside the bay, concerned that it, too, might hit some shoals.[8]

Now, the fight was down to the *Hyder Ally* and the *General Monk*. The *General Monk* was a captured rebel privateer out of Charlestown, originally named *General Washington*. Its new name honored a seventeenth-century general who had helped restore the monarchy after Cromwell's death. Josias Rogers had captained the *General Monk* since December 1780; under him, the ship took sixty rebel prizes. Rogers, 27, joined the British navy in 1771; his first captain was Andrew Snape Hamond, who later became governor of Halifax. Like Barney, Rogers had been a prisoner of war, captured after being driven ashore off Delaware Bay during a storm. He escaped from the enemy while on parole in Philadelphia in 1777. He received command of the *General Monk* after distinguishing himself in the British capture of Charlestown.[9]

The *General Monk* was larger than the *Hyder Ally*, had more— and heavier—guns, and a larger crew. Rogers judged "from the appearance of the *Hyder Ally* that she was an easy prize," a British sympathizer said. "We shall have the Yankee ship in five minutes," Rogers told a crewman. He closed in to board it. Seeing this— according to Whig accounts—Barney told his men to follow the "rule of contrary," meaning his next order would be the reverse of what he said. And Barney said it loud enough so Rogers heard. Rogers was fooled. The *Hyder Ally*'s rigging got entangled with the

General Monk's boom in a way that gave the rebel ship a good position to rake its enemy, firing twenty broadsides in twenty-six minutes.[10]

Rogers told a different story. As he neared the *Hyder Ally*, according to a contemporary biographer, "he found she was so full of men, and so well-provided with defenses against board[ing]," that he began a cannonade. But his cannon became overheated, and many came off their moorings. That was the sole reason for his surrender, he told the Admiralty.[11]

Both sides agreed on the result: the *General Monk* was devastated. Twenty of its 136-man crew were dead, and thirty-three were wounded, including Rogers, who was wounded in his foot and couldn't stand. (The *Hyder Ally* had four killed and eleven wounded.) "The *General Monk*'s decks were, in every direction, besmeared with blood, covered with the dead and wounded, and resembled a charnel house," said an eyewitness. Barney himself was surprised at his victory. "When we were about to engage it, it was the opinion of myself, as well as my crew, that she would have blown us to atoms, but we were determined she should gain her victory dearly."[12]

Rogers was so badly wounded in the battle that he was forced to use crutches for at least two years, and was limited in walking for another five. After the war, he served on smuggling duty, and in 1790, was promoted to flag captain. Ironically, in the West Indies, he commanded the *Québec*—the frigate that was unable to help him with the *Hyder Ally*. Before leaving for England in 1795, he stopped at Grenada to suppress a French-incited slave rebellion. After two months of successfully stabilizing the situation for the whites, he caught yellow fever and died in his *Québec* cabin.

Barney became a successful Baltimore businessman. He was a less-successful politician, twice defeated for Congress. He served in France's navy from 1795 to 1802, then distinguished himself trying to defend Chesapeake in the War of 1812. While en route to a new home in Kentucky in 1818, he died in Pittsburgh, where he was buried. By his own count, he fought in twenty-six battles and was captured six times. Over the years, the navy named four ships after him.

Gillon, after failing to bring Barney and other passengers to America, but later helping the Spanish to seize the Bahamas, sailed the *South Carolina* to Philadelphia, where John Joyner, an experienced South Carolina captain, took command.

He didn't command it for long. On December 19, three British ships spotted the *South Carolina* off Delaware Bay. They chased it for eighteen hours, then fought it for another two before Joyner surrendered. (One crew member charged that Joyner stayed in his cabin preparing his full-dress uniform and newly powdered hair, then "shamefully surrendered without resistance." But a 1784 court-martial acquitted Joyner.) The *South Carolina* ended the war as a troop transport, carrying Hessians back to Europe.[13]

Chesapeake Bay inlets made it possible for Loyalist privateers to sail directly to rebel properties, burn them, and steal their livestock, slaves, and other valuables. In response, the Maryland legislature created a small state fleet of barges funded by confiscations and sales of Loyalist property. With sails and oars, the barges were able to negotiate both shallow and deeper water. Captain Zedekiah Walley (also spelled "Whaley") led the fleet in the *Protector*, built for sixty men and armed with a large cannon that was able to swivel.[14]

Walley had success from the start, capturing at least six prizes from mid-1781 to fall 1782. When, in November, he heard reports of Tory raiders near the bay's entrance, he left Baltimore with three other barges and a schooner to try to capture them. On the 15th, he saw two Loyalist barges and captured one. Twelve days later, sixty miles from the bay's mouth, Walley saw more enemy ships. He sent for reinforcements from Onancock, a small town fifteen miles to the east on the bay's eastern shore in Virginia. There, Walley found enough volunteers to man two captured Loyalist barges, as well as a new second-in-command. Lieutenant Colonel John Cropper was a veteran Continental officer who had fought at Brandywine, Germantown, and Monmouth, and he stayed with the army at Valley Forge. He resigned in 1779 to help protect his neighbors on the Chesapeake from marauding Tories and British detachments.[15]

With Cropper and reinforcements, Walley left Onancok on November 29 after scouts told him the enemy was now in Cagey's Strait (now Kedges), about twenty miles northwest. The next day, he found the enemy fleet, led by Captain John Kidd, a Virginia native and successful raider. Two months before, on September 18, Kidd had captured a Pennsylvania privateer in Delaware Bay that was returning to Philadelphia from Cuba with £5,000 in gold and silver as well as a cargo of sugar. A rebel account said Kidd or one of his men killed the captain after he had surrendered. Kidd cashed in his prize in British-held New York. Kidd manned his six barges with Loyalist refugees and escaped slaves.[16]

The *Protector* sailed faster than its colleagues, and Walley was first to engage Kidd in what became known as the Battle of the Barges. When Kidd's barges began firing, about 300 yards away, Walley's other ships disappeared. "This dastardly conduct of our comrades brought on our barge the whole fire of the enemy, which was very severe," Cropper said. Then things got worse. A small powder magazine blew up, "the explosion of which burned three or four people to death, caused five or six more, all afire, to leap overboard, and the alarm of the barge blowing up made several others swim for their lives. . . . There was one continual shower of musket balls, boarding pikes, cutlasses, cold shot, and iron . . . for eight or 10 minutes."

Of the *Protector*'s sixty-five men, twenty-five were killed or drowned, and another twenty-nine wounded, some mortally. Only eleven escaped. Cropper described his own wounds: "Myself was wounded by a cutlass on the head, slightly by a pick on the face and thigh, slightly by a cutlass on the shoulder, and after the surrender, was knocked down by a four-pound rammer, the blow of which was unfortunately near upon the same place where the cutlass hit."[17]

The Loyalists suffered nineteen killed or wounded. Kidd agreed to parole his captives and return them to Onancock, provided Cropper arrange for care of the Loyalist wounded. Cropper agreed. Cropper's wounds led to an unexpected tragedy: In December, his wife was changing his bandages, holding several pins in her mouth. She accidentally swallowed one and died, presumably from choking or internal bleeding. After the war, Cropper continued to be active in the militia, served in Maryland's legislature, and was county sheriff. As a state senator, he once threated to cut off the ears of a man who abused Washington's memory.[18]

Joseph Wheland Jr. (also spelled Whalen) was another Loyalist privateer working the bays. He was arrested in 1776 for burning a Whig sloop in his native Maryland, then released after making restitution and promising he'd behave. He later commanded a tender to a British warship and started his privateer career by seizing a wreck. Rebel militia arrested him again, but he escaped from a Baltimore jail.[19]

A Whig captain, John Greenwood, lost his merchant ship to Wheland in fall 1781, and he left a description: "Captain Whalen appeared to me to be as great a villain as ever was unhung. . . . He was a tall, slim, gallows-looking fellow, in his shirt sleeves, with a gold-laced jacket on that he had robbed from some old trooper on the Eastern Shore." Greenwood recognized one of Whelan's crewmen as a six-foot-tall "mulatto," an escaped slave. Another man Greenwood knew personally. When he asked if the man had joined "these pirates," Whelan interjected that his commission was as good as any captain's in the British navy.[20]

From 1781 into 1783, Wheland and his fleet of four barges successfully attacked rebel shipping. On February 17, 1783, he raided the village of Benedict, more than twenty miles up the Patuxent River, which feeds into the bay. Maryland's governor complained to Washington, saying Britain's pledge to end offensive operations "have been most shamefully violated by the enemy's barges and armed vessels . . . There are now in the bay 11 barges and one sloop and two schooners who proceed in detached parties not only capturing our vessels, but landing on our shores and wasting and plundering the property of the people of this state." He used the Wheland raid as an example. Wheland "plundered the town," burning one home and stealing the slaves of another. Other Tories "make incursions up the rivers on the Eastern Shore robbing and plundering."[21]

At the start of 1783, the Continental navy had three ships. John Manley captained one of them, the *Hague*.

British-born Manley was in his early fifties. He is a cipher until 1757, when he lived in Massachusetts. An early British historian said his life until then was that of a "master of a merchantman before he took arms against his sovereign."[22]

Colonel John Glover, leader of a trusted Whig amphibious regiment (despite, in Washington's view, its African-American crewmen), recommended Manley for "Washington's navy," the pre-Continental fleet that supported the army. Manley had its first success in November 1775, capturing five prizes within a month, including a British ordnance ship that gave Washington needed arms and ammunition. "Captain Manley's good fortune seems to stick to him," one of Washington's officers said. Whig civilians honored him with a poem: "Brave Manley he is stout, and his men have proved true; by taking of those English ships, he makes their jacks to rue."[23]

In mid-1776, Congress named him captain of one of the two newly built Continental frigates, but within half a year, he was fighting with the other captains over seniority and tactics. A Boston politician said Manley was a "blunt, honest, and, I believe, brave officer," but Captain John Paul Jones described him as "despicable" and "altogether unfit to command a frigate." He wasn't alone in detesting Manley.[24]

British captain George Collier (who would later defeat the rebels at Penobscot) helped capture Manley in summer 1777. When he was exchanged a year later, no Continental captaincies were available, so he turned to privateering. The British captured Manley again in 1779, but he escaped. In mid-year, they captured him again, and this time sent him to an English prison. There, he wrote to Franklin, pleading for his help in getting exchanged. "I am the unfortunate Manley that commanded the ship *Hancock* in the service of the United States . . . and am still desirous of retaliating for the ill treatment I daily receive which without any recourse to humanity."[25]

In late 1781, Manley was exchanged. He arrived home in Boston in spring 1782. There, he waited. In September, Manley became captain of the Continental frigate the *Hague*, originally named *Deane*, after a diplomat who had become persona non grata.[26]

The next month, he sailed for the West Indies. In mid-January, the *Hague* ran into five British warships. Discretion meant sailing to the French harbor at Guadeloupe, but Manley didn't make it before the British caught up with him. "I have been drove on shore after a 36-hour chase by a 50-gun ship and lay at the mercy of her incessant fire for two days, who, with the assistance of a 74[-gun ship] and two other sail of the line to back her up, were not sparing of a heavy and brisk cannonade," he reported. But he made it to

Guadeloupe on January 13, with just one man killed and one slight-ly wounded.[27]

The cruise turned out to be profitable: He captured five prizes, including a merchant ship, the *Baille*. Manley had captured the rebel navy's first prize of the war; the *Baille* was the navy's last prize of the war.[28]

Manley died in Boston in 1793, but historians know little about his postwar years. Three U.S. navy ships were named after him, the most recent being a destroyer that was decommissioned in 1983.

John Barry, 38, a more successful captain—the British wounded him, but never captured him, allowing him to amass dozens of prizes—commanded the other surviving Continental frigate, the *Alliance*. Barry was an Irish-born son of a malt-house clerk. He went to sea as a youth, and at fifteen settled in Philadelphia. By the time the war began, Barry was a wealthy ship owner.

When the war began, he joined the navy as a captain, and made the Continental navy's first capture of a British navy ship. Although he lost two battles during the war, forcing him to either burn or scuttle his ships, his success earned him Congress's trust. In 1780, it named him commander of the *Alliance*, a two-year-old, Massa-chusetts-built 32-gun frigate.

The third surviving Continental ship was the 20-gun *Duc de Lauzun*, a former British customs ship that Congress bought in Europe in late 1782. It rendezvoused with Barry and the *Alliance* in Philadelphia in January 1783. Their orders were to sail to Cuba and bring back 576,000 reales, or 72,000 "pieces of eight," there being eight reales to the Spanish dollars, a widely accepted currency (at least $1.4 million today).[29]

In February or early March, they arrived in Havana, and then soon sailed north with the money, intended for Congress. (The money's source is unclear, but the French often used Havana as a transfer point for both loans to Congress and money to sustain their American army.)

On March 10, 1783, they were off the Florida coast when they saw three British ships bearing down on them. Because the *Alliance*, with a copper bottom, was faster, it was carrying the money. Barry told the slower *Lauzun* to jettison its guns and make a run for it. It escaped and arrived in Philadelphia eleven days later. The *Alliance* was headed for an uneven battle with the British when a strange ship appeared. It was a French warship, and two British ships left the scene.[30]

That left the *Alliance* to fight the British *Sibyl* (also spelled *Sybille*), a smaller ship with four fewer guns and fewer men. The British captured it from the French in Chesapeake Bay a year before. Its captain, James Vashon, 41, had fought as a young sailor in the Seven Years' War. He earned a promotion to captain in 1779 after sailing through a storm with a prize and two hundred French prisoners. Rodney appointed Vashon flagship captain, and together they fought at the Saintes. Later, in 1782, Vashon took command of the *Sibyl*.[31]

Now, Vashon fought Barry. The American account was that after half an hour, the *Sibyl*'s "guns were silenced and nothing but musketry was fired from her. She appeared very much injured in her hull." After another fifteen minutes, Vashon retreated. Barry reported one killed and nine wounded. "My sails, spars, and rigging hurt a little, but not so much but they would all do again."[32]

Vashon had a different report. He said it was the *Alliance* that sailed off and ended the fight. Rebel propaganda that Vashon had praised Barry's skills "is an entire fabrication," an early British historian said. With a French ship nearby, Barry "seems to have had very little cause to boast, but on the contrary, we think his courage might reasonably be called in question for running away as he did." The *Sibyl*'s casualties were similar to the *Alliance*'s: two killed, seven or eight wounded.[33]

Barry still had to deliver the money, and he headed to Philadelphia. But off Delaware Bay, he saw two British ships through clearings in a fog, believed he had "great reason to suppose the coast was lined with the enemy's ships," and didn't want to jeopardize the money, "belonging to the public which I shall take care of." He changed course for Rhode Island, and arrived in Newport on March 20.[34]

Barry's fight with Vashon was the last of the war for the Continental navy. Barry went on to fight as senior captain and later commander in the Barbary Wars in 1794 and the Quasi-War with France in 1798 and 1799. He headed the U.S. navy starting in 1801, and earned the name, "Father of the American Navy." He died in

1803. Parks, ships, schools, monuments, and a postage stamp com-
memorate his service.

Vashon led British commands in the Mediterranean, the
Channel, and the Caribbean. His friend, explorer, and fellow officer,
Captain George Vancouver, named what is now a Seattle bedroom
community after him: Vashon Island.

PART SIX

The Mediterranean

35. "Calamity Has Come On Us"

CHARLES O'HARA'S FATHER, JAMES, WAS MINORCA'S GOVERNOR for nine years. His assignment ended when he was promoted to Gibraltar's governorship in 1756. Charles made his own mark on Gibraltar, first as lieutenant governor thirty-six years later, then, in 1795, as governor himself until his death in 1802.

Gibraltar and Minorca were British strongholds in the Mediterranean: Gibraltar, a 2.3-square-mile peninsula guarding the northern side of the Mediterranean's nine-mile-wide outlet to the Atlantic; Minorca, a twenty-nine-mile-long island off the Spanish coast, and two hundred forty miles south-southwest of the French naval base at Toulon. Both were Spanish until the early eighteenth century, when Spain lost a war to Britain. It agreed in the peace treaty that Britain would own the posts "with all manners of right forever, without any exception of impediment whatsoever."[1]

Immediately, Spain had loser's remorse. In 1779, the only way France could persuade Spain to enter the revolution was to promise to keep fighting until Gibraltar was again Spanish. Once it entered the war in June 1779, Spain refused to cooperate with France on any campaign that didn't either protect its Western Hemisphere colonies or work toward seizing Gibraltar. This meant a mostly defensive campaign. "The King should preserve his fleet so as to cover the seas and guard the coasts, [and] protect trade in the Indies," a Spanish official said. Besides, Spanish finances were as bad as those of the American rebels. "There is not a *reale* in the navy treasury nor any hope of receiving anything for a long while past."[2]

The same month Spain declared war on Britain, it began to blockade and besiege Gibraltar, with the intent of starving it into surrender. Recovering Gibraltar obsessed Spain—as it does to this day. ("We are just one shot away from military conflict," a British headline read during a 2013 dispute.) Minorca, in comparison, was an annoyance. Spain saw it as a privateer's haven, and believed that eliminating its British base might help in the effort to take Gibraltar. Also, Spain was none too happy when Britain attempted to sell the island to Russia in exchange for its support.[3]

Spain ignored Minorca for two years. Then, in early 1781, Lieutenant General Louis de Balbe de Berton, Duc de Crillon, 64, began planning a joint Spanish-French invasion. He came from a family of honored French military men, and had fought in two Franco-Anglo wars. When, in 1762, he was passed over for command of a French military expedition, he shifted loyalties, and Spain welcomed him. "Who hath not heard of the name of Crillon?" a colleague asked Franklin rhetorically. A British general wished that Crillon "never will command an army against my Sovereign, for his military talents are as conspicuous as the goodness of his heart."[4]

"Behead me," Crillon told Spanish king Charles III, if Minorca didn't fall within three months.[5]

On August 19, 1781, Crillon and 8,000 men landed at multiple locations on Minorca and, unopposed, seized most of the island and its 27,000 people. The British were so surprised that they didn't fire on the 52-ship fleet as it sailed past fortifications. The only part of the island Crillon didn't capture was Fort St. Philip, a stronghold that guarded the harbor of the capital, Mahón. The harbor was one of the Mediterranean's best.

The next day, Crillon demanded that the British governor surrender St. Philip. The governor, Lieutenant General James Murray, refused. Surprised by Murray's answer, Crillon began digging in for a siege. It took a month for the Spanish and French to amass a siege force of nearly 15,000 men and the guns and mortars needed to pummel the fort. Murray had about 2,200 men, of which one in five were invalids.[6]

In early September, Murray made a statement: His men raided and destroyed a Spanish battery and captured 100 men. In mid-

September, the allies began a constant bombardment. Another month passed, and the enemies remained at a stalemate.

Then, Madrid ordered Crillon to bribe Murray into surrender. "In short," Crillon told Murray through an intermediary, "your general may have what sum he pleases." He said Spain had information that Murray was "ill-treated by some people at home . . ." Murray was offended. "The King of Spain charged you to assassinate the character of a man whose birth is as illustrious as your own. . . . I can have no further communication with you, but in arms. If you have any humanity, pray send clothing to your unfortunate prisoners in my possession." Crillon replied: "Your letter places us each in our proper station. It confirms me in the esteem I have always had for you."[7]

Using a ship that broke through the blockade, Murray told London that Crillon will find St. Philip "a harder nut to break than he imagines." He might have been describing himself.[8]

Murray, 59, was a Scot, the fifth son and fourteenth child of a baron. He rose through army ranks and served in the West Indies, Colombia, Cuba, and Flanders, where he was seriously wounded in 1745. He was familiar with sieges. In 1758, then a lieutenant colonel, he commanded a brigade at the three-month siege of Louisbourg, in Nova Scotia. "Murray . . . has acted with infinite spirit," his commander said. "The public is much indebted to him for great services in advancing . . . this siege." After leading a wing at the British victory on the Plains of Abraham, he commanded Québec city during a winter that saw 1,000 men die from disease.[9]

From 1760 to 1763, he was military governor—virtually dictator—of the Québec colony, wrested from the French and with a largely Catholic, French-Canadian population. It was a difficult occupation. Murray didn't want to alienate French residents; as a result, British settlers and merchants complained to London that he acted against their interests. By the time Murray was recalled to England, he believed the British Canadians were "the most cruel, ignorant, rapacious fanatics, who ever existed." The French Canadians were "perhaps, the best and bravest race on the globe," despite being "impecunious, haughty, tyrannical, contemptuous of trade and authority, [and] attached to French rule."[10]

A 1766 British council of inquiry concluded that the charges against Murray were "groundless, scandalous, and derogatory." He resumed his career, was named Minorca's lieutenant governor in

1774, and governor in 1779. Before accepting the Minorca job, he insisted on being paid a fixed salary, rather than relying on a share of taxes and fees, which he felt would undermine his credibility. "My salary should be fixed independent of such disgraceful emoluments," he said.[11]

Murray found a weak Minorca garrison. "I take the liberty to put you in mind how unequal the troops I have here are to the defense," he told London in 1776. Three years later, he pleaded for "a reinforcement to this sickly garrison. . . . The inhabitants have suffered equally with the troops." In another letter: "The two British regiments [here] look more like ghosts than soldiers."[12]

Murray suffered personal loss while in Minorca. His ill wife returned to England and died just after reaching their home. (During the siege, he married the eighteen-year-old daughter of a British consul in Minorca.) One of his brothers died, leaving him £15,000 pounds. He wrote the estate lawyer telling him to give the money to the dead brother's children. He added that he wished his brother "had left me nothing and showed more attention to my [other] brother, George. . . . I wish George and my other relations had paid more attention to him. . . . You know how much they used to tease and torment him."[13]

Before Crillon's invasion, Murray put Minorca into a state of emergency that included price controls, forced sale of cattle, and searches of homes and churches. He also welcomed a small reinforcement of fifty Corsican soldiers. At the same time, he feuded with his second-in-command, Lieutenant General William Draper, who despised Murray.[14]

In early November 1781, Murray sent out another sortie, and like the one in September, it was successful, capturing eighty-six Spanish soldiers. A third sortie failed. By December, Murray acknowledged that his worst enemy wasn't the allies, but scurvy, not surprising "when I consider that one-half the troops has lived eleven years on salt provisions, the other half not less than six." In January 1782, Murray had 776 men fit for duty. Crillon increased the bombardment, firing 750 rounds an hour. "They never stopped firing, and we as well returned it," a British officer said.[15]

That month, Murray's officers began pleading with him to surrender. Murray refused. Then, on February 2, Murray told his officers, "Calamity has come on us."[16]

He surrendered on February 4, and explained to London the circumstances: "The most inveterate scurvy which I believe ever had infected mortals reduced us to this situation. . . . Of the 660 able to do duty, 560 were actually tainted with the scurvy . . . A more tragic scene was never exhibited than that of the march of the garrison of St. Philip's through the Spanish and French armies. It consisted of no more than 600 old, decrepit soldiers, 200 seamen, 120 of the royal artillery, 20 Corsicans, and 25 Greeks, Turks, Moors, Jews, etc. Such was the distressing figures of our men that many of the Spanish and French troops are said to have shed tears as they passed them."[17]

Murray returned home to a court-martial, which cleared him of most charges, and praised him for "great zeal, courage, and firmness." George III waived a reprimand for the two minor convictions. He retired in 1783 as a full general. In 1789, he wrote a Québec friend: "I, at the age of 66, enjoy perfect health and happiness, truly contented with my lot of independent mutton. . . . [I] am only anxious for the prosperity of my two delightful children and the cultivation and increase of my fields and garden." He died five years later at his home.[18]

36. The Great Siege of Gibraltar

JOHN DRINKWATER, FIFTEEN, HAD NO SOONER JOINED THE BRITISH army in 1777 than he was sent to Gibraltar. By twenty, he was a captain there, but his greatest service wasn't military: After the war, he published the journal he had kept, and that journal is the core of most accounts of the Great Siege of Gibraltar.[1]

Gibraltar's location, Drinkwater said, "commanding the entrance of the Mediterranean . . . is, perhaps, more singular and curious than that of any fortress in the world." Its bay is "commodious and seems intended by nature to command the Straits. There are opportunities, however, when a fleet may pass unobserved by the garrison, for such is the impenetrable thickness of the mists . . . that many ships have baffled the vigilance of the cruisers and gone through unnoticed."[2]

A nineteenth-century officer praised Gibraltar's fortifications as "some of the most formidable in the universe. . . . Every spot from whence a gun can be brought to bear is occupied by cannon."[3]

The Gibraltar Peninsula is connected to the Spanish mainland by a low, sandy isthmus. Rising from the isthmus is the Rock, a nearly 1,400-foot high promontory that rises precipitously on its northern, Spain-facing side, and its eastern, Mediterranean side, "both naturally very steep and totally inaccessible," Drinkwater said. On the peninsula's west, facing the bay, is "a gradual slope, interspersed with precipices." Ships docked within one of Gibraltar's three "moles"—massive stone breakwaters. On the western shore, the Old Mole dated from 1309; the New Mole, from 1620. The British had built a southern mole beyond the range of Spanish guns by the time of the Great Siege.[4]

Also on the western shore is the town of Gibraltar. In 1779, about 3,600 civilians lived there, of whom one in seven were British. The rest were Spanish, Moroccan, and, classified separately, Jewish. For their water, they collected rain in tanks and cisterns. Summers were droughty. Growing vegetables in the rocky soil was difficult.[5]

Within the Rock itself are natural caves, used by people since prehistoric times. With each new war, the army expanded and modified the caves for defensive purposes.[6]

The siege began slowly, on June 21, 1779. Almost six miles across the bay, Spain fortified the small town and port of Algeciras. Its main naval base, however, remained in Cádiz, on the Atlantic, 100 miles from Algeciras by sea. At the Gibraltar isthmus' northern end, Spain built trenches and gun batteries. By October, the allied garrison had grown to 14,000 Spanish and French soldiers, enough for a siege, but not enough for an assault. The allied fleet blockaded the peninsula, but, as Drinkwater noted, the blockade was porous.[7]

On the British side, Lieutenant General George Augustus Eliott, the governor, dug in.

Eliott, 62, a Scot, educated at the University of Leyden in Holland—common for the son of a baronet—and, during a peace between wars, at a French military college. His first war experience was fighting for the Prussian army. He later returned to England for training as a military engineer. He served in a cavalry regiment his uncle commanded, and in 1743, now a captain, was wounded in fighting on the continent.

When the Seven Years' War began, he was married (to an heiress) and a lieutenant colonel. George III appointed him as an aide-de-camp, and he distinguished himself in battle as a cavalry commander. Toward the war's end, the now-Major General Eliott was second-in-command of an expedition that captured Havana. He became wealthier with the prize money he earned. After a brief assignment as commander-in-chief in Ireland, London named him, in 1776, Gibraltar's governor. He took command there in May 1777.[8]

He was "singular and austere in his manner," an officer said. Others called him "sour" and "intractable." Eliott may have been "the most abstemious man of his age," because he never ate meat or drank strong liquor, but lived "chiefly on vegetables, puddings, and water." He ruled his men with by-the-book discipline. In the siege's early days, after a soldier said he'd join the Spanish army if Spain took Gibraltar, Eliott ruled the man insane, ordered his head shaven, his body blistered and bled, straight-jacketed, and fed only bread and water. He executed soldiers not only for desertion, but also for plundering, robbery, and drunkenness. He even ordered soldiers' wives flogged for buying stolen goods. His officers chafed under him. To discourage drinking, he forced them to pay tax on liquor. He fined some officers after they not only reneged on paying debts to two Jews, but also beat them up. Eliott angered other officers for requiring goods that got through the blockade to be sold in public, rather than privately or in the black market.[9]

But Eliott seemed to be the right man for Gibraltar, with its 5,382-man garrison. (The garrison would grow to 7,100–7,500 men, depending on estimate, by fall 1782 as ships carrying reinforcements broke through the blockade. At the same time, the civilian population diminished when they sailed on outbound ships through the blockade.)[10]

When Eliott arrived, he ordered a team of military engineers to improve defenses. He cross-trained infantry so they could use artillery. As the siege began, Eliott ordered horses shot because they ate too much food. He prohibited his men from powdering their hair, because the flour they used needed to be conserved. (One rumor said that Eliott was hoarding all the flour so he could use it in his puddings.) In 1778, he started experimenting with "red-hot shot"; this involved heating cannonballs and other iron projectiles in a way that didn't blow up your own cannon when lit. Used against wooden ships or gunpowder magazines, red-hot shot caused fires and explosions.[11]

As 1780 began, Gibraltar was feeling the siege's effects. "No vessel has got in here," Eliott wrote London. "The Spanish cruisers are so vigilant, consequently no supplies—our provisions daily consuming—many inhabitants near starving." (The British sent multiple copies of messages of such letters on different ships and boats, often belonging to Italian or Muslim entrepreneurs who ran the blockade.)[12]

London chose Admiral George Rodney to lead a Gibraltar expedition, hoping he would not only bring Eliott relief, but then proceed to the West Indies. Rodney didn't disappoint. He left England on December 29, 1779, with the relief convoy, twenty-two warships, and additional frigates. About two hundred miles west of Gibraltar, a Spanish squadron half the size spotted the British sails. Thinking it was just a few warships guarding the convoy, Admiral Juan Francisco de Lángara y Huarte attacked. In night action—the "Moonlight Battle"—the British captured six Spanish warships, sank another, and made Lángara a prisoner. Rodney's ships sailed unmolested into Gibraltar January 19–25, unloaded reinforcements and supplies, and left for the West Indies.

At the end of 1780, Eliott again was running out of food and supplies. Again, London responded with a second relief fleet, led by Vice Admiral George Darby. Darby evaded the allies en route to Gibraltar, but once he entered the harbor on April 12, 1781, his one hundred-ship fleet came under heavy fire from Spanish batteries. But, like Rodney, Darby unloaded the supplies and reinforcements, and left without major losses.

Darby's expedition marked the start of an escalation. For the next twenty-one months, the allies would bombard Gibraltar day and night. In the first week alone, the guns killed twenty-three men and wounded seventy-five. Soon, they destroyed most of the town, although Eliott's fortifications suffered relatively little damage.[13]

"Death and slaughter continue to be our visitants," wrote Samuel Ancell, a regimental clerk, in September 1781. "On every hand impending ruin hourly upon us, seemingly studiously meditating our overthrow." Desertion and attempted desertion were common. In October, crewmen on a navy cutter plotted a mutiny with the intent of sailing to Algeciras. Eliott discovered the plot and jailed the ringleaders.[14]

In November, the Spanish finished new trenches and batteries on the isthmus closer to British lines. Eliott's guns were ineffective in stopping them, so he chose another tactic. On the night of November 26, he sent 2,500 men across the lines to destroy the new batteries. In an hour, they succeeded. "The enemy," Eliott reported, "after a scattering fire of short duration, gave way on all sides, and abandoned their stupendous works with great precipitation. . . . Many of the enemy were killed upon the spot." His men returned to safety by 5 A.M. the next morning. Four were killed, twenty-five were wounded, and one was declared missing. They took twelve prisoners. Because of the dark, they couldn't estimate the number of Spanish casualties.[15]

Drinkwater described the damage: "The principal magazine blew up with a tremendous explosion, throwing up vast pieces of timber, which, falling into the flames, added to the general conflagration. Although the enemy must have been early alarmed, not the smallest effort was made to save or avenge their works. The fugitives seemed to communicate a panic to the whole."[16]

By the end of 1781, the British were again in distress. Not only were they running low on arms and men, but scurvy appeared. Two American rebels, held prisoner by the British, escaped to Algeciras, where they said Gibraltar was "devoured with the scurvy . . . but that of other articles of provision they have plenty, and flatter themselves that they shall soon receive a fresh supply."[17]

The information was accurate. Six of Eliott's boats successfully ran the blockade, sailed to Portugal, and returned in late February 1782 with supplies—and lemons. "The garrison grows daily more and more healthy," Eliott said. By spring, Eliott's scouting boats, allied deserters, and blockade-runners were bringing him intelligence that something different was happening in Algeciras. A French military engineer had had an idea.[18]

Jean-Claude-Éléonore le Michaud, Chevalier d'Arçon, had a passion for weapons. Although his father wanted him to become a priest, d'Arçon studied at the French royal engineering school. He had firsthand knowledge of sieges: During the Seven Years' War, he was one of the besieged at Cassel, a French-held German town that fell in one of the war's final European actions.[19]

In March 1780, d'Arçon, 47, was a colonel. Breaching Gibraltar's defenses became d'Arçon's personal challenge, and he made a proposal to Spain's ambassador in France. Spain agreed the idea had merit. It sent for d'Arçon, and he arrived in Algeciras in July 1781.[20]

D'Arçon's idea was to sail ten floating gun batteries close to the weakest spot in Gibraltar's defenses, destroy it, and land an invasion force. Why wouldn't the British destroy the floating batteries first? D'Arçon proposed using advanced technology so they would be "*insubmergibles et incombustibles*"—unsinkable and unburnable. The ships' sides and enclosed decks would use timber a yard thick to repel cannonballs. Within the ship's walls, d'Arçon implanted wet sand and cork. To protect against British red-hot shot, pump-driven water would keep the timber soaked. The ten batteries would have 152 heavy guns. With gunboats and land batteries, the allies would direct a total of 398 guns against a British position near the town defended by eighty-six.[21]

The allies began preparation. In June 1782, they erected large tents in Algeciras to shelter the men as they converted old merchant ships into the floating batteries. French admiral Guichen arrived in Algeciras with twelve ships and an additional four thousand French troops. In July, the Spanish fleet repositioned itself from the Atlantic, where it had captured eighteen ships of a British convoy headed to Canada.[22]

By mid-August, the allies had forty-seven warships, forty gunboats with heavy artillery, three hundred troop landing ships, and scores of frigates, xebeques, gallies, and other boats—in addition to d'Arçon's ten-ship armada. More than 27,000 Spanish and 4,000 French soldiers manned gun batteries or waited to land on the Gibraltar beach. Altogether, 100,000 men opposed Eliott's garrison of no more than 7,500 men, of whom four hundred were hospitalized and unable to fight. To lead the massive and complex operation, the allies chose a man who was comfortable wearing both uniforms: the victor at Minorca, Crillon.[23]

Crillon arrived on August 15, and four days later announced his arrival to Eliott. He wrote about "the pleasure to which I look forward to becoming your friend, after I shall have learned to render myself worthy of the honor by facing you as an enemy." He then made a gesture: "I know you live entirely upon vegetables," and he offered to provide some if Eliott would tell him what he preferred. Eliott politely declined.[24]

Crillon and his naval counterpart, the Spanish admiral, Don Luis de Córdoba, were skeptical that d'Arçon's batteries would work. "You have a fatherly love for your batteries, and are only anxious for their preservation," Crillon told d'Arçon. "Should the enemy attempt to take possession of them, I will burn them before his [the enemy's] face." To cover himself, Crillon wrote Madrid. He pledged to support d'Arçon "by every means," and if the allies succeeded, he would give "all the glory of this feat of arms" to him. But if the operation failed, "no reproaches can be made to me, since I have taken no part in the project."[25]

Except for the date, the attack was now common knowledge. Some eighty thousand spectators lined the hills. The Spanish built a grandstand for dignitaries.

Eliott didn't wait for the allies. On September 8, he began his own offensive with a steadily escalating bombardment of the allied position on the north side of the isthmus. "The effect of the red-hot shot and carcasses [incendiary bombs] exceeded our most sanguine expectations," Drinkwater said.[26]

The attack forced Crillon's hand. Concerned that the British would destroy the isthmus batteries, Crillon "determined to avoid the blow . . . by opening his batteries, even in their unfinished state." He also had received intelligence that another British relief fleet would arrive soon. But D'Arçon said the batteries needed more testing, at least a trial run. The man named to command the ten batteries, Rear Admiral Bonaventura Moreno, also wanted to delay. Crillon knew Moreno well, because he had led the navy's blockade at Minorca. "If you do not proceed to an instant attack, you are a man devoid of honor," Crillon replied.[27]

The attack began around 9 A.M. on September 13.

At first, the attack went well for the allies, despite currents that caused most of the batteries to anchor out of position. The British fired and "to our great astonishment, we found they [balls] rebounded from their sides and roofs," Ancell said. "The fire was returned on our part without intermission, and equally maintained by the foe."[28]

The allied bombardment from sea and land took its toll. Ancell saw "a soldier before me, lying on the ground, and his head somewhat raised, and supported on his elbows. I ran to him, imagining the man had life, and lifted him up, when such a sight was displayed to my view that I think I never shall forget—a 26-pound ball had gone through his body, and his entrails, as they hung out from the orifice, were of a most disagreeable resemblance."[29]

At this point, the British fired only cold shot; artillerymen were still heating up the red-hots. None would be fired until noon, and their full use wouldn't begin for two hours after that. But by late afternoon, the red-hot shot took hold. A fire began on the floating battery d'Arçon was aboard, and Córdoba sent an oared boat to bring him back to land. Then Moreno's flagship battery was afire, and he was evacuated. Another battery was helpless on a sandbar. By 7 P.M., crewmen were shooting few of the batteries' cannons.[30]

"The continual discharge of red hot balls kept up by us was such as rendered all the precautions taken by the enemy . . . of no effect, for the balls lodging in their sides, in length of time, spread the fire throughout," Ancell said.[31]

To Guichen's and other admirals' frustration, Córdoba refused to send reinforcements, because, a Spanish newspaper said later, sending them "could not possibly be carried into execution on account of the rise of the wind and sea." The reporter described what happened overnight and into daylight hours of the 14th: "A constant and heavy fire from all the enemy's batteries . . . were more numerous than we imagined." The red-hot balls, by burying themselves in the batteries' sides, "spread the fire throughout." Moreno's ship "began to burn with such violence as made it impossible to save her. . . . All the other batteries began to be nearly in the same situation." Boats sent to rescue battery crews turned back due to "the enemy's dreadful fire of grape shot . . . The enemy sunk several of the small craft." Later, when it was clear the batteries couldn't function any longer, British gunboats began rescuing the crewmen, "making prisoners of all the troops that remained in the floating batteries." By mid-morning, "the floating batteries blew up one after the other except three, which burnt to the water's edge."[32]

The British gunboat commander, who had fired on the allied rescue boats because he thought they were reinforcements, described the "dreadful" scene after the allies left the battery crews "to our mercy, or to the flames." There were "men crying from amidst the flames, some upon pieces of wood in the water, others appear in the ships where the fire had as yet made but little progress, all expressing, by speech and gesture, the deepest distress and all imploring assistance, formed a spectacle of horror not easily to be described." He saved 357 men. All told, 1,500 allied soldiers and sailors drowned, were killed or wounded, or went missing during the battle. Fifteen British soldiers died; sixty-eight were wounded.[33]

"Everything is lost and through my fault," d'Arçon wrote a friend. (Later, he decided it wasn't his fault and wrote a defense of his actions.) The British stopped the invasion, but the siege and bombardment continued. Eliott needed urgent relief.[34]

The third relief expedition was on its way, led by a failed admiral who, as a friend said, "had not enjoyed the smiles" of George III and his government.[35]

Richard Howe, 56, was London-born, but spent three of his early years in Barbados, where his father was governor. His mother was a member of George III's household. Howe's navy career crisscrossed the Atlantic, from Portugal to the Caribbean, South America (as far as Cape Horn) to Africa, the North Sea to North America. Concurrently, he had a long Parliamentary career and, as an admiral, sought diplomatic assignments.

Howe's contemporaries acknowledged his personal courage, even as they described him as introverted and inarticulate. "Lord Howe's ideas were commonly either so ill-conceived by himself, or so darkly and ambiguously expressed, that it was by no means easy to comprehend his precise meaning," one MP said. Another contemporary said Howe had "a shyness and awkwardness in his manner, which to a stranger at first sight gave a rather unfavorable impression." A friend conceded Howe's "very peculiar manner of explaining himself," but explained that "his mind was always clear, prompt, and willing to communicate with every person who consulted him, and who could get rid of the apparent coldness of his manner." Others disagreed. Walpole talked about Howe's "want of sense," and a French diplomat said he was "very muddled."[36]

Howe was down-to-earth and unflamboyant. "We cannot make a rake of Lord Howe, tho' we have got him to a supper party and kept him there 'til one," said a general who attempted to get Howe to enjoy himself. "Pains were taken to get him to play vingt-et-un, but he is as virtuous as yourself and could not be prevailed upon."[37]

Howe's men were fond of him and nicknamed him "Black Dick," for both his dark complexion and his manner. One crewman said Howe would "go below after an action and talk to every wounded man, sitting by the sides of their cradles, and constantly ordering his livestock and wines to be applied to their use at the discretion of the surgeon, and at all times for the sick on board." Another friend said Howe was "most deservedly popular with seamen" despite "no spice of the tar in his personal behavior anywhere."[38]

Horatio Nelson complimented Howe to his face as "the first and greatest sea-officer the world has ever produced." Privately, Nelson said he "certainly is a great officer in the management of a fleet, but that is all."[39]

In 1776, London sent Howe and his younger brother, General William Howe, to be the respective commanders-in-chief for the navy and army in North America. At their request, they were vested with powers to negotiate with the rebels and reach a settlement. Although they met with Franklin and John Adams, the negotiations never began: The rebels already had declared independence, and they demanded recognition, not reconciliation. This the Howes "could not accept."[40]

As the war escalated, and rebel privateers began seizing British ships, the Howes lost their political support. After the Saratoga debacle, they asked to be relieved. Richard returned to England in October 1778. For three and a half years, the government and the navy ignored him. Then, in March 1782, the government fell. A month later, the new ministry promoted Howe to full admiral and named him commander of the Channel fleet.

Over the summer, the cabinet debated whether it was worth the risk to send Howe with a relief expedition to Gibraltar. Howe's absence could expose England to invasion, and there was no certainty that his fleet could get through safely. In late August, the government reached its conclusion: Send Howe.

Between Howe and Gibraltar were Córdoba and the allied fleet. Córdoba, 76, had a distinguished record, although like most Spanish admirals, he preferred defensive tactics. He had fought Algerians, Austrians, and the English, serving in Italy, both Americas, and North Africa. He was co-commander of an allied fleet that was to invade England in 1779, but bad weather and a typhus outbreak in the fleet ended the plan. The next year, Córdoba became a national hero by capturing a fifty-five-ship British convoy. He did it again in 1781, capturing twenty-four more ships. Córdoba's name lives on—in Alaska, where a Spanish explorer named the city of Cordova after him.[41]

Howe's thirty-five warships and eight frigates left England on September 11, 1782, escorting 130 transports. Córdoba's allied fleet sailed from Cádiz to find Howe, but failed. One day before Howe reached Gibraltar, high winds damaged four of Córdoba's ships in Gibraltar Bay. Howe's convoy rode out the storm. On October 11, because of bad nighttime visibility, continuing winds, and inattention, all but a frigate and four supply ships missed Gibraltar and sailed past it into the Mediterranean.[42]

Again Córdoba chased Howe, but the winds favored the British. The convoy reached Gibraltar over three days, followed by Howe himself on October 18. Howe would later tell a friend that his relief and maneuvers at Gibraltar were "the greatest he had ever performed, and . . . the only one of which he claimed the sole merit to himself."[43]

He left the next day with his warships for England, but Córdoba hadn't given up the chase. On October 20, off Cape Spartel, Africa's Atlantic entrance to the Gibraltar strait, Córdoba's forty-three warships (including his French ally Guichen) sighted Howe's fleet. The enemies fought for several hours, and each side lost about sixty men. Then they parted, but who sailed away first became a debate. Córdoba described the battle as a victory in which the defeated Howe was able to flee the Spanish and French only because the British ships, with their coppered bottoms, were faster. Howe disagreed. He said he would have fought on, but Córdoba was the one who refused close action.[44]

A French captain later praised Howe's expedition. "There were neither separations, nor collisions, nor casualties; and there occurred none of those events so frequent in the experiences of a squadron which often oblige admirals to take a course wholly contrary to the end they have in view. . . . If it is just to submit that Lord Howe displayed the highest talents, it should be added that he had in his hands excellent instruments."[45]

The encounter with Howe was Guichen's last action. He had been in the French navy for fifty-two years. He died in France a little more than seven years later.

Back in Gibraltar, the allies gradually decreased their bombardment, although in January 1783, eighteen British soldiers were killed, and British and allied gunboats fought on January 29. Eliott ignored the peace rumors. When he saw his garrison relaxing, he prohibited entertainment.[46]

But peace was near. The British estimated that during the siege's three years and seven months, their enemy suffered nearly 3,800 killed or missing. The British lost more men from disease than from enemy shells: 1,036 from illness versus 471 killed or disabled in action. Another forty-three deserted.[47]

On February 5, 1783, Crillon sent Eliott a message that the allies had lifted the siege. The diplomats had signed a preliminary peace treaty in Paris. When, a month later, Eliott confirmed the peace with a dispatch from a British frigate, he and Crillon agreed to meet. Crillon and his aides rode into Gibraltar on March 12. When he and Eliott saw each other, Drinkwater said, "both instantly dismounted and embraced. When the salutations were over, they conversed about a half an hour, and then returned to their respective commands." Eleven days later, Eliott dined with Crillon within Spanish lines. At month's end, Eliott gave Crillon a tour of Gibraltar. "Gentlemen," Crillon told Eliott's staff, "I would rather see you here as friends than on your batteries as enemies, where you never spared me."[48]

Gibraltar destroyed Crillon's reputation. It was the last of his sixty-eight battles and twenty-two sieges. He died in Madrid in 1796. Unlike Crillon, D'Arçon wasn't blamed for the debacle. He wrote an account of the siege, as well as a military engineering book. In the early 1790s, he fought with the French revolutionary army, until ill health forced him to resign. He then became a professor of fortification at a military college. In 1799, Napoleon appointed him to the senate. He died a year later near Paris.

Eliott remained Gibraltar's governor until his death, but with the siege lifted, he made several trips home. The king elevated him to a peerage: Lord Heathfield, baron of Gibraltar. He is buried near his English estate. The plate on his coffin was melted down from a gun recovered from a floating battery.[49]

Gibraltar completed Howe's rehabilitation. He became first lord of the Admiralty after the war, but because he was charged to downsize the navy, he made enemies. Still, after Rodney died in 1792, Howe succeeded him as vice admiral of England. When war with the French resumed, he won a major victory off Ushant in

1794, dubbed the "Glorious First of June." Although semi-retired in 1797, he helped end a mutiny over wages by offering concessions and a royal pardon. It was Howe's last official act. He died two years later.

Drinkwater's journal of the Gibraltar siege, published in 1785, became a best-seller. He founded the Garrison Library, which remains open to the public to this day. He later followed O'Hara to fight the French in Toulon and ultimately retired as a colonel. He died in England in 1844.

PART SEVEN

The Battle for India

37. Hyder Ali: "The Most Formidable Enemy"

WHEN CHARLES CORNWALLIS, O'HARA'S SUPERIOR AT YORKTOWN, returned to Britain, the government saw him as a talented victim of circumstances. Twice, in 1782 and 1784, he turned down offers to be British India's governor because he believed civil authority without corresponding military command was doomed to fail. In 1786, the government agreed to his demand.

That the British continued to have any Indian presence was in question during the revolution's last eighteen months.

A European feeding frenzy to grab a share of Indian trade—or monopolize it—began when the Portuguese reached its western coast in 1498. Four years later, they built their first fort. The French, British, Dutch, and Danish followed, and even Swedes, Flemish, Austrians, and Prussians attempted to establish posts. Within India, invaders, dynasties, and empires fought each other when they weren't allied with each other. European wars and hostilities spilled into India, and each nation sought native allies, who, like Native American nations, played the European parties against each other for their own self-interests and survival.

Pondicherry (now Puducherry), on India's southeastern coast, was typical. It changed hands at least thirteen times over the centuries until the French were pressured to cede it to an independent India in 1954.

Private East India companies, chartered by their governments, led the European advance, but not even their monopoly status guaranteed financial success. The French government took over its company's assets in the 1760s. The Dutch East India Company gave way to its government in the 1790s. During the revolution, the British Parliament's attempts to reform the British East India Company resulted in a confusing structure that caused conflicts between the government and company, and within the company. Adam Smith, the economist, reflected many MPs' views: The company is corrupt, "the plunderers of India . . . so perfectly indifferent about the happiness or misery of their subjects, the improvement or waste of their dominions, the glory or disgrace of their administration."[1]

The company divided its rule into three semi-autonomous "presidencies": Fort William in Bengal's Calcutta (Kolkata today) in the northeast; Bombay (Mumbai) on the western Malabar Coast, 2,400 miles from Bengal by ship; and Fort St. George in Madras (Chennai) on the southeastern Coromandel Coast, 900 miles to Calcutta, 1,500 to Bombay.

The king appointed a governor general to represent the national interest over the three presidencies. The government allowed the company to make treaties with non-Christian nations; sometimes, the company's army imposed the treaties. Native and European mercenaries, along with the British army and navy, complemented the company's army. Often, British military commanders and company administrators and their councils argued over mutually exclusive interests.

India produced wealth: cotton, tea, coffee, indigo, saltpeter (used to make gunpowder), spices, diamonds, gold, and silver. But it also was a difficult land. Famine, caused by ceaseless wars and drought, was common, as were floods. Like the Caribbean's hurricane season, India's seasons affected military operations: Heavy monsoon rains occurred from June through September; high monsoon winds arrived in October and stayed through December.

In Madras, Europeans "seem to be chiefly employed in avoiding the excessive heat of the climate, and, indeed, it is not to be wondered at for, to me, it feels intolerable," a British captain said. As with the Caribbean and American South, India also took its toll in the form of tropical diseases. (In 2001, malaria alone affected 15 million Indians.)[2]

For ships supplying and defending the European settlements, scurvy and typhus were ever-present. "Their crews were packed together like sardines in humid, confined, and filthy spaces below decks, fed a wretched diet lacking fresh vegetables, fruits, and meats; and denied adequate quantities of water for drinking and bathing."[3]

Adding to the challenges was the lack of harbors where ships could be overhauled. Even Madras was inadequate for the British navy; its ships sailed to Bombay or Calcutta for major refitting. Between Madras and the Dutch settlement at Negapatam (Nagapattinam) 200 miles to the south, the coastline was smooth, and few towns could handle European ships: Dutch Sadras, French Pondicherry, and Danish Tranquebar (Tharangambadi). The tip of Ceylon (Sri Lanka) lay sixty-five miles to the south of Negapatam. Only after sailing another 150 miles to the southeast did ships arrive at Trincomalee, one of the world's largest natural harbors, and a key military objective.[4]

On July 7, 1778, British governor general Warren Hastings, 46, based in Calcutta, received the four-month-old news that the French had entered the American war. He was an India veteran of twenty-eight years, who "in the face of overwhelming danger . . . showed a master spirit fitted to grapple with every emergency, and equally capable of saving or creating an empire," an admirer said.[5]

Hastings immediately ordered government, company, and native troops to attack French positions. By September, they had expelled the French from the Bengal region and taken France's main port at Pondicherry, south of Madras. The only remaining French posts were on the western Malabar Coast.

Now, Hastings erred. He made an enemy of a powerful general, Hyder Ali of the Mysore kingdom. Mysore was the size of modern Pennsylvania and South Carolina combined. Militarily, it dominated southern India from the Malabar to within fifty to one hundred miles of Madras on the eastern Coromandel Coast.

American rebels might not have heard of Hyder in 1778, but they honored him in 1782: Joshua Barney sailed the *Hyder Ally* to his Delaware Bay battle. Hyder was born in Mysore between 1716 and 1728; most historians guess 1721. His father, a military man, died when Hyder was 5, and he and his older brother were raised by a cousin with influence in the Mysorean court. He rose to prominence as a volunteer in his brother's cavalry unit. Within a couple of years, he had his own command, and in 1755, became military governor of a frontier fort. There, he organized his own army, gaining loyalty by sharing plunder equally with his men, but insisting on accurate records backed up by auditors. He didn't tolerate corruption.[6]

Hyder also worked with French advisors to gain modern military technology, supplies, and tactics. "He was attentive and exact in observing everything that passed in the French camp," an officer said. When Mysore's ruler died in 1759, Hyder assumed all power, but allowed a puppet prince to remain on the throne. Within three more years, he built a dockyard and navy.[7]

For the rest of his life, he was at war, fighting rival nations, rebellions, or British-led or inspired invasions. The still-definitive history of southern India, written by British colonel Mark Wilks, who had served in the company's army during the war, has more than five pages of Hyder references in its index. Most refer to military events: "Besieges Nunjeraj . . . Undertakes to conquer Bâramahâl . . . Defeats an English detachment . . . Defeat of, by Kundè Row . . . Takes Balipoor by assault . . . Retreat of, to Seringapatam . . . Recovery of Malabar . . . His narrow escape from Afghans . . . His dreadful devastations . . . Surrender of Colonel Baille to . . ."[8]

The British knew him well. From 1767 to 1769, they fought him in the First Anglo-Mysore War—and lost. With his army camped five miles from a feeble Madras, he dictated the peace treaty: It included a mutual defense clause that Hyder intended to invoke if attacked by enemies.[9]

He was, said a nineteenth-century biographer and British commissioner to Mysore, "a bold, an original, and an enterprising commander, skillful in tactics and fertile in resources, full of energy and never desponding in defeat." A British military engineer saw that "Hyder possessed great courage and abilities, which have appeared both in his military and civil capacity, and which should have taught the servants of the British East India Company to have endeavored to make him their friend, and not to have provoked him to become their enemy."[10]

His greatest opponent, General Eyre Coote, talked about him in a way that eighteenth-century Englishmen rarely spoke of native Indians: "Hyder had taken every measure which could occur to the most experienced general to distress us and to render himself formidable; and his conduct in his civil capacity had been supported by a degree of political address unequalled by any power that had yet appeared in Indostan." Even when Coote forced Hyder to retreat, "There was no consternation on his part, no trophies on ours."[11]

Although Hyder's relationship with his French allies had its ups and downs, the French conceded that they couldn't win British India without him. "Hyder Ali is the only Indian power who can assist the French advantageously in their projects. His forces are considerable; he has a martial character, the abilities of a general, and most important, his interests harmonize perfectly with ours, being the ruin and debasement of English power in India," one general reported.[12]

By 1769, when a company official met him, Hyder "had no eyebrows nor, indeed, a single hair left on any part of his face," and an attendant plucked any hairs that grew out. Hyder explained that he didn't want anyone in Mysore who looked like him. He was about five feet six, with a "rather thick" lower lip. When not fighting in uniform, he wore a simple white robe with a turban.[13]

To Europeans, "his manners, voice, and deportment were most soft and ingratiating whenever he wished to please or affected to be gracious and benign, but he was terrible and often ferocious in his anger." Former prisoners accused him of torture, starvation diets, and even forced circumcision. For those caught before his army, "miserable inhabitants, flying from their flaming villages, in part were slaughtered; others, without regard to sex, to age, to the respect of rank, or sacredness of function; fathers torn from children, husbands from wives; enveloped in a whirlwind of cavalry, and amidst the goading spears of drivers, and the trampling of pursuing horses, were swept into a captivity in an unknown and hostile land." He was "as vindictive and merciless as he was active and powerful. Thousands of unresisting and innocent natives were murdered in cold blood."[14]

But there was another side to him. He created a meritocracy. "What religion people profess, or whether they profess any at all, that is perfectly indifferent to him. He has none himself and leaves everyone to his choice," a British army chaplain said. "He cared not one jot what faith his officials followed so long as they obeyed his orders," a later British official wrote.[15]

Hyder was an innovator. Unlike other Indian leaders who hired mercenaries, Hyder centralized his army's recruiting and training. He broke tradition by building a large cavalry the British conceded was tactically superior to theirs. And he used advanced weapons the Europeans didn't have: Long-range rockets launched from bamboo tubes lined with iron. Pointed horizontally at an enemy, they did "great damage, particularly amongst cavalry and ammunition tumbrils," a British officer said. Hyder would "readily adopt whatever European improvements appeared most essential to secure his government, to extend his empire, and to render his name immortal." George Macartney, the company's Madras governor, explained to London about the military challenge: "The Indians have less terror of our arms; we, less contempt for their opposition."[16]

To Edmund Burke, Hyder and his allies were "the declared enemy of the human species." Another MP later compared Hyder to Napoleon, "the most formidable enemy with whom we had to contend in the East."[17]

In 1771, a neighboring kingdom invaded Mysore. Hyder asked for British help under the mutual-defense terms of the treaty they had signed two years before. The British refused. Hyder complained to a company envoy that they "had broken their solemn engagements and promise, but that nevertheless he was willing to live in peace with them."[18]

He kept his word. When Hastings and the British seized French posts in 1778, Hyder remained neutral, despite French requests for help. But then, Hyder learned that the British were considering an attack on Mahé, a French port on the Malabar. Although the French occupied Mahé, the town wasn't French territory: It was Mysorean, and it was a conduit for French supplies to Hyder. Hyder explicitly warned the British to avoid Mahé. "Should the English create a disturbance in the French factory [post] of Mahé, he would punish them by devastating the whole country from Madura [Madurai] to Madras. He would totally efface them from the face of the Earth," a translator said.[19]

He sent another warning on March 19, 1779, that he would consider an attack on Mahé a hostile act. That same day, the French peacefully surrendered Mahé to a British army outside its gates. The company tried to smooth relations with Hyder by sending him an envoy. Hyder replied, "I was convinced that the King of England and the company were one, and that there would not be the smallest deviation from the treaties made by the company, but I now think otherwise from your proceedings."[20]

That winter, Hyder joined a coalition of other native states united against the British. Hastings reported to London of "a war, actual or impending, in every quarter and with every power."[21]

38. Coote and Hughes to the Rescue

HYDER AND HIS ARMY OF 90,000 INFANTRY AND CAVALRY, including a few French officers, attacked the Madras presidency's posts defended by 11,000 men. By the end of October 1780, he had defeated a company-and-mercenary army, killed or captured nearly 3,800 men, and threatened Madras.[1]

Hastings ordered his Calcutta commander, Lieutenant General Eyre Coote, 54, south to Madras to stiffen up the British defense, which was down to 1,600 regulars (although reinforcements were on the way), plus assorted mercenaries.[2]

Coote was the fourth son of an Irish minister, a distant cousin of a seventeenth-century New York governor. He entered the infantry as an ensign in 1744 at the relatively old age of eighteen. Two years later, he fought in a losing battle against Scottish rebels. Accused of cowardice when he fled from the battle, Coote was convicted of a minor offense; the jury concluded that he ran away only to keep the regimental colors out of enemy hands.[3]

In 1754, Coote went to India to fight the French and their allies. Within five years, he was a lieutenant colonel commanding the Madras army. At the end of 1759, he and his British-native troops took several enemy posts, before the French besieged his position at Wandiwash (Vandavasi), seventy miles southwest of Madras. Two months later, he broke out and defeated the larger French force. The victory was a turning point. Working with the navy, Coote routed the French again in 1761 at their capital, Pondicherry. He returned to England the next year, bought an estate, and began serving in Parliament. When the new war against the French began,

Britain promoted him to lieutenant general and commander-in-chief in Calcutta, where he arrived in spring 1779.[4]

"Age and sickness had impaired, in a certain degree, the physical strength and mental energy of this distinguished veteran," said Wilks, who served under him. But even ill, Coote showed "a bodily frame of unusual vigor and activity, and mental energy always awake . . . restrained from excessive action by a patience and temper which never allowed the spirit of enterprise to outmarch the dictates of prudence."[5]

Company officials recognized that his military abilities were a match for Hyder's, but they detested him personally. Hastings complained, "My letters have been all friendly to him; his to me, all petulant and suspicious; I know not why or for what. I bear with him, and will bear, for I am lost if he abandons me." Macartney, the Madras governor, also complained about Coote. "It is very difficult to keep on good terms with him. He is now no longer what he was. Soured by disappointment, grown old, impaired in health, jealous and fractious . . . , I court him like a mistress and humor him like a child."[6]

Coote frequently threatened to resign. "He was of a fretful temper, and a love of gain had grown up side-by-side with his pursuit of glory," said a military historian one generation removed. "He was strongly impressed with his own merits, and like many excellent officers, he was ever prone to deem himself slighted or neglected."[7]

For his part, Coote made sure to inform Macartney and Hastings of their inability to properly supply him, his own failing health, and Hyder's strategy:

> "My state of health is very indifferent and being yesterday the whole day obliged to expose myself on horseback to an intense sun, is, at this present time, severely felt by me."
>
> His situation was "truly distressing . . . for the want of proper magazines, means of field subsistence, and carriage for it.
>
> "Numbers have died by hunger and the inclemency of the weather. . . . In short, the scene exhibited was more like a field of battle than a line of march.
>
> "Hyder always takes care to be certain that there is impeding or impossible ground between his army and ours. Thus, he is always sure of its being optional with him to draw off his guns in safety before our army can act offensively."[8]

Nevertheless, Coote went on the offensive and helped inspire other British commanders. From January 1781 through August 1782, Coote relieved besieged garrisons, fought bloody battles with Hyder, and put him on the defensive. In 1782, the Mysoreans and British fought eleven major land battles.[9]

Hyder trapped Coote in February 1781 in the port of Cuddalore, 115 miles south of Madras. Hyder besieged him by land, and a French squadron led by Admiral Thomas d'Estienne, Comte d'Orves, prevented relief from sea. Hyder asked d'Orves to land a regiment to support the siege. D'Orves not only refused; he sailed away, citing orders against dangerous operations and the need to return to Île-de-France (Mauritius). British reinforcements with supplies sailed into Cuddalore. Coote was down to his last two days of provisions.[10]

Hyder had come to expect such French lethargy. In 1773, when the French failed to react to a British attack on a native district, he rhetorically asked his liaison officer: "Are the French really interested in India? If they are, why do they fumble? Why do not their vessels come more often? If they decided to fight the English, will they indicate this plan to me, so that I can join in this enterprise?" He also warned France against territorial greed: "If the English are eliminated, and you aspire to succeed in their place, then I will battle you with the same tenacity as I do now against them. You are all Europeans, and I do not wish to see you in my neighborhood."[11]

In July 1781, Coote's army again was an underdog, this time at Porto Novo (Parangipettai), fifty miles south of Cuddalore. His eight thousand men were outnumbered by Hyder's sixty thousand, but by the end of the day Hyder withdrew his forces. Coote was unable to pursue for lack of cavalry and transport. Nor was Coote able to retake Hyder's arsenal town of Arcot, seventy miles west of Madras. In February 1782, the Mysoreans and a small French unit killed or captured two-thirds of a 2000-man British and native detachment.[12]

After another battle with Hyder in June 1782, this time at Arnee (Arani), ninety miles west of Madras, Coote said that he "most assuredly" would have defeated Hyder there and ended the war "had I possessed the means of sustenance"—namely, supplies and provisions for his army.[13]

By September, Coote couldn't continue. His health deteriorated, and he returned to Calcutta for rest and cure. There, he stayed until

April 1783, when he felt restored enough to return to Madras. But two French ships chased his transport, and, a contemporary said, "his anxiety was indeed so great that it kept him almost constantly on deck." He died—from "the heat, the fatigue, the night air, and above all, the agitation of mind"—on April 26, two days after arriving in Madras.[14]

While Coote staunched the bleeding in Madras, the British navy attacked Hyder, the French, and, after they entered the war, the Dutch.

A squadron under Vice Admiral Edward Hughes destroyed the Mysorean navy at Mangalore on the Malabar Coast in December 1780. A joint army-navy expedition took Dutch Negapatam in November 1781. On January 11, 1782, the last Dutch fortification on Ceylon's Trincomalee harbor surrendered to Hughes's marines. "The enemy lost but few men as they mostly threw down their arms, and their forfeited lives were spared by that disposition to mercy which ever distinguishes Britons," Hughes said.[15]

From France's entry into the war through 1781, the British commanded the oceans around India and Ceylon, and Hughes commanded the British. "He is a short, thick-set, fat man," the *Bengal Gazette* said. "His skin fits remarkably right about him, has very rosy gills, and drivels a little at the mouth from the constant use of quids [chewing tobacco]."[16]

Although competent, Hughes was not a Rodney-like, loose-cannon admiral. The Admiralty appreciated it. "He will not wander out of the path that may be prescribed to him to follow any schemes or whims of his own, nor never will study to find faults with his orders, but always how he may best execute them," the navy comptroller said. Indeed, Hughes thought the enemy's innovative naval tactics were unchivalrous.[17]

But, like Coote, he had his arguments with the company. He refused to take orders from it and resented its leadership presuming "to arrogate to themselves a dictatorial power over the officer commanding his Majesty's squadron in the East Indies." When the company pressured him to action before he was done refitting, he replied that "I was the judge when to sail, being myself only accountable for my conduct, and that, too, not to you." He reminded the company of his request for reinforcements, which they hoarded—tens of thousands of men "at enormous expense parading round . . . , eating up the small supplies of provisions that come to Madras."[18]

Hughes treated his men well, although some thought he was too soft. Regardless, it didn't hurt his performance. The French admiral whose name would be soon linked with Hughes in history described him as "brave, skillful, and in every respect, a very able officer" with "consummate skills and abilities equal to any man I have ever had to deal with in my profession."[19]

His birth was obscure—about 1720. His father was a small-town official of Hertford, England. As with most career officers, he entered the navy as a young teen and saw action in each of Britain's wars, from South America to Europe to Canada. In 1747, he was promoted to captain, and in ensuing years he commanded progressively larger ships. After a period of unemployment following the Seven Years' War, Hughes commanded the East India Squadron from 1774 to 1777 out of Bombay. He returned home for two years. Then, in January 1778, the king promoted him to rear admiral, knighted him, and reassigned him back to India as the naval commander-in-chief. On his way, in March 1779, he ousted the French from the slaving port of Gorée (now part of Dakar, Senegal), on the West African coast.

Hughes arrived in Madras in January 1780, and started his successful offensive against Hyder, the French, and the Dutch.

39. Suffren's "Lust for Action"

I N PARIS, THE GOVERNMENT KNEW IT HAD TO REINFORCE INDIA, OR it would lose it. "Attack the English, united or separated, wherever possible," the navy ministry ordered its commanders in Île de France (now Mauritius) in March 1781. The man to lead the offensive would be d'Orves, who, unknown to Paris, had already refused to disobey his orders and work with Hyder to trap Coote at Cuddalore.[1]

But the ministry intended to give d'Orves some help in the form of an aggressive second-in-command on the seas, and a general who would command on the land and be the admiral's superior. The general didn't arrive in India until mid-1782. The new *chef d'escadre* (the equivalent of a rear admiral), didn't wait for him.

If southern Whigs found a general in Nathanael Greene, the French in India found an admiral in Pierre André de Suffren. "He is an excellent and resourceful tactician, full of audacity and lust for action," his superior said. The naval ministry recommended him to the king: "This captain will perhaps be the best squadron commander that His Majesty could have."[2]

A generation later, Napoleon rued not having Suffren in his navy: "Oh, why did not Suffren live till my time, or why did I not light on a man of his stamp?" With an aide, he discussed Suffren's merits: He "possessed genius, invention, ardor, ambition, and inflexible steadiness . . . Suffren, who was harsh, capricious, egotistical, and a very unpleasant companion, was loved by nobody, though he was valued and admired by all. He was a man with whom no one could live on good terms."[3]

A British traveler who met Suffren in India wrote a memorable description: "He looked much more like a little fat vulgar English butler than a Frenchman of consequence. In height, he was about five feet five, very corpulent, scarce any hair upon the crown of his head, the sides and back tolerably thick. Although quite grey, he wore neither powder nor pomatum [pomade] nor any curl, having a short queue of three to four inches tied with a piece of old spun yarn. He was in slippers, or, rather, a pair of old shoes, the straps being cut off, blue cloth breeches unbuttoned at the knees, cotton or thread stockings (none of the cleanest) hanging about his legs, no waistcoat or cravat, a coarse linen shirt entirely wet with perspiration, open at the neck, the sleeves being rolled up above his elbows as if just going to wash his hands and arms." Despite his obesity, Suffren was agile—"as quick and as light as any midshipman."[4]

In habits, he usually ate with his fingers, and preferred spicy food. During battle, he wore a lucky beaver hat an older brother had given him; it helped him stay visible to his men. He often chewed on a cigar. Despite his own appearance, he tried to keep his crews healthy by requiring them to use soap.[5]

To critics, he became known as "Admiral Satan"—"*l'amiral Satan*"— a mid-twentieth-century French biographer reported. The nickname might be apocryphal, but his behavior wasn't. One contemporary said he had inborn authority, genius, ardor, ambition, and an iron character, but was egotistic, a bad comrade, liked by none, but admired and appreciated by all. "Courageous even to rashness, he showed an inflexible rigor toward officers whom he suspected of weakness or cowardice," said another.[6]

Suffren was about nine years older than Hughes, born in 1729 to a modestly wealthy, noble family. As a younger son, however, he had to earn a living. He chose the navy, and started his apprenticeship just before a French-English war broke out. From 1744 to 1747, he crossed the Atlantic three times. His first battle was at Toulon, where, 50 years later, another war would result in Charles O'Hara's capture. Before the war ended, the British captured Suffren and he spent three months in an English prison.[7]

Between wars, Suffren joined the Maltese navy and the career path of a knight of the Order of Malta, protecting Mediterranean shipping from pirates. As a knight, he took an oath of celibacy; historians haven't found any accounts of mistresses or bastard children. During the Seven Years' War, he was again with the French navy, fighting first at Minorca, and then captured again off Portugal. This time, he was a prisoner for two years. After the war, he returned to the Maltese navy, where he was a frigate captain, again fighting pirates.

With the American rebellion, Suffren returned to the French navy and commanded his first large warship. Off Rhode Island in 1778, he forced two British frigates to beach and burn themselves. Later that year, he saw action in the Caribbean. Like Kempenfelt, Suffren sent a litany of suggestions to the ministry he believed would improve the fleet: Copper the ships' hulls. Require the sailors to wash with soap. Install fire pumps. Attach lightning rods. Add more launches. Use mortars to fire grapeshot.

Suffren never seemed to alienate his superiors, but in private letters—many to Marie-Thérèse de Perrot de Seillans, the Countess d'Alès, a close friend, possibly a distant cousin—he railed against them and his peers. January 5, 1779: "You cannot imagine the idiotic maneuvers that have been made. . . . They have gotten annoyed with me for wanting to attack seven small ships with 12 big ones, simply because the former were defended by some land batteries." January 8: "I am extremely disgusted . . ." April 2: "Imagine a fleet commander whose least fault is to be not one whit a seaman." July 10: "Had his seamanship matched his courage, we would not have let four dismasted British ships escape."[8]

By late 1780, at 51, he returned to France a squadron commander who, although respected, played no major role in the war. About that time, the navy minister lost a political battle and was replaced. Suffren immediate lobbied the new minister for an expanded role. The new minister gave him a choice: Return to North America, or go to India.

In March 1781, Suffren and his small squadron sailed out of Brest with Grasse's fleet, which was headed for the Caribbean and, ultimately, Yorktown. Near Madeira, Suffren left the fleet, veering south for India via the Cape Verde Islands, Cape Town, and Île de France. One of his orders was to land reinforcements for the Dutch fort at the Cape to ensure the British wouldn't attack the strategic port, as intelligence said they were planning.

Off the town of Porto Praya (Praia) at Portugese Cape Verde on April 15, Suffren saw a British squadron, presumably the one headed for Cape Town. He attacked—violating Portuguese neutrality—and damaged the enemy ships. When the fighting broke off at sundown, Suffren immediately left for Cape Town, where he arrived in mid-June. The British arrived from Porto Praya in July, but seeing the reinforcements and Suffren's squadron, they sailed away, some returning to Britain, others reinforcing Hughes in India.

It's 2,565 miles from Cape Town to Île de France, and bad weather and the need for refitting delayed Suffren's sailing until September. He arrived in the Île de France capital, Port Louis, on October 25. There, he found his superior officer, d'Orves, ill; d'Orves's officers insubordinate because Suffren refused to follow seniority in naming captains (d'Orves overruled Suffren); and "the military spirit has been forgotten."[9]

The Île-de-France governor told d'Orves that "Madras is the important object that we cannot attend to too soon; the quicker we attack this place, the less resistance it will offer." D'Orves now commanded a squadron of eleven warships, three frigates, assorted other ships and transports, 8,550 sailors, and 3,100 army troops. They left port on December 7—but didn't head to Madras as Suffren and the governor wanted. Instead, the fleet sailed toward Trincomalee, which, unknown to d'Orves, was now British. On the way, in mid-January 1782, Suffren captured a British warship, thus augmenting the squadron. Other than that action, Suffren chafed—but not for long. On February 3, 1782, d'Orves' health worsened, and he turned command over to Suffren. D'Orves died six days later.[10]

Suffren immediately changed plans. He told his captains to change course for Madras. And unlike traditional French navy strategies that focused on defense and keeping a line in battle, Suffren told his captains to use their own judgment in attacking the enemy.[11]

He was, a French admiral later wrote, "the first to disdain the routine . . . of ranging the squadron in one single line of battle. He cared not for the traditions which required one to fight at a moderate distance. He engaged within pistol-shot." Suffren's objectives—to attack, not defend; to concentrate fire, not dilute it along the line—were "too original for his officers' mentality," said another admiral. By the time Suffren was done in India, he had fired nine captains, returning them to France in disgrace, three of them under arrest.[12]

Again and again, Suffren complained to Île de France and Paris that annihilation of the British fleet was thwarted by captains who didn't obey his orders. "I am absolutely brokenhearted by the most general of defections," he wrote the navy minister after one battle. "I just missed the chance to destroy the English squadron." He described his second-in-command as "the born enemy of his commanders, and he would go into despair if they did well. You understand how awful it is to have such a second. I dare not speak to you about the others [captains]."[13]

Suffren also felt at a disadvantage because few of his ships had coppered bottoms, making them slower and needing more frequent maintenance. And, with the loss of Trincomalee to Hughes, Suffren had no major harbor where he could shelter his ships from the monsoons or adequately resupply the fleet.

40. The Final Battles

SUFFREN'S SQUADRON ARRIVED OFF MADRAS ON FEBRUARY 14, 1782. There, he saw Hughes's ships anchored under the town's land batteries. Suffren sent most of his transports to Porto Novo (which Coote had abandoned). Hughes left the harbor to engage Suffren. What followed was the first of five battles between Suffren and Hughes over the next seventeen months:

SADRAS: Sunday, February 17, 1782. Hughes chased Suffren to the waters off Sadras (Kalpakkam), about forty miles south of Madras, but Suffren attacked first. The enemies fought from the late afternoon until sunset. Although Hughes captured six French transports, his ships suffered severe damage—one ship, he said, "reduced almost to the state of a wreck." Both sides suffered roughly the same number of casualties: about thirty dead and one hundred wounded. Suffren blamed four of his captains for the battle's inconclusiveness; those captains refused to obey his orders to close, firing their weapons only from a distance. Hughes sailed his squadron to Trincomalee for repairs; Suffren sailed to Porto Novo.[1]

At Porto Novo, he talked with Hyder's envoys and agreed to leave 2,000 to 3,000 troops there, including an African regiment, that Hyder could use to take Cuddalore. That town fell to the Mysoreans and French in early May. Suffren promised that more reinforcements were on the way from France. In March, Suffren received new orders, written in France: Return to Île de France to refit his ships and wait for the reinforcements. He refused to do so, angering more of his captains. "It would be better to sink the squadron under the walls of Madras than to retire from before Sir Edward Hughes," he told them. Relations with Hyder were too fragile, Suffren believed, and he wasn't going to give Hughes five months of peaceful sailing. "I take this step, though the only right one, with regret, for it will please no one and be disapproved by all," he said. He then sailed to Ceylon in hopes of a rendezvous with promised reinforcements and the possibility of taking Trincomalee itself. (Île-de-France's governor supported Suffren's disobedience: "The brave decision by M. de Suffren may save India.")[2]

PROVEDIEN: Friday, April 12, 1782. While Suffren worked with Hyder's envoys at Porto Novo, Hughes returned to Madras. Then, hearing from scouts that Suffren was headed to Ceylon, Hughes returned to Trincomalee to shore up its defenses with his squadron and army reinforcements. He arrived there on April 8. For three days, the French and British stayed in sight of each other, but Suffren couldn't attack because of unfavorable winds.

Despite what one contemporary called "baffling and uncertain" winds, the squadrons engaged on the 12th off the coast of Provedian (probably Challitivu Islet), thirty miles south of Trincomalee. The battle was again indecisive, with both squadrons being crippled, and Suffren again complained about his captains. Suffren's flagship lost one of its masts and became difficult to sail; he was forced to move to another ship. The French had about 1,300 wounded or ill men; the British had nearly 1,900. Hughes said his vessels were "more like hospital ships than men-of-war."[3]

For several days after the battle, the enemies eyed each other from a distance. At one point, the two admirals discussed a prisoner exchange, but Hughes refused, saying he didn't have the power to authorize one. Possibly, he might have wanted Suffren to remain burdened with guarding and feeding them. Suffren didn't let that happen. He eventually handed over his prisoners to Hyder, "clearly contrary to the custom of civilized war" because Hyder was "in reality, a barbarian," the British said. Hyder's mistreatment of British prisoners became part of anti-Suffren propaganda and the post-war subject of horrific first-person accounts. When some prisoners got a message to Suffren about their treatment, he indignantly replied that their leaders had refused an exchange. "It is them you are to thank." He later apologized for his sarcasm, saying he was reacting to the notorious British treatment of French and American rebel prisoners in New York, "crowded into a prison ship and dying of an epidemical disease." He ordered his prisoners' rations increased.[4]

(Hyder himself refused at least one exchange with the British. In December 1781, when offered one thousand native troops for his Europeans prisoners, Hyder replied that "he knew better than to exchange European prisoners for a set of dastardly scoundrels whose heads, to a man, when they return to him, he would assuredly chop off.")[5]

At a standoff, Hughes returned to Trincomalee, and Suffren sailed seventy miles south to the still-Dutch town of Batacola (Batticaloa). His squadron, like Hughes's, was in bad shape. "Scurvy was making frightful ravages in the fleet," an officer said. "The country round Batacola was unhealthy, and . . . it was impossible to get either fruits or vegetables. . . . Our supply of rope exhausted; the provisions running short; the crews, sadly diminished in number, overworked; the certainty of more battles in which we could not promise ourselves any advantage more decisive than in those we had fought—all these were considerations that threw a dark cloud over our future prospects, and gave rise to the most embarrassing reflections."[6]

NEGAPATAM: Saturday, July 6, 1782. Suffren left Batacola on June 3 with some provisions, got more at neutral Danish Tranquebar on the Indian mainland several days later, and captured a few British supply ships en route. The squadron arrived in Cuddalore on June 20. There, he learned that the French general left in command—who would be superseded by the new general that Paris promised—had alienated Hyder and refused to work with him to attack Negapatam, 80 miles to the south.

Suffren repaired relations with his ally, and they agreed to proceed with the attack. The first step, however, was to defeat Hughes, who had learned about Suffren's moves, and sailed to defend Negapatam. On July 5, Suffren sailed near the town and saw that Hughes beat him to the anchorage. Suffren signaled for an attack, but a sudden squall damaged one of his ships and gave Hughes the advantage of the wind. Suffren disengaged from a battle.

The next day was different. The enemies began fighting in midmorning. It was another bloody battle. Hughes seemed to have the upper hand when the wind shifted against his favor around 12:30 P.M. Had the wind not changed, "I have good reason to believe it would have ended in the capture of several of their line-of-battle ships," he said. Suffren again blamed his captains for disobeying orders. He later arrested three of them: One had tried to surrender, but his officers mutinied to save their ship. Another simply refused to fight, saying he hadn't had time to repair damage. Hughes thwarted Suffren's attempt to take Negapatam, and his ships killed nearly 180 French sailors, while wounding more than six hundred—significantly higher losses than the British suffered. Suffren sailed back to Cuddalore, but Hughes's ships were too damaged to pursue.[7]

On July 20, Hughes arrived back in Madras. "After three long and severe engagements," he said, "there was not a line of battleship in the squadron that had not to stop their holes . . ."[8]

The French also suffered. "I assure you it is no easy matter to keep to sea on a coast without money, without magazines, with a squadron in many respects badly furnished, and after having sustained three combats," Suffren wrote Île de France. "I am at the end of my resources. . . . The squadron has 2,000 men in hospital, of whom 600 are wounded."[9]

Hyder and Suffren met on July 26 for the first time at Hyder's camp outside Cuddalore. The Mysorean leader praised the first Frenchman who was as aggressive as he was. "At last, the English have found their master," he told Suffren. "Here is the man who will help me to exterminate them." He called Suffren "extraordinary." He also was impressed by Suffren's appetite at a banquet; apparently, Suffren inhaled the spicy Indian food. The two men discussed strategy over the course of three days. Suffren promised Hyder that once reinforcements arrived, he would attack Hughes, and "God willing, I shall destroy him." Hyder replied, "Suffren, now that I have seen you, I have seen all." Suffren's report to Paris was equally enthusiastic: "If we had known how to deal with him from the start, we could have had him do anything we wanted. My only cunning in dealing with him was to use none and to tell him always what was strictly true."[10]

But where were the long-awaited reinforcements?

The general that Paris chose to send to India as commander was an India veteran.

Charles-Joseph Patissier, the Marquis de Bussy-Castelnau, 64, had lost his father at a young age. He joined the army and, in 1737, went to India as a soldier of fortune with the French East India Company army. He trained native troops, led them against the British company army, and earned for France territory and concessions. In 1750, with 1,250 native and European troops, he defeated a native army of ten thousand. A decade later, however, Bussy met his match: Coote captured him. The British released him on parole, and he retired to a French estate, where he suffered from periodic bouts of malaria and gout. When the government asked him to prepare a plan for conquering India, he recommended not relying on native allies or demanding concessions from them. In 1781, Bussy agreed to return to India, but only if an army of nine thousand French soldiers accompanied him, and, to coordinate fighting, he commanded both the army and navy. The government agreed to the command, but could promise only six to seven thousand men.[11]

Suffren complained to the ministry that Bussy didn't understand the navy. But he promised, "I will do my best to prevent harm arising." Harm, however, had already come to Bussy. He left Cádiz, Spain, on January 4, 1782, but with only four thousand men. Kempenfelt's victory over Guichen on December 12 meant many of Bussy's supplies never arrived. The men on his expedition suffered from scurvy, and Bussy himself had a serious, two-month-long illness. He didn't arrive in Île de France until the end of May, minus 1,700 men he left in Cape Town for its defense.[12]

Another convoy, sent to reinforce Bussy, was star-crossed. It was hit by scurvy, and by the time it arrived in Île-de-France, seven hundred men were dead, 2,800 soldiers needed hospitalization, and of these, 1,200 would die.[13]

A small French convoy—two warships, a frigate, nine transport ships, and eight hundred soldiers—finally arrived in July in Dutch Galle on Ceylon's south shore, three hundred miles from Trincomalee and Batacola. Suffren wrote Bussy, still in Île de France, that his squadron intended to attack Trincomalee in an effort to defeat Hughes before expected British reinforcements arrived. "Of all the imaginable combinations, there is only one—in which I defeat the English squadron before their reinforcements come—that can give us an existence in India." Suffren arrived there on August 9, and reinforcements arrived starting on August 18.[14]

With those reinforcements came a message: The Order of Malta had promoted Suffren to Bailli, its highest honor. Suffren used that title, rather than his French rank, for the rest of his life.

TRINCOMALEE: Tuesday, September 3, 1782. Suffren arrived at Trincomalee the night of August 25. He landed 2,300 soldiers and 500 marines, then prepared to besiege the British at Fort Ostenburg, which overlooked the harbor. Suffren opened fire on August 29; the British surrendered the next day, extracting from Suffren a pledge to return the 150 European and three hundred native troops to Madras.

Hughes appeared off Trincomalee on September 2, unaware the port was lost. Suffren planned to attack, but some of his captains hesitated, wanting to stay in the harbor under Fort Ostenburg's guns. Suffren replied, "If the enemy had more ships than I have, I would abstain. If he had an equal number, I could scarcely refrain. But as he has fewer, there is no choice: We must go out and fight him."[15]

The fight started the next day at mid-afternoon and continued until dark. Again, Suffren's captains failed to get good position: Two collided with each other; three couldn't raise their anchors. Even a British account said the French captains were "unworthy to serve so great a man." The *Calcutta Gazette* said Suffren was "badly seconded."[16]

And again, the battle was indecisive. Both enemies suffered severe damage. It took Suffren three days to maneuver four damaged ships back to Trincomalee.[17] Three of Hughes's ships were in danger of sinking. He couldn't chase Suffren because, he said, "The ships of our squadron had apparently suffered so much as to be in no condition to pursue them." Both sides lost about the same number of men: the French had eighty-two killed and 255 wounded, the British fifty-one killed and 282 wounded.[18]

Hughes made his way back to Madras, and eventually to Bombay, to refit during the monsoons.

Suffren found himself with a mixed blessing: Four of his captains resigned, three ostensibly for health reasons, the fourth for personal reasons. Suffren's dilemma was that while Trincomalee was a great harbor, the area, as Wilks said, was "utterly destitute of every resource." Suffren sailed first to Cuddalore to land reinforcements, and then one thousand miles east to neutral Achin (Aceh), Sumatra.[19]

Over the winter, Suffren heard that on the same day he fought Hughes off Provedien, Grasse was captured at the Battle of the Saintes.

A second piece of news directly affected Suffren. Hyder died from an infected abscess on December 7, 1782. His court biographer reported his last days: "Hyder, on hearing that it was a deadly boil which had appeared on his neck, became certain that his last hour had arrived. But without allowing fear or apprehension to take place in his mind, he remained, as usual, absorbed in the order and regulation of his army and kingdom. . . ." He sent for his son to assume command, authorized a bonus for his soldiers, sent cavalry out to frighten villages (presumably to divert attention), then "swallowed a little broth and laid down to rest. The same night, his ever-victorious spirit took its flight to Paradise."[20]

Hyder's son and successor, Tipu Sultan, was born around 1753. (He wasn't a sultan; it's a common name.) He was an experienced and successful commander. Like his father, he was controversial. Wilks heard secondhand that Hyder believed his son's intellect "was of an inferior order, and his disposition wantonly cruel, deceitful, vicious, and intractable." Others accused Tipu of forced conversions to Islam—"a reign of Islamic terror and oppression." An eighteenth-century British admirer said, "He acted with so much equity and mildness that no prince was ever more popular in his own dominions. . . . He was seldom deceived in his politics as a statesman or cruel to his captives as a conqueror." Nonetheless, he worked toward a greater role for Islam in India, with Europeans reduced to trading stations only. Most modern Hindu writers, however, argue that Tipu was "a great patriot, a nationalist, and a freedom fighter" slandered by the British, who "hated him because he was an ardent fighter for national integration." Forcing Hindus to convert to Islam was something some of his governors did; fourteen of Tipu's twenty-four cabinet ministers were Hindu.[21]

Tipu's immediate concern were attacks by the British and their allies against Mysorean positions on the Malabar. Accordingly, he left the east and the French in Cuddalore to address his enemies in the west. A British force had taken Mangalore; it would be several months before Tipu retook the town and defeated the British.

Suffren needed to be closer to the action. He left Achin for Cuddalore before 1782 was out. At that point, he didn't know that Bussy had finally left Île-de-France having survived an epidemic there. Bussy said the knowledge that the government was depending on him, "constrain me to sacrifice the little health that remains to me, and depart for India, despite the weakness of my present means."[22]

CUDDALORE: June 20, 1783. For the first part of 1783, the enemies did little. They captured a few of each other's ships. Tipu besieged Mangalore. Hughes refitted in Bombay. Suffren sailed from Cuddalore to Trincomalee to complete his refitting. Food was scarce in southeastern India. In Madras, the British garrison was on rations; a famine killed thousands in the region. "Wretched mothers might be seen loaded with grief and affliction, offering to enslave their darling children for as much rice as would only prolong their miseries for perhaps eight dreadful days," an officer wrote. "Crows, vultures, and jackals, allured by the scent of death, flocked in crowds to the scene."[23]

On March 10, Bussy finally arrived in Trincomalee. He brought with him three warships, a frigate, and transports carrying 2,300 troops. Suffren escorted them to India, dropping Bussy and his men off to reinforce Porto Novo and then Cuddalore. In Cuddalore, Bussy found a garrison of six hundred French soldiers, four thousand native soldiers, and eight thousand of Tipu's cavalry. Suffren, needing further refitting, returned to Trincomalee.

In April, Bussy passed on to Suffren the intelligence that a combined British land–sea expedition against Cuddalore was imminent. He wrote Suffren pleading for "food, wood, bullets—but above all food." The intelligence was correct. Hughes had arrived in Madras on April 13. Coote's successor, Major General James Stuart, vowed to Hughes: "Our next campaign will, I trust, put an end to French consequence in India." Their plan was for Hughes to besiege Cuddalore from the sea and maintain a supply chain to Stuart. Stuart would march from Madras to Cuddalore and capture a suitable beach outside the town for Hughes's supply ships.[24]

Stuart was one of Coote's trusted and experienced generals. During the Seven Years' War, Stuart had fought in Nova Scotia, Martinique, and France, rising to lieutenant colonel and serving as a quartermaster general. He was posted to India in 1775. There, on orders of the Madras presidency, Stuart arrested the governor. The company board in London suspended him. He was cleared by a court-martial five years later, given back pay, promoted to brigadier general (and later, major general), and restored to the Madras command. In a battle against Hyder, a cannonball shot away one of Stuart's legs. Like Coote, he fought with Governor Macartney.[25]

Stuart and 15,000 men left Madras for Cuddalore on April 21, 1783. What he had planned as an eleven-day march, took forty-seven days. Hampered by sickness, weather, difficult terrain, and low food supplies, he didn't arrive on the outskirts of Cuddalore until June 7.[26]

Bussy, once an aggressive general, didn't attack. Instead, he abandoned his outer defense perimeter and, one eyewitness said, stayed "invisible in his tent like a rich nabob." (Failing health might have been a factor; he died in India in 1785.)[27]

Hughes, who arrived off Cuddalore on June 6, landed reinforcements and supplies for Stuart at the beachhead. Now, Bussy was besieged, and his only chance of relief was from Tipu, still on the Malabar, or Suffren, still refitting in Trincomalee.

On the 13th, Stuart attacked Bussy's inner defense perimeter. "A most bloody and desperate conflict ensued," said one fighter. "The usual carnage," Wilks said. At the end of the day, the British and their allies suffered one thousand men killed, wounded, or missing. The French and their allies suffered half that number. Still, Bussy was pessimistic about his ability to hold Cuddalore with Hughes's 18 warships sailing off the coast between Porto Novo and Cuddalore, protecting British transports that supplied Stuart. Now, Bussy waited for Suffren.[28]

Suffren, with three fewer warships than Hughes, five of them commanded by lieutenants, approached the coast off Porto Novo on June 13. Thanks to their fast scouting ships, the two admirals knew roughly where the other was. For the next seven days, without favorable winds, they eyed each other, jockeying for position. In the meantime, Suffren seized the Cuddalore anchorage, where his officers conferred with Bussy. They concluded that Cuddalore would be lost if Suffren couldn't defeat Hughes, and Bussy loaned Suffren more than one thousand men.[29]

Finally, in the mid-afternoon of June 20, the winds cooperated, and the battle began. Cuddalore became the largest naval battle fought in the Indian Ocean during the sailing era. As with the previous four battles, the casualties were similar—about one hundred dead and four hundred wounded on each side. But as evening came, Hughes withdrew, sailing back to Madras. In the preceding month, three thousand of his men contracted scurvy; although he had more ships, he had fewer sailors—half their normal complement. What's more, he was running out of water.[30]

The next day, Suffren re-anchored at Cuddalore, returned the borrowed soldiers, added some of his marines, and went ashore where he was carried through the streets as the hero of the day. Bussy greeted him with four words: "Messieurs, voila notre sauveur." ("Gentlemen, behold our savior.")[31]

But Stuart's army remained camped outside Cuddalore's walls. Stuart had seen the French ships return and his British lifeline disappear. This, he said, gave the French "infinite superiority" to him. His position was "almost insupportable." As for him personally, "this is now nine days since our fleet and provision ships left us . . . my mind is upon the rack without a moment's rest."[32]

Bussy attacked Stuart around 3 A.M. on June 25. The sortie was a disaster. He had sent too few men led by an incompetent commander, a "recognized disability," a French officer said. The result was forty dead Frenchmen and one hundred prisoners.[33]

Suffren now planned a sea bombardment of Stuart's position.

But on an overcast Sunday, June 29, at 1:30 P.M., with a fresh wind coming from the southwest, Suffren wrote in his journal that one of his ships "reported a sail to the North-Northeast." Because of the wind, it took ten hours for the *Medea*, a British frigate flying a white flag, to position itself next to Suffren's ship. *Medea*'s Captain Erasmus Gower had a message from Hughes and Macartney for Suffren and Bussy.[34]

Twelve days before, on June 17, someone gave Madras officials a newspaper that reported details of the preliminary Anglo-French peace treaty. The treaty had been signed in Paris five months to the day that the Battle of Cuddalore was fought. As soon as Hughes returned to Madras from the battle, he and Macartney dispatched the *Medea* with a ceasefire proposal. "It is somewhat strange that the saving of many thousands of lives of ours was literally owing to one private gentleman sending a newspaper to another," Gower said.[35]

The truce held, although the French and British didn't receive official word of the treaty until late August. The Mysoreans, however, weren't a party to the treaty, and Tipu and the British continued to skirmish until March 1784, when they signed the Treaty of Mangalore. It provided for a prisoner exchange and mutual restoration of territory, but some British considered it a diplomatic victory for Tipu since it positioned him better to fight neighboring kingdoms.[36]

For the French, the ceasefire was "most unfortunate," because if they had defeated Stuart's army, all southern India would have been theirs. Suffren complained to Paris, "If everything sent from France had arrived in time, we should now be masters of India." To his close friend, he was modest: "The consideration in which I am held in India is almost incredible: verses, songs, letters, the lot. But it could have been otherwise. The smallest thing can turn handclaps into hisses."[37]

Hughes also was reflective. He acknowledged to Parliament his inability to destroy Suffren's squadron. Nonetheless, "I have, however, with the assistance of the brave men who served with me, been able effectually to disappoint and defeat all their designs of conquest in this part of the world."[38]

The careers of Hughes and Suffren were effectively over. Promoted to admiral in 1793, Hughes never held another command. Suffren arrived home in 1784, was celebrated as a hero, given a large pension, and ignored for any active command. "Here I am," he wrote, "once a man of importance, now fallen to the humble state of a bourgeois of Paris." In 1788, while eating dinner, he collapsed, probably from a heart attack. Suffren lay in a Paris cemetery for four years until the French Revolution, when his bones were dug up and scattered. Seven navy ships have been named after Suffren, as well as a Parisian avenue, at least one bar, restaurant, and hotel.[39]

Tipu fought two more wars with the British, but never achieved his father's success. Cornwallis, then in India, defeated Tipu in 1792, and forced him to cede half his kingdom to the East India Company and its allies. In 1799, the British invaded Mysore. Tipu was killed on May 4, when his enemies stormed the capital. The British exiled his family to Calcutta, and their descendants became impoverished. In 2009, a state government, acknowledging Tipu's contributions to nationalism, agreed to give one descendant a house and pay for his children's education. Tipu and Hyder are buried in their capital city in a mausoleum.[40]

The mutual hatred between Madras governor Macartney and Stuart intensified when Macartney suspended Stuart after Cuddalore and ordered him to England. Four years later, Stuart challenged him to a duel. Macartney accepted, and Stuart wounded Macartney in the shoulder. Stuart is sometimes confused with

Lieutenant Colonel James Stuart (1741–1815), who was under General Stuart's command at Cuddalore. The lieutenant colonel also became a general.[41]

Cuddalore was the last battle of the American Revolution. But it wasn't yet the end.

PART EIGHT

Washington and Carleton

41. New Leader, Old Leader

AFTER YORKTOWN, HENRY CLINTON, BRITAIN'S COMMANDER IN North America, lost the war of finger-pointing. London allowed him to resign, and he left New York for England shortly after his replacement arrived on May 5, 1782.

"The country will have more confidence in a new man," George III said. "I believe, without partiality, that the man who would, in general, by the army be looked on as the best officer is Sir Guy Carleton."[1]

Lieutenant General Carleton, 58, came from a family of modest landowners in Ireland. He worked his way up the ranks by demonstrating competence to powerful patrons. He befriended the future general and military wunderkind, James Wolfe, as well as the Duke of Richmond, a future field marshal. While George II wasn't fond of Carleton, George III appointed Carleton an aide-de-camp. When Carleton was named commander-in-chief, that led to the resignation of cabinet eminence George Germain, with whom Carleton had an ancient, bitter feud. And even Germain acknowledged Carleton's "reputation of a resolute and persevering officer."[2]

Carleton's personality didn't match his competence. "He is one of the most distant, reserved men in the world," said a lieutenant who served with him in Canada. "He has a rigid strictness in his manner, very unpleasing, and which he observes even to his most particular friends and acquaintances. At the same time, he is a very able general and brave officer; has seen a great deal of service; and rose from a private life ... by mere merit to the rank he at present bears. In time of danger, he possesses a coolness and steadiness . . . which few can attain, yet he was far from being the favorite of the army."[3]

An MP described Carleton as "a grave man . . . too reserved to betray himself if he was not what he was reckoned." The prime minister, Lord North, said Carleton didn't play games: "so much of a soldier, and so little of a politician; such a resolute, honest man, and such a faithful and dutiful subject."[4]

Unlike other military leaders of his time, Carleton refused to tolerate corruption as General William Howe did or get rich in the questionable ways that Admiral Rodney did. George III complained about Carleton being "too cold and not as active as might be wished," but his "uncorruptness is universally acknowledged."[5]

He came to North America during the Seven Years' War as quartermaster general and de facto chief engineer for Wolfe. At the 1759 Battle of the Plains of Abraham outside Québec, he commanded a battalion. Wolfe was killed; Carleton, wounded in the head. Two years later, Carleton was seriously wounded again during an attack against an enemy position off the French coast. Star-crossed, he was wounded a third time during a 1762 assault on Havana.

After the war, he was promoted to lieutenant governor of Québec. In fact, he served as de facto governor general, because the existing governor general, James Murray (the future hero of Minorca), was recalled. Five years later, in 1768, Carleton became governor and commander in name. Canada then (as now) was split by language and ethnic divisions. Carleton was an autocratic reformer who, like Murray, championed the majority French-Canadian population over British merchants and traders. One of his early actions was to suppress government and military officials from enriching themselves by taking a cut of fees imposed on the population. "There is a certain appearance of dirt, a sort of meanness, in exacting fees on every occasion," he said.[6]

His reforms ran the gamut: promoting agriculture and mining; opposing a manufacturing ban; lifting bans on fur traders traveling in Indian country; indemnifying residents who owned old French paper money; repairing roads; regulating bakers and river pilots. Carleton spent four years in London helping to shape what became the Québec Act of 1774; it extended Canada's boundary to the Ohio River, guaranteed French-Canadian civil rights, and allowed

Catholics to hold office. British merchants and American rebels denounced it.

Those rebels invaded Canada in fall 1775 and captured Montréal. Carleton escaped the city disguised as a peasant and narrowly avoided capture. Soon, however, he organized and led the defense of a besieged Québec, repulsed a new year's attack, and kept it in British hands until it was relieved in May 1776. Although he defeated a weak rebel armada on Lake Champlain in October, he failed to pursue the remnants of the rebel army—citing the late time of year—and refused to allow allied Indians to attack the enemy. That month, as a conciliatory gesture, he released all his prisoners.

London praised him for Québec's defense, but it ordered another general, John Burgoyne, to assume command of an invasion force for 1777. Carleton resigned in protest, although he made a good-faith effort to support Burgoyne while waiting for a new governor. Burgoyne's expedition ended in defeat at Saratoga. From 1778 to 1782, Carleton lived in England, working on a commission that audited military expenditures. Then, the king named him Clinton's replacement.

As Carleton prepared to leave London for New York, Lord North's ministry fell, and Parliament voted to end offensive military actions against the American rebels and to treat captured rebels as prisoners of war, not practitioners of treason. The new prime minister, Shelburne, confirmed Carleton's appointment, and agreed that he should follow up on the demonstrations of Britain's good faith with a goal of achieving reconciliation with the rebels short of independence. This would allow Britain to focus its military efforts against the more dangerous enemies, France, Spain, and Holland.

Carleton's first priority, Shelburne said, was to "provide for withdrawing the garrison, artillery, provisions, stores of all kinds, every species of public property" from Savannah, Charlestown, and New York. If he was attacked while evacuating, he was authorized to make "an early capitulation" if he could do so on favorable terms. Avoid "an obstinate defense of the place without hope of answering any rational purpose by it." In addition, by "reconciling the minds and affections of His Majesty's subjects by such open and generous conduct as may serve to captivate their hearts and remove every suspicion of insincerity" would help sever their alliance and dependence on the French.[7]

On May 7, two days after arriving in New York, Carleton wrote Washington an introductory letter, talked about Britain's new "pacific disposition," and said he would match conciliatory acts in kind. He especially hoped the two generals could reduce atrocities and "acts of retaliation" by Whig and Loyalist militias.[8]

Beyond relations with Washington, Carleton assessed the situation he inherited from Clinton. It wasn't good. For lack of transports, he would be unable to carry out his orders to evacuate the city in 1782. Worse, Clinton had neglected New York's defenses; a combined French-rebel attack could well succeed. Carleton immediately ordered fortifications strengthened and to emphasize it, he rode out every morning to inspect a different part of British-controlled territory.[9]

Loyalists chafed under British military rule—and corruption. Within a month, Carleton began to correct what one MP called "enormous abuses." A German-born minister, the Reverend Ewald Gustav Schaukirk, described Carleton's impact after just two weeks: "The new commander-in-chief makes many wholesome changes to the great saving of public expenses. . . . A couple of hundred of deputy commissioners in different departments have been or will be dismissed, hundreds of carpenters and other workmen have been turned off. . . . No officer will be allowed to have vessels, wagons, etc. to carry on any [personal or contraband] trade. We rejoice that the chain of enormous, iniquitous practices will be at last broken! . . . The inhabitants have also been relieved from working on the fortifications every fifth day." Nine months later, Schaukirk recorded that the prices of flour, rum, molasses, and coffee "have fallen surprisingly." This showed that before Carleton arrived, merchants practiced "avarice and extortion."[10]

But Carleton couldn't be everywhere. British colonel Benjamin Thompson, who had fought successfully against Francis Marion in South Carolina, showed how British troops—actually, Loyalist troops—turned neutral or even loyal civilians into rebels. He stationed his 400-man King's American Dragoons in Huntington, Long Island. There, he demolished a Presbyterian church for its timber; forced civilians to build a fort; used gravestones for fireplaces, tables, and ovens; pitched his tent in a graveyard; and as his troops left, burned all the fence rails in the area. He did all this, a Whig resident said, "without any assignable purpose except that of filling his own pockets," and to "gratify a malignant disposition by vexing the people."[11]

(Thompson had an illustrious postwar career. With British government permission, he moved to Munich, where he served as Bavarian war minister and modernized its army. Munich built a monument to him and named him Count von Rumford, after his New Hampshire hometown [now Concord]. President John Adams offered him a military position. Rumford declined with thanks. In Dublin, Rumford improved hospital and workhouse conditions. Back in London, he invented ways to reduce smoky chimneys, and contributed ideas in physics. He moved to Paris in 1805 and married the widow of the French scientist, Lavoisier. There, he died. Part of his estate went to Harvard University to create a still-active endowed chair.)

Thompson wasn't alone in alienating civilians. As with many modern-day insurgencies, the British army, even after six years of occupation, couldn't distinguish between friends and enemies; experienced breakdowns in discipline that resulted in civilians being robbed, their property confiscated, their persons abused; and failed to compensate adequately, if at all, for goods. The military government often failed to convict soldiers guilty of crimes, or commuted their sentences. The army caused food and fuel shortages, and inflation. Admiral Rodney, visiting New York in 1780, called it "a long train of leeches."[12]

Prisoners of war were another of Carleton's problems. Clinton had paroled 130 rebels in January 1782 from one of the brutal New York prison ships that had mortality rates estimated from thirty-five to seventy percent. When the ex-POWs arrived in Connecticut, a Whig paper reported, "It is enough to melt the most obdurate heart of anyone (except a Briton) to see these miserable objects continually landing here . . . sick and dying, and the few rags they have on covered with vermin and their own excrements." Carleton paroled another eight hundred prisoners in May. By the end of the year, a prison ship officer said he was "left here with about 700 miserable objects, eaten up with lice, and daily taking fevers, which carry them off fast."[13]

Carleton, however, wanted reciprocity. He and Washington named commissioners in September to negotiate a general exchange. The talks failed because the Whigs felt the British commissioners didn't have enough authorization to do the kind of deal they wanted. Then, the Whigs demanded compensation for the upkeep of the British POWs. Carleton told Washington that the easiest way to ease that burden would be for Congress to release all the prisoners on parole. The British ended up sending clothing and blankets. Despite the commission's failure, by year's end, Carleton had paroled hundreds of enemy prisoners.[14]

The rebels frustrated Carleton. "I have not found the least disposition in the rulers of the provinces to come into pacific measures," he told Shelburne. Some said the country is controlled by the French minister, Washington, and Robert Morris (the superintendent of finance), and that Congress is their puppet. If so, Carleton said, " 'tis not surprising America should be sacrificed to the interests of France."[15]

The rebels' chain of command—Washington's insistence that he could make no decisions about what he defined as civil matters—confused Carleton. In one letter about prisoner exchanges, Carleton asked Washington for clarification. "Am I, sir, to apply to Congress, that persons appointed by me, may be admitted to conferences at Philadelphia? Or can any deputation be sent by Congress to your camp for this purpose, to be there met by persons empowered by me? Or will you, sir, undertake to manage our common interest? All I wish for is: that an end in which our common honor and humanity is engaged may be substantially obtained."[16]

Washington had his own problems. The Continental army returned in November 1781 from Yorktown to its main encampments along the lower Hudson River north of New York City. Thanks to French money, its twelve thousand men were now the best equipped in its history.[17]

However, the soldiers worked for a bankrupt government with no taxing authority and no ability to pay them. The situation gnawed at Washington, who confided to a former aide: "The predicament in which I stand as citizen and soldier is as critical and delicate as can well be conceived. It has been the subject of many contemplative hours. The sufferings of a complaining army on one hand, and the inability of Congress and tardiness of the states on the other, are the forebodings of evil."[18]

The evil was an army mutiny or even a coup. In the war's eight years, there would be fifty-six documented mutinies or attempted mutinies in the Continental army. New England troops suppressed a mutiny by New Jersey troops in January 1782. A march by Connecticut troops on the state capital in May ended when their leader was shot. The Pennsylvania line threatened Congress in June 1783; Washington ended the mutiny by sending 1,500 troops against them. Congress pardoned the ringleaders.[19]

Two months earlier, in Newburgh, New York, Washington personally quashed a potential rebellion among his officers at an emotional meeting. By deferring to civil authorities, he said, "you will, by the dignity of your conduct, afford occasion for posterity to say, when speaking of the glorious example you have exhibited to mankind, 'Had this day been wanting, the world had never seen the last stage of perfection to which human nature is capable of attaining.' " At one point, Washington pulled out his reading glasses— most officers had never seen him use them—and, said an eyewitness, excused himself because "he had grown gray in their service, and now found himself growing blind."[20]

Washington also had problems maintaining the size of his army due to desertion and expiring enlistments. Recruiting standards fell, but even so, in spring 1782, Washington court-martialed an officer for recruiting French deserters, small boys, a lame Negro, and an "idiot."[21]

Another concern was contraband. Since the British could pay gold for goods and food, a continuous flow of supplies streamed across the lines. It made Washington's own efforts to supply his men that much more difficult.[22]

Just as the rebel's chain of command frustrated Carleton, the British strategy of conciliation struck Washington as inexplicable and possibly dangerous. "I hardly know what to think or believe," he wrote Nathanael Greene in August 1782. "I confess, I am induced to doubt everything—to suspect everything." Now more than ever, the Continental army needed to be on guard "whatever the real intention of the enemy may be." Two months later, he was still convinced that the British had ulterior motives. "Notwithstanding all the pacific declarations of the British, it has constantly been my pre-

vailing sentiment [that their] principal design was to gain time by
lulling us into security . . . and in the interim to augment their naval
force and wait the chance of some fortunate event to decide their
future line of conduct."23

Carleton's delay in evacuating New York because of inadequate
transports might have been an excuse. Washington thought that
"nothing short of a military force would ever free the city."24

42. Refugees and the *Book of Negroes*

MEANWHILE, TORY AND REBEL MILITIAS AND GANGS FOUGHT A vicious civil war in the New York area. One historian documented nineteen skirmishes in New Jersey, Long Island, Connecticut, and the Hudson River Valley in 1782 and 1783. Another found thirty-five. A third lists forty-nine. Counting small-party incidents of terrorism, there were many more.[1]

In May 1782, for example, a Loyalist whaleboat off Mattituck, Long Island, attacked Whig militia killing one and wounding one. Later that month, off Sandy Hook, New Jersey, Whig militia attacked 25 enemy, killing or wounding thirteen. In September, near Morristown, New Jersey, Whig militia killed one Loyalist and captured another.

As late as spring 1783, the enemies fought. Loyalist captain John Bacon's band of about two dozen men had regularly raided Whig property in central New Jersey, sometimes fighting heated battles with enemy militia. In early 1782, the Whigs captured him, but he escaped. In October, he reputedly killed nearly all of a crew of Whig privateers sleeping on a beach after unloading a captured cargo. With the help of local residents, Bacon fought off militia two months later. Another militia posse caught up with him on April 3, 1783, in an Egg Harbor tavern. After a scuffle, he surrendered and was granted quarter. That didn't stop one of the Whigs, who believed Bacon had killed a brother, from running him through with a bayonet. Wounded, Bacon tried to escape and was shot dead.[2]

One series of revenge killings became an international incident. In the early hours of March 24, 1782, a Loyalist militia force of 120 men attacked two dozen Whig militia in Toms River, New Jersey, led by Captain Joshua Huddy. The Loyalists suffered eight casualties; the Whigs, eleven, with thirteen captured—including Huddy, whom the Loyalists took to a New York jail. Six days later, Whigs captured Philip White, a Loyalist and former Huddy neighbor. He was shot trying to escape, although Loyalists believed it was a setup and revenge killing because White had previously killed one of the Whigs' fathers. Now the Loyalists demanded revenge. They got permission to remove Huddy from New York, ostensibly as part of a prisoner exchange. Loyalist militia Captain Richard Lippincott commanded the group that took Huddy back to New Jersey where they hung him. They pinned a note on his chest: "Up goes Huddy for Philip White," and cited "the cruel murders of our brethren." Local residents now petitioned Washington to take action. Washington demanded Lippincott's extradition. Clinton, who still commanded in New York, refused, saying Lippincott would receive a British court-martial. Washington then ordered a British officer chosen by lot for execution. The unlucky officer was Captain Charles Asgill, 19, son of a former London mayor. A month after Carleton arrived, Lippincott's court-martial acquitted him. Washington was cornered by his pledge to execute an innocent man. Asgill's mother appealed to the French king, who asked Congress for clemency. Congress acceded to its ally's request; Washington released Asgill in December.[3]

In June 1782, Shelburne wrote Carleton that the government had agreed to American independence as a basis for peace negotiations. Carleton's efforts, he said, should be focused only on evacuation and treating Loyalists with "the tenderest and most honorable care, giving them every assistance." Carleton got the news in late July. He submitted his resignation on August 14, saying he had accepted the New York command from "an ardent desire to see these colonies reconciled to Great Britain." Now, he could no longer render "any considerable service." To a cabinet member, he confided that he was not prepared to be a "mere inspector of embarkations." But the government persuaded Carleton to do exactly that.[4]

He notified Washington of the policy change on August 2. The king would support "the independency of the Thirteen Provinces," and hope that Loyalists would be allowed to return home or be fully compensated for "whatever confiscation may have taken place." The next day, Carleton announced the news publicly. There would be a cessation of hostilities.[5]

It shocked and angered the Loyalists, some of whom refused to believe it. "This information struck me as the loss of all I had in the world and my family with it," said the chief justice.[6] The Reverend Schaukirk said it was impossible to describe "what an alarming effect this so unexpected news has upon the minds of the people; they were enraged against the Ministry. Some were for defending themselves to the last extremity and make their own conditions."[7]

Outside the city proper, Loyalists faced a grim situation. Between 1776 and the war's end, the states passed 213 laws against Tories—including fifty-three from 1782 to 1785—limiting their freedom of speech and action; requiring loyalty oaths; removing them from office and disenfranchising them; quarantining, banishing, or exiling them; making it treason to support Britain in any way; and taxing or confiscating their property.[8]

Now, Whig militia, gangs, and bandits increased their terrorism, while their Loyalist counterparts responded with diminished efforts. The Whigs "have cast off all appearance of a desire to be reconciled to the Loyalists who remained among them," Carleton told London. "Almost all those [Loyalists] who have attempted to return to their homes have been exceedingly ill-treated, many beaten, robbed of their money and clothing, and sent back."[9]

One Connecticut refugee said he was "secured and dragged by a licentious and bloodthirsty mob and hung up by the neck . . . taken down, stripped, and whipped with a cat o' nine tails in a most inhuman manner and then tarred and feathered and again hung up at the yard arm as a public spectacle." They sent him to New York with a warning to never return, or he would be killed.[10]

Loyalist militia, who had provided some protection, now deserted en masse. In May 1782, a Bergen Point, New Jersey, Loyalist unit of 350 whites and two hundred blacks (presumably escaped slaves) helped supply New York. Four months later, the unit was down to forty-nine whites.[11]

Tens of thousands of refugees filled New York. Food was scarce. People scuffled in the streets, with too few troops to police them. In mid-December, the "greatest snow storm in 30 years" fell. "The rebels breathe the most rancorous and malignant spirit everywhere. Committees and associations are formed in every colony, and resolves passed, that no refugees shall return nor have their estates restored. . . . In short, the mob now reigns," one Loyalist wrote.[12]

In mid-1783, Carleton told Congress that it should blame itself for delaying the evacuation. "The violence in the Americans, which broke out soon after the cessation of hostilities, increased the number of their countrymen who look to me for escape from threatened destruction. But these terrors have of late been so considerably augmented that almost all within these lines conceive the safety both of their property and of their lives depend upon their being removed by me, which renders it impossible to say when the evacuation can be completed."[13]

He protested to Washington about "the shedding of American blood by American hands."[14] A Whig writer acknowledged the situation. Loyalists "had everything to fear if the British troops withdrew and left them to the clemency of their countrymen, now elated by success, and more hardened against the feelings of humanity by the cruel scenes of war they had witnessed."[15]

The chancellor of New York (who, in 1789, would administer the oath of office to President-elect Washington) observed a "violent spirit of persecution which prevails here . . . In some few, it is a blind spirit of revenge and resentment, but in more, it is the most sordid interest. One wishes to possess the house of some wretched Tory. Another fears him as a rival in his trade or commerce, and a fourth wishes to get rid of his debts by shaking off his creditor."[16]

Timothy Dwight, 25, a Continental army chaplain (and future Yale University president) served "for some time" in New York's Westchester County. He later remembered the civilians he saw caught between the two armies:

They feared everybody who they saw and loved nobody. . . . Fear was, apparently, the only passion by which they were animated. The power of volition seemed to have deserted them. They were not civil, but obsequious; not obliging, but subservient. . . . Both their countenances and motions had lost every trace of animation and feeling. . . . Their houses, in the meantime, were, in a great measure, scenes of desolation. Their furniture was extensively plundered or broken to pieces. The walls, floors, and windows were injured both by violence and decay, and were not repaired because they had not the means of repairing them, and because they were exposed to the repetition of the same injuries. Their cattle were gone. Their enclosures were burnt where they were capable of becoming fuel, and in many cases thrown down, where they were not. Their fields were covered with a rank growth of weeds and wild grass.[17]

Washington replied skeptically to Carleton's August 2, 1782, announcement that the British would suspend hostilities. Why didn't it extend to naval operations? Why were Indian-Loyalist raids continuing on the frontier? Such raids, fueled by British arms, certainly weren't happening "without directions from the commander-in-chief in Canada."[18]

Carleton replied that since American independence—the issue of contention—is now a given, "I disapprove of all hostilities both by land and sea." As for "the savages," Carleton said he had sent messengers to end raids; subsequent fights, such as those in Ohio, were "necessary for self-defense."[19]

Proof of good intentions came on March 19, 1783. Carleton wrote Washington that he received the news that a preliminary peace treaty was signed on November 30 in Paris. What was the best way, Carleton asked, to communicate that news to Congress? But Congress already had the news, courtesy of Captain Joshua Barney who arrived in Philadelphia on March 12. Washington learned of it the day Carleton wrote. Now, even the American general believed it. "The news of peace (tho' not official) is nevertheless so positive and the certainty that hostilities were to cease . . . is so great" that he ordered everything his army had captured "be given up and returned to the British Lines, without the least injury or delay."[20]

The next month, Carleton shared more news with Washington. The American allies, France and Spain, had signed their respective preliminary peace treaties in January. Accordingly, he would announce the peace publicly in two days, April 8, 1783, end all further hostilities, and release remaining prisoners. Moreover, he expected Congress to abide by the treaty's provision for restitution of the Loyalists' confiscated estates so that "the blessings of peace should universally prevail."[21]

Washington agreed to the cessation of hostilities, but deferred on the release of prisoners he held until he got the official word from Congress, which came shortly thereafter. "I beg, sir," he told Carleton, "that you will please to accept a tender from me of reciprocal goodwill . . . and with an earnest wish that . . . it may prove as lasting as it is happy."[22]

But the generals' war wasn't over. When Loyalists heard the news read to them in front of City Hall, they responded with "groans and hisses . . . bitter reproaches and curses upon their king for having deserted them," a paper reported. "It is surprising what England gives up," said the Reverend Schaukirk. "It is shameful how the Loyalists are abandoned." (The king acknowledged his own bitterness in a speech before Parliament. In conceding American independence, "I have sacrificed every consideration of my own to the wishes and opinion of my people." After the speech, he asked an observer, "Did I lower my voice when I came to that part of my speech?")[23]

For Carleton, months would pass before his work was done: the logistics of transporting an army to new assignments, and resettling a refugee city in other colonies, primarily Atlantic Canada.

Washington's work was to furlough most of his army—without pay—and keep a core to observe the British and maintain order until civilian authorities took over. "No disorder or licentiousness must be tolerated," he warned his army. "No military neglects or excesses shall go unpunished." He urged patience. You are "gallant and persevering men . . . with well-earned laurels." You have "shared in the toils and dangers of effecting this glorious revolution, of rescuing millions from the hand of oppression . . . and establishing an asylum for the poor and oppressed of all nations and religions."[24]

When Washington talked about an asylum for the oppressed, he made one exception—an exception Carleton refused to accept.

The exception was African Americans. The British had promised freedom to those blacks who deserted the rebel army or escaped from rebel slavery.[25] But the preliminary peace treaty prohibited the

British from "carrying away Negroes or other property" that belonged to Whigs. At stake were significant quantities of such "property." In New Jersey alone before the war, about 11,000 slaves accounted for 8 percent of the population. In New York and its four adjacent counties, more than 7,700 African Americans—some free, but most enslaved—represented fifteen percent of the whole.[26]

Returning the escaped slaves was on Washington's agenda at his only face-to-face meeting with Carleton. The May 6, 1783, conference was held on the west bank of the Hudson River about twenty-five miles north of New York near what is now Piermont. The generals talked about prisoner releases, and evacuation of the city and frontier posts. According to one Whig account, when Washington asked about "obtaining the delivery of all Negroes and other property," Carleton mentioned that among the six thousand Loyalists already evacuated, some of them were blacks. Washington "expressed his surprise" that this had happened in contradiction to the terms of the treaty. Carleton explained that it couldn't have been the intention of the British government to violate its "faith to the Negroes who came into the British lines" and deliver them to their former masters for punishment or even execution. This would be "a dishonorable violation of the public faith pledged to the Negroes."

Besides, if the two governments concluded that his position contradicted the treaty, Britain would compensate the American owners for their loss, Carleton said. To facilitate this, the British kept a register—the *Book of Negroes*—of all former slaves who were evacuated. Washington replied that "it was impossible to ascertain the value of the slaves" from such a register.[27]

To make sure Carleton understood how unhappy he was, Washington followed up with a letter to him that same day. "I cannot, however, conceal from your excellency, that my private opinion is that the measure is totally different from the letter and spirit of the Treaty." But Carleton wouldn't budge. He told Washington that although he has stopped future emigration of blacks, for those who escaped across the lines prior to the treaty, "I had no right to deprive them of that liberty I found them possessed of."[28]

Lord North, who had returned to the British cabinet, backed up Carleton. Not only did the evacuation not violate the treaty, but "the removal of the Negroes . . . is certainly an act of justice due to them from us."[29]

The *Book of Negroes* register would grow to three thousand people, two-thirds of them escapees from the South. The British also evacuated 1,200 additional African Americans; as slaves owned by Loyalists, they remained slaves. Some criminal Britons captured escaped slaves and resold them to their Whig owners. In other cases, British military courts ordered escapees returned to their owners. Another group—the sick, frail, and aging—were abandoned to the Whigs. Still, the British evacuated thousands of formerly enslaved African Americans throughout North America to freedom, the common estimate being about twenty thousand. Hundreds more escaped in private ships.[30]

43. Evacuation Day

AS TRANSPORTS ARRIVED THROUGHOUT 1783, CARLETON EVACUATED refugees, their slaves and servants, and Loyalist and British troops, but it wasn't fast enough for Washington. In May, shortly after their conference, Carleton told him that "it is impossible to tell when the evacuation of this city can be completed; in truth, I cannot guess the quantity of shipping that will be sent me, nor the number of persons that will be forced to abandon this place."[1]

When the British left Westchester County, immediately north of Manhattan, civil authorities couldn't maintain order, and robberies and violence against Loyalists spiked. Washington sent in Continental troops. In mid-June, he was able to reassure a Congressman that "no outrages . . . have been experienced—and I hope e'er long that good order and regularity of government may prevail in that distressed county."[2]

The colonel in charge of these advance troops reported to Washington in early July that not only was all calm, but he and his British counterpart across the lines engaged in "a friendly intercourse," and conducted reciprocal visits. Washington immediately ordered the colonel to stop the visits, something "I have carefully endeavored to avoid."[3]

Still, Loyalists were hounded. In August, a British intelligence report said sarcastically: "The spirit of doing equal justice seems to prevail in the country: from tarring and feathering Tories, the remedial administration are now turned to the officers who have retired from our service, of which some are beat, others mobbed, and others compelled to fly from the rage of an ungrateful race of miscreants."⁴

Meanwhile, Carleton continued to make progress with the evacuations, and Washington responded by steadily dismissing the Continental army. He discharged all but several hundred men on November 2. Washington thanked the troops for "their extraordinary patience in suffering, as well as their invincible fortitude in action." He then bid "a final adieu to the armies" he "so long had the honor to command."⁵

Ten days later, Carleton sent Washington an update. The British would evacuate northern Manhattan and parts of Long Island on November 21, and the remainder of the posts "as soon after as may be practicable." The "practicable" time turned out to be noon on the 25th. When the last British soldier left, Washington, with the New York governor at his side, accompanied by eight hundred of the remaining Continental infantry, as well as a number of militia, entered New York City.⁶

Anchored in the harbor with his fleet, Carleton wrote Washington on December 1: He expected to sail three days later "if wind and weather permit." Washington returned the courtesy the next day, thanking him for the notice. "I . . . sincerely wish that your excellency, with the troops under your orders, may have a safe and pleasant passage." Washington also would leave then, first for Congress, then for home.⁷

Carleton had evacuated more than 35,000 Loyalist refugees and 20,000 soldiers. The government rewarded him for his American service with a peerage—he became Lord Dorchester—and, in 1786, a new assignment: governor of Canada's now three provinces and commander-in-chief. As governor, he again tried to balance the needs of French Canadians and the now-significant population of English Canadians. "I confess myself as yet at a loss for any plan likely to give satisfaction," he said. He resigned in 1794 and returned home in 1796. Although he kept an interest in politics, he spent much time breeding horses and managing his three estates.⁸

Throughout the day, Wednesday, December 4, Staten Island residents stood on a bank overlooking the Narrows, the channel through which the British fleet sailed to leave New York harbor for the ocean.

"We were very boisterous in our demonstrations of joy," said an eyewitness whose words were passed down to a nineteenth-century historian. "We clapped our hands, we waved our hats, we sprang into the air, and some few, who brought muskets with them, fired a *feu-de-joie*. A few others, in the exuberance of their gladness, indulged in gestures, which though very expressive, were neither polite nor judicious."

A British ship responded to the gestures by firing a cannon shot that landed on a nearby bank. It scattered some of the spectators.

"A few rods from us stood another group, composed of men and women, who gazed silently, and some tearfully, upon the passing ships—for some of the females had lovers, and some, husbands, on board of them, who were leaving them behind, never, probably, to see them again.

"It was long after dark when the last ship passed through the Narrows."[9]

NOTES

ABBREVIATIONS

BF	*Papers of Benjamin Franklin*
CE	*Canadian Encyclopedia*
DAR	*Documents of the American Revolution*
DCAR	*Diplomatic Correspondence of the American Revolution*
DCB	*Dictionary of Canadian Biography Online*
DNB	*Dictionary of National Biography*
EB	*Encyclopedia Britannica*, 11th Edition
FO	Founders Online
GW	*George Washington Papers*
HMC	Historic Manuscripts Commission
JA	*Adams Papers Digital Editions*
NBS	*Nothing But Blood and Slaughter*, Patrick O'Kelley
NCHP	North Carolina History Project
NG	*The Papers of Nathanael Greene*, Dennis M. Conrad
NPS	National Park Service
OED	*Oxford English Dictionary*
WPA	Works Progress Administration

INTRODUCTION: HOW TO END A WAR

1. David Halberstam, *The Making of a Quagmire* (New York: Random House, 1965); Johnson to Richard Russell, March 6, 1965, http://millercenter.org/scripps/archive/presidentialrecordings/johnson/1965/03_1965.

2. Richard Eder, "Aiken Suggests U.S. Say It Has Won War," *New York Times*, October 20, 1966, ProQuest Historical Newspapers, 1, 16.

3. John W. Mashek, *Politico*, August 3, 2009, http://www.politico.com/news/stories/0809/25710.html; Eugene Robinson, *Washington Post*, June 9, 2011,

http://www.washingtonpost.com/opinions/a-plan-for-afghanistan-declare-victory—and-leave/2011/06/09/AGz8LrNH_story.html.

4. James K. Polk, Third Annual Message, December 7, 1847, *American Presidency Project*, University of California Santa Barbara, http://www.presidency.ucsb.edu/ws/index.php?pid=29488#ixzz2ixcK9fDu.

5. Mason Locke Weems, *The Life of George Washington* (Philadelphia: Joseph Allen, 1837), 112; Greg Walker and Mort Walker, *Beetle Bailey* (King Features Syndicate, October 17, 2010); NPS, Colonial National Historical Park, "Yorktown Battlefield," http://www.nps.gov/york/index.htm.

6. Margaret MacMillan, *Dangerous Games: The Uses and Abuses of History* (New York: Modern Library, 2009), 169.

7. NG, 10:xxii; Calloway (2013), xii; Thomas Hutchinson, August 8, 1774: *Diary and Letters of His Excellency Thomas Hutchinson, Esq.*, ed. Peter Orlando Hutchinson (London: Sampson Low, 1883), 215.

CHAPTER ONE: THE TREATY

1. François Boucher, *American Footprints in Paris* (New York: George H. Doran, 1921), 100; Daniel Jouve, Alice Jouve, and Alvin Grossman, *Paris: Birthplace of the U.S.A.* (Paris: Gründ, 1995), http://www.waymarking.com/waymarks/WMV9D_Hotel_de_Valentinois_Paris_France.

2. Elénor-François-Elie, Comte de Moustier, to Armand Marc, Comte de Montmorin, September 8, 1789, Kaminski, 279; Joshua Loring to Jonathan Palfrey, May 13, 1790, Stahr, 277-278; Robert Livingston, Stahr, 285.

3. Emma Lawton and Shannon Wait, "Finding aid for David Hartley Papers, 1783-1785," May 2011, William L. Clements Library, http://quod.lib.umich.edu/c/clementsmss/umich-wcl-M-196har?view=text; Wraxall (1884), 124.

4. Charles James Fox, Fleming, 249.

5. John G. Blair, "The Story behind the Proclamation of Peace," Blair House Publisher, http://peaceproclamation.com/proclamation_story.html.

6. Franklin, 572.

7. Washington to Henry Knox, February 1, 1783, FO.

CHAPTER TWO: O'HARA'S WARS

1. *The Times*, December 16, 1793, 2; Samuel Hood, Ireland, 252.

2. Roger Lee, "The War List," *The History Guy*, http://www.historyguy.com/War_list.html#warlist2.

3. Ireland, 238.

4. Elliot to Lady Elliot, November 24, 1793, Elliot, 190.

5. Bonaparte to Marmont, 1798, Browning, 244.

6. Elliot, 195.

7. David Dundas, *The Times*, December 26, 1793, 2.

8. O'Meara, 126-127; Elliot, 193-194.

9. O'Meara, 126-127.

10. Bourrienne, 21; Browning, 256.

11. Baskin, "Charles O'Hara"; Thomas Carlyle, *The French Revolution*, vol. 3 (London: George Bell, 1902), 248, GB.

12. Alan Valentine, *The British Establishment 1760-1784*, vol. 2 (Norman: University of Oklahoma Press, 1970), 659; Baskin, "Charles O'Hara."

13. Donald N. Moran, "King George III's Soldiers, Brigadier General Charles O'Hara." Sons of Liberty Chapter, SAR, http://www.revolutionarywar archives.org/ohara.html; Baskin, "Charles O'Hara"; DNB, "O'Hara, Charles," 42:61-62; Christopher Bryant, correspondence with author.

14. John Moore in G. C. Moore Smith, *The Life of John Colborne, Field-Marshal Lord Seaton* (London: John Murray, 1903), 65.

15. Thomas Hamilton, *The Youth and Manhood of Cyril Thornton* (Edinburgh: William Blackwood & Sons, 1868), 216-217; Horace Walpole to Mary Berry, April 15, 1791, Lewis (1866), 301.

16. NPS, Gateway National Recreation Area, *Sandy Hook Lighthouse* (rev. 2005).

17. Clinton (1954), 100.

18. O'Hara to Grafton, November 1, 1780, O'Hara, 159-160.

19. O'Hara to Grafton, April 20, 1781, O'Hara, 174.

20. O'Hara to Grafton, April 20, 1781, O'Hara, 175; Lamb, 345.

21. Baskin, "Charles O'Hara"; Cornwallis to Germain, March 17, 1781, Tarleton, 317.

22. O'Hara to Grafton, April 20, 1781, O'Hara, 177.

23. Greene to Anthony Wayne, July 24, 1781, NG, 9:75; *Public Advertiser,* June 19, 1781, Lutnick, 471.

24. Urwin, 59, 67-68.

25. Jefferson to William Gordon, July 16, 1788, FO.

26. Cornwallis, Riley, 178; Selesky, 1292; Quarles, 141; Urwin, 75-78.

27. Quarles, 142; Selesky, 1295.

28. Clinton, Riley, 41.

29. O'Hara and Cornwallis letters, August 5-17, 1781, Sylvia R. Frey, "Between Slavery and Freedom: Virginia Blacks in the American Revolution," *Journal of Southern History,* 49:3, August 1983, 393.

30. Frey, op. cit., 394; John Graves Simcoe, *Simcoe's Military Journal* (New York: Bartlett and Welford, 1844), 303.

31. Johann Ewald, Tustin, 342; Stephen Popp, "Popp's Journal, 1777–1783," *Pennsylvania Magazine of History and Biography,* 26:2, 1902, 246.

32. Denny, 45.

33. Abbé Claude Robin, *New Travels Through North America (Nouveau Voyage dans l'Amérique Septentrionale).* (New York: *New York Times* Arno Press, [1783] 1969), 65; Edward Hand, "Edward Hand to Jasper Yeates on the Siege of Yorktown in 1781." *Bulletin of the New York Public Library,* 6:8, August 1902, 286.

34. Johann Ewald, Tustin, 335-336.

CHAPTER THREE: ROCHAMBEAU AND WASHINGTON

1. Selig (2007), 43; Christopher Bryant, email to author.

2. Eliphalet Dyer to Joseph Trumbull, June 17, 1775, Stahr, 108.

3. Charles Royster, *The Fabulous History of the Dismal Swamp Company* (New York: Vintage Books, 2000), 21; Dorothy Twohig, Chernow (2010), 23.

4. John Adams to John Taylor, June 9, 1814, FO.

5. Chernow (2010), 457.

6. Robert Morris to John Jay, July 4, 1781, Rappleye, 231.

7. George Washington to John Laurens, April 9, 1781, FO.

8. Selesky, 994; Selig (2007), 9. Selig says Laurens and Rochambeau accompanied each other, but there is no evidence in other accounts.

9. Richard Peters Jr. to William Henry Harrison, January 12, 1818, Henry Simpson, *The Lives of Eminent Philadelphians* (Philadelphia: William Brotherhead, 1859), 705-707.

10. Claude Blanchard, *The Journal of Claude Blanchard*, ed. Thomas Balch (New York: Arno Press, [1876] 1969), 121-122.

11. *London Packet*, Martha Laurens to John Adams, January 16, 1782, FO, n1.

12. St. George Tucker, "St. George Tucker's Journal of the Siege of Yorktown, 1781," *William and Mary Quarterly*, series 3, 5:3, July 1948, 392-393; Lossing, 518.

13. Franklin and Mary Wickwire, *Cornwallis: The American Adventure* (Boston: Houghton Mifflin, 1970), 3; Arnold Whitridge, *Rochambeau* (New York: Macmillan, 1965), 226.

14. Lee (1827), 370-371; Closen, 153; James Thacher, *Military Journal of the American Revolution* (Hartford: Hurlbut, Williams, 1862), 288-290.

15. Thacher, op. cit.; Mathieu Dumas, *Memoirs of His Own Time, including the Revolution, the Empire, and the Restoration*, vol. 1. (London: Richard Bentley, 1839), 69-70n.

16. Clifford K. Shipton, "Benjamin Lincoln: Old Reliable," *George Washington's Generals*, ed. George Athan Billias (New York: William Morrow, 1964), 193.

17. Betsy Knight, "Prisoner Exchange and Parole in the American Revolution," *William and Mary Quarterly*, 48:2, April 1991, 214.

18. Johnathan Trumbull, "Minutes of Occurrences respecting the Seige [*sic*] and Capture of York in Virginia," *Proceedings of the Massachusetts Historical Society, 1875–1876* (Boston: MA Historical Society, 1876), 337; Cromot du Bourg in Stephen Bonsal, *When the French Were Here* (Garden City: Doubleday, Doran, 1945), 167-178.

19. O'Hara, 179.

20. Clinton (1954), 587.

21. Wraxall (1904), 293-297.

22. Germain description, Wraxall (1904), 398.

23. Wraxall (1904), 401.

24. *Annual Register . . . for the Year 1782* (London: G. Auld, 1800), 291-292, GB.

25. Lutnick, 478; John W. Fortescue, *The Correspondence of George the Third from 1760 to December 1783*, vol. 5 (London: Macmillan, 1928), 313-314.

26. Probus, *Morning Chronicle*, December 11, 1781, and Regulus, *Morning Chronicle*, December 14, 1781, in Alfred Grant, *Our American Brethren* (Jefferson, NC: McFarland, 1995), 117-118.

27. Vergennes to Lafayette, 1er Xbre [December] 1781, in Henri Doniol, *Histoire de la participation de la France à l'établissement des Etats-Unis d'Amérique . . .*, vol. 4 (Paris: Imprimerie Nationale, 1890), 688.

28. Adams to John Jay, November 26, 1781, FO.

29. Francis Dana to Robert Livingston, March 5, 1782, DCAR (1857), IV:611.

30. Franklin to Robert Morris, March 9, 1782, FO; Franklin to Washington, April 2, 1782, FO.

31. Greene to Thomas Nelson, October 24, 1781, NG, 9:473; to Thomas McKean, October 24, 1781, NG, 9:483; to Francis Marion, November 11, 1781, NG, 9:558; to Alexander Martin, November 14, 1781, NG, 9:570-571.

32. Washington to Greene, November 16, 1781, NG, 9:580.

33. Barnet Schecter, *George Washington's America: A Biography Through His Maps*

(New York: Walker, 2010), 192, 209; Greene to John Rutledge, January 21, 1782, NG, 10:229.

34. Richard Henry Lee, *The Floyd E. Risvold Collection*, vol. 1. (New York: Spink Shreves Galleries, January 27, 2010), 9.

35. John Jay to Gouverneur Morris, October 13, 1782, Spahr (2006), 161.

36. Washington to John Laurens, July 10, 1782, GW; to James McHenry, September 12, 1782, GW.

37. Washington to Greene, October 31, 1781, NG, 9:504-505.

38. Washington to Marquis de Chastellux, January 4, 1782, FO.

39. Washington to Greene, October 31, 1781, NG, 9:504-505.

CHAPTER FOUR: RICE AND THE LOW COUNTRY

1. Unknown writer: Cheves, 309.

2. Coastal Service Center (NOAA) and S.C. Dept. of Natural Resources, *Characterization of the Ashepoo-Combahee-Edisto (ACE) Basin* (Charleston: Coastal Service Center, 2000); Lawrence Sanders Rowland, et al., *The History of Beaufort County, South Carolina: 1514-1861*, vol. 1 (Columbia: University of South Carolina Press, 1996), 86.

3. Unknown writer, 1671: Cheves, 308-309.

4. William Feltman, *The Journal of Lieut. William Feltman, of the First Pennsylvania Regiment, 1781-'82* (Philadelphia: Henry Carey Baird, 1853), 33-34, 39, 47.

5. Tilden, 217, 227.

6. McDowell, 311.

7. Denny, 46.

8. Edelson, 38-41.

9. Joyce E. Chaplin, "Tidal Rice Cultivation and the Problem of Slavery in South Carolina and Georgia, 1760-1815," *William and Mary Quarterly*, 49:1, January 1992, 31; Clifton, 273; Jennifer Payne, "Rice, Indigo, and Fever in Colonial South Carolina," http://jenpayne10.info/indigo.html; Henry C. Dethloff, "The Colonial Rice Trade," *Agricultural History*, 56:1, January 1982, 232-233.

10. Rob Martin, "Cowes Rice Trade," Isle of Wright History Center, http://free-space.virgin.net/robmar.tin/rice/rice; Jean M. West, "Rice and Slavery: A Fatal Gold Seede," *Slavery in America*, http://www.slaveryinamerica.org/history/hs_es_rice.htm.

CHAPTER FIVE: GENERAL LESLIE COMES TO CHARLESTOWN

1. Clinton (1954), 354.

2. Kenneth Rutherford Davis, *The Rutherfords in Britain: A History and Guide* (Gloucester, UK: Alan Sutton, 1987), 42-45; Debrett (1828), 526; Richard L. Blanco, ed., *The American Revolution, 1775-1783, An Encyclopedia* (New York: Garland, 1993), 919; H. G. Purdon, *An Historical Sketch of the 64th Regiment*, http://web.archive.org/web/20010911013815/http://www.cvco.org/sigs/reg64/64th_sketch.html; Baskin, "Alexander Leslie"; Essex Institute, 325.

3. John Peebles and Ira D. Gruber, *John Peebles' American War . . .* (Stroud, UK: Sutton, 1998), 179; Ann Hulton, *Letters of a Loyalist Lady . . .* (Cambridge: Harvard University Press, 1927), 63; *Massachusetts Spy*, March 2, 1775: Endicott, 38.

4. Account from Endicott, 13-31; David Hackett Fischer, *Paul Revere's Ride*. (New York: Oxford University Press, 1994), 58-63; Robert S. Rantoul, "Some Claims of

Salem on the Notice of the Country," *Historical Collections of the Essex Institute*, vol. 32, 1896, 3-13.

5. Endicott, 25-26.

6. Selesky, 620; Essex Institute, 325, and Debrett (1828), 526, incorrectly describe the relationship. See: "Capt. Hon. William Leslie," http://www.silverwhistle.co.uk/lobsters/index.html.

7. Cornwallis to Germain, March 17, 1781, Baskin, "Alexander Leslie."

8. DAR, 20:252.

9. HMC, 2:360.

10. HMC, 2:463; Leslie to Clinton, December 27, 1781, DAR, 20:288.

11. Clinton (1954), 356; HMC, 2:357; *Pennsylvania Packet,* June 4, 1782, NG, 11:140, n3.

12. HMC, 2:463; George Smith McCowen Jr., *The British Occupation of Charleston, 1780–'82* (Columbia: University of South Carolina Press, 1972), 87.

13. DAR, 20:254; Leslie to Clinton, November 30, 1781, Clinton (1954), 589.

14. Leslie to Clinton, December 27, 1781, DAR, 20:288.

15. Leslie to Germain, January 3, 1782, HMC, 2:378-379.

CHAPTER SIX: THE DEPUTY SAVIOR

1. Thomas Mifflin, Thomas Fleming, *Washington's Secret War* (New York: HarperCollins, 2005), 102; McCrady, 730.

2. McCrady, 720; Edmund Randolph to James Madison, August 16, 1782, Burnett, 455n2.

3. Dennis M. Conrad, August 26, 2009, National Archives and Records Administration, CSPAN recording; Greene to Washington, November 9, 1776, Carbone, 42.

4. Carbone, 10.

5. Greene to Sammy Ward, Carbone, 11.

6. Carbone, 3-5, 16.

7. Estimates of Caty's birth date range from 1753 to 1756. Her gravestone says she died in 1814 at age 59, http://www.findagrave.com/cgi-bin/fg.cgi?page=pv&GRid =33086947&PIpi=55800232; Elizabeth F. Ellet, Stegeman, 10; Greene to Caty Greene, October 14, 1780, Stegeman, 81; Johnson (1851), 390.

8. Washington to Congress, March 18, 1777, GW.

9. Knox to Judge Henry William de Saussure, Garden, 76.

10. Greene to Washington, April 24, 1779, FO.

11. Washington to John Mathews, October 23, 1780, GW.

12. Greene to Caty Greene, December 7, 1780, NG, 6:542.

13. Garden, 76.

14. Greene to Chevalier de la Luzerne, April 28, 1781, NG, 8:168; Greene to Jeremiah Wadsworth, July 8, 1781, NG, 9:41; Knox to John Adams, October 21, 1781, FO.

15. John Mathews, April 12, 1782, Massey (2000), 216.

16. William McDowell, March 23, 1782; May 5, 1782; May 28, 1782; July 2, 1782, McDowell, 314-325.

17. Greene to Benjamin Lincoln, February 6, 1782, NG, 10:322.

18. Greene to Washington, January 24, 1782, NG, 10:256; March 9, 1782, NG, 10:471-472.

19. Greene to John Hanson, NG, 11:50.

20. Greene to John Mathews, April 1, 1782, NG, 10:568.

21. Greene to Robert Morris, April 22, 1782, NG, 11:93-94.

22. Greene to Jeremiah Wadsworth, February 9, 1782, NG, 10:338.

23. Greene to Joseph Reed, February 27, 1782, NG, 10:414.

24. Oscar Reiss, *Medicine and the American Revolution* (Jefferson, NC: McFarland, 1998), 3-31; J. R. McNeill, *Mosquito Empires; Ecology and War in the Greater Caribbean, 1620–1914* (New York: Cambridge University Press, 2010), 43, 52-53.

25. Denny, 46-47; William McDowell, diary, NG, 11:679n1; Greene to Leslie, September 24, 1782, NG, 11:694; McCrady, 487.

26. Greene to Charles Pettit, November 2, 1782, NG, 11:398n1.

CHAPTER SEVEN: THE "BLOODIEST, CRUEL WAR"

1. O'Hara to Grafton, January 6, 1781, O'Hara, 171.

2. James Henry Craig to Cornwallis, May 28, 1781, Lawrence E. Babits and Joshua B. Howard, *Long, Obstinate, and Bloody: The Battle of Guilford Courthouse* (Chapel Hill: University of North Carolina Press, 2009), 5; Gray, 145; John Doyle to Francis Marion, November 20, 1781, NG, 9:595.

3. William Pierce to St. George Tucker, July 20, 1781, Pierce, 434; Aedanus Burke to Arthur Middleton, January 25, 1782, Middleton, 192.

4. January 8, 1782, A. S. Salley Jr., ed., *Journal of the House of Representatives of South Carolina*, January 8, 1782–February 26, 1782 (Columbia: Historical Commission of SC: 1916), 9-10.

5. Greene to Rev. Ezra Stiles, September 29, 1782, NG, 11:708; Greene to Caty Greene, January 12, 1781, NG, 7:103.

6. Anthony Wayne, March 20, 1782, F. D. Lee and J. L. Agnew, *Historical Record of the City of Savannah* (Savannah: J. H. Estill, 1869), 66; Justin S. Liles, "The Reluctant Partisan: Nathanael Greene's Southern Campaigns, 1780–1783," MA thesis, University of North Texas, May 2005, 28; Nisbet Balfour, March 3, 1781; Francis Marion, March 7, 1781, Ben Rubin, "The Rhetoric of Revenge: Atrocity and Identity in the Revolutionary Carolinas," *Journal of Backcountry Studies*, 5:2, Fall 2010, 8; Wayne E. Lee, *Crowds and Soldiers in Revolutionary North Carolina* (Gainesville: University Press of Florida, 2001), 179; William Pierce to St. George Tucker, July 20, 1781, Pierce, 434; Stephen Drayton to Thomas Burke, July 16, 1781: Clark, 15:512; Moses Hall, Dann, 202-203; Henry Reid, 1787 statement, Lee (2001), 190.

7. Ward (2002), 225, 226ff; William Henry Foote, *Sketches of North Carolina* (New York: Robert Carter, 1846), 279; Moultrie, 299-300.

8. John Marshall, *The Life of George Washington*, vol. 4 (Philadelphia: G. P. Wayne, 1805), 537.

9. Moultrie, 1802, 301, 303.

10. Pastor Simpson, November 5, 1783; George Howe, *History of the Presbyterian Church in South Carolina*, vol. 1 (Columbia: Duffie and Chapman, 1870), 465; Moultrie, 354-355.

11. Greene to John Rutledge, December 19, 1781, NG, 10:20-21.

12. Greene to John Steward, December 26, 1781, NG, 10:107; to John Rutledge, January 21, 1782, NG, 10:229; Lee (1812), 445.

13. Greene to Washington, May 19, 1782, NG, 11:213.

14. Washington to Greene, September 23, 1782, NG, 11:693.

15. Washington to Greene, April 23, 1782, NG, 11:110; Greene to John Eager Howard, June 6, 1782, NG, 11:294.

16. Clinton to Germain, October 29, 1781, DAR, 20:252; Francisco de Miranda, NG, 9:642-643; Leslie to Clinton, December 1, 1781, Davies, 1979, 267-268.

17. Leslie to Clinton, November 30, 1781, Clinton (1954), 589.

18. Leslie proclamation, December 15, 1782, *Scots Magazine* (Edinburgh: A. Murray and J. Cochran, 1782), 44:28-29.

19. Leslie to Germain, April 23, 1782, HMC, 2:463.

20. Leslie to Clinton, March 27, 1782, HMC, 2:434; to Carleton, June 27, 1782, HMC, 2:543-544.

21. Earl of Shelburne, prime minister, to Guy Carleton, April 4, 1782, DAR, 21:53.

22. Leslie to Carleton, June 27, 1782, HMC, 2:543-544.

23. James Chastillier, NG, 11:117; Leslie to Clinton, January 29, 1782, HMC, 2:388; Hans von Knoblauch–Baron von Jumgkenn, March 9, 1782, NG, 10:419n3.

CHAPTER EIGHT: NORTH CAROLINA: TWO COMBUSTIBLE COMMANDERS

1. Mcgeachy, 8.

2. Leslie to Germain, November 13, 1781, HMC, 2:348.

3. MacDonald, 139; Mcgeachy, 24.

4. Jean-Pierre Wallot, "Sir James Henry Craig," DCB; Henry Bunbury, *Narratives of Some Passages in the Great War with France from 1790 to 1810* (London: Richard Bentley, 1854), 182-183.

5. Hairr, 92; Mcgeachy, 4-5.

6. William Dickson, McGeachy, 6-7.

7. Caruthers (1856), 352.

8. Graham, 355.

9. Craig to Nisbet Balfour, May 28, 1781, Mcgeachy, 7; Greene to Alexander Martin, September 27, 1781, NG, 9:400.

10. Gray, 156.

11. *Royal Gazette*, Charlestown, SC, February 20, 1782, Ward (2002), 225; Archibald Maclaine to George Hopper, ca. 1783, Clark, 16:966.

12. Greene to Rutherford, October 18, 1781, NG, 9:452.

13. Samuel A. Ashe et al., eds., "Griffith Rutherford," *Biographical History of North Carolina from Colonial Times to the Present* (Greensboro: Charles L. Van Noppen, 1905), 381-385; Harding; MacDonald, 14-15.

14. Harding; Ashe, op. cit.; MacDonald, 8, 18-19, 22.

15. Ashe, op. cit.; MacDonald, 42, 47-48.

16. MacDonald, 57; Ashe, op. cit.; Harding.

17. Rutherford to William Christian, August 5, 1776, MacDonald, 73.

18. Cornwallis to Henry Clinton, August 29, 1780, Clark, 15:276.

19. Hairr, 156-157; MacDonald, 128-132, 138, 143.

20. Graham, 55-56; NBS, 3:375-376; MacDonald, 147-148; NG, 9:484; Craig to Nesbit Balfour, October 22, 1781, Hairr, 160.

21. Graham, 369-370.

22. John D. Jones in Mcgeachy, 24.

23. NBS, 3:395-397.

24. MacDonald, 162-164, 176; Harding.

25. Hairr, 65; Allen; Selesky, 351; Johnson (1851), 569; NCHP; Caruthers (1854), 144-145.
26. OED; Fanning (1865), x.
27. Caruthers (1854), 140.
28. Caruthers (1854), 145; NCHP; Hairr, 10-13.
29. Fanning (1865), x; Fanning (1908), 9.
30. NCHP; Fanning (1908), 13.
31. NCHP; Caruthers (1854), 157.
32. Caruthers (1854), 165-168, 194.
33. Fanning (1908), 23-24.
34. Craig to Nesbit Balfour, October 22, 1781, Hairr, 163-164.
35. Fanning (1908), 18-19.
36. Fanning (1908), 27-32; NBS, 3:40-44.
37. NBS, 3:59-60; Hairr, 183-189.
38. NCHP; Allen.

CHAPTER NINE: GEORGIA: "MAKING BRICKS WITHOUT STRAW"

1. Greene to Washington, January 24, 1782, NG, 10:256.
2. Evan Edwards to Walter Stewart, February 1, 1782, NG, 10:176.
3. Alastair W. Massie, "Clarke, Sir Alured (1744–1832)," *Oxford Dictionary of National Biography* (Oxford University Press, [2004] 2008); DNB, "Clark, Alured," 10:415; Peter Burroughs, "Sir Alured Clarke," DCB.
4. HMC, 2:128.
5. Moultrie, 336; Greene to John Martin, January 9, 1782, NG, 10:173.
6. Foster, 16; Jones (1883), 496.
7. Charlton, 3, 59, 63-64.
8. Charlton, 1, 7; Selesky, 561-562.
9. Foster, 17-20; Peckham, 92; Jackson to Nathan Brownson, November 7, 1781, Jackson, 56.
10. DAR, 20:260.
11. John Twiggs to Greene, December 3, 1781, NG, 10:67, NG, 10:19n5.
12. James Wright to George Germain, December 18, 1781, DAR, 20:279.
13. Jones (1883), 506; Daniel T. and Rita Folse Elliott, *Seasons in the Sun: 1989 and 1990 Excavations at New Ebenezer* (Savannah: LAMAR Institute, 1991), 6.
14. NG, 10:177n1.
15. [Isaac Wayne], "Biography of General Wayne," *Casket*, 4:11, November 1829, 498.
16. Wayne to Greene, April 28, 1782, NG, 11:139.
17. Wayne to Washington, July 4, 1779, Nelson (1985), 3.
18. Alexander Graydon, Nelson (1985), 3; Greene to James McHenry, July 24, 1781; Hugh F. Rankin, "Anthony Wayne: Military Romanticist," *George Washington's Generals*, ed. George Athan Billias (New York: William Morrow, 1965), 282; Lee (1827), 443.
19. Ebenezer Elmer, 1776, Nelson (1985), 2.
20. Washington, March 9, 1792, Opinion of General Officers, GW.
21. John Armstrong, "Life of Anthony Wayne," *The Library of American Biography*, vol. 4 (Boston: Hilliard, Gray, 1835), 4.
22. Stillé, 8-10.

23. Nelson (1985), 57-58; Washington, November 1, 1777, General Orders.

24. Wayne to Walter Stewart, June 7, 1779, *Register of Pennsylvania*, 4:3, July 18, 1829, 34.

25. Nelson (1985), 137.

26. Greene to Wayne, January 9, 1782, NG, 10:175.

27. Greene to Wayne, January 22, 1782, NG, 10:236.

28. Charlton, 38; Foster, 18.

29. Wayne to Greene, February 6, 1782, NG, 10:326; February 22, 1782, NG, 10:397-398; February 28, 1782, NG, 10:423.

30. James Wright to Germain, January 23, 1782, DAR, 21:29; Wayne to Greene, January 26, 1782, NG, 10:267; Harrington, 32.

31. NG, 10:302-303.

32. Stillé, 289; Harrington, 33; Jones (1883), 507.

33. Benjamin Fishbourne to Greene, March 25, 1782, NG, 11:537.

34. Peckham, 95; NG, 11:76n1, 3; Wayne to Greene, April 18, 1782, NG, 11:76n1, 3; NG, 11:169-170n1; Wayne to Greene, May 7, 1782, NG, 11:169.

35. William Gordon, *The History of the Rise, Progress, and Establishment of the Independence of the United States of America* (London, Charles Dilly: 1788), 299.

36. Wayne to Greene, June 24, 1782, NG, 11:365-367; Capt. Alexander Parker, from Lee, NG, 11:3675.

37. Wayne to Greene, June 24, 1782, NG, 11:366; Thomas Brown to the Earl of Shelburne, September 23, 1782, NG, 11:367n1.

38. Harrington, 33; NG, 10:397n3. Sir Patrick is sometimes confused with his father of the same name, who died before the war.

39. Wayne to Greene, March 11, 1782, NG, 10:486; Nelson (1985), 169; Kenneth Coleman, *The American Revolution in Georgia, 1763–1789* (Athens: University of Georgia Press, 1958), 143.

40. Leslie to Clinton, March 12, 1782, HMC, 2:418.

41. Nelson (1985), 172-173.

42. Smith (2007).

43. Wayne to Greene, July 12, 1782, NG, 11:440.

44. Jackson, 60.

45. Jasanoff, 70-72; Harrington, 34; NG, 11:346n2.

46. Henry Nase, July 11, 1782: Jasanoff, 70.

47. Nelson (1985), 178; Smith (2007).

48. Greene to Wayne, August 2, 1782, NG, 11:479-482.

49. Lossing, 741.

50. Wayne to Greene, February 28, 1782, NG, 10:423.

51. Foster, vii-viii, 22.

CHAPTER TEN: LESLIE'S WORK

1. A. S. Salley Jr., "Col. Miles Brewton and Some of His Descendants," *South Carolina Historical and Genealogical Magazine*, 2:2, April 1901, 142-143; Josiah Quincy Jr., March 7, 1773, George C. Rogers Jr., *Charleston in the Age of the Pinckneys* (Columbia: University of South Carolina Press, 1980), 69-70; Esther Singleton, *The Furniture of Our Forefathers, Part VII* (New York: Doubleday, Page, 1906), 494.

2. Coy, 28.

3. Lambert, 137, 162-163.

4. Leslie to Carleton, July 17, 1782, HMC, 3:24; Leslie to Carleton, June 10, 1782, HMC, 2:518.

5. McCrady, 492-493, NG, 9:xlvii.

6. Leslie to Don Juan Manuel Cagigal, June 12, 1782, Leslie, *Letterbooks*, 15593.

7. Ramsay, 62-63, 229, 234, 243.

8. Ramsay, 121; John André, 1780: Quarles, 112.

9. Quarles, 157.

10. Birkin, 2005, 125; Schama, 8-9; Selesky, 923; Quarles, 122-126.

11. Frey (1991), 121-123, 138; Olwell, 255; Farley, 75-76.

12. Schama, 124.

13. Thomas Sumter to Francis Marion, February 20, 1781, Frey (1991), 139; Pinckney to Arthur Middleton, August 13, 1782, Olwell, 259; William Matthews, January 17, 1782, Olwell, 258-259; William Bull to Germain, March 25, 1782, DAR, 21:51.

14. NG, 11:91-92n7; Olwell, 259; William Seymour, Seymour, 393.

15. Greene to Washington, April 15, 1782, NG, 11:65.

16. Leslie to Carlton, June 27, 1782, Farley, 84.

17. Leslie to Francis Marion, April 4, 1782, Gibbes, 153.

18. Leslie to Greene, April 4, 1782; Mathews to Leslie, April 12, 1782, NG, 10:583-584n3.

19. Leslie to Francis Marion, April 4, 1782, Gibbes, 153; Leslie to Thomas Fraser, March 27, 1782, Frey (1991), 137.

20. Carleton to Leslie, May 23, 1782, Leslie, *Letterbooks*, no. 15587; Carleton to Leslie, July 15, 1782, HMC, 3:19-20.

21. Franklin to Joseph Galloway, May 11, 1782, DAR, 21:73.

22. Leslie to Greene, May 23, 1782, NG, 11:235.

23. Greene to President John Hanson, May 21, 1782, NG, 11:227-228.

24. Washington to Lafayette, October 20, 1782, GW.

CHAPTER ELEVEN: "HOWLINGS OF A TRIPLE-HEADED MONSTER"

1. NG, 10:xi.

2. John Laurens to Washington, June 11, 1782, GW; Wayne to Robert Morris, September 2, 1782, Nelson (1985), 180; O'Kelley, 579; General Orders, April 20, 1782, NG, 11:80; April 22, 1782, NG, 11:87-88.

3. Greene to Marion, April 28, 1782, NG, 11:134.

4. Seymour, 387-391.

5. Lee to Greene, January 26, 1782, NG, 10:264; Rankin (1973), 275-277.

6. Chorlton, 119-120; Clifton, 281-282; Edelson, 200.

7. Henry Laurens to Smith and Clifton, July 17, 1755; Henry Laurens to John Laurens, August 14, 1776, Chorlton, 120.

8. Martha Laurens to Adams, January 16, 1782, JA, n1.

9. Wallace, 464-465.

10. Laurens to James Laurens, April 17, 1772, Simms (1867), 13-14; Massey (2000), 68-69.

11. Lafayette to John Lewis Gervais, October 8, 1777, Massey (2000), 75.

12. James McHenry to Elias Boudinot, July 2, 1778, Massey (2000), 110.

13. John Laurens to Henry Laurens, January 22, 1778, Simms (1867), 110-111; Henry Laurens to John Laurens, July 26, 1778, Massey (2000), 113.

14. Massey (2000), 125; Nancy Isenberg, *Fallen Founder: The Life of Aaron Burr* (New York: Viking Penguin, 2007), 47.

15. Caroline V. Hamilton, "The Erotic Charisma of Alexander Hamilton," *Journal of American Studies*, 45:1, April 12, 2010, 14-15; Chernow (2004), 95; Hamilton to Laurens, April 1779, Chernow (2004), 123; Laurens to Hamilton, July 14, 1779, FO.

16. Moultrie, 1:402-404.

17. Laurens to Washington, May 25, 1780, GW.

18. Lafayette to Adrienne de Noialles de Lafayette, February 2, 1781, Idzerda, 3:310.

19. Lafayette to Laurens, February 3, 1781, Idzerda, 3:315.

20. Hamilton to Laurens, February 4, 1781, Massey (2000), 176.

21. Vergennes to Lafayette, April 19, 1781, Wallace, 482; Vergennes to La Luzerne, May 11, 1781, Perkins, 335.

22. Franklin to William Carmichael, August 24, 1781, FO.

23. Franklin to Robert Livingston, July 22, 1783, FO; Adams to Robert Livingston, February 21, 1782, FO.

24. 1 *livre* is equivalent to 18 cents (Hamilton to Ternant, June 23, 1792, FO); Wallace, 484-486; Laurens to John Adams, April 28, 1781, JA, n2-3; Rappleye, 241; Franklin to William Carmichael, August 24, 1781, FO; Perkins, 335-336.

25. Hamilton to Lafayette, October 15, 1781, FO.

26. Laurens to Francis Kinloch, spring 1776, Wallace, 475; John Laurens to Henry Laurens, January 14, 1778, Simms (1867), 108.

27. David Ramsey to William Henry Drayton, September 1, 1779, Farley, 81.

28. Chernow (2010), 212-213; Washington to Laurens, February 18, 1782, FO.

29. Greene to John Rutledge, December 9, 1781, NG, 10:22.

30. Aedanus Burke to Arthur Middleton, February 5, 1782, Middleton, 194.

31. Rutledge to Arthur Middleton, February 8, 1782, NG, 10:229n4.

32. William Pierce to St. George Tucker, February 6, 1782, NG, 10:230n4; Greene to Robert Livingston, April 12, 1782, NG, 11:35.

33. Laurens to Washington, May 19, 1782, GW; Washington to Laurens, July 10, 1782, GW.

34. Coy, 44; Farley, 85; Leslie to Clinton, March 12, 1782, HMC, 2:417; Quarles, 108.

CHAPTER TWELVE: THE SWAMP FOX MEETS HIS MATCH

1. McDowell, 319.

2. Tilden, 217.

3. Moultrie, 341.

4. Leslie (1782).

5. *Pennsylvania Gazette*, July 31, 1782, Ward (2002), 175-176.

6. Lee (1812), 415; NG, 11:86n1.

7. Dorchester background, Daniel J. Bell, *Old Dorchester State Park Visitor's Guide* (South Carolina: SC Department of Parks, Recreation, and Tourism, 1995); Steven and Mindy Steele, "Early Dorchester," *Swamp Fox Brigade: South Carolina in the American Revolution*, http://swampfoxbrigade.blogspot.com/2011/11/early-dorchester.html.

8. Greene to John Rutledge, December 3, 1781, NG, 10:3-4.

9. In the mid-twentieth century, Walt Disney produced a TV series about the Swamp Fox that was short-lived, but often rerun. In 2000, *The Patriot*, with superstar

Mel Gibson, showed Marion as a nonslaveholder (contrary to facts) and "exaggerated the Swamp Fox legend for a whole new generation." Amy Crawford, "The Swamp Fox," *Smithsonian*, July 1, 2007, http://www.smithsonianmag.com/history-archaeology/fox.html.

10. William Dobein James, *A Sketch of the Life of Brig. Gen. Francis Marion*, ed. Alan R. Light (Charleston: Gould and Riley, 1821), ch. 2.

11. William Moultrie, James, op. cit., ch. 1.

12. Rankin (1973), 45.

13. Greene to Marion, December 4, 1780, NG, 6:520.

14. Otho Williams, "A Narrative of the Campaign of 1780," rpt. in William Johnson, *Sketches of the Life and Correspondence of Nathanael Greene* (Charleston: A. E. Miller, 1822), 488.

15. Henry Lee IV, son of Henry "Light-Horse Harry" Lee, Lee (1827), 433.

16. John W. T. Watson, Lossing, 772.

17. Cornwallis to Henry Clinton, December 3, 1780, Tarleton, 205; Tarleton, 174; Gray, 144.

18. Marion to Greene, November 18, 1781, NG, 9:589-590.

19. Adjutant general of Alexander Stewart, McCardy, 1902, 489-490.

20. "Memoir of the Late Lieutenant-Colonel William Brereton," *United Service Journal and Naval and Military Magazine*, 1831, Pt. 1 (London: Henry Colburn and Richard Bentley, 1831), 516-517; H. G. Purdon, *Memoirs of the Services of the 64th Regiment* (London: W. H. Allen, 1882), 8ff.

21. My Heritage, "Joseph Henry Videau," http://www.myheritage.com/person-3005506_114888091_114888091/joseph-henry-videau#!events; Leslie to Clinton, January 29, 1782, HMC, 2:389.

22. Marion to Greene, January 15, 1782, NG, 10:197n1.

23. Ellis, 8.

24. Ellis, 7.

25. Thompson to the Rev. Timothy Walker, December 24, 1774, Ellis, 68.

26. Samuel Curwen, May 24, 1781, Ellis, 114.

27. Thompson to Germain, January 15, 1782, Brown (1979), 328n12.

28. Marion to Greene, January 15, 1782, NG, 10:196.

29. *Rivington's Royal Gazette*, April 13, 1782, Brown (1979), 83; Parker, 59; Rankin (1973), 272-273; NG, 10:499n2.

30. Thompson to Leslie, February 25, 1782, HMC, 2:406-407.

31. NG, 10:420-421n6.

32. Rankin (1973), 280-282; NBS, 3:74.

CHAPTER THIRTEEN: "BLOODY BILL" CUNNINGHAM RAIDS THE BACK-COUNTRY

1. Ward (1845), 643, 648.

2. Moultrie, 302; Ward (1845), 646.

3. Selesky, 293; Lambert, 147; Ward (1845), 639.

4. Ward (1845), 640.

5. Thomas Sumter to Greene, November 14, 1781, NG, 9:575-576; Ward (1845), 644.

6. Lambert, 147-148.

7. Greene to Thomas Sumter, November 2, 1781, NG, 9:517-518.

8. Lambert, 148; NG, 9:651-653n3.

9. LeRoy Hammond to Greene, December 2, 1781, NG, 9:651-653.

10. Lambert, 148-149; John W. Gordon, *South Carolina and the American Revolution: A Battlefield History* (Columbia: University of South Carolina Press, 2003), 171-172.

11. Ward (1845), 646.

12. Thomas Sumter to Greene, November 14, 1781, NG, 9:575-576.

13. Parker, 295.

14. NG, 9:651-653n4.

15. NBS, 3:387.

16. NBS, 3:387.

17. NBS, 3:401.

18. NG, 9:651-653n5.

19. Maham to Greene, May 20, 1782, NG, 11:226.

20. NBS, 4:96; McCrady, 630-631.

21. Ward (1845), 647; Wilbur H. Siebert, *Loyalists in East Florida 1774 to 1785*, vol. 2 (Deland: Florida State Historical Society, 1929), 315; Selesky, 293; J. B. O'Neal, "Random Recollections of Revolutionary Characters and Incidents," *Southern Literary Journal and Magazine of Arts*, vol. 4, no. 1, July 1838, 40-45.

22. Leslie to Carleton, September 8, 1782, NG, 11:607-608n2-7.

23. Leslie to Carleton, September 8, 1782, NG, 11:607-608n2-7.

24. Marion to Greene, August 30, 1782, NG, 11:607.

CHAPTER FOURTEEN: LAURENS AND HIS GLORY

1. Greene to Lee, December 21, 1781, NG, 10:85.

2. Leslie to Clinton, November 30, 1781, NG, 10:145n2.

3. McDowell, 311.

4. McDowell, 311-312.

5. Greene to John Rutledge, January 16, 1782, NG, 10:206.

6. Greene to Lee, April 22, 1782, NG, 11:90-91.

7. McDowell, 315-316.

8. Greene to Otho Williams, September 17, 1782, NG, 11:670; Greene to Lee, June 6, 1782, NG, 11:295; McDowell, 324.

9. Laurens to Greene, August 3, 1782, NG, 11:484.

10. Laurens to Greene, August 3, 1782, NG, 11:484; August 5, 1782, NG, 11:489-490; August 13, 1782, NG, 11:536.

11. Leslie to Greene, August 13, 1782, NG, 11:538.

12. Greene to John Hanson, August 28, 1782, NG, 11:584.

13. Leslie to Carlton, September 8, 1782, Leslie (1782).

14. Jeff Grigg, "A Brief History of Combahee Ferry for the Harriet Tubman Bridge Dedication, October 18, 2008," http://sc150civilwar.palmettohistory.org/combaheehistory.pdf.

15. Leslie to Brereton, August 21, 1782, Leslie, *Letterbooks*, no. 15637.

16. Estimates are 500–1,200; 800 is in Johnson (1822), 336; "An Historical Sketch of the 64th Regiment," Robertson.

17. William Pierce Jr. to Gist, August 23, 1782, NG, 11:570.

18. Selesky, 435-436; Richard J. Cox, "A Guide to the Microfilm Edition of the Mordecai Gist Papers," Maryland Historical Society, 1975, http://www.mdhs.org/findingaid/gist-papers-1772-1813-ms-390.

19. Laurens to Greene, August 24, 1782, NG, 11:570.

20. Gist to Greene, August 27, 1782, NG, 11:579. Tar Bluff has also been called Chehaw Point, although it's on the Combahee, not the Chehaw.

21. Gist to Greene, August 27, 1782, NG, 11:579; McDowell, 328.

22. Johnson (1822), 340.

23. Brereton to Leslie, August 27, 1782, NG, 11:581n3.

24. Gist to Greene, August 27, 1782, NG, 11:579.

25. Seymour, 392; Brereton to Leslie, August 27, 1782, NG, 11:581-582n5.

26. "An Historical Sketch of the 64th Regiment," Robertson; Johnson (1822), 340.

27. Casualty numbers vary by source. NG, 11:582n9; Leslie to Carleton, September 8, 1782, Leslie (1782).

28. Gist to Greene, August 27, 1782, NG, 11:579-580.

29. Brereton to Leslie, August 27, 1782, NG, 11:581n7; Leslie to Carleton, September 8, 1782, Leslie (1782); NG, 11:581n3; "Memoir of the Late Lieutenant-Colonel William Brereton," *United Service Journal and Naval and Military Magazine*, 1847:2 (London: Henry Colburn and Richard Bentley, 1831), 516-517.

30. Gist to Greene, August 27, 1782, NG, 11:581.

31. Charlestown *Royal Gazette*, September 7, 1782, Wallace, 490-491.

32. Greene to Washington, August 29, 1782, Washington; Washington to Greene, October 18, 1782, GW.

33. Washington to William Gordon, March 8, 1785, GW.

34. Greene to Otho H. Williams, September 17, 1782, NG, 11:670.

35. Hamilton to Greene, October 12, 1782, FO.

36. Chernow (2004), 173.

37. Washington to Lafayette, October 20, 1782, GW.

38. Adams to Henry Laurens, November 6, 1782, FO.

39. Henry Laurens to Mary Laurens, December 20, 1782, Chesnutt, 110-112.

CHAPTER FIFTEEN: AT LAST, THE EVACUATION

1. Greene to Thomas Burke, February 24, 1782, NG, 10:407.

2. Leslie to Clinton, December 27, 1781, DAR, 20:288.

3. Leslie to Greene, August 5, 1782, NG, 11:492; Greene to Leslie, August 9, 1782, NG, 11:508-509.

4. Prisoners aboard *Lord Howe* to Greene, August 12, 1782, NG, 11:529.

5. Washington to William Stephens Smith, January 22, 1783, Washington; Jones (1979), 277.

6. *Royal Gazette*, August 7, 1782, Lambert, 180.

7. Jones (1979), 270; Frey (1991), 177.

8. Leslie to Carleton, August 2, 1782, NG, 11:490n4; Leslie to Carleton, September 8, 1782, Leslie (1782).

9. Carleton to Leslie, August 15, 1782, HMC, 3:71; Leslie to Carleton, September 8, 1782, Leslie (1782); Leslie to Carleton, November 18, 1782, DAR, 21:40.

10. Greene to Anthony Wayne, December 12, 1782, NG, 12:281; Christopher Gadsden to Francis Marion, November 13, 1782, ed. John Bennett, "Marion–Gadsden Correspondence," *South Carolina Historical and Genealogical Magazine*, 41:2, April 1940, 55, accessed via JSTOR.

11. Leslie to Carleton, November 18, 1782, DAR, 21:140.

12. Jones (1979), 273; Lambert, 172.

13. Parker, 56; Olwell, 31, 98.
14. Jasanoff, 74.
15. Leslie to Carleton, June 27, 1782, HMC, 2:544.
16. Leslie to Carleton, October 3, 1782, HMC, 3:150.
17. Leslie to Carleton, October 1782 (no date), HMC, 3:195.
18. Leslie to Carleton, October 18, 1782, HMC, 3:175-176.
19. Carleton to Leslie, July 15, 1782, HMC, 3:20.
20. Jasanoff, 75; Jones (1979), 274-275; Lambert, 181; Frey (1991), 178.
21. Leslie to Carleton, November 18, 1782, DAR, 21:140.
22. Jones (1979), 272.
23. George W. Kyte, "Thaddeus Kosciuszko at the Liberation of Charleston, 1782," *South Carolina Historical Magazine*, 84:1, January 1983, 11-21.
24. Denny, 48.
25. Wayne to Greene, December 13, 1782, NG, 12:290.
26. NG, 12:291n2; Jones (1979), 278.
27. Denny, 49.
28. Bull to Thomas Townsend, January 19, 1783, DAR, 21:148.
29. Denny, 49.
30. Unnamed soldier, *South Carolina Weekly Gazette*, May 31, 1783, Barnwell, 11-12.
31. Schama, 133.
32. Rivington's *Royal Gazette*, January 4, 1783, Barnwell, 15.
33. Lambert, 183; Bull to Thomas Townsend, January 19, 1783, Lambert, 184.
34. General orders, December 15, 1782, O'Kelley, 583.
35. Greene to Elias Boudinot, December 19, 1782, NG, 12:301; Greene to Washington, December 19, 1782, FO.
36. Morris to Greene, February 21, 1783, NG, 12:388.
37. Interview, E. Lee Spence, June 15, 2015, who cites *South Carolina Weekly Advertiser*, April 2, 1783; *Gazette of the State of Georgia*, April 10, 1783; *South Carolina Weekly Gazette*, April 5, 1783. Because of the different descriptions of type of ship, Spence believes there is no question that at least two vessels were destroyed. *See also*: Spence, "Spence's List 1520-1865," *Shipwrecks of South Carolina and Georgia* (Sullivan's Island, SC: Sea Research Society, 1984), 268-269.
38. Ward (2002); Parker, 164-165; Schama, 125-126; Charles C. Jones Jr., *The Life and Services of the Honorable Maj. Gen. Samuel Elbert of Georgia* (Cambridge: Riverside Press, 1887), 47.
39. Coy, 2000, 9.
40. Greene to Charles Pettit, November 2, 1782, NG, 12:136-137; Greene to Gist, January 1, 1783, NG, 12:364.
41. General Orders, June 21, 1783, NG, 12:44-46.
42. Carbone, 234-235; Wayne to James Jackson: Charlton, 134; Washington to Rochambeau, July 31, 1786, NG, 13:701; Washington to Jeremiah Wadsworth, October 22, 1786, GW.
43. Wayne to Caty Greene, August 1, 1786, Stegeman, 153-154.
44. Stegeman, 161, 170.
45. http://batman.neoseeker.com/wiki/Batman.
46. John Kay, *A Series of Original Portraits and Caricature Etchings*, vol. 2, pt. 1 (Edinburgh: Hugh Paton, 1842), 79; Peter Charles Hoffer, *Prelude to Revolution: The Salem Gunpowder Raid of 1775* (Baltimore: Johns Hopkins University Press, 2013),

105; *Times*, December 22, 1794, 1, accessed via Gale NewsVault.

47. *True Briton*, January 2, 1795, issue 629, 3, accessed via Gale NewsVault.

CHAPTER SIXTEEN: INDIANS

1. Philbrick, 69, 71.

2. Calloway (1995), 1.

3. Johnson to William Tryon, October 22, 1773, O'Callaghan, 458-459.

4. Filson, 52-54.

5. Silver, 11; Calloway (1995), 19; Peter H. Wood, "The Changing Population of the Colonial South," *Powhatan's Mantle: Indians in the Colonial Southeast*, eds. Gregory A. Waselkov et al. (Lincoln: University of Nebraska Press, 2006), 61-62; Louise Phelps Kellogg, *Frontier Retreat on the Upper Ohio, 1779–1781* (Madison: State Historical Society of Wisconsin, 1917), 21.

6. Frederick Jackson Turner, *The Frontier in American History* (New York: Henry Holt, 1920), 4-6.

7. Delaware Indians to George Thomas, January 3, 1741, Silver, 8; Pachgantschihilas (Buckongahelas), April 1781, Sipe, 651.

8. Taylor, 43-45; Glatthaar, 69; Calloway (2013), 2-13, 73-75.

9. Thomas Gage to Lord Shelburne, June 13, 1767, Taylor, 42.

10. Washington to William Crawford, September 21, 1767, GW.

11. Johnson to Earl of Dartmouth, June 20, 1774, O'Callaghan, 459-461.

12. John Stuart, Calloway (1995), 23.

13. Franklin to John Sevier, December 16, 1787, BF; St. Clair to Territorial Legislature, November 5, 1800, William Henry Smith, *The St. Clair Papers . . .* (Cincinnati: Robert Clarke, 1882), 503.

14. Fauquier to Pennsylvania John Penn, December 11, 1766, Silver, 154.

15. Doddridge, 206.

16. Silver, 41-42, 56-58; Graymont, 18; Knowles, 188-190, 204, 208-214.

17. Heckewelder (1876), 217-219.

18. Stone, xii-xiv, xvi.

19. Adams to James Warren, June 7, 1775; Washington to Commissioners of Indian Affairs, March 13, 1778; Jefferson to Theodorick Bland, June 8, 1779, FO.

20. Silver, xix-xx, 85, 89, 195, 228.

21. Brackenridge, 36-38.

22. Lamb, 78.

23. Graymont, 237; William L. Stone, *Border Wars of the American Revolution*, vol. 2 (New York: A. L. Fowle, 1900), 173-174, 184.

24. "A Whig," *Pennsylvania Packet*, August 5, 1779, Frank Moore, *Diary of the American Revolution*, vol. 2 (New York: Charles Scribner, 1860), 166-167.

25. William Bradford, Philbrick, 178; Knowles, 165.

26. Allan Maclean to Frederick Haldimand, December 16, 1782, Griffin (2007), 170.

27. Philbrick, 320; James Clinton to Goose Van Schaick, Stone, 404; Tiouganda, December 11, 1782, Taylor, 98.

28. Peter Oliver, *Peter Oliver's Origin and Progress of the American Rebellion*, eds. Douglass Adair and John A. Scutz (San Marino: Huntington Library, 1961), 133.

29. Unnamed veteran, Calloway (1995), 124-125.

30. Heckewelder (1876), 342.

31. Hugh Percy to Thomas Gage, April 20, 1775, Graymont, 62.

32. Thomas Brown to Thomas Townshend, January 12, 1783, Griffin (2007), 170.

33. Sayenqueraghta, late 1782, Graymont, 256.

34. Oneidas to Jonathan Trumbull, March 1775, Graymont, 58.

35. Half King, Calloway (1995), 39.

36. Washington to Philip Schuyler, April 19, 1776, FO; Massachusetts Provincial Congress to Samuel Kirkland, Andrew McFarland Davis, "The Employment of Indian Auxiliaries in the American War," *English Historical Review*, 2:8, October 1887, 714-715; George Rogers Clark, July 1778, Griffin (2007), 143; Allen, Graymont, 68.

37. Gage to Guy Johnson, February 5, 1775, Graymont, 61; John Butler to Iroquois council, late May or early June 1776, Graymont, 98.

38. Calloway (1995), 167-168; Griffin (2007), 152; Selesky, 551.

39. Calloway (1995), 49-54.

40. Charles Stedman, *The History of the Origin, Progress, and Termination of the American War* (London: J. Murray, 1794), 73.

CHAPTER SEVENTEEN: THE DEATH OF COLONEL BUTLER

1. WPA, *New York: A Guide to the Empire State* (New York: Oxford University Press, 1940), 317-319.

2. Glatthaar, 47, 62, 86, 73, 98, 106, 110, 123; Cruikshank (1893), 5.

3. Glatthaar, 87; Jasanoff, 40-41; Wilbur H. Siebert, *The Loyalists and Six Nation Indians in the Niagara Peninsula*, Transactions of the Royal Society of Canada, series 3, vol. 9 (Ottawa: Royal Society of Canada, 1915), 83, 86.

4. Washington to Sullivan, May 31, 1779, FO.

5. Graymont, 235.

6. George Clinton to Congress, February 5, 1781, Graymont, 238; Johansen, 225; Graymont, 242-243; Glatthaar, 272-273, 284; Hanson, 111-112.

7. Marquis de Chastellux, *Travels in North-America, in the Years 1780-'81-'82* (New York: White, Gallaher, and White, 1827), 182-184; Taylor, 102.

8. Willett, 11, 13-24; Ketcham, "Marinus Willett."

9. Willett, 57-58.

10. Washington to Willett, February 2, 1783, FO; Willett, 72-73.

11. Willett to Washington, July 6, 1781, FO.

12. Hanson, 118-119.

13. Haldimand to Ross, September 1781, Cruikshank (1893), 98.

14. Preston.

15. Graymont, 247.

16. Haldimand to Lord Germain, November 1781, Cruikshank (1895), 298; John Johnson, July 16, 1778, Cruikshank (1895), 286-287; Haldimand to John Butler, February 12, 1780, Swiggett, 208.

17. Swiggett, ch. 11, 249, 266-267.

18. Swiggett, 21, 36-37; Ketcham, "Walter Butler"; Cruikshank (1895), 285.

19. Cruikshank (1895), 285.

20. Swiggett, 92, 96; Cruikshank (1895), 285.

21. Graymont, 164; Cruikshank (1895), 286.

22. Alexander Macomb to Henry Hamilton, February 4, 1779, Swiggett, 159; Butler to Bolton, November 17, 1778, Cruikshank (1893), 56.

23. Butler to Philip Schuyler, November 12, 1778, Swiggett, 158; Butler to James

Clinton, February 18, 1779, Cruikshank (1893), 57-58; Charters.

24. Willett, 87.

25. Haldimand to Germain, November 23, 1781, DAR, 20:262.

26. Willett to George Clinton, Willett to Clinton, November 16, 1781, Clinton (1904), 505; Haldimand to Germain, November 23, 1781, DAR, 20:262.

27. Cruikshank (1895), 99-101, 296.

28. Haldimand to Germain, November 23, 1781, DAR, 20:263; Graymont, 248.

29. Willett to George Clinton, November 2, 1781, Clinton (1904), 472-474.

30. Willett to George Clinton, November 2, 1781, Clinton (1904), 472-474.

31. Willett to George Clinton, November 2, 1781, Clinton (1904), 472-474; Cruikshank (1895), 297.

32. Haldimand to Ross, November 16, 1781, Swiggett, 244.

33. Leonard Gansevoort Jr. to Leonard Bronck, Ketcham, "Walter Butler."

34. Willett, 88-89.

35. Swiggett, 279-280.

36. Preston.

37. Graymont, 251, 254; Willett to Washington, July 21, 1782, FO.

38. Washington to Frederick Visscher, June 30, 1782, FO.

39. James Duane to George Clinton: Glatthaar, 286.

40. Washington to Willett, December 18, 1782, FO.

41. Willett to Washington, February 19, 1782, FO; NG, 169-170.

42. Washington to Willett, March 5, 1782, FO.

43. Haldimand to Thomas Townsend, DAR, 21:163.

CHAPTER EIGHTEEN: MASSACRE AND REVENGE

1. Heckewelder (1820), 423-424, 427.

2. Biography, Daniel J. Brock, "David Zeisberger," DCB; Bliss, viii-xx.

3. Colwell, 35; Silver, 265.

4. January 16, 1782, February 1, 1782, February 13, 1782, Bliss, 61, 64, 66.

5. William Croghan to Michael Gratz, April 26, 1782, Silver, 267-268, 276.

6. Von Pilchau, 293-294.

7. Dorsey Pentecost to William Moore, May 8, 1782, *Pennsylvania Archives*, series 1, 9:540, Silver, 268.

8. Contemporary descriptions based on two eyewitness accounts publicized by missionaries, Heckewelder (1820); Leonard Sadosky, "Rethinking the Gnadenhutten Massacre," *The Sixty Years' War for the Great Lakes, 1754-1814*, eds. David Curtis Skaggs and Larry L. Nelson (East Lansing: Michigan State University Press, 2001), 198-199; Silver, 268-273.

9. Irvine to Anne Callender Irvine, April 12, 1782, Butterfield (1882), 343-344.

10. Croghan to William Davies, June [July] 6, 1782, James, *Clark Papers*, 71; Rose, May 28, 1782, Von Pilchau, 141.

11. Zeisberger, March 14, 1782, March 23, 1782, Bliss, 73, 78-81.

12. Franklin to James Hutton, July 7, 1782, FO.

13. Irvine to Washington, February 2, 1782, FO.

14. Noncommissioned officers, 7th Virginia Regiment, to Irvine, March 1782, Butterfield (1882), 103n1; Albert (1916), 139.

15. Arthur Lee, late 1783, Albert (1916), 152.

16. Dorsey Pentecost to William Moore, May 8, 1782, Sipe, 658.

17. Irvine to Washington, May 21, 1782, FO.
18. Von Pilchau, 129-136.
19. Irvine to Washington, May 21, 1782, FO.
20. Crawford to Washington, December 6, 1770, May 5, 1772, May 8, 1774, FO.
21. Washington to Crawford, June 9, 1781, FO.
22. Von Pilchau, 293.
23. Washington to Crawford, February 2, 1777, FO.
24. Butterfield (1882), 367-378.
25. Cruikshank (1893), 106.
26. Von Pilchau, 148-151.
27. Tierney to DePeyster, June 7, 1782, DAR, 21:86; Angus McCoy, Dann, 312.
28. Von Pilchau, 151-152.
29. Williamson to Irvine, June 13, 1782, Butterfield (1882), 366.
30. Von Pilchau, 153-156.
31. Brackenridge, 8; Brown (1987), 60.
32. Heckewelder (1876), 284-288.
33. Brown (1987), 53-59.
34. Brackenridge, 9.
35. Butterfield (1890), 96; Heckewelder (1876), 152.
36. James T. Morehead, Butterfield (1890), 395.
37. John Mason Brown, *An Oration: Delivered on the Occasion of the Centennial Commemoration of the Battle of Blue Licks* (Frankfort: Major, Johnson, and Barrett, 1882), 9.
38. Grey, 183-184.
39. Butterfield (1890), 5; Colwell, 41n10; author interview with descendant Ken Girty, Renfrew, PA, November 11, 2013.
40. Butterfield (1890), 41, 45; Colwell, 32.
41. Kulina, 10; S[arepta] Kussart, *The Early History of the 15th Ward of the City of Pittsburgh* (Bellevue/Pittsburgh: Suburban Printing, 1925), 6-7; Butterfield (1890), 50, 52; Colwell, 32.
42. Butterfield (1890), 80, 98; Douglas Leighton, "Simon Girty," DCB; Lofaro, 123; William K. Beall, "Journal of William K. Beall, July–August, 1812," *American Historical Review*, 17:4, July 1912, 801 (IA); Grey, 183-184.
43. William Renwick Riddell, "Two Incidents of Revolutionary Time," *Journal of Criminal Law and Criminology*, 12:2, 1921, 226-227; Leighton, op. cit.; Johansen, 112; Butterfield (1890), 95, 130-131, 323-324.
44. Brackenridge, 9-12.
45. Caldwell to A. S. DePeyster, June 11, 1782, Butterfield (1882), 370-371n.
46. Cruikshank (1893), 107.
47. Butterfield (1882), 372n; Irvine to Washington, July 11, 1782, FO; William Croghan, July 6, 1782, Colwell, 37-38; Mrs. Alexander McCormick, Colwell, 39; Brown (1987), 62; Johansen, 115; Butterfield (1890), 174-175; Kulina, 10.
48. DePeyster to Alexander McKee, June 6, 1782, Cruikshank (1893), 107; DePeyster to Haldimand, August 18, 1782, Butterfield (1882), 373n; Haldimand to Carleton, July 28, 1782, Butterfield (1882), 373n.
49. Caldwell to DePeyster, June 11, 1782, Butterfield (1882), 370-371n.
50. Washington to Irvine, July 10, 1782, FO.
51. Irvine to Lincoln, July 1, 1782, Butterfield (1882), 174-175; Irvine to Lincoln,

April 16, 1783, Butterfield (1882), 187.

52. Albert, 1916, 290-291, 297-298.

53. Richard Coulter, *Pennsylvania Argus*, Greensburg, PA, 1836, Albert, 1916, 301-307.

54. Huffnagle to Irvine, July 14, 1782, July 17, 1782, Albert, 1916, 308-309.

CHAPTER NINETEEN: AMBUSH AT BLUE LICKS

1. Caldwell to DePeyster, August 26, 1782, Roosevelt, 2:393-394.

2. Biography, Kulisek; Recker.

3. John Butler, July 12, 1778, Selesky, 1288; Cruikshank (1893), 44-47, 52.

4. Cruikshank (1893), 53.

5. Calloway (1995), 22.

6. Calloway (2013), 86-87.

7. Calloway (1995), 190.

8. Lofaro, 143-144; William A. Galloway, "Daniel Boon," *Ohio Archaeological and Historical Quarterly*, 8:2, April 1904, 277.

9. McGary to Henry, February 27, 1777, Hammersmith, 127-128.

10. John Floyd to John May, April 8, 1782, Henry Steele Commager and Richard B. Morris, eds., *The Spirit of 'Seventy-Six: The Story of the American Revolution as Told by Participants* (Edison, NJ: Castle Books, 2002), 1057-1058.

11. Boone, "Autobiography," Filson, 45.

12. Caldwell to DePeyster, August 26, 1782, Roosevelt, 2:393-394; Filson, 46.

13. Filson, 46-47.

14. Alexander McKee to DePeyster, August 28, 1782, DAR, 21:115.

15. Carter; Nancy O'Malley, "Perceiving Class Relations through Material Culture: Three Households from Kentucky," University of Kentucky, no date given, http://www.uky.edu/~omalley/Papers/Considering%20Class%20SHA%202010%20latest.docx; Hammersmith, 116-117, 125-126, 142.

16. Levi Todd to Benjamin Harrison, September 11, 1782, Palmer, 3:300-301; Arthur Campbell to William Davies, October 3, 1782, Palmer, 3:337.

17. [William?] Madison, Hammersmith, 205.

18. Filson, 46-47.

19. Todd to Harrison, September 11, 1782, Palmer, 3:300-301.

20. Caldwell to DePeyster, August 26, 1782, Roosevelt, 2:393-394.

21. Peter Houston, in purported 1842 manuscript published in 1887, Lofaro, 128.

22. Boone et al. to Harrison, September 11, 1782, Palmer, 3:301.

23. Lofaro, 138-139; Hammersmith, 147-185, 256-267; Carter.

24. Recker; Kulisek.

CHAPTER TWENTY: FINAL FIGHTS ON THE OHIO

1. WPA, *West Virginia: A Guide to the Mountain State* (New York: Oxford University Press, 1941), 283.

2. De Hass, 332, 335; Thrapp, 3:1619; Washington diary, October 24, 1770, FO; Selesky, 1309.

3. Cole, 672; De Hass, 266, 277; A. B. Brooks, "Story of Fort Henry," *West Virginia History*, 1:2, January 1940, http://www.wvculture.org/history/journal_wvh/wvh1-2.html.

4. Ebenezer Zane to William Irvine, July 22, 1782, Butterfield (1882), 390.

5. Butterfield (1890), 200.

6. "Captain Andrew Bradt's Company," *Butler's Rangers*, http://iaw.on.ca/~awoolley/brang/brang.html; Cruikshank (1893), 91; Noelle [only name given], "U.E.L. Captain Andries 'Andrew' BRADT\BRATT," *Rootsweb*, http://wc.rootsweb.ancestry.com/cgi bin/igm.cgi?op=GET&db=nlbrown&id=I2377; Hanson, 137-139; Charters.

7. Zane to William Irvine, September 17, 1782, Butterfield (1882), 397-398; Charles McKnight, *Our Western Border* . . . (Philadelphia: J. C. McCurdy, 1875), 523-528.

8. Cole, 673, 675.

9. Zane Grey's West Society, "The Genealogy of Zane Grey" by Thelma Frazier, http://www.zgws.org/sf8.php; Grey, 272, 275.

10. William Hintzen, "Betty Zane, Lydia Boggs, and Molly Scott: The Gunpowder Exploits at Fort Henry," *West Virginia History*, vol. 55, 1996; Cole, 675.

11. Cole, 675; Thrapp, 3:1619; De Hass, 336; Selesky, 1309.

12. McKnight, op. cit.; De Hass, 263.

13. Albert (1916), 405; Sipe, 673-674; Doddridge, 217-219.

14. Cruikshank (1893), 109.

15. Irvine to Washington, October 29, 1782, FO.

16. Harrison to George Rogers Clark, March 24, 1782, James, *Clark Papers*, 49-50.

17. Clark memoir: Indiana Historical Bureau, http://www.in.gov/history/2426.htm; Calloway (1995), 48.

18. WPA, *Ohio Guide* (New York: Oxford University Press, 1940), 594.

19. Clark to Thomas Nelson, October 1, 1781, Connelley, 184; James, *Clark Papers*, xxxiv-xxxvi.

20. Boone et al. to Harrison, September 12, 1782, Connelley, 186; Arthur Campbell to William Davies, October 3, 1782, Palmer, 3:337; Harrison to William Fleming et al., October 16, 1782, James (1926), 131-132; Harrison to Levi Todd, October 14, 1782, James (1926), 128.

21. Clark to Harrison, November 20, 1782, James, *Clark Papers*, 161-163.

22. Clark to Oliver Pollock, October 25, 1782, James, *Clark Papers*, 48.

23. Joseph Crockett to Harrison, October 24, 1782, James, *Clark Papers*, 142.

24. Connelley, 186-187; James, *Clark Papers*, liv-lv; Irvine to Clark, November 7, 1782, James, *Clark Papers*, 149.

25. Clark to Harrison, November 27, 1782, Palmer, 3:381; English, 758-759.

26. Wryneck, spring 1781, Calloway (1995), 172.

27. DePeyster, summer 1783, Calloway (1995), 173.

28. Supreme Executive Council of PA, April 29, 1783, Sipe, 682; John Cummins to John Dickinson, March 29, 1783, Sipe, 681.

29. English, 751-752.

30. Colwell, 41n19.

31. Butterfield (1890), 210.

32. Johansen, 115-117; Butterfield (1890), 210-286, 313-329.

CHAPTER TWENTY-ONE: SEVIER HUNTS FOR DRAGGING CANOE

1. WPA, *Tennessee: A Guide to the State* (New York: Viking Press, 1945), 31; Francis M. Turner, *Life of General John Sevier* (Washington, D.C.: Neale Publishing, 1910), 25.

2. Jefferson to Edmund Pendleton, August 13, 1776, FO.

3. Parmenter, 118; Dragging Canoe, reported by Henry Stuart, 1776, Calloway (1995), 191.

4. Cherokee Heritage Documentation Center, "Dragging Canoe," http://cherokeeregistry.com/Dragging_Canoe.pdf; Alexander Cameron, 1774, Parmenter, 119; Black Fox's eulogy for Dragging Canoe, June 28, 1792, Parmenter, 131.

5. WPA, *Tennessee*, 38-39; Parmenter, 125-126.

6. The Raven, 1781, Calloway (1995), 204.

7. Thomas Brown to Carleton, January 1, 1782, HMC, 3:326; to Lord Germain, April 6, 1782, DAR, 21:55.

8. Old Tassel to Martin, September 25, 1782, James R. Gilmore, *The Rear-Guard of the Revolution* (New York: D. Appleton, 1889), 310; Harrison to Martin, November 12, 1782, O'Donnell, 128.

9. Martin to John Sevier, February 11, 1782, Gilmore, op. cit., 308-309.

10. Richard J. Hooker, ed., *The Carolina Backcountry on the Eve of the Revolution* (Chapel Hill: University of North Carolina Press, 1953), 52, 56, 61.

11. Williams, 223.

12. George Washington Sevier, Sevier, 18, 22.

13. Roosevelt, 2:356-359.

14. July 28, 1781, Sevier, 53-54.

15. Sevier, 56; Greene, 11:635n7-8; Joseph Martin to Arthur Campbell, September 18, 1782, ed. Colyer Meriwether, "General Joseph Martin and the Cherokees," *Publications of the Southern History Association*, 9:1, January 1905, 27, GB.

16. Maj. James Sevier, Sevier, 56.

17. Parmenter, 129-132.

CHAPTER TWENTY-TWO: ARKANSAS POST AND THE SPANISH FRONTIER

1. Calloway (1995), 213, 222.

2. St. Jean, 273-274.

3. Coleman (1987), 51-58; James Alton James, "Spanish Influence in the West during the American Revolution," *Mississippi Valley Historical Review*, 4:2, September 1917, 195-199, 202.

4. Anna Lewis, *Along the Arkansas* (Dallas: Southwest Press, 1932), 172; James, op. cit.; *Texas and the American Revolution* (San Antonio: University of Texas at San Antonio, 1975), 26; J. Barton Starr, *Tories, Dons, and Rebels: The American Revolution in British West Florida* (Gainesville: University of Florida Press, 1976), 78-88.

5. Piomingo, Calloway (1995), 213; John Stuart, May 1777, Calloway (1995), 223; St. Jean, 276.

6. Calloway (1995), 214.

7. Colbert to Benjamin Harrison, July 25, 1783, Catherine 'Erin' Serafina Liora Spiceland, "James Logan Colbert," http://www.geni.com/people/James-Logan-Colbert/6000000019790613785; Bearrs, 1974, 19; Guy B. Braden, "The Colberts and the Chickasaw Nation," *Tennessee Historical Quarterly*, 17:3, September 1958, 223.

8. Congressional Committee on Indian Affairs, May 28, 1784, *Journals of the Continental Congress*, 462-463, Library of Congress, http://memory.loc.gov/cgi-bin/query/D?hlaw:1:./temp/~ammem_CrXN:::; Silbestre Labadie, May 1782, Bearrs, 1974, 34.

9. Floridablanca to Charles Gravier, comte de Vergennes, March 30, 1779, Paul Chrisler Phillips, "The West in the Diplomacy of the American Revolution," *University of Illinois Studies in the Social Sciences*, 11:2-3, October 1913, 93.

10. Lafayette to Robert Livingston, March 2, 1783, DCAR (1830), X:34, 37.

11. Jay to Samuel Huntington, May 26, 1780, Stahr, 132; John Adams to William Lee, April 13, 1780, FO; Rappleye, 207-209.

12. Lewis (1980), 83-84, 90-91.

13. Calloway (1995), 225; Din (1981), 9; Gálvez to Esteban Rodriguez Miró, July 21, 1782, Houck, 232-233.

14. Din (1981), 8-9.

15. Francisco Bouligney, 1782, Atkinson, 111-112.

16. Bernard Romans, *A Concise Natural History of East and West Florida* (New York: R. Aitken, 1776), 59-61.

17. St. Jean, 277.

18. Gilbert C. Din, "Esteban Rodríguez Miró," *The Louisiana Governors*, ed. Joseph G. Dawson III (Baton Rouge: Louisiana State University Press, 1990), 61.

19. Bearss, 25-25; Williams, 242.

20. Bearss, 24; D. C. [Duvon Clough] Corbitt, "James Colbert and the Spanish Claims to the East Bank of the Mississippi," *Mississippi Valley Historical Review*, 24:4, March 1938, 458-459; Silbestre Labadie, May 1782: Bearss, 27-29.

21. Miró debriefing of Cruzat, May 30, 1782, Houck, 221-223, 227, 230.

22. Miro to Gálvez, June 5, 1782, Houck, 214-217.

23. Gálvez to Miró, July 21, 1782, Houck, 232-233.

24. Gálvez to José de Gálvez, Minister of the Indies, August 5, 1782, Houck, 211-212.

25. Colbert to Miró, October 6, 1782, Bearss, 41-42.

26. Bearss, 46-47; Atkinson, 112-114; Miró to Louis de Villars, October 18, 1782, Calloway (1995), 230.

27. Bearss, 47, 50; Din (1981), 22.

28. Din (1981), 4, 10.

29. Bearss, 61-62.

30. Arnold (1993), 70; Capt. Balthasar de Villiers to Gálvez, July 11, 1781, Bearss, 22, 68-69.

31. Din (1981), 21-22; Dubreuil to Miró, February 21, 1783, Bearss, 50.

32. Bearss, 25, 76; Din (1981), 18-19; Coleman (1987), 65; Arnold (1996), 64.

33. Unless noted, ensuing quotes are from Dubreuil to Miró, May 5, 1783, Lewis (September 1943), 262-265; Bearss, 54.

34. Din (1981), 25.

35. St. Jean, 278.

36. Din (1981), 25.

37. Bearss, 46.

38. Dubreuil to Colbert, [May?], Lewis (March 1943), 52-53.

39. Colbert to Dubreuil, August 3, 1783, Lewis (March 1943), 53-54; Bearss, 59.

40. Dubreuil to Miró, August 26, 1783, Lewis (March 1943), 54-55.

41. Rickey Butch Walker, *Chickasaw Chief George Colbert: His Family and His County* (Killen, AB: Bluewater Publications, 2012), 42-43.

42. Dubreuil to Miró, May 5, 1783, Lewis (September 1943), 266.

43. Gilbert C. Din, " 'For Defense of Country and the Glory of Arms': Army Officers in Spanish Louisiana, 1766–1803," *Louisiana History*, 43:1, Winter 2002, 24, 30; Lawrence and Lucia B. Kinnaird, "War Comes to San Marcos," *Florida Historical Quarterly*, 62:1, July 1983, 26, 38; Roscoe R. Hill, *Descriptive Catalogue of the Documents Relating to the History of the United States in the Papeles Procedentes de Cuba* . . . (Washington: Carnegie Institution, 1916), xxxvii, GB.

44. Frey (1991), 182.

CHAPTER TWENTY-THREE: BETWEEN TWO HELLS

1. Brown to Shelburne, September 25, 1782, DAR, 21:122.
2. William Christian to Harrison, December 16, 1782, Palmer, 3:398.
3. July 9, 1782, O'Donnell, 125.
4. Brant to Johnson, December 25, 1782, E. [Ernest] Cruikshank, "Joseph Brant in the American Revolution," *Transactions of The Canadian Institute*, vol. 7 (Toronto: Canadian Institute, 1904), 406-407.
5. *Pennsylvania Packet*, November 7, 1782, Silver, 263.
6. Irvine to Benjamin Lincoln, October 28, 1782, Burnett, 542n2.
7. Roosevelt, 2:373-374.
8. O'Donnell, 129-130.
9. Calloway (1995), 276.
10. Graymont, 260.
11. Calloway (1995), 273.
12. Haldimand to Lord North, June 2, 1783, DAR, 21:176.
13. Maclean to Haldimand, May 18, 1783, Taylor, 112-113.
14. McArthur to Carleton, May 19, 1783, HMC, 4:89.
15. [Hansard], *The Parliamentary History of England from the Earliest Period to the Year 1803*, vol. 23 (London: T. C. Hansard, 1814), 382, 384-385, 410.
16. Worcester vs. Georgia, 31 U.S. 542-543 (1832).
17. Worcester vs. Georgia, 31 U.S. 538-539 (1832); Wikipedia, "Cherokee treaties," http://en.wikipedia.org/wiki/Historic_treaties_of_the_Cherokee.
18. Captain Johnny, May 18, 1785, Colin G. Calloway, " 'We have always been the frontier': The American revolution in Shawnee country," *American Indian Quarterly*, 16:1 (Winter 1992), 174.
19. News release, Gov. Andrew M. Cuomo, May 16, 2013, http://www.governor.ny.gov/press/05162013-agreement-with-state-oneida-nation-and-oneida-and-madison-counties.

TWENTY-FOUR: RICHES

1. NG, 11:173n3.
2. Leslie to Clinton, May 9, 1782, HMC, 2:485; NG, 11:141n2; HMC, 2:450; Edward Mathew to Carleton, July 2, 1782, HMC, 3:2.
3. DNB, 42:61-62.
4. William Hotham, William D. Griffin, "General Charles O'Hara," *Irish Sword*, 10:179, Summer 1972, 187; "Obituary, with Anecdotes, of Remarkable Persons," *Gentleman's Magazine*, 72:1, March 1802, 278.
5. O'Shaughnessy (2000), 32.
6. Blane, 203; James, *British Navy*, 86; O'Shaughnessy (2000), 32.
7. Blane, 90, 203.
8. George Rodney reporting about Adm. Samuel Graves to Joshua Rowley, June 30, 1782, Rodney, 475-476.
9. Smith (1904), IV.7.76; Dunn, 312.
10. Deerr, 1:116-119.
11. James, *British Navy*, 86.
12. O'Shaughnessy (2000), 60-62, 72.
13. Smith (1904), I.11.42; Charles Leslie, 1739: T. G. Burnard, " 'Prodigious riches':

the wealth of Jamaica before the American Revolution," *Economic History Review*, 54:3, 2001, 506, 520.

14. Tuchman (1988), 139.

15. James, *British Navy*, 85; Robert and Isabelle Tombs, *That Sweet Enemy: The French and the British from the Sun King to the Present* (New York: Alfred A. Knopf, 2007), 111; Killion, 68-69.

16. Smith (1904), III.2.10.

17. George III to John Montagu, Earl of Sandwich, 1779: Tuchman (1988), 136.

18. O'Shaughnessy (2013), 295-296.

19. Patton, 71; O'Shaughnessy (2000), 158.

20. George Macartney to Germain, October 22, 1777, O'Shaughnessy (2013), 296, 49; Samuel Hood, Mackesy, 228.

21. "Chevaliér de Goussencourt," a pseudonym, Bradford, 107.

22. "Martinique," *Jewish Encyclopedia*, http://www.jewishencyclopedia.com/articles/10444-martinique; O'Shaughnessy (2000), 30, 298-299; Andrews, 135-138.

23. O'Shaughnessy (2000), 29; Chartrand (2008), 34-35; Maria Alessandra Bollettino, "Slavery, War, and Britain's Atlantic Empire: Black Soldiers, Sailors, and Rebels in the Seven Years' War," Ph.D. diss., University of Texas, December 2009, 3, 12.

24. Smith (1904), IV.7.76; Ramsay, 52-53; Dunn, 224; Andrews, 127.

25. Deerr, 2:289.

26. George Rodney, Mundy, 425-429.

27. Dunn, 224; Deerr, 2:278-280; Bryan Edwards, *The History, Civil and Commercial, of the British Colonies in the West Indies,* abridged edition (London: B. Crosby, 1798), 121-122.

28. Deerr, 2:317 and Ch. 20; Jamaican assembly to George III, December 31, 1773, O'Shaughnessy (2000), 51, 152; Goslinga, 464-492.

29. George Germain to John Vaughan, February 2, 1780, O'Shaughnessy (2013), 178; Lewis (1980), 84-85; Mackesy, 309-310.

TWENTY-FIVE: THE GOLDEN ROCK

1. Morse, "Eustatius"; Burke, May 14, 1781, Burke, 247.

2. A. Grenfell Price, "White Settlement in Saba Island, Dutch West Indies," *Geographical Review*, 24:1, January 1934, 42; Burke, May 14, 1781, Burke, 247; Tuchman (1988), 21; Goslinga, 141; Beatson, 5:163.

3. Andrews, 135-138.

4. Jameson, 685-686; Tuchman (1988); the first salute to any Whig ship, in this case, a privateer, was the month before in Danish St. Croix: "U.S. Took Ownership of the Virgin Islands March 31, 1917," Library of Congress, http://www.americas-library.gov/jb/jazz/jb_jazz_virgin_3.html; O'Shaughnessy (2013), 291; Goslinga, 146; James, *British Navy*, 255; Patton, 217.

5. O'Shaughnessy (2013), 291; George Rodney to Philip Stephens, August 12, 1780, Rodney, 5.

6. Manifesto, December 20, 1780, *Parliamentary Register . . . during the First Session of the Fifteenth Parliament*, vol. 1 (London: J. Almon and J. Debrett, 1781), 315-318, GB.

7. Lord Sandwich et al. to Rodney, December 20, 1780, Mundy, 8; Beatson, 5:161; Rodney to Stephens, February 4, 1781, Mundy, 9-11; Johannes de Graaf and Jacobus Seys to Rodney and Vaughan, February 3, 1781, Beatson, 5:164;

O'Shaughnessy (2013), 300-301.

8. Spinney, 146; Mundy, 370.

9. Breen, 230-234.

10. John Marr to Lord Northampton, March 23, 1772, Spinney, 257; Robert Gregson to Shelburne, Mackesy, 320.

11. Richard Cumberland, *Memoirs of Richard Cumberland* . . . , vol. 1 (London: Lackington, Allen, 1807), 405.

12. Sandwich to Rodney, July 7, 1781, Rodger, 284-287.

13. Rodney to Bayard, March 29, 1781, Spinney, 369; Rodney to Stephens, March 6, 1781, Mundy, 43-44.

14. Rodney to Lady Rodney, February 7, 1781, Mundy, 18-19; Dull (1975), 238; Rodney to George Germain, February 6, 1781, Mundy, 15-16; James, *British Navy*, 255; O'Shaughnessy (2013), 304.

15. Jameson, 705; Goslinga, 150; Burke, 250-256.

16. Burke, May 14, 1781: Burke, 248, 261; Horace Walpole to Horace Mann, October 18, 1781, Jameson, 706.

17. Jameson, 706-707; Beatson, 5:170; Duffy, 257-258; Mackesy, 417.

18. Rodney to Bouillé, March 23, 1781, Mundy, 73.

19. Bouillé to Rodney, March [ND] 1781, Mundy, 74-75.

20. Balch, 62-63; *Anti-Jacobin*, 225.

21. Bouillé (1906), 15-16.

22. L. G. [Louis] Gabriel] Michaud, "Bouillé," *Biographie Universelle*, vol. 5 (Paris: Chez Michaud Frères, Libraires, 1812), 511-513.

23. *Anti-Jacobin*, 226; Speech, February 4, 1782, Burke, 326.

24. Goslinga, 151; Beatson, 5:201.

25. Beatson, 5:203; Lafayette to Washington, January 18, 1782, FO.

26. Goslinga, 152; Beatson, 5:204.

27. Rodney to Lady Rodney, March 9, 1782, Mundy, 199-200; Beatson, 5:201; Fortescue (1911), 414.

28. Rodway, *History*, 116-118; "Lieutenant Colonel Cockburn," 112-116; Beatson, 5:204-205; DNB, "Cockburn, James," 11:188; Robert and Harry A. Cockburn, *The Records of the Cockburn Family* (London: T. N. Foulis, 1913), 96-97.

TWENTY-SIX: MORE BRITISH HUMILIATIONS

1. R. Montgomery Martin, *History of the West Indies* . . . , vol. 2 (London: Whittaker, 1837), 8-9, ch. 4.

2. Raynal, 1798, 239; Martin, op. cit., 3; De Villiers, 8-12, 19.

3. C. A. Harris and J. A. J. de Villiers, *Storm's Gravesande: The Rise of British Guiana*, vol. 1 (London: Hakluyt Society, 1911), 104; Goslinga, 432, 440, 443; Raymond T. Smith, *British Guiana* (London: Oxford University Press, 1962), 18-19; De Villiers, 14; Laurens Storm van 's Gravesande, 1772, De Villiers, 18.

4. Beatson, 5:172-174, 6:259-260; Goslinga, 455.

5. EB, "Kersaint," 15:759.

6. Beatson, 5:459-460; Rodway, 1-4.

7. Rodney to Stephens, March 14, 1782, Rodney, 289-290; Schomberg, 5:358; British National Archives, ADM 6/342/6, ff, 26-29, *Sarah Tahourdin, widow of William Tahourdin, Captain Royal Navy who died 1 May 1804; Will of William Tahourdin of Byfleet, May 30, 1804*, PROB 11/1409/229.

8. Rodway, 11-18.

9. George Washington Parke Custis, *Recollections and Private Memoirs of Washington* (Philadelphia: J. W. Bradley, 1861), GB.

10. "Account of the Life and Military Service of the Comte de Grasse," *European Magazine and London Review*, August 1782, 83-84.

11. Louis Guillouet, Comte d'Orvilliers, Lewis (1945), 49; Léon Guéron, *Histoire Maritime de la France*, 1844, Bradford, 21.

12. Grasse to Rochambeau, October 28, 1781, Lewis (1945), 197.

13. Morse, "Christophers"; Andrews, 120, 130; Tornquist, 81.

14. Lewis (1945), 208-209; Clowes, 3:510; Beatson, 5:458.

15. James, *British Navy*, 322; Tornquist, 81; Robertson, "Saint Kitts" by Chris Woolf; G. E. [George Edward] Cokayne, ed., *Complete Baronetage*, vol. 5 (Exeter: William Pollard, 1906), 252.

16. John Montagu, Earl of Sandwich, to Rodney, September 25, 1780, Breen, 240; Duffy, 257.

17. Hood to Rodney, April 1, 1781, Hannay, 17.

18. Hood to Middleton, April 16, 1782, March 31, 1782, April 3, 1782, August 9, 1782, Barham, 151-154, 157, 164, 206.

19. Hood to Jackson, June 24, 1781, April 16, 1782, Hannay, 22-23, 105-106; Hood to Stephens, December 10, 1781, Hannay, 50; August 30, 1782, Barham, lxii.

20. Hood to Middleton, May 4, 1781, Barham, 108-109; Hood to Jackson, May 21, 1781, Breen, 239.

21. Nelson to Frances Nelson, September 12, 1794, Nicolas, 487; Adm. William Hotham: A. M. W. Stirling, *Pages and Portraits from the Past*, vol. 2 (London: Herbert Jenkins, 1919), 43-44.

22. Jenkins, 172-173; James, *British Navy*, 323, 325.

23. Robert Manners to Duke of Rutland, February 8, 1782, James, *British Navy*, 325; Lewis (1945), 214-217.

24. Mackesy, 456; "Chevaliér de Goussencourt," a pseudonym, Bradford, 103.

25. Fraser, February 24, 1782: Beatson, 6:327-328n278.

26. Bradford, 105; Lewis (1945), 219-220.

27. Duffy, 260.

28. Rodney to Stephens, March 15, 1782, Rodney, 295; Mahan, 202; Mahan, *The Influence of Sea Power upon History* (Boston: Little, Brown, 1891), 476.

TWENTY-SEVEN: BATTLE OF THE SAINTES

1. Wraxall (1904), 457.

2. A common spelling was "François," reflecting an older pronunciation, but still meaning "French," not a man's name.

3. Hood to Jackson, March 31, 1782, Hannay, 95; Rodney to Hood, March 29, 1782, Rodney, 329.

4. Duffy, 261; James, *British Navy*, 331-333; Tornquist, 88.

5. Bradford, 101-102n1.

6. Hood to Jackson, April 16, 1782, James, *British Navy*, 335.

7. Tornquist, 90.

8. Tuchman (1988), 117, 123-124; O'Shaughnessy (2013), 314; Sébastien-François Bigot de Morogues, *Tactique Navale*, 1763, Killion, 24.

9. Breen, 244; John Creswell, *British Admirals of the Eighteenth Century* (Hamden, CT: Archon Books, 1972), 163.

10. Charles Douglas to Middleton, April 28, 1782, Barham, 280; Lewis (1945), 246.
11. "Notes on Sailing Warships: Cannon and Carronades," https://web.archive.org/web/20070528195028/http://www.cronab.demon.co.uk/gen1.htm; Hood to Middleton, April 13, 1782, Barham, 160-161.
12. Jenkins, 179.
13. Jenkins, 179; *Memoirs*, Lewis (1945), 247.
14. Lord Cranston, Wraxall (1904), 463.
15. Sir Gilbert Blane to Lord Dalrymple, April 22, 1782, Mundy, 236-237.
16. Blane, 479; Spinney, 443-445; Beatson, 5:473-474, 6:336n287.
17. Bouillé (1797), 1-2, 24-25.
18. Journal, June 15, 1782, BF; Washington to Rochambeau, April 28, 1788, FO.
19. Hood to Jackson, April 30, 1782, Hannay, 136-137; Mundy, 248-250; Hood to Middleton, April 16, 1782, Barham, 162; Rodney to Philip Stephens, Secretary of the Admiralty, April 14, 1782, Rodney, 357-358.
20. Wraxall (1904), 460-462, 467.
21. Rodney, March 1788, Spinney, 422; O'Shaughnessy (2013), 318-319.
22. Royal Naval Museum Library, "Biography: Samuel Hood," http://www.royal-navalmuseum.org/info_sheets_samuel_hood.htm; Daniel A. Baugh, "Sir Samuel Hood: Superior Subordinate," rpt. in *George Washington's Opponents*, ed. George Athan Billias (New York: William Morrow, 1969), 319; Duffy, 261.
23. Adams to Robert Livingston, June 9, 1782, FO.
24. Francisco de Saavedra, April 21, 1782, Padrón, 320.
25. Greene to Henry Knox, May, 20, 1782, NG, 11:217.
26. Mundy, 245n.

TWENTY-EIGHT: FLIP-FLOPS IN CENTRAL AMERICA

1. David W. Jones and Carlyle A. Glean, "The English-speaking Communities of Honduras and Nicaragua," *Caribbean Quarterly*, 17:2, June 1971, 50; Floyd, 59; Dawson, 677.
2. Morse, "Black River"; Floyd, 56; Dawson, 678-679, 682.
3. Journal, August 5, 1780, Kemble, 36; O'Shaughnessy (2000), 189.
4. John Dalling to Honduras governor, May 29, 1780, Kemble, 236.
5. Albert, "Gálvez."
6. Chávez, 162-163; Floyd, 156.
7. Archibald Campbell to Rodney, June 4, 1782, Rodney, 440; Jay, 131-133.
8. Charles Oman, *The Unfortunate Colonel Despard and Other Studies* (New York: Burt Franklin, 1922), 2ff; Jay, 85, 135ff; Floyd, 160-161; Dawson, 701.
9. Albert, "Gálvez"; Chávez, 165.

TWENTY-NINE: A FUTURE HERO

1. Yves-Joseph Kerguelen[-Trémarec], *Histoires des Évènements de la Guerre Maritimes* . . . (Paris: Imprimerie de Patris, 1796), 337, GB; Beatson, 6:258n1.
2. Archibald Duncan, *The British Trident* . . . , vol. 3 (London: James Cundee, 1805), 132-133; Marley, 346; Nelson to Hood, March 9, 1783, Nicolas, 74.
3. Nicolas, 70n7.
4. Marley, 346; Nelson to Hood, March 9, 1783, Nicolas, 74.
5. James Trevenen to his mother, April 5, 1783, Christopher Lloyd and R. C. Anderson, eds., *A Memoir of James Trevenen* (London: Navy Records Society, 1959), 56-57.

6. Dull (1975), 299-301.

7. Tornquist, 122.

8. Georges Lacour-Gayet, *La marine militaire de la France sous le règne de Louis XVI* (Paris: Honoré Campion, 1905), 436-437; Barham, 406; Tornquist, 123.

9. Balch, 246-248.

10. His cousin with a similar name, Juan Manuel Cagigal y Niño, was a future governor of Cuba. See Caicedo, AGEOD Forums, "Spanish commanders," October 27, 2008, http://www.ageod-forum.com/archive/index.php/t-11158.html; Lewis (1991), 4-5, 8; Padrón, 100n72; Beerman, 83.

11. Gillon biography, Coy, 9, 39; D. E. Huger Smith, "Commodore Alexander Gillon and the Frigate South Carolina," *South Carolina Historical and Genealogical Magazine*, 9:4, October 1908, 189-216; Beerman, 85-90; Lewis (1991), 10-17, 21-33; Chávez, 208.

12. Gálvez to José de Gálvez, January 23, 1782, Beerman, 86.

13. John Maxwell to Thomas Townsend, May 14, 1782, *Remembrancer*, 2:148; Lewis (1991), 29.

14. Chávez, 209; Beerman, 93; Caicedo; Lewis (1991), ch. 3.

15. Claraco, May 6, 1782, Craton, 169; Lewis (1991), 55-59, 66.

16. Craton, 169; Johnson (1851), 175-179; Edward Rutledge to Arthur Middleton, March 16, 1782, *The Papers of Eliza Lucas Pinckney and Harriott Pinckney Horry Digital Edition*, ed. Constance Schulz, http://rotunda.upress.virginia.edu/founders/PIHO-01-01-02-0538; Deveaux to Carleton, June 3, 1783, Crary, 356-357.

17. Johnson (1851), 179-180; Craton, 170; Lewis (1991), 63-67; Crary, 355.

18. Lewis (1991), 76-78.

19. Craton, 171; Lewis (1991), ch. 6.

THIRTY: BRITANNIA DOESN'T RULE THE WAVES

1. May 18, 1782, Wraxall (1904), 461.

2. O'Shaughnessy (2013), 330; Clowes, 3:339; Conrad.

3. Clowes, 4:112-116; Greenwood (1915), 136.

4. Tuchman (1988), 129; Blane, 79, 86, 209-210.

5. Blane, 83-84.

6. Henry Atwill Carper, May 16, 1782, Rodney, 406-408; Blane, 203-204.

7. James, *British Navy*, 85-86; Killion, 25.

8. Rodger, 273.

9. E. Gordon Bowen-Hassell, Dennis M. Conrad, and Mark L. Hayes, *Sea Raiders of the American Revolution: The Continental Navy in European Waters* (Washington, D.C.: Naval Historical Center, 2003), 34.

10. Eller, 265; Bowen-Hassell, op. cit.

11. Patton, 230, 236; Maclay, viii-ix; Selesky, 940; Patton, 241.

12. Benjamin Rush to Richard Henry Lee, December 21, 1776, Patton, 124; D. Hamilton Hurd, *History of Essex County, Massachusetts*, vol. 1 (Philadelphia: J. W. Lewis, 1888), 192-193; Patton, 111-112.

13. Maclay, 7.

14. Quarles, 83-92, 152-154.

15. Maclay, 114; Eller, 280; Conrad.

16. Kellow.

17. O'Shaughnessy (2013), 332.

THIRTY-ONE: FRENCH DISASTER, BRITISH TRAGEDY

1. William Langewiesche, "Storm Island," *Atlantic*, December 1, 2001, http://www.theatlantic.com/magazine/archive/2001/12/storm-island/302357/?single_page=true.
2. Jenkins, 171; Syrett, 150, says the convoy had 100 ships.
3. Jenkins, 182; EB, "Guichen," 12:686.
4. Syrett, 149.
5. Syrett, 62; Charles Middleton, Mackesy, 283; DNB, "Kempenfelt, Richard," 30:395-396.
6. Kempenfelt to Middleton, December 28 [1779?], Barham, 308; Edward Hawke Locker, *Memoirs of Celebrated Naval Commanders* (London: Harding and Lepard, 1832), 8.
7. Kempenfelt to Middleton, August 9, 1779, October 17, 1779, Barham, 294, 302.
8. Kempenfelt to Stephens, December 14, 1781, *Remembrancer*, 1:50.
9. Barham, 360; Syrett, 150; accounts vary on prisoner numbers; Kempenfelt to Stephens, January 1782, *Remembrancer*, 1:117.
10. Kempenfelt to Stephens, December 14, 1781, *Remembrancer*, 1:50; Kempenfelt to Middleton, December 14, 1781, Barham, 357.
11. Jenkins, 172; Mackesy, 450.
12. Washington to John Laurens, March 22, 1782, FO.
13. Franklin to Robert R. Livingston, March 4, 1782, FO.
14. William Cowper, *Loss of the Royal George*, http://www.bartleby.com/106/129.html.
15. Barrington to Stephens, April 25, 1782, *Remembrancer*, 1:316.
16. Cust, 335; Clowes, 4:82; Mackesy, 478.

THIRTY-TWO: SECRET MISSION TO THE ARCTIC

1. Dunmore, 133-134; Tornquist, 106.
2. Ann M. Carlos and Frank D. Lewis, "Agents of Their Own Desires," *University of Colorado at Boulder*, 2001, http://www.colorado.edu/economics/papers/papers01/wp01-10.pdf.
3. Mackinnon.
4. David Thompson, *David Thompson's Narrative of His Explorations in Western America, 1784–1812*, ed. J. B. Tyrrell (Toronto: Champlain Society, 1916), 10-14, 24; Umfreville, 11-13.
5. Thompson, op. cit.; Mackinnon.
6. Dunmore, 152-155; Umfreville, 136-137.
7. Umfreville, 138-139; Mackinnon.
8. Umfreville, 127-129; Elizabeth A. Fenn, *Pox Americana: The Great Smallpox Epidemic of 1775–'82* (New York: Hill and Wang, 2001), 189-191.
9. Dunmore, 158.
10. Madison to Edmund Randolph, December 10, 1782, FO, n13; Dunmore, 151.
11. Umfreville, 134.
12. Mackinnon.
13. Dunmore, 168; Étienne Taillemite, "Jean-François de Galaup, Comte de Lapérouse," DCB.

THIRTY-THREE: COASTAL WAR: HALIFAX TO BOSTON

1. L. F. S. Upton, "John Julien," DCB; WPA, *Maine: A Guide 'Down East'* (Boston: Houghton Mifflin, 1937), 302.
2. Samuel Phillips Jr., February 8, 1783, to Washington, FO.
3. Clinton to Francis McLean, February 11, 1779, HMC, 1904, 381; Norman Desmarais, *The Guide to the American Revolutionary War in Canada and New England* (Ithaca: Busca, 2009), 51.
4. HMC, 1906, 13.
5. Abigail Adams to James Lovell, December 13, 1779, FO.
6. James Phinney Baxter, ed., *Documentary History of the State of Maine*, vol. 19 (Portland: Lefavor-Tower, 1914), 423-425.
7. *New England Chronicle*, Boston, October 3, 1782, 15:761, 1; Sharon Cummins, "The Revolutionary War Battle of Cape Porpoise, Maine," http://mykennebunks .com/revolution.htm.
8. Rochambeau to Vaudreuil, July 30, 1782 (attachment to Washington, July 30, 1782), FO; Vaudreuil to Washington, July 26, 1782, FO; Washington to Vaudreuil, August 18, 1782, FO.
9. Washington to Lafayette, March 23, 1783, FO.
10. Hamond to Percy Brett, April 21, 1782, May 8, 1782, Gwyn, 74.
11. Julian Gwyn, *Frigates and Foremasts: The North American Squadron in Nova Scotia Waters* (Vancouver: UBC Press, 2003), 74-75.
12. Nova Scotia Archives, "Lunenburg by the Sea: 250 Years; Lunenburg before 1800," http://www.gov.ns.ca/nsarm/virtual/lunenburg/results.asp?SearchList1=1 &Language=English; DesBrisay, 22.
13. DesBrisay, 62-65, 434.
14. J. Murray Beck, "John Creighton," DCB.
15. "Sack of Lunenburg, 1 July 1782," *American War of Independence at Sea*, http://www.awiatsea.com/incidents/1782-07-01%20Sack%20of%20 Lunenburg.html; Leonard C. Rudolf, July 1, 1782, DesBrisay, 63-64.
16. Ralph M. Eastman, *Some Famous Privateers of New England* (Boston: State Street Trust, 1928), 61-62.

THIRTY-FOUR: COASTAL WAR: DELAWARE TO CHESAPEAKE

1. Morse, "Baltimore"; Selesky, 903.
2. Richard Barnes to Thomas Sim Lee, February 18, 1781, Eller, 234; Unnamed, August 1, 1782, Eller, 280.
3. "Vessels of the Continental Navy," *U.S. Navy, Naval History Center*, http://www.history.navy.mil/wars/revwar/contships.htm.
4. Norton, 71-72; Barney, 112-113.
5. Barney, 3-5, 10-11, 26.
6. Norton, xxi-xxii.
7. John Trumbull, August 12, 1782, John Trumbull, *Autobiography* (New York: Wiley and Putnam, 1841), 82, GB.
8. Gilpin, 54-56; Norton, 74-75; Barney, 113-114; Matthew Ridley to Franklin, June 10, 1782, FO.
9. EB, "Rogers, Josias," 49:134-135; Gilpin, 24-38; EB, "Rogers, Josias," 49:134-135.
10. Matthew Ridley to Franklin, June 10, 1782, FO; Barney, 113-114, 308.

11. Gilpin, 57-58.

12. Norton, 79; Gilpin, 57-58; Barney, 115, 308.

13. Clowes, 4:91; Johnson (1851), 132-133; Marley, 346; Lewis (1991), 33-34; Gerhard Spieler, "John Joyner: Early South Carolina naval figure," *Island Packet*, June 5, 2001, http://www.lowcountrynewspapers.net/archive/node/123724.

14. Wise, 283; Eller, 205, 210, 234-235; Robert Armistead Stewart, *The History of Virginia's Navy of the Revolution* (Baltimore: Genealogical Publishing, 1993), 128-130.

15. Eller, 235, 240-242; Wise, 278-283, 291.

16. Kellow; Eller, 241.

17. Cropper to William Davies, December 6, 1782, Wise, 298-299.

18. Wise, 243-244, 303-310; Wise, 302.

19. Eller, 381-383.

20. Isaac J. Greenwood Jr., "Cruizing on the Chesapeake in 1781," *Maryland Historical Magazine*, 5:2, June 1910, 126-130.

21. William Paca to Washington, February 21, 1783, FO.

22. Greenwood, 17-18; Smith (1977), 5.

23. Greenwood, 17-18; Stephen Moylan to William Watson, December 13, 1775, Smith (1977), 13; Smith (1977), 14.

24. James Warren to Samuel Adams, July 5, 1778; Jones to Joseph Hewes, January 12, 1777, Smith (1977), 43, 45.

25. Smith (1977), 4, 89, 92; Manley to Franklin, June 4, 1781, BF.

26. Greenwood, 127.

27. Manley to Andrew Johannot and Francis Mulligan, January 26, 1783, Greenwood, 132.

28. Greenwood, 129, 139-142; Patton, 214; Selesky, 674.

29. "Duc de Lauzun," *Dictionary of American Fighting Ships*, http://www.history.navy.mil/danfs/d6/duc_de_lauzun.htm.

30. Griffin (1903), 220.

31. Clowes, 4:93; DNB, "Vashon, James," 58:154-155.

32. John Kessler and March 20, 1783 Barry report, Griffin (1903), 221, 223.

33. J. Ralfe, *The Naval Biography of Great Britain*, vol. 3 (London: Whitemore and Fenn, 1828), 190-192.

34. Barry report, March 20, 1783, Griffin (1903), 221.

THIRTY-FIVE: "CALAMITY HAS COME ON US"

1. Treaty of Utrecht, 1713, Chartrand (2006), 13.

2. Cesáreo Fernández Duro, *Armada Española*, Petrie, 194-195.

3. *Express*, November 19, 2013, http://www.express.co.uk/news/world/443937/GIBRALTAR-We-are-just-one-shot-away-from-military-conflict-warns-MP-amid-new-standoff; Coxe, 449; Gregory, 187.

4. William Carmichael to Franklin, October 25, 1780, FO; Cust, 346; Chartrand (2006), 20; Murray to Earl of Hillsborough, February 16, 1782, *Remembrancer*, 1:239.

5. Gregory, 188.

6. Chartrand (2006), 54-55; Gregory, 189; EB, "Murray, James," 39:373-376.

7. John La Rivière account, Mahon, 400; Murray to Crillon; Crillon reply, October 16, 1782, *Remembrancer*, 1:126.

8. Murray to Viscount Hillsborough, November 12, 1781, Gregory, 189.

9. EB, "Murray, James," 39:373-376; G. Peter Browne, "Murray, James," DCB.

10. Browne, op. cit.

11. Murray to Lord Rochfort, November 20, 1774, Mahon, 381.

12. Murray to Weymouth, 1776, Mahon, 384; Murray, January 1779, Mahon, 387; Murray to Germain, January 13, 1779, Fortescue (1911), 305.

13. Mahon, 388, 395.

14. Gregory, 91; Mahon, 393; EB, "Murray, James," 39:373-376.

15. Murray, December 28, 1781, Mahon, 403; Gregory, 191; Captain Dixon, January 9, 1782, Chartrand (2006), 55.

16. Gregory, 191-192.

17. Murray to Earl of Hillsborough, February 16, 1782, *Remembrancer*, 1:238-239.

18. Gregory, 193; EB, "Murray, James," 39:373-376; Mahon, 436.

THIRTY-SIX: THE GREAT SIEGE OF GIBRALTAR

1. McGuffie, 196.

2. Drinkwater, 40, 45.

3. Gilbard, 51-52.

4. Gilbard, 46; Drinkwater, 26, 29.

5. Chartrand (2006), 33; McGuffie, 14.

6. Gilbard, 42-43.

7. Drinkwater, 1, 25, 41-42; Petrie, 186; Chartrand (2006), 33, 36.

8. DNB, "Eliott, George Augustus," 17:195-196; McGuffie, 24-25.

9. Fortescue (1911), 421, 426; Chartrand (2006), 18; McGuffie, 25, 81-82, 89, 103, 108, 128

10. McGuffie, 101, 183.

11. McGuffie, 27, 41-44; Eliott to Lord Weymouth, April 10, 1778, Fortescue (1911), 305; Edward A. St. Germain, "Artillery," http://www.americanrevolution.org/artillery.html; Fortescue (1911), 426.

12. Eliott to Lord Weymouth, January 8, 1780, Chartrand (2006), 37; McGuffie, 48.

13. Chartrand (2006), 42; McGuffie, 105.

14. Ancell, 129; McGuffie, 115, 142.

15. Eliott to Earl of Hillsborough, November 28, 1781, *Remembrancer*, 1:65-66; McGuffie, 119-124.

16. Drinkwater, 201.

17. Unnamed, February 28, 1782, *Remembrancer*, 1:265.

18. Chartrand (2006), 57.

19. Bernard Girard, "Jean Claude Eléonore le Michaud d'Arçon," *Racines Comtoises*, http://www.racinescomtoises.net/?Jean-Claude-Eleonore-Le-Michaud-d; Cust, 347.

20. Chartrand (2006), 58.

21. Cust, 347; Mackesy, 482-483; McGuffie, 157.

22. Drinkwater, 236; Chartrand (2006), 58; Mackesy, 478.

23. Cust, 344; James, *British Navy*, 373; Chartrand (2006), 62-63; McGuffie, 156.

24. Crillon to Eliott, August 19, 1782, Petrie, 200.

25. Chartrand (2006), 61; Coxe, 463; Petrie, 201.

26. Drinkwater, 273.

27. Fortescue (1911), 422; Drinkwater, 275; Chartrand (2006), 66; Coxe, 464.

28. Ancell, 225-226.

29. Ancell, 222.

30. Chartrand (2006), 75-78; McGuffie, 159-160.

31. Ancell, 225-226.

32. *Madrid Gazette*, September, 24, 1782, *Remembrancer*, 2:300-301.

33. Capt. Roger Curtis to Stephens, September 15, 1782, *Remembrancer*, 2:357.

34. Coxe, 466.

35. Wraxall (1904), 363.

36. Wraxall (1904), 363-364; Barrow (1838), 402; Walpole, 44; Adm. Robert Stopford, Barrow (1838), 119; Comte de Garnier to Joseph Matthais Gérard de Rayneval, May 8, 1776, Gruber, 86.

37. Robert Pigot to Lord Percy, March 20, 1777, Gruber, 190.

38. Mason, 83-84, 110.

39. Nelson to Howe, January 8, 1799, Roger Knight, "Richard, Earl Howe," *Precursors of Nelson: British Admirals of the Eighteenth Century*, eds. Peter Le Fevre and Richard Harding (Mechanicsburg, PA: Stackpole Books, 2000), 279; Nelson to Rev. Dixon Hoste, June 22, 1795, Nicolas, 46.

40. DNB, "Howe, Richard," 28:92-102.

41. Juan Antonio Jiménez Castro, "Córdoba y Córdoba, Luis de (1706–1796)," *La Web de las Biografías*, http://www.mcnbiografias.com/app-bio/do/show?key=cordoba-y-cordoba-luis-de.

42. Historians disagree on the convoy numbers. The low estimate: James, *British Navy*, 450-451.

43. James, *British Navy*, 376; Mason, 50.

44. McGuffie, 169, 174; Mackesy, 484 and n1.

45. Mahan, 232-233.

46. Chartrand (2006), 85; McGuffie, 181.

47. Chartrand (2006), 86.

48. Drinkwater, 340-343.

49. McGuffie, 195.

THIRTY-SEVEN: HYDER ALI: THE "MOST FORMIDABLE ENEMY"

1. Smith (1904), V.1.115

2. Munro, 25; World Health Organization, http://www.ncbi.nlm.nih.gov/books/NBK1720/figure/pg69.f7/?report=objectonly.

3. Killion, 369

4. Mackesy, 496

5. Dupuy, 241-242; Wilks, I, 285

6. Ram Chandra Rao, *Memoirs of Hyder and Tippoo* (Madras: Simkins, 1849), 1n3, 33n3; Wilks, 1:246, 351; Fernandes, 21; Maistre, 33; B. L. Rice, *Mysore and Coorg* (Calcutta: Superintendent of Government Printing, 1908), 22.

7. Maistre de la Tour, Maya Jasanoff, *Edge of Empire* (New York: Alfred A. Knopf, 2005), 155.

8. Wilks, 3:514-520.

9. Fernandes, 47-48; Majumdar, 683.

10. Bowring, 113; Beatson, 5:330-331.

11. Debrett (1786), 389; Barrow (1807), 118.

12. Guillaume de Bellecombe to Antoine de Sartine, August 22, 1777, Das, 208.

13. Josias Du Pré to John Macpherson, Wraxall (1884), 128-129; Maistre, 15-16.

14. Wraxall (1884), 129; James Scurry, *The Captivity, Sufferings, and Escape of James Scurry* (London: Henry Fisher, 1824), 48-67; Debrett (1786), 365; Barrow (1807), 81.

15. Rev. Christian Friedrich Schwartz, Wilks, 1:576; Bowring, 109-110.

16. Manimugdha S. Sharma, "Evolution of Indian Military: From Panipat to Festubert," *Times of India*, September 26, 2014, http://timesofindia.indiatimes .com/india/Evolution-of-Indian-military-From-Panipat-to-Festubert/arti-cleshow/43541983.cms; Munro, 122, 132; Macartney to Board of Directors, Barrow (1807), 97.

17. Burke, December 1, 1783, Burke, 423; Wraxall (1884), 126.

18. Fernandes, 61.

19. Ali, 178; Sen, 52.

20. Hyder to Thomas Rumbold, undated, Ali, 200.

21. Majumdar, 684.

THIRTY-EIGHT: COOTE AND HUGHES TO THE RESCUE

1. Killion, 103-106; Malleson, 5.

2. Mackesy, 495.

3. Wylly, 3-4, 12-15.

4. DNB, "Coote, Sir Eyre," 12:159-160.

5. Wilks, 1:286, 408.

6. Hastings, 1779, Earl Stanhope, Lord Mahon, *The Rise of Our Indian Empire* (London: John Murray, 1876), 141; Wylly, 276.

7. Cust, 312.

8. Coote to Macartney, January 1, 1782, January 11, 1782, January 14, 1782, Wylly, 267-268; Coote to company leaders, November 29, 1781, Wylly, 254.

9. Fortescue (1911), 472-478.

10. Malleson, 6, 8-9; Richmond, 107-109; Mackesy, 496.

11. Das, 202, 204.

12. Richmond, 115-116; Dupuy, 246; Fortescue (1911), 473.

13. Coote to Macartney, June 11, 1782, Wylly, 424.

14. Beatson, 5:609.

15. John Campbell, *Naval History of Great Britain* . . . (London: John Stockdale, 1813), 342.

16. Richmond, 90-91.

17. Hugh Palliser to Lord Sandwich, August 11, 1773, Killion, 297; Richmond, 215.

18. Richmond, 262-263.

19. Cavaliero, 94; Suffren, Hickey, 55.

THIRTY-NINE: SUFFREN'S "LUST FOR ACTION"

1. Castries to Souillac and d'Orves, March 1, 1781, Killion, 467.

2. Count D'Estaing to Antoine de Sartine, March 1, 1780, Cavaliero, 45; Sartine to Louis XVI, 1779, Killion, 198.

3. Diary, November 6, 1816, Las Cases, 82-83.

4. Hickey, 51, 63-64.

5. Cavaliero, 24-25, 28.

6. Jean B. de La Varende, *Suffren et Ses Ennemis* (Paris: Ed. de Paris, 1948), 209; Emmanuel-Augustin-Dieudonné-Joseph, comte de Las Cases, Richmond, 141;

Joseph Francois Gabriel Hennequin, Malleson, 77.

7. Biographical, Moran, 316, 318, 323; Cavaliero, 7-10, 26, 48; Malleson, 12; Killion, 200, 203-204, 265.

8. Suffren to Seillans, Killion, 196-198.

9. Suffren, letter, December 4, 1781, Cavaliero, 83-84.

10. François de Souillac to d'Orves, November 27, 1781, Killion, 280; Malleson, 19-20.

11. Cavaliero, 88.

12. Bouët Willaumez, *Batailles de Terre et de Mar*, Malleson, 77; Richmond, 140; Raoul Castex, Moran, 323; Cavaliero, 87.

13. Suffren to Castries, September 29, 1782, Killion, 436-437; Suffren to Jean-Baptiste-Antoine Blouin, April 4, 1782, Killion, 329-330.

FORTY: THE FINAL BATTLES

1. Hughes to Philip Stephens, April 4, 1782, Killion, 322; Malleson (1884), 23-24; Wilks, 2:375-376; Killion, 324-326.

2. Richmond, 206-207; Cavaliero, 133; Killion, 336; Souillac to Castries, June 18, 1782, Cavaliero, 134.

3. Schomberg, 2:110; Hughes: Richmond, 214, 222, 228; Malleson, 25-26; Wilks, 2:383; Killion, 392.

4. Laughton, 121; Suffren to *Hannibal* officers, July 19 and July 29, 1782, Schomberg, 2:122-123.

5. Munro, 261.

6. Jacques Trublet de la Villejégu, Laughton, 122-123.

7. Richmond, 246; Malleson, 36-39.

8. Hughes to Admiralty, October 20, 1782, Killion, 417.

9. Suffren to de Souillac, July 30, 1782, Malleson, 41-42.

10. Cavaliero, 165-169.

11. Surjit Mansingh, *Historical Dictionary of India* (Lanham, MD: Scarecrow Press, 2006), 126; G. B. [George Bruce] Malleson, *History of the French in India* (London: W. H. Allen, 1893), 262-263; Cavaliero, 129-131.

12. Suffren to Castries, July 31, 1782, Killion, 355; Cavaliero, 134-135.

13. Killion, 370-371.

14. Suffren to Bussy, July 30, 1782, Killion, 413.

15. Malleson, 49.

16. Killion, 425; Malleson, 55.

17. Killion, 434.

18. Richmond, 281.

19. Wilks, 2:396.

20. Mir Hussain Ali Khan Kirmani, Fernandes, 70-71.

21. Fernandes, 23; Wilks, 2:565-566; I. M. Muthanna, *Tipu Sultan X'Rayed* (Mysore: Usha Press, 1980); Debrett (1786), 488-489; V. Jalaja Sakthidasan, *Tippu Sultan, a Fanatic?* (Madras: Nithyananda Jothi Nilayam, 1990), 5; "A Tete a Tete with Bhagwan Gidwani," *Sindhishaan*, http://www.sindhishaan.com/article/personali-ties/pers_05_01b.html; Kabir Kausar, *The Secret Correspondence of Tipu Sultan* (New Delhi: Light and Life Publishers, 1908); Bhagwan S. Gidwani, *The Sword of Tipu Sultan*, a best-selling, fact-based, fictional hagiography.

22. De Bussy, *Journal*, December 1782, Killion, 377.

23. Munro, 298-300.

24. Bussy to Suffren, April 10, 1783, Richmond, 347; Stuart to Hughes, Richmond, 342.

25. DNB, "Stuart, James," 55:88.

26. Richmond, 343-344; Malleson, 63.

27. Malleson, 63-64.

28. Wilks, 2:436; Debrett (1786), 502-503; Richmond, 361.

29. Malleson, 70.

30. Killion, 476; Mackesy, 500; Richmond, 371; Malleson, 70-72.

31. Cavaliero, 237.

32. Stuart to Select Committee at Madras, June 25, 1783, *Political Magazine . . . for the Year M,DCC,LXXXIV*, 6:12, 1784, GB.

33. Malleson, 73-74.

34. Suffren, 282.

35. Gower to Philip Carteret, January 18 or 25, 1784, Cavaliero, 238.

36. Sen, 53; Majumdar, 685.

37. Malleson, 75; Suffren to Vergennes, October 15, 1783, Cavaliero, 240; Suffren to Seillans, September 13, 1783, Cavaliero, 241.

38. May 16, 1785, Richmond, 379.

39. Moran, 325; Cavaliero, 253.

40. *Telegraph*, July 31, 2009, http://www.telegraph.co.uk/news/worldnews/asia/india/5940701/Tipu-Sultan-descendants-to-have-royal-status-restored.html.

41. DNB, "Stuart, James," 55:88-89.

FORTY-ONE: NEW LEADER, OLD LEADER

1. George III to Germain, December 15, 1781, Nelson (2000), 137.

2. Biographical, Nelson (2000); Browne, "Carleton"; Germain to John Montagu, Earl of Sandwich, Mackesy, 76.

3. James Phinney Baxter, ed., *The British Invasion from the North* (Albany: Joel Munsell's Sons, 1887), 156-157.

4. Walpole, 500; Browne, "Carleton."

5. George III to North, December 13, 1776; December 15, 1781, Nelson (2000), 11-12.

6. Carleton to Charles Townsend, November 17, 1766, Nelson (2000), 40.

7. Shelburne to Carleton, April 4, 1782, DAR, 21:53-54.

8. Carleton to Washington, May 7, 1782, FO.

9. Carleton to Shelburne, May 14, 1782, DAR, 21:75; Schecter, 365.

10. Walpole, 501; Schaukirk, 441, 444.

11. Brown (1979), 87-89; Silas Wood, Ellis, 134-137.

12. Rodney to Germain, December 22, 1980, Joseph S. Tiedemann, "Patriots by Default: Queens County, New York, and the British Army, 1776-1783," *William and Mary Quarterly*, 43:1, January 1986, 43.

13. Edwin G. Burrows, *Forgotten Patriots* (New York: Basic Books, 2008), 180, 186, 195, 200.

14. GW to Carleton, October 2, 1782; Carleton to GW, October 25, 1782, FO.

15. Carleton to Shelburne, June 18, 1782, DAR, 21:87.

16. Carleton to Washington, July 7, 1782, FO.

17. Young, 95.

18. Washington to Hamilton, March 4, 1783, FO.

19. John A. Nagy, *Rebellion in the Ranks: Mutinies of the American Revolution* (Yardley, PA: Westholme Publishing, 2007).
20. Washington to officers, March 15, 1783, FO; Samuel Shaw, *The Journals of Maj. Samuel Shaw* (Boston: Wm. Crosby and H. P. Nichols, 1847), 104, GB.
21. Young, 80.
22. Van Tyne, 205-206; Fowler (1960), 27.
23. Washington to Greene, August 6, 1782, October 17, 1782, FO.
24. Washington to Lafayette, October 20, 1782, FO.

FORTY-TWO: REFUGEES AND THE *BOOK OF NEGROES*

1. Todd Braisted, TOLIFALS, *The On-line Institute for Advanced Loyalist Studies*, http://www.royalprovincial.com; Peckham, 94-99; John Robertson, Patrick O'Kelley, Ken Kellow, "Land and Sea Battles of the American Revolution," http://www.revwar75.com/battles/index.htm.
2. Ward (2002), 108-111.
3. Ward (2002), 64-67.
4. Shelburne to Carleton, June 5, 1782, Fowler (2011), 112; Nelson (2000), 148; Carleton to Shelburne, August 14, 1782, DAR, 21:111; Carleton to Henry Seymour Conway, Browne, "Carleton."
5. Carleton to Washington, August 2, 1782, FO.
6. William Smith, diary, Schecter, 367.
7. Schaukirk, 442.
8. Van Tyne, 327-341.
9. Carleton to Thomas Townshend, May 27, 1783, DAR, 21:172.
10. Memorial, Prosper Brown to Carleton, June 4, 1783, Crary, 370.
11. Chopra, 200.
12. Fowler (2011), 120; Schaukirk, 443; Anonymous, 1783, Crary, 360.
13. Carleton to Elias Boudinot, August 17, 1783, DAR, 21:208.
14. Carleton to Washington, August 29, 1782, FO.
15. Mercy Warren, *History of the Rise, Progress, and Termination of the American Revolution*, vol. 3 (Boston: E. Larkin, 1805), 256.
16. Robert R. Livingston to Hamilton, August 30, 1783, FO.
17. Timothy Dwight, *Travels in New-England and New-York* (London: William Baynes and Son, 1823), 470-472.
18. Washington to Carleton, September 8, 1782, FO.
19. Carleton to Washington, September 12, 1782, FO.
20. Carleton to Washington, March 19, 1783, FO; William S. Baker, *Itinerary of General Washington* (Philadelphia: J. B. Lippincott, 1892), 291; Washington to Capt. John Pray, March 30, 1783, GW.
21. Carleton to Washington, April 6, 1783, FO.
22. Washington to Carleton, April 9, 1783.
23. *Pennsylvania Packet*, Schecter, 369; Schaukirk, 444; George III, December 5, 1782, John Heneage Jesse, *Memoirs of King George the Third*, vol. 3 (Boston: L. C. Page, 1902), 431.
24. General Orders, transcript, April 18, 1783, GW.
25. Chopra, 115.
26. Jasanoff, 88-89; Ward (2002), 61; Evarts B. Greene and Virginia D. Harrington, *American Population before the Federal Census of 1790* (New York: Columbia University Press, 1932), 102-104.

27. Conference report by George Clinton, John Morin Scott, Engelbert Benson, and Jonathan Trumbull Jr., May 6, 1783, FO.

28. Washington to Carleton, May 6, 1783, FO; Carleton to Washington, May 12, 1783; Quarles, 1966, 171.

29. North to Carleton, August 8, 1783, DAR, 21:202.

30. Chopra, 208, 214; Quarles, 1966, 172-173.

FORTY-THREE: EVACUATION DAY

1. Carleton to Washington, May 12, 1783, FO.

2. Washington to Ralph Izard, June 14, 1783, FO.

3. William Hull to GW, July 7, 1783; Washington to Hull, July 8, 1783, FO.

4. August 11, 1783, HMC, 4:272.

5. Orders to the Army, November 2, 1783, FO.

6. Carleton to Washington, November 12, 1783, FO.

7. Carleton to Washington, December 1, 1783; Washington to Carleton, December 2, 1783, FO.

8. Jasanoff, 86; Carleton to Thomas Townshend Sydney, June 13, 1787, Nelson (2000), 207.

9. J. [John] Clute, *Annals of Staten Island from Its Discovery to the Present* (New York: Chas. Vogt, 1877), 126-127.

BIBLIOGRAPHY AND
ACKNOWLEDGMENTS

I GREW UP IN NEW YORK'S MOHAWK VALLEY READING THE *Schenectady Union-Star* (1911–1969). Back then, compositors set type using hot lead to make printing plates. If there were odd spaces at the end of columns, they'd fill those spaces with, well, "fillers." Usually, the fillers were one- or two-sentence trivia bits. One filler that stuck with me said the last battle of the revolution took place at Fort Henry, Virginia. The information wasn't correct, but the concept led to this book. I am grateful for those newspapers still in business.

I could not have researched the book without modern technology. I'm grateful to the institutions and companies that digitalize out-of-copyright publications, as well as online library card catalogs. Internet Archive, Google Books, WorldCat, the British National Archives database, "Founders Online" (sponsored by the U.S. National Archives and University of Virginia Press), and, yes, Wikipedia, are indispensable.

The web also provides an outlet to unaffiliated researchers—I won't use the term "amateur," because their work is professional. Among them: John Robertson's *Gazetteer of the American Revolution*; Marg Baskin's *Oatmeal for the Foxhounds*; J. L. Bell's *Boston 1775*; and Todd Andrlik, Hugh Harrington, and Don Hagist from the rigorous, but fun, online *Journal of the American Revolution*.

I owe debts to libraries around the world, but especially to the great Seattle Public Library and the University of Washington Libraries. I also used Seattle University's Lemieux Library and the New York Public Library. Among the individuals who helped are: Bob Sullivan, Schenectady Public Library; Melissa Tacke, Schenectady County Historical Society; Bonnie Johnson, Princeton, Indiana, Public Library; Patrick Kerwin, Manuscript Division,

Library of Congress; Sandra Kroupa, University of Washington; and Thomas R. Evans, Rhode Island State Library.

Park and museum staff were eager to share. They included Ashley Chapman, Colonial Dorchester State Historic Site, South Carolina; Alan Stello and John Young, The Powder Magazine, South Carolina; Judith Kramer and Gary Kaushaugen, Caw Caw Interpretive Center, South Carolina; Frank Doughman and Jason Collins, George Rogers Clark National Historical Park, Indiana; Robert Sherman, Middleton Place, South Carolina; and Joseph Herron, Arkansas Post National Memorial, Arkansas.

Academics also contributed. They included Gilbert C. Din, E. Lee Spence, Patrick D. Bellegard, Barbara Vance, Deborah Jenson, Nadève Ménard, Wendy Bennett, and Paul Young.

Some unclassifiable folks also helped. Pulitzer Prize winner Joseph Ellis gave me valuable feedback on some early excerpts. Art dealer and military expert Christopher Bryant was an intermediary in getting certain permissions, but I'm also indebted to him for correcting some of my many errors. Ken Girty provided information about his ancestor, Simon. My friend, Jeff Siddiqui, offered perspectives about India. Al Oickle, my mentor when I was a college student and an inspiration as a historian, encouraged me all the way. My agent, Roger S. Williams, from New England Publishing Associates, is worth the price of a college education. Bruce H. Franklin of Westholme Publishing saw my potential, and he contributes greatly to our nation's knowledge banks. Alex Kane, my editor, saved me from much embarassment.

Finally, as they say, I stand on the shoulders of giants, including: Colonel Mark M. Boatner III and his *Encyclopedia of the American Revolution* (updated by Harold E. Selesky et al.); Dennis M. Conrad and other editors of *The Papers of Nathanael Greene*; Benjamin Quarles, who wrote the seminal history of African Americans in the Revolution; Piers Mackesy for British perspectives; Barbara Tuchman, whose books taught me important lessons about writing history; and Barbara Graymont and Colin G. Calloway for their groundbreaking work about Native Americans during the war.

Note: Websites were accessed from 2009 through 2014. Conversions of eighteenth-century currency to 2011–2013 dollars were made using the conservative end of MeasuringWorth.com calculators.

PRIMARY SOURCES

Adams Papers Digital Editions. Massachusetts Historical Society.
http://www.masshist.org/publications/apde/index.php.

Ancell, Samuel. *A Journal of the Late and Important Blockade and Siege of Gibraltar.* Edinburgh, 1786.

Andrews, Evangeline, ed. *Journal of a Lady of Quality* . . . New Haven: Yale University Press, 1921.

Anti-Jacobin Review and Magazine. "The Marquis de Bouille." February 1801.

Barham, Lord (Charles Middleton). *Letters and Papers of Charles, Lord Barham,* vol. 1. England: Navy Records Society, 1907.

Barney, Mary, ed. *Biographical Memoir of the Late Commodore Joshua Barney.* Boston: Gray and Bowen, 1832.

Barrow, John. *Some Account of the Public Life, and a Selection from the Unpublished Writings, of the Earl of Macartney,* vol. 1. London: T. Cadell and W. Davies, 1807.

Beatson, Robert. *Naval and Military Memoirs of Great Britain from 1727 to 1783,* vols. 5-6. London: Longman, Hurst, Rees, and Orme, 1804.

Blane, Gilbert. *Observations on the Diseases Incident to Seamen.* London: Joseph Cooper, 1785.

Bliss, Eugene F. *Diary of David Zeisberger,* vol. 1. Cincinnati: Robert Clarke, 1885.

Bouillé, Marquis de. *Memoirs Relating to the French Revolution.* London: Cadell and Davies, 1797.

Bouillé, Marquis de (Louis-Joseph-Amour). *Souvenirs et fragments pour servir aux mémoires de ma vie et de mon temps, par le marquis de Bouillé,* vol. 1. Paris: Alphonse Pigard et Fils, 1906.

Bourrienne, Louis Antoine Fauvelet de. *Memoirs of Napoleon Bonaparte,* vol. 1. London: Richard Bentley, 1836.

Brackenridge, H. H. [Hugh Henry]. *Narratives of a Late Expedition against the Indians.* Philadelphia: Francis Bailey, 1783.

Burke, Edmund. *The Speeches of the Right Honourable Edmund Burke* . . . , vol. 2. London: Longman, Hurst, Rees, Orme, and Brown, 1816.

Burnett, Edmund, ed. *Letters of Members of the Continental Congress,* vol. 6. Washington, D.C.: Carnegie Institution of Washington, 1933.

Butterfield, Consul Willshire. *Washington-Irvine Correspondence.* Madison: David Atwood, 1882.

Chesnutt, David R., ed., and C. James Taylor. *The Papers of Henry Laurens,* vol. 16. Columbia: University of South Carolina Press, 2003.

Cheves, Langdon, ed. "The Shaftsbury Papers and Other Records Relating to Carolina." *Collections of the South Carolina Historical Society,* vol. 5. Richmond, VA: South Carolina Historical Society, 1897.

Clark, Walter, ed. *The State Records of North Carolina, 1782-'83,* vols. 15, 16, and 19. Goldsboro: Nash Brothers, [1898] 1901.

Clinton, George. *Public Papers of George Clinton*, vol. 7. Albany: Oliver A. Quayle, State Legislative Printer, 1904.

Clinton, Sir Henry. *The American Rebellion*. William B. Willcox, ed. New Haven: Yale University Press, 1954.

Closen, Ludwig, Baron von. Evelyn Martha Acomb, ed. *The Revolutionary Journal of Baron Ludwig von Closen, 1780–1783*. Chapel Hill: Institute of Early American History and Culture, University of North Carolina Press, 1958.

Conrad, Dennis M., Richard K. Showman, and Roger Parks, eds. *The Papers of Nathanael Greene*, vols. 2, 6-13. Chapel Hill: University of North Carolina Press, 1980–2005.

Crary, Catherine S., ed. *The Price of Loyalty: Tory Writings from the Revolutionary Era*. New York: McGraw-Hill, 1973.

Davies, K. G., ed. *Documents of the American Revolution* (Colonial Office Series), vols. 20-21. Dublin: Irish University Press, [1979] 1981.

Debrett, J., pub. *Transactions in India . . .* London: J. Debrett, 1786.

Debrett, John. *Debrett's Peerage of the United Kingdom of Great Britain and Ireland*, vol. 2. London: G. Woodfall, 1828.

Denny, Ebenezer. *Military Journal of Major Ebenezer Denny*. Philadelphia: J. B. Lippincott, 1859.

Drinkwater, John. *A History of the Late Siege of Gibraltar*. London: T. Spilsbury, 1786.

Elliot, Sir Gilbert. *Life and Letters of Sir Gilbert Elliot*, vol. 2. London: Longmans, Green, 1874.

Ellis, George E. *Memoir of Sir Benjamin Thompson, Count Rumford, with Notices of His Daughter*. Boston: American Academy of Arts and Sciences, 1871.

Endicott, Charles M. *Account of Leslie's Retreat at the North Bridge, on Sunday, Feb'y 26, 1775*. Salem: Wm. Ives and Geo. W. Pease Printers, 1856.

Fanning, David. *The Narrative of Colonel David Fanning*. New York: Reprinted for Joseph Sabin, 1865.

Fanning, David, and A. W. Savary. *Col. David Fanning's Narrative . . .* Toronto: Reprinted from *Canadian* magazine, 1908.

Filson, John. *The Discovery, Settlement, and Present State of Kentucky*. London: John Stockdale, 1793.

Founders Online, National Archives. http://founders.archives.gov.

Franklin, Benjamin. *Memoirs of Benjamin Franklin*, vol. 1. Philadelphia: McCarty and Davis, 1834.

Franklin, Benjamin. *Papers of Benjamin Franklin*. Sponsored by the American Philosophical Society and Yale University; digital edition, The Packard Humanities Institute. http://franklinpapers.org.

George Washington Papers at the Library of Congress. Washington, D.C.: Manuscript Division, Library of Congress. Includes transcriptions from

John C. Fitzpatrick, ed. *The Writings of Washington from the Original Manuscript Sources, 1745–1799*, 39 vols. Washington, D.C.: Government Printing Office, 1931-1944; rpt. in New York: Greenwood Press, 1970. http://memory.loc.gov/ammem/gwhtml/gwhome.html. Also available in an electronic edition. Frank E. Grizzard Jr., ed. Washington Resources at University of Virginia Library. http://etext.virginia.edu/washington/fitzpatrick/.

Gibbes, Robert Wilson. *Documentary History of the American Revolution: 1781–1782.* New York: D. Appleton and Company, 1857.

Gilpin, William. *Memoirs of Josias Rogers, Esq.* London: T. Cadell and W. Davies, 1808.

Gray, Robert. "Colonel Robert Gray's Observations on the War in Carolina." *South Carolina Historical and Genealogical Magazine*, XI:3, July 1910.

Hannay, David, ed. *Letters Written by Sir Samuel Hood.* London: Navy Records Society, 1895.

Heckewelder, John. *A Narrative of the Mission of the United Brethren Among the Delaware and Mohegan Indians . . .* Philadelphia: M'Carty and Davis, 1820.

Heckewelder, Rev. John. *History, Manners, and Customs of the Indian Nations Who Once Inhabited Pennsylvania and the Neighbouring States.* Philadelphia: Publication Fund of the Historical Society of Pennsylvania, 1876.

Hickey, William. *Memoirs of William Hickey*, vol. 3. Alfred Spencer, ed. London: Hurst and Blackett, 1913.

Historic Manuscripts Commission. *Report on American Manuscripts in the Royal Institution of Great Britain.* His Majesty's Stationery Office: vol. 1, London, 1904; vol. 2, Dublin, 1906; vols. 3-4, Hereford, 1907, 1909.

Idzerda, Stanley J. *Lafayette in the Age of the American Revolution: Selected Letters and Papers, 1776–1790.* Ithaca: Cornell University Press, 1980.

Jackson, James. "Miscellaneous Papers of James Jackson." Lilla M. Hawes, ed. *Georgia Historical Quarterly*, 37:1, March 1953.

James, James Alton, ed. *George Rogers Clark Papers 1781–1784.* Springfield: Illinois State Historical Library, 1926.

Kaminski, John P., ed. *The Founders on the Founders.* Charlottesville: University of Virginia Press, 2008.

Kemble, Stephen. *The Kemble Papers*, vol. 2. New York: New York Historical Society, 1885.

Lamb, Roger. *An original and authentic journal of occurrences during the late American war from its commencement to the year 1783.* Dublin: Wilkinson and Courtney, 1809.

Las Cases, [Emmaneul], Count de. *Memoirs of the Life, Exile, and Conversations of the Emperor Napoleon*, vol. 4. New York: Redfield, 1855.

Lee, Henry. *Memoirs of the War in the Southern Department of the United States*, vol. 2. Philadelphia: Bradford and Inskeep, 1812.

Lee, Henry. *Memoirs of the War in the Southern Department of the United States*. Washington: Peter Force, 1827.

Leslie, Alexander. *Letterbooks*. New York Public Library, Emmet Collection, Manuscripts and Archives Division, *ZL-261, Reel 10.

Leslie, Alexander, letter, Sept. 8, 1782, to Sir Guy Carleton, CO 5/107 America and West Indies, Original Correspondence: Military despatches. August–November 1782, British National Archives.

Lewis, Anna, and Jacobo du Breuil. "Some Spanish Letters Written from Arkansas Post." *Arkansas Historical Quarterly*, 2:1, March 1943.

Lewis, Theresa, ed. *Extracts from the Journals and Correspondence of Miss Berry*. London: Longmans, Green, 1866.

"Lieutenant Colonel Cockburn's Defence and Evidence." *Political Magazine and Parliamentary, Naval, Military, and Literary Journal*, vol. 6. London: J. Bew, 1783.

Maistre de la Tour (M.M.D.L.T.). *The History of Hyder Shah*. Revised and corrected by Golam Mohammed. Calcutta: Sanders, Cones, 1848.

McDowell, William. "Journal of Lieut. William McDowell, of the First Penn'a Regiment, in the Southern Campaign, 1781–1782." *Journals and Diaries of the War of the Revolution with Lists of Officers and Soldiers, 1775-1783*. William Henry Egle, ed. Harrisburg: E. K. Meyers, State Printer, 1893.

Middleton, Arthur. "Correspondence of Hon. Arthur Middleton, Signer of the Declaration of Independence." Joseph W. Barnwell, ed. *South Carolina Historical and Genealogical Magazine*, 26:4, October 1925.

Morse, Jedidiah. *The American Gazeteer*. Boston: S. Hall and Thomas and Andrews, 1797.

Moultrie, William. *Memoirs of the American Revolution* . . . New York: David Longworth, 1802.

Mundy, Major-General [Godrey Basil]. *The Life and Correspondence of the Late Admiral Lord Rodney*, vol. 2. London: John Murray, 1830.

Munro, Innes. *A Narrative of the Military Operations on the Coromandel Coast* . . . London: T. Bensley, 1789.

Nicolas, Nicholas Harris, ed. *The Dispatches and Letters of Vice Admiral Lord Viscount Nelson*, vol. 1. London: Henry Colburn, 1845.

O'Callaghan, E. B., ed. *Documents Relative to the Colonial History of the State of New York*, vol. 8. Albany: Weed, Parsons, 1857.

O'Meara, Barry E. *Napoleon in Exile; or, A Voice from St. Helena*, vol. 1. New York: Redfield, 1853.

Padrón, Francisco Morales, ed., and Aileen Moore Topping, trans. *Journal of Don Francisco de Saavedra de Sangronis* . . . Gainesville: University of Florida Press, 1989.

Palmer, William P. *Calendar of Virginia State Papers*, vol. 3, January 1, 1782 to December 31, 1784. Richmond: James E. Goode, 1883.

Ramsay, James. *An Essay on the Treatment and Conversion of African Slaves in the British Sugar Colonies.* London: James Phillips, 1784.

Remembrancer, The, or Impartial Repository of Public Events for the Year 1782. London: J. Debrett, 1782.

Rodney, Lord George. *Letter-books and Order-book of George, Lord Rodney,* vol. 1. New York: New York Historical Society, 1932.

Schomberg, Isaac Capt. *Naval Chronology* . . . London: T. Egerto, 1802.

Seymour, William. "A Journal of the Southern Expedition, 1780–1873." *Pennsylvania Magazine of History and Biography,* 7:4, 1883.

Simms, William Gilmore, ed. *The Army Correspondence of Colonel John Laurens in the Years 1777–'78.* New York: Bradford Club, 1867.

Suffren, Bailli de. *Journal de Bord du Bailli de Suffren dans L'Inde.* Henri Moris, ed. Paris: Chez Challamel, 1888.

Tarleton, Banastre. *A History of the Campaigns of 1780 and 1781 in the Southern Provinces of North America.* Dublin: Colles, Exshaw, White, et al., 1787.

The Times. TimesOnline database. London: various dates, 1788–1796.

Tilden, John Bell. "Extracts from the Journal of Lieutenant John Bell Tilden, Second Pennsylvania Line, 1781–1782 (continued)." *Pennsylvania Magazine of History and Biography,* 19:2, 1895.

Tustin, Joseph P. ed. *Diary of the American War, A Hessian Journal, Captain Johann Ewald, Field Jäger Corps.* New Haven: Yale University Press, 1979.

Umfreville, Edward. *The Present State of Hudson's Bay.* London: Charles Stalker, 1790.

Von Pilchau, George Pilar, and William L. Stone. "Journal of a Volunteer Expedition to Sandusky, from May 24 to June 13, 1782." *Pennsylvania Magazine of History and Biography,* 18:2, 1894.

Walpole, Horace. *Journal of the Reign of King George the Third,* vol. 2. London: Richard Bentley, 1859.

Ward, George Atkinson, ed. *Journal and Letters of the Late Samuel Curwen.* New York: Leavitt, Trow, 1845.

Wilks, Mark. *Historical Sketches of the South of India* . . . vol. 1 (1820), vols. 2 and 3 (1817). London: Longman, Hurst, Rees, Orme, and Brown.

Willett, William M. *A Narrative of the Military Actions of Colonel Marinus Willett, Taken Chief from his Own Manuscript.* New York: G., C., and H. Carvill, 1831.

Wise, Barton Haxall. "Memoir of General John Cropper of Accomack County, Virginia." *Proceedings of the Virginia Historical Society.* Richmond: Virginia Historical Society, 1892.

Wraxall, Nathaniel William. *The Historical and Posthumous Memoirs of Sir Nathaniel William Maxwell, 1772–1784.* Henry B. Wheatley, ed. London: Bickers and Son, 1884.

Wraxall, Nathaniel William. *Historical Memoirs of My Own Time*. London: Kegan, Paul, Trench, Trubner, 1904.

SECONDARY SOURCES

Albert, George Dallas. "The Frontier Forts of Western Pennsylvania." *Report of the Commission to Locate the Site of the Frontier Forts of Pennsylvania*, vol. 2. Thomas Lynch Montgomery, ed. Harrisburg: Wm. Stanley Ray, State Printer, 1916.

Albert, Salvador Bernabéu. "Gálvez y Gallardo, Matías (1717–1784)." *Las Web de las Biografías.* http://www.mcnbiografias.com/app-bio/do/show?key=galvez-matias-de.

Ali, B. Sheik. *British Relations with Haidar Ali*. Mysore: Rao and Raghavan, 1963.

Allen, Robert S. "David Fanning." DCB.

Arnold, Morris S. *Colonial Arkansas, 1686-1804: A Social and Cultural History*. Fayetteville: University of Arkansas Press, 1993.

Atkinson, James R. *Splendid Land, Splendid People: The Chickasaw Indians to Removal*. Tuscaloosa: University of Alabama Press, 2004.

Balch, Thomas. *The French in America During the War of Independence of the United States*, vol. 2. Philadelphia: Porter and Coates, 1895.

Barnwell, Joseph W. "The Evacuation of Charleston by the British in 1782." *South Carolina Historical and Genealogical Magazine*, 11:1, January 1910.

Barrow, John. *The Life of Richard Earl Howe, K. G.* London: John Murray, 1838.

Baskin, Marg. *Oatmeal for the Foxhounds: Banastre Tarleton and the British Legion*. http://home.golden.net/~marg/bansite/btfriends.html.

Bearss, Edwin C. *Special History Report: The Colbert Raid*. Denver: Denver Service Center, Historic Preservation Team, NPS, November 1974. http://www.nps.gov/arpo/historyculture/upload/Colberts-Raid_Special-History-Report-with-notes_reduced.pdf.

Beerman, Eric. "The Last Battle of the American Revolution: Yorktown. No, the Bahamas." *Americas*, 45:1, July 1988.

Bowring, Lewin B. *Haidar Ali and Tipu Sultan*. Oxford: Clarendon Press, 1899.

Bradford Club. *The Operations of the French Fleet under the Count de Grasse* . . . New York: Bradford Club, 1864.

Breen, Kenneth. "George Bridges, Lord Rodney." *Precursors of Nelson: British Admirals of the Eighteenth Century*. Peter Le Fevre and Richard Harding, eds. Mechanicsburg, PA: Stackpole Books, 2000.

Brown, Parker B. "The Historical Accuracy of the Captivity Narrative of Doctor John Knight." *Western Pennsylvania Historical Magazine*, 70:1,

January 1987. http://ojs.libraries.psu.edu/index.php/wph/article/view/4040.

Brown, Sanborn C. *Benjamin Thompson, Count Rumford.* Cambridge: MIT Press, 1979.

Browne, G. Peter, "Carleton, Guy." DCB.

Browning, Oscar. *Napoleon, The First Phase.* London: John Lane, 1905.

Butterfield, Consul Willshire. *History of the Girtys.* Cincinnati: Robert Clarke, 1890.

Caicedo, Ernesto Wilson. "Cajigal y Montserrat, Juan Manuel de." https://sites.google.com/site/grancol1819/bio/cajigal-y-monserrat-juan-manuel.

Calloway, Colin G. *The American Revolution in Indian Country.* New York: Cambridge University Press: 1995.

Calloway, Colin G. *Pen and Ink Witchcraft.* New York: Oxford University Press, 2013.

Canadian Encyclopedia. http://www.thecanadianencyclopedia.com.

Carbone, Gerald M. *Nathanael Greene: A Biography of the American Revolution.* New York: Palgrave Macmillan, 2008.

Carter, William G. "Col. Hugh McGary Sr." *Find a Grave* (1993). http://www.findagrave.com/cgi-bin/fg.cgi?page=grandGRid=70660902.

Caruthers, Eli Washington. *Revolutionary Incidents and Sketches of Character Chiefly in the "Old North State,"* pts. 1 and 2. Philadelphia: Hayes and Zell, 1854, 1856.

Cavaliero, Roderick. *Admiral Satan: The Life and Campaigns of Suffren.* London: I. B. Tauris Publishers, 1994.

Charlton, Thomas U. P. *The Life of Major General James Jackson.* Augusta: Geo. F. Randolph and Company, [1809] 1897.

Charters, David A. "Walter Butler." DCB.

Chartrand, René. *Gibraltar 1779–'83: The Great Siege.* Oxford: Osprey Publishing, 2006.

Chartrand, René. *American Loyalist Troops, 1775–'84.* Oxford: Osprey Publishing, 2008.

Chávez, Thomas. *Spain and the Independence of the United States.* Albuquerque: University of New Mexico Press, 2002.

Chernow, Ron. *Alexander Hamilton.* New York: Penguin Press, 2004.

Chernow, Ron. *Washington: A Life.* New York: Penguin Press, 2010.

Chopra, Ruma. *Unnatural Rebellion: Loyalists in New York City During the Revolution.* Charlottesville: University of Virginia Press, 2011.

Chorlton, Thomas Patrick. *The First American Republic, 1774–1789.* Bloomington: AuthorHouse, 2011.

Clifton, James M. "The Rice Industry in Colonial America." *Agricultural History,* 55:3, July 1981.

Clowes, William Laird. *The Royal Navy: A History from the Earliest Times to the Present*, vols. 3-4. London: Sampson Low, Marston, 1898, 1899.

Cole, Adelaide M. "Did Betty Save Fort Henry?" *Daughters of the American Revolution Magazine*, 114:5, May 1980.

Coleman, Roger. *The Arkansas Post Story*. Santa Fe: NPS, Southwest Cultural Resources Center, 1987. http://www.nps.gov/history/history/online_books/arpo/history.pdf.

Colwell, David G. "The Causes and Accuracy of the Reputation of Simon Girty in American History." *Pittsburgh History*, 77:1, Spring 1994.

Connelley, William Elsey and E. M. Coulter. *History of Kentucky*, vol. 1. Chicago: American Historical Society, 1922.

Conrad, Dennis. "Naval Warfare in the American Revolution." Speech, September 24, 2014. http://www.c-span.org/video/?321666-1/discussion-naval-warfare-american-revolution.

Coxe, William. *Memoirs of the Kings of Spain* . . . London: Longman, Hurst, Rees, Orme, and Brown, 1813.

Coy, Mary Clark. *The Revolutionary War Walking History Book*. Charleston, SC: Mary Clark Coy, 2009.

Craton, Michael, and Gail Saunders. *Islanders in the Stream: A History of the Bahamian People*. Athens: University of Georgia Press, 1999.

Cruikshank, Ernest. *The Story of Butler's Rangers and the Settlement of Niagara*. Welland, Ontario: Tribune Printing House, 1893.

Cruikshank, Ernest. "Memoir of Captain Walter Butler." *Transactions of the Canadian Institute*, 4:8, pt. 2, December 1895.

Cust, Edward. *Annals of the Wars of the Eighteenth Century*. London: Mitchell's Military Library, 1859.

Dann, John C. *The Revolution Remembered*. Chicago: University of Chicago Press, 1980.

Das, Sudipta. *Myths and Realities of French Imperialism in India, 1763–1783*. New York: Peter Lang, 1992.

Dawson, Frank Griffith. "William Pitt's Settlement at Black River on the Mosquito Shore . . ." *Hispanic American Historical Review*, 63:4, November 1983.

De Hass, Wills. *History of the Early Settlement and Indian Wars of Western Virginia*. Wheeling: H. Hoblitzell, 1851.

De Villiers, John Abraham Jacob. "The Foundation and Development of British Guiana." *Geographical Journal*, 38:1, July 1911.

Deerr, Noel. *The History of Sugar*, vols. 1-2. London: Chapman and Hall, 1949, 1950.

DesBrisay, Mather Byles. *History of the County of Lunenburg*. Toronto: William Briggs, 1895.

Dictionary of Canadian Biography Online. University of Toronto and Université Laval. http://www.biographi.ca/en/index.php.

Din, Gilbert C. "Arkansas Post in the American Revolution." *Arkansas Historical Quarterly*, 40:1, Spring 1981.

Doddridge, Joseph. *Notes on the Settlement and Indian Wars of the Western Parts of Virginia and Pennsylvania from 1763 to 1783*. Pittsburgh: John S. Ritenour and Wm. T. Lindsey, 1912.

Duffy, Michael. "Samuel Hood, First Viscount Hood." *Precursors of Nelson: British Admirals of the Eighteenth Century*. Peter Le Fevre and Richard Harding, eds. Mechanicsburg, PA: Stackpole Books, 2000.

Dull, Jonathan R. *The French Navy and American Independence*. Princeton: Princeton University Press, 1975.

Dunmore, John. *Where Fate Beckons: The Life of Jean-François de la Pérouse*. Fairbanks: University of Alaska Press, 2007.

Dunn, Richard S. *Sugar and Slaves: The Rise of the Planter Class in the English West Indies, 1624–1713*. New York: W. W. Norton, 1973.

Dupuy, R. Ernest, Gay Hammerman, and Grace P. Hayes. *The American Revolution: A Global War*. New York: David McKay, 1977.

Edelson, S. Max. *Plantation Enterprise in Colonial South Carolina*. Cambridge: Harvard University Press, 2006.

Eller, Ernest McNeill, ed. *Chesapeake Bay in the American Revolution*. Centreville, MD: Tidewater Publishers, 1981.

Encyclopædia Britannica, 11th Edition. Cambridge, England: University of Cambridge, 1910–1911.

English, William Hayden. *Conquest of the Country of the River Ohio 1778–1783 and Life of George Rogers Clark*, vol. 2. Indianapolis, Kansas City: Bowen-Merrill, 1897.

Essex Institute. "The Affair at the North Bridge, Salem, February 26, 1775." *Historical Collections of the Essex Institute*, 38:4, October 1902.

Farley, M. Foster. "The South Carolina Negro in the American Revolution, 1775–1783." *South Carolina Historical Magazine*, 79:2, April 1978.

Fernandes, Praxy. *Storm over Seringapatam: The Incredible Story of Hyder Ali and Tippu Sultan*. Bombay: Thacker, 1969.

Fleming, Thomas. *The Perils of Peace*. New York: HarperCollins, 2007.

Floyd, Troy S. *The Anglo-Spanish Struggle for Mosquitia*. Albuquerque: University of New Mexico Press, 1967.

Fortescue, John W. *A History of the British Army*, vol. 3. London: Macmillan, 1911.

Foster, William Omer Sr. *James Jackson: Duelist and Militant Statesman 1757–1806*. Athens: University of Georgia Press, 1960.

Fowler, William M. Jr. *American Crisis. George Washington and the Dangerous Two Years After Yorktown, 1781–1783*. New York: Walker and Company, 2011.

Frey, Sylvia. *Water from the Rock: Black Resistance in a Revolutionary Age*. Princeton, NJ: Princeton University Press, 1991.

Garden, Alexander. *Anecdotes of the American Revolution.* Charleston: A. E. Miller, 1822.

Gilbard, G. J., ed. *A Popular History of Gibraltar* . . . Gibraltar: Garrison Library Printing Establishment, 1881.

Glatthaar, Joseph T., and James Kirby Martin. *Forgotten Allies: The Oneida Indians and the American Revolution.* New York: Hill and Wang, 2006.

Goslinga, Cornelius Ch. *The Dutch in the Caribbean and in the Guianas, 1680–1791.* Assen/Maastricht, The Netherlands: Van Gorcum, 1985.

Graham, Major William A. *General Joseph Graham and His Papers on North Carolina Revolutionary History.* Raleigh: Edwards and Broughton, 1904.

Graymont, Barbara. *The Iroquois in the American Revolution.* Syracuse: Syracuse University Press, 1972.

Greenwood, Isaac J. *Captain John Manley.* Boston: C. E. Goodspeed, 1915.

Gregory, Desmond. *Minorca, the Illusory Prize.* Rutherford: Fairleigh Dickinson University Press, 1990.

Grey, Zane. *Betty Zane.* New York: Grosset and Dunlap, 1903.

Griffin, Martin I. J. *Commodore John Barry.* Philadelphia, 1903.

Griffin, Patrick. *American Leviathan: Empire, Nation, and Revolutionary Frontier.* New York: Hill and Wang, 2007.

Gruber, Ira. D. *The Howe Brothers and the American Revolution.* Chapel Hill: Institute of Early American History and Culture at Williamsburg, Virginia, 1972.

Hairr, John. *Colonel David Fanning: The Adventures of a Carolina Loyalist.* Erwin, NC: Averasboro Press, 2000.

Hammersmith, Mary Powell. *Hugh McGary, Senior: Pioneer of Virginia, North Carolina, Kentucky, and Indiana.* Wheaton, IL: Nodus Press, 2000.

Hanson, Willis T. *A History of Schenectady During the Revolution.* Brattleboro, VT: Private printing [E. L. Hildreth and Co.], 1916.

Harding, Gary Rutherford. "General Griffith Rutherford." http://freepages.genealogy.rootsweb.ancestry.com/~rutherford/general_griffith_rutherford.htm.

Harrington, Hugh T. "'The Enemy are Hounded': Gen. 'Mad' Anthony Wayne's 1782 Savannah Campaign." *Southern Campaigns of the American Revolution,* 3:4, April 2006. http://www.southerncampaign.org.

Houck, Louis. *The Spanish Regime in Missouri.* Chicago: R. R. Donnelley and Sons Company, 1909.

Ireland, Bernard. *The Fall of Toulon: The Last Opportunity to Defeat the French Revolution.* London: Cassell Military Paperbacks, 2005.

James, Captain Wm. M. *The British Navy in Adversity.* London: Longmans, Green, 1926.

Jameson, J. Franklin. "St. Eustatius in the American Revolution." *American Historical Review,* 8:4, July 1903.

Jasanoff, Maya. *Liberty's Exiles: American Loyalists in the Revolutionary World*. New York: Alfred A. Knopf, 2011.

Jay, Mike. *The Unfortunate Colonel Despard*. London: Bantam Books, 2004.

Jenkins, E. H. *A History of the French Navy*. London: Macdonald and Jane's, 1973.

Johansen, Bruce Elliott, and Barbara Alice Mann, eds. *Encyclopedia of the Haudenosaunee: Iroquois Confederacy*. Westport: Greenwood Press, 2000.

Johnson, Allen. "Barry, John." *Dictionary of American Biography*, vol. 1. New York: Charles Scribner's Sons, 1928.

Johnson, Joseph. *Traditions and Reminiscences Chiefly of the American Revolution in the South*. Charleston: Walker and James, 1851.

Johnson, William. *Sketches of the Life and Correspondence of Nathanael Greene*. Charleston, SC: A. E. Miller, 1822.

Jones, Charles C. *The History of Georgia*, vol. 2. Boston: Houghton, Mifflin, 1883.

Jones, Eldon, "The British Withdrawal from the South, 1781–'85." *The Revolutionary War in the South: Power, Conflict, and Leadership*. W. Robert Higgins, ed. Durham: Duke University Press, 1979.

Kellow, K. N. *American War of Independence—at Sea*. http://www.awiatsea.com/Incident.html.

Ketcham, Greg. *Drums Along the Mohawk: The American Revolution on the New York Frontier*. http://www.nyhistory.net/~drums/index.html.

Killion, Howard Ray. "The Suffren Expedition: French Operations in India during the War of American Independence." Ph.D. diss., Duke University, 1972.

Knowles, Nathaniel. "The Torture of Captives by the Indians of Eastern North America." *Proceedings of the American Philosophical Society*, 82:2, March 1940.

Kulina, Anna. *In the Footsteps of Renegades: A Virtual Tour of Greenfield*. Pittsburgh: Brandt Street Press, 2010. http://www.brandtstreetpress.com/Ebook-Renegades.pdf.

Kulisek, Larry L. "William Caldwell." DCB.

Lambert, Robert Stansbury. *South Carolina Loyalists in the American Revolution*. Clemson, SC: Clemson University Digital Press, 2010.

Laughton, John Knox. *Studies in Naval History Biographies*. London: Longmans, Green, 1887.

Lewis, Anna, and Jacobo du Breuil. "An Attack Upon the Arkansas Post, 1783." *Arkansas Historical Quarterly*, 2:3, September 1943.

Lewis, Charles Lee. *Admiral de Grasse and American Independence*. Annapolis: United States Naval Institute, 1945.

Lewis, James A. "Las Damas de la Havana, el Precursor, and Francisco de Saavedra: A Note on Spanish Participation in the Battle of Yorktown." *Americas*, 37:1, July 1980.

Lewis, James A. *The Final Campaign of the American Revolution*. Columbia: University of South Carolina Press, 1991.

Lofaro, Michael A. *Daniel Boone: An American Life*. Lexington: University of Kentucky Press, 2003.

Lossing, Benson J. *The Pictorial Field-Book of the Revolution . . .* , vol. 2. New York: Harper and Bros., 1852.

Lutnick, Solomon M. "The Defeat at Yorktown: A View from the British Press." *Virginia Magazine of History and Biography*, 72:4, October 1964.

MacDonald, James M. "Politics of the Personal in the Old North State: Griffith Rutherford in Revolutionary North Carolina." Ph.D. diss., Louisiana State University, 2006. http://etd.lsu.edu/docs/available/etd-03022006-111555/unrestricted/Mac_Donald_dis.pdf.

Mackesy, Piers. *The War for America, 1775–1783*. Lincoln: University of Nebraska Press, Bison Book Edition, 1993.

Mackinnon, Charles Stuart. "Samuel Hearne." DCB.

Maclay, Edgar Stanton. *A History of American Privateers*. New York: D. Appleton, 1899.

Mahan, A. T. [Alfred Thayer]. *Major Operations of the Navies in the War of American Independence*. Boston: Little, Brown, 1913.

Mahon, R. H. [Reginald Henry]. *Life of General The Hon. James Murray*. London: John Murray, 1921.

Majumdar, R. C., H. C. Raychaudhuri, and Kalikinkar Datta. *An Advanced History of India*. London: Macmillan, 1961.

Malleson, G. B. [George Bruce]. *Final French Struggles in India*. London: W. H. Allen, 1884.

Marley, David F. *Wars of the Americas*. Santa Barbara: ABC-CLIO, 1998.

Mason, George. *The Life of Richard Earl Howe*. London: C. Roworth, 1803.

Massey, Gregory D. *John Laurens and the American Revolution*. Columbia: University of South Carolina Press, 2000.

McCrady, Edward. *The History of South Carolina in the Revolution 1780–1783*. New York: Macmillian, 1902.

McGeachy, John A. "Revolutionary Reminiscences from the 'Cape Fear Sketches.' " Paper, North Carolina State University, History 590, 2001. http://www4.ncsu.edu/~jam3/1781-3.pdf.

McGuffie, T. H. *The Siege of Gibraltar 1779–1783*. London: B. T. Batsford, 1965.

MeasuringWorth.com. "Annual Inflation Rates in the United States, 1775–2009, and United Kingdom, 1265–2009." http://www.measuringworth.com/inflation.

Moran, Charles. "Suffren, The Apostle of Action." *United States Naval Proceedings*, 64:3, March 1938.

Nelson, Paul David. *Anthony Wayne, Soldier of the Early Republic*. Bloomington: Indiana University Press, 1985.

Nelson, Paul David. *General Sir Guy Carleton, Lord Dorchester*. Madison, Teaneck: Fairleigh Dickinson University Press, 2000.

Norton, Louis Arthur. *Joshua Barney: Hero of the Revolution and 1812*. Annapolis: Naval Institute Press, 2000.

O'Donnell, James H. III. *Southern Indians in the American Revolution.* Knoxville: University of Tennessee Press, Newfound Press, 1973. http://www.newfoundpress.utk.edu/pubs/odonnell/.

O'Hara, Charles. "Letters of Charles O'Hara to the Duke of Grafton." George C. Rogers Jr., ed. *South Carolina Historical Magazine,* 65:3, July 1964.

O'Kelley, Patrick. *Unwaried Patience and Fortitude: Francis Marion's Orderly Book.* West Conshohocken, PA: Infinity Publishing.com, 2006.

Olwell, Robert. *Masters, Slaves, and Subjects.* Ithaca: Cornell University Press, 1998.

O'Shaughnessy, Andrew Jackson. *An Empire Divided: The American Revolution and the British Caribbean.* Philadelphia: University of Pennsylvania Press, 2000.

O'Shaughnessy, Andrew Jackson. *The Men Who Lost America.* New Haven: Yale University Press, 2013.

Papas, Phillip. *That Ever Loyal Island: Staten Island and the American Revolution.* New York: New York University Press, 2007.

Parker, John C. Jr. *Parker's Guide to the Revolutionary War in South Carolina.* Patrick, SC: Hem Branch Publishing, 2009.

Parmenter, Jon W. "Dragging Canoe (Tsi'yu-gunsi'ni) Chickamauga Cherokee Patriot." *The Human Tradition in the American Revolution.* Nancy L. Rhoden and Ian K. Steele, eds. Rowman and Littlefield, 2000.

Patton, Robert H. *Patriot Pirates.* New York: Pantheon Books, 2008.

Peckham, Howard H. *The Toll of Independence: Engagements and Battle Casualties of the American Revolution.* Chicago: University of Chicago Press, 1974.

Perkins, James Breck. *France in the American Revolution.* Boston: Houghton Mifflin, 1911.

Petrie, Charles. *King Charles III of Spain.* New York: John Day, 1971.

Philbrick, Nathaniel. *Mayflower.* New York: Viking, 2006.

Pierce, William. "Southern Campaign of General Greene, 1781–'82." *Magazine of American History,* 7:6, December 1881.

Preston, Richard A. "John Ross." DCB.

Quarles, Benjamin. *The Negro in the American Revolution.* With a new foreword by Thad W. Tate. Chapel Hill: University of North Carolina Press for the Institute of Early American History and Culture, 1996.

Rankin, Hugh F. *Francis Marion: The Swamp Fox.* New York: Thomas Y. Crowell, 1973.

Rappleye, Charles. *Robert Morris.* New York: Simon and Schuster, 2010.

Recker, Marvin. United Empire Loyalists Association of Canada. "William Caldwell/Baby Family Date Line." January 15, 2013. http://www.uelac.org/Loyalist-Info/extras/Caldwell-William/Caldwell-William-from-Marvin-Recker-Time-Line.pdf.

Richmond, H. [Herbert] W. *The Navy in India, 1763–1783.* Aldershot, U.K.: Gregg Revivals, 1993 reprint.

Riley, Edward M. "Yorktown during the Revolution," pts. 1 (22-43) and 2 (176-188, 274-285). *Virginia Magazine of History and Biography,* 57:1-3. January–July 1949.

Robertson, John. *Global Gazetteer of the American Revolution.* http://www.gaz.jrshelby.com/index.htm.

Rodger, N. A. M. *The Insatiable Earl: A Life of John Montagu, Fourth Earl of Sandwich 1718-1792.* New York: W. W. Norton, 1993.

Rodway, James. *History of British Guiana,* vol. 2. Georgetown: J. Thomson, 1893.

Roosevelt, Theodore. *The Winning of the West.* New York: Book of Reviews Company, 1910.

Schama, Simon. *Rough Crossings: Britain, the Slaves, and the American Revolution.* New York: HarperCollins, 2006.

Schaukirk, Ewald Gustav. "Occupation of New York City by the British." *Pennsylvania Magazine of History and Biography,* 10:4, January 1887.

Schecter, Barnet. *The Battle for New York: The City at the Heart of the American Revolution.* New York: Walker and Company, 2002.

Selesky, Harold E., and Mark Mayo Boatner. *Encyclopedia of the American Revolution,* second edition: Library of Military History. Detroit: Charles Scribner's Sons, 2006.

Selig, Robert. *The March to Victory: Washington, Rochambeau, and the Yorktown Campaign of 1781.* U.S. Army Center for Military History, 2007. http://www.history.army.mil/html/books/rochambeau/ CMH_70-104-1.pdf.

Sen, Sailendra Nath. *An Advanced History of Modern India.* Delhi: Macmillian Publishers India, 2010.

Sevier, Cora Bales, and Nancy S. Madden. *Sevier Family History.* Washington, D.C.: Kaufmann Printing Company, 1961.

Silver, Peter. *Our Savage Neighbors: How Indian War Transformed Early America.* New York: W. W. Norton, 2008.

Sipe, C. Hale. *The Indian Wars of Pennsylvania.* Harrisburg: Telegraph Press, 1929.

Smith, Adam. *An Inquiry into the Nature and Causes of the Wealth of Nations.* Edwin Cannan, ed. London: Methuen, 1904. Library of Economics and Liberty. http://www.econlib.org/library/Smith /smWN.html.

Smith, Gordon B. "The British Evacuate Savannah Georgia." *SAR,* Spring 2007. http://www.revolutionarywararchives.org/savannah.html.

Smith, Philip Chadwick Foster. *Fired by Manley Zeal.* Salem: Peabody Museum, 1977.

Spinney, David. *Rodney.* London: George Allen and Unwin, 1969.

Stahr, Walter. *John Jay, Founding Father.* New York: Hambledon and Continuum, 2006.

Stegeman, John F., and Janet A. Stegeman. *Caty: A Biography of Catharine Littlefield Greene.* Athens: Brown Thrasher Books, University of Georgia Press, 1977.

Stephen, Leslie, and Sidney Lee, eds. *Dictionary of National Biography.* London: Smith, Elder, and Co., 1885–1900.

Stillé, Charles J. *Major-General Anthony Wayne and the Pennsylvania Line in the Continental Army.* Philadelphia: J. B. Lippincott, 1893.

St. Jean, Wendy. "The Chickasaw-Quapaw Alliance in the Revolutionary Era." *Arkansas Historical Quarterly,* 68:3, Autumn 2009.

Stone, William L. *Life of Joseph Brant (Thayendanegea),* vol. 1. Albany, NY: J. Munsell, 1865.

Swiggett, Howard. *War Out of Niagara: Walter Butler and the Tory Rangers.* Port Washington: Ira J. Friedman, Inc., and Columbia University Press, 1963.

Syrett, David. *The Royal Navy in European Waters during the American Revolution.* Columbia: University of South Carolina Press, 1998.

Taylor, Alan. *The Divided Ground: Indians, Settlers, and the Northern Borderland of the American Revolution.* New York: Vintage Books, 2006.

Thrapp, Dan L. *Encyclopedia of Frontier Biography.* Glendale: Arthur H. Clark, 1988.

Tornquist, Karl Gustaf. *The Naval Campaigns of Count de Grasse during the American Revolution, 1781–1783.* Philadelphia: Swedish Colonial Society, 1942.

Tuchman, Barbara W. *The First Salute.* New York: Ballantine Books, 1988.

Urwin, Gregory J. W. "When Freedom Wore a Red Coat . . ." *The U.S. Army and Irregular Warfare, 1775–2007.* Richard G. Davis, ed. Washington, D.C.: Center of Military History, U.S. Army, 2008.

Van Tyne, Claude Halstead. *The Loyalists in the American Revolution.* New York: Macmillan, 1902.

Wallace, David Duncan. *The Life of Henry Laurens With a Sketch of the Life of Lieutenant-Colonel John Laurens.* New York: G. P. Putnam's Sons, 1915.

Ward, Harry M. *Between the Lines: Banditti of the American Revolution.* Westport, CT: Praeger, 2002.

Williams, Samuel Cole. *Tennessee During the Revolutionary War.* Nashville: Tennessee Historical Commission, 1944.

Wylly, H. C. [Harold Carmichael]. *A Life of Lieutenant-General Sir Eyre Coote, K. B.* Oxford: Clarendon Press, 1922.

Young, Alfred F. *Masquerade: The Life and Times of Deborah Sampson, Continental Soldier.* New York: Vintage Books, 2004.

INDEX

Abermarle, 249

Adams, Abigail, 274

Adams, John, 17, 23, 82, 85, 112, 132, 192, 243, 252, 305, 347

African Americans, 12-15, 48, 61, 72, 76, 78, 193, 199, 356-358; *see also* slaves

Aiken, George D., xv-xvi

Alatamaha River, 69

Albermarle, 250

Ali, Hyder, 313-323, 328-331, 334, 336, 338

Allen, Ethan, 135, 143

Alliance, 286-287

Alligator, 89

Amherst, Jeffrey, 228

Angaska, 198-202

Appalachian Mountains, 129-130, 167-168, 184

Arctic Ocean, 270

Arkansas Post, 197-199, 201-203

Arkansas River, 189, 197-199

Arnold, Benedict, 66, 140, 143

Asgill, Charles, 352

Ashley River, 30, 81, 89

Astrée, 268, 271

Bacon, John, 351

Baille, 286

Bald Eagle Creek, 154

Barbary Wars, 287

Barges, battle of, 283

Barney, Joshua, 279-282, 313, 355

Barnwell, John, 80

Barry, John, 286-287

Bay of Fundy, 276

Bay of Honduras, 245

Beall, William K., 162

Bengal Gazette, description of Edward Hughes and, 321

Berbice River, 229

Berry, Mary, 213

Black Brigade, 77

Black Dragoons, 78

Black Pioneers, 77

Black River, 245-247

Blue Ridge Mountains, 182

Bonaparte, Napoleon, 7-8, 251, 307, 316, 323

Book of Negroes, 357-358

Boone, Daniel, 167-171, 178-179, 182

Boone, Nathan, 168

Bouëxic, Luc Urbain de, 264-267, 301, 303, 306, 332

Bougainville, Louis-Antoine de, 239-241

Brackenridge, Hugh Henry, 132, 159, 162-163

Braddock, Edward, 17, 94, 167

Bradt, Andries, 174-176, 384n6

Brandywine, battle of, 17, 40, 66, 82, 94, 282

Brant, Joseph, 138-139, 142-143, 147, 162, 178, 205, 208

Brant, Molly, 127, 134, 138-139, 141, 145

Brereton, William, 94-95, 107-110

Brewton, II, Miles, 74

Brick House, 55

British East India Company, 312, 314

Brown, Thomas, 204

Bryan's Station, 169-170, 175

Bull, William, 118-119

Bunker Hill, 50, 227

Burgoyne, John, 174, 345

Burke, Edmund, 221-222, 225, 243, 316

Burke, Thomas, 58

Burkhart, John, 180

Butler, James, 102

Butler, John, 146-147, 166, 174
Butler's Rangers, 142, 144
Butler, Walter, 138, 142-146, 166

Cagey's Strait, 282
Cagigal, Juan Manuel de, 251-255
Calcutta Gazette, Suffren's captains and, 333
Caldwell, Billy, 172
Caldwell, William, 147, 157-158, 163-164, 166-167, 169-172, 175-176
Calloway, Colin G., xvii
Campbell, John, 193, 196
Cape Fear River, 50, 55
Cape Town, 56, 72, 325-326, 332
Cape Verde Islands, 325
Cap Français, 238-239, 242, 268, 270
Carleton, Guy, 48, 71, 78, 114-117, 143, 164, 234, 343-350, 352-357, 359-360
Catawba River, 11
Catcher in the Rye, 122
Cesar, 202
Ceylon (Sri Lanka), 313, 321, 329, 332
Charles III, 292
Charlestown, British evacuation of, 12, 19, 37, 44-45, 48, 79-80, 102, 106-107, 114, 117-120
Chehaw River, 29, 108-109, 377n20
Chernow, Ron, 112
Cherokees, 54, 89, 91, 99, 102, 129, 149, 167, 182-184, 186-187, 204, 207
Chesapeake Bay, 13, 19, 51, 279, 282, 287
Chickamauga Creek, 183
Chickamaugas, 183, 186-187
Chickasaws, 149, 189-191, 193-194, 196-199, 202, 207-208
Choctaws, 69, 72, 189, 193, 206-207
Churchill River, 270-271
Church of England, 61
Claraco, Antonio, 253-255
Clarke, Alured, 61-63, 68-72
Clark, George Rogers, 177-180, 186, 194, 384n17
Clark, William, 179
Clinton, George, 139-140
Clinton, Henry
  Benjamin Lincoln surrender and, 19
  Charles O'Hara and, 9-10

concern about Charlestown and the rest of the South, 32
concern of French attack on New York and, 13
defeat at King's Mountain and, 35
defeat of Whig armies in the South and, 40
Leslie's strategies and, 47-48, 75, 104
Lippincott's extradition and, 352
neglected New York's defenses and, 346
New York prison ships and, 347
ordering O'Hara to the Caribbean and, 213-214
ordering troops from Halifax to fortify Penobscot and, 274
promising freedom to escapees from the rebels and, 76
refugee problem and, 37
urging London to send "a superior fleet" to America and, 21
war of finger-pointing and, 343
Cockburn, James, 227-228
Coëtnempren, Armand Guy Simon de, 230-231
Colbert, James Logan, 191, 193-197, 199-202, 385n7
Coldstream Guards, 9
Collier, George, 274, 285
Colonial Dorchester State Historic Site, 90
Combahee Ferry, 108-109, 376n14
Combahee River, 29, 107-109, 376n14, 377n20
Comte de Grasse, 18, 25, 231-233, 236-242, 249, 260, 264, 266, 274, 325, 334
Comte de Kersaint, 230-231
Continental Congress, 3, 82, 385n8
Cooper, James Fenimore, 168
Cooper River, 110
Coote, Eyre, 314-315, 318-321, 323, 328, 332, 336
Córdoba, Don Juan de, 301, 303, 305-306, 397n41
Cornstalk (Hokoleskwa), 136
Cornwallis, Charles
  absence at surrender and, 20-21
  Alexander Leslie and, 35-36
  anniversary of surrender and, xvi
  Anthony Wayne and, 67

attempted rescue of, 231, 260
capturing of Rutherford and, 54
Charles O'Hara and, 9, 11-12, 32, 311
defeat of Tipu Sultan and, 338
defeat of two Whig armies in the South and, 40
Francis Marion and, 93
James Henry Craig and, 50
John Laurens and, 19
Marquis de Lafayette and, 16
moving north into Virginia and, 35
slaves and, 116
surrounded by the rebel and French armies, 14
Cornwallis, Edward, 276
Cowan's Ford, 11, 35
Cowper, William, 267
Craig, James Henry, 50-52, 54-58, 61, 75, 104-105
Crawford, John, 164
Cree Indians, 270
Creek Indians, 36, 68-70, 89, 127-128, 149-150, 183, 187, 202-203, 207
Creighton, John, 276-277
Crillon, Louis de Balbe, 292-294, 301-302, 307
Croghan, William, 151, 153
Cropper, John, 282-283
Cruzat, Doña Anicanova Ramos de, 195-196
Cuddalore, battle of, 320, 323, 328, 330-331, 333-339
Cumberland Gap, 168
Cumberland Island National Seashore, 122
Cunningham, John, 100
Cunningham, William "Bloody Bill", 99-103

Daniel Boone, 168
Darby, George, 299
d'Arçon, Jean-Claude-Éléonore, 300-304
Darwin, Charles, 271
Deane, 285
Declaration of Independence, 86, 133
Delaware Bay, 278-280, 282-283, 287, 313
Delaware Indians, 130, 136, 149-151, 157-160, 162, 169, 173, 179

Delaware River, 156
Demerara River, 229
Denny, Ebenezer, 30
DePeyster, Arent Schuyler, 157, 163-164, 174, 176-177, 180
desertion, 14, 18, 36, 71, 75, 80-81, 83, 114-115, 166, 178, 298-299, 349
Despard, Edward Marcus, 247-248
d'Estienne, Thomas, 320, 323, 326
Deveaux, Andrew, 254
Digby, Robert, 235
Don Juan (Byron), 168
Douglas, Charles, 235
Dragging Canoe, 183, 187, 385n4
Draper, William, 294
Drinkwater, John, 296-297, 300, 302, 307
Dubreuil, Jacobo, 198-203
Duc de Lauzun, 286
Duke of Richmond, 343
Dunmore's Ethiopian Regiment, 77
Dunmore's War, 130, 159, 161, 166, 173, 177, 180, 186, 189
Dutch Curaçao, 225
Dutch East India Company, 312
Dwight, Timothy, 354-355
East Florida, 24, 35-36, 59, 62, 102, 119, 189, 203
East India Squadron, 322
Egg Harbor tavern, 351
Eliott, George Augustus, 297-302, 304, 307, 396n11
Eliza, 120
Elliot, Gilbert, 7-8
Emistisiguo, 70
Engageant, 268, 271
English Channel, 234, 259, 264
Eutaw Springs, battle of, 93

Fair American, 280
Falkland Islands, 190
Fallen Timbers, battle of, 122
Fanning, David, 56-59, 98
Fauquier, Francis, 131
Feltman, William, 30
First Anglo-Mysore War, 314
Fish, 160
Fitzmaurice, William Petty, 4
Fitzroy, Augustus Henry, 10
Floridablanca, José Moñino de, 191
Floyd, John, 180

Fort Carlos III, 197-199, 203
Fort Dalling, 247
Fort Fincastle, 173
Fort Frontenac, 140
Fort Jefferson, 194
Fort Johnson, 91
Fort Kijkoveral, 229
Fort McIntosh, 153-154
Fort Montague, 253-254
Fort Moultrie, 122
Fort Nassau, 253-254
Fort Niagara, 143, 166
Fort Pitt, 150-158, 160-161, 165-166,
    173-174, 176-180, 205
Fort Prince of Wales, 269-271
Fort Quepriva, 247
Fort Randolph, 136
Fort Stanwix, 140
Fort St. George, 312
Fort St. Joseph, 192
Fort St. Philip, 292-293, 295
Fort Sumter National Monument, 122
Fort Ticonderoga, 66
Fort William, 312
Francis Marion National Forest, 103
François-Claude-Amour, 225-227,
    231, 233, 236, 238, 242, 246,
    274
Franklin, Benjamin, 3-5, 23, 46, 65,
    79, 82, 85, 130, 153, 187, 242,
    266,
    285, 292, 305
Franklin, William, 79
Fraser, Thomas, 102-103, 107, 234,
    236
French and Indian War, 17
French East India Company, 332
French Martinique, 219
French Revolution, 7, 231, 251, 307,
    338
French Saint-Domingue, 219, 233
French West Indies, 219, 225

Gage, Thomas, 33, 228
Gálvez, Bernardo de, 190, 192-196,
    201, 246-248, 251-253
Gálvez, Matías de, 246-247
Ganey, Micajah, 97-98, 103
Garrison Library, 308
Gaspée, 39
Gates, Horatio, 54, 90-92, 117
General Monk, 280-281

General Washington, 280
George III, 3-5, 22-23, 61, 133, 217,
    244, 265, 295, 297, 304, 343-
    344, 365n13
Georgia Legion, 62, 66
Germain, George, 22, 95-96, 343,
    396n11
Gibraltar, 50, 72, 190, 192, 214, 224,
    291-292, 296-301, 305-308
Gillon, Alexander, 251-253, 261, 279,
    282
Girty, George, 169, 176
Girty, Simon, 159-164, 169, 176, 180-
    181
Gist, Mordecai, 108-110, 376n18
Gist, Nathaniel, 80
Glover, John, 284
Gnadenhütten, 150-155, 159, 164
Grand River, 172, 208
Grasse-Briançon, Marquis de, 249
Great Slave Lake, 270
Greene, George Washington, 121
Greene, Nathanael, xvii
    African American soldiers and, 78
    alarming reports from the back-
        country and, 100
    Anthony Wayne and, 36, 64-65
    attacking British post on Johns
        Island and, 104
    British strategy of conciliation and,
        349
    Cornwallis's new, risky strategy
        and, 11
    dealing with small mutinies and,
        120-121
    death of, 121
    early years of, 38-39
    eigteenth-century horrors and, 42
    enlistments of Continental soldiers
        and, 23-24
    Hannastown and, 165
    impressions of, 38
    information from spies and, 114-
        115
    Johnson Square monument and,
        122
    learning of Laurens death and, 110
    Leslie's ceasefire proposal and, 79
    Marion's report to, 94
    meeting Francis Marion and, 92-93
    mercy as wise military strategy and,
        61

methodical terrorism of southern
    war and, 43
military strategy and, 46
named quartermaster general and,
    40
orders to Wayne in georgia and, 67
prisoner exchange and, 113-114
problem with his generals and, 60
relief of Gates and, 92
Rutherford's treatment of Tories
    and, 52
southern Whigs and, 323
troops movements in South
    Carolina and, 80-87
Greenwich Hospital, 224, 243
Greenwood, John, 284
Grey, Thomas de, 207
Grey, Zane, 175, 384n9
Guadeloupe, 216, 226, 239-240, 285
Guiana (Guyana), 229, 245
Guichen, Luc Urbain de, 264-267,
    301, 303, 306, 332
Guilford Courthouse, 11-12, 35
Gulf of Alaska, 272
Gulf of Mexico, 190

Hague, 284-285
Haldimand, Frederick, 141-142, 146,
    148, 164, 206
Hamilton, Alexander, 83-85, 111-112,
    237
Hamilton, Henry, 177
Hamond, Andrew Snape, 275-276,
    280
Hancock, 285
Hancock, John, 82
Harrison, Benjamin, 176-179, 184,
    385n7
Hartley, David, 3-5, 364n3
Harvard University, 347
Hastings, Warren, 313, 316-319
Hayes, Joseph, 101
Hayes Station, 101
Hearne, Samuel, 269-271
Henderson, William, 80
Henry, Patrick, 168, 174, 177, 190
Hessians, 20, 37, 70-71, 282
Hill, Aaron, 206
Hoboi-Hili-Miko, 206
Hodgson, Robert, 247
Hondo River, 245-246

Hood, Samuel, 223-225, 232, 235-
    239, 241-243, 249-250,
    391n11, 391n22
Horry, Peter, 81, 96-97
Houston, Patrick, 70
Howe, Richard, 304-307
Howe, William, 228, 344
Huddy, Joshua, 352
Hudson River, 66, 137, 255, 348, 351,
    357
Hudson's Bay Company (HBC), 269-
    271
Hudson Strait, 270-271
Huffnagle, Michael, 165
Hughes, Edward, 321-322, 324, 326-
    338
Hunter, Elizabeth Catherine, 61
Hyder Ally, 279-281, 313

Île de France, 320, 323, 325-328, 331-
    332, 335
Immaculada Concepción de
    Honduras, 247
Indian Ocean, 268, 336
Iroquois Indians, 128, 130, 134-141,
    149-150, 160, 167, 206-208
Irvine, William, 152-156, 158-159,
    163-165, 174, 176-177, 179, 205

Jackson, Andrew, 172, 188
Jackson, George, 235
Jackson, James, 62-63, 68-69, 72-73,
    122
Jamaica, 72, 75, 77, 110, 116, 119, 140,
    194, 201, 213-214, 216, 218-
    220, 224, 237-238, 243, 246-
    247, 250-251, 388n13, 388n28
Jamaica Rangers, 77
James Island, 104-105, 117
Jay, John, 3-5, 24, 192, 252
Jefferson, Thomas, 12, 73, 132, 182
Jemy, 64
Jews, 218, 225, 230, 295, 298
Johns Island, 75, 104
Johnson, John, 132, 142-143, 205
Johnson, Lyndon B., xv
Johnson, William, 127-128, 130, 132,
    134, 138, 142, 145, 149, 167,
    205
Jones, John Paul, 285
Joyner, John, 282, 395n13

Kanonraron, 206
Kayashuta, 165
Kempenfelt, Richard, 265-267, 325, 332
Kickapoos, 197
Kidd, John, 283
King's American Dragoons, 96, 346
King's Mountain, 35, 186
Kip's Bay, 17, 34
Knight, John, 155, 159, 162-164
Knox, Henry, 40, 232
Kosciuszko, Thaddeus, 117-118

Lafayette, Marquis de, 16, 20, 23, 63-64, 67, 82, 84-85, 112, 192, 227
Lake Marion, 103
Lake Nicaragua, 246
Lake Ontario, 35, 135, 138, 140, 142, 147
La Marseillaise, 242
Lángara, Juan Francisco de, 299
Lapérouse, Jean-François de, 268-272
Lapérouse Bay, 272
Last of the Mohicans (Cooper), 168
Laurens, Henry, 81-83, 112, 182
Laurens, John, 18-19, 24, 81-87, 91, 97, 104-106, 108-112, 117, 122, 365n8
Lauzun, 286
Lawrie, James, 247
Lee, Charles, 83, 190
Lee, Henry "Light-Horse Harry", 81, 89, 104, 106
Lee, Richard Henry, 24
Lee's Legion, 81
Leeward Islands squadron, 224
Leslie, Alexander
    Anthony Wayne and, 118
    assumes command in the Southern District and, 32-37
    Benjamin Thompson and, 96-97
    Black Dragoons regiment and, 77
    Craig's vulnerability to attack and, 105
    defensive line at Quarter House and, 47
    expense of occupation and, 74
    foraging and cattlegrazing for supplies and, 104
    Henry Clinton and, 48, 75, 213
    Hessian Regiments and, 71
    illness and, 75
    Indian offensive operations and, 204
    Nathanael Greene and, 40, 42-43, 46, 73, 79-80, 88, 106-107, 113-114, 118
    organizing an evacuation and, 50, 79, 106-107, 114, 118, 213
    prisoner exchanges and, 113-114
    privateering and, 261
    return to Scotland and, 122-123
    sending troops to Jamaica and, 75
    slaves and, 76, 78, 115-117
    vulnerability of Marion's force and, 94
Lewis and Clark Expedition, 179
Licking River, 170
Lincoln, Benjamin, 19-21, 54, 83-84, 91-92, 164
Lippincott, Richard, 352
Littlefield, Catharine "Caty", 39, 44, 121-122
Little Turkey, 206
Long Island, battle of, 34
Lord Byron, 168
Lord Dunmore's War, 130, 159, 161, 166, 173, 177, 180, 186, 189
Lord North, 344-345, 357
Louis XVI, 231, 242, 244
Loyalists, xvii
    Alexander Leslie and, 46, 48, 75-76, 78-79, 114-115, 117
    attack by Georgia Whigs and, 69
    attack on Fort Henry and, 174
    attacking settlements along southern frontier and, 182
    battle near Monck's Corner and, 88
    battle of the Barges and, 283
    chafing under British military rule and, 346
    David Fanning and, 56-59
    defeat at Kings Mountain and, 185
    execution of rebel soldiers and, 45
    fleeing the Mohawk Valley and, 138
    forced flight to Canada and, 143
    Francis Marion and, 98, 103
    Georgia Legion and, 62
    Griffith Rutherford and, 52
    Guy Carleton and, 352-354, 357
    hanging of Oliver Toles and, 101
    ill treatment of, 36, 58-59, 69, 119-120, 134, 185, 359
    Indian raids and, 132-133

James Lawrie and, 247
James Logan Colbert and, 197, 199
John Campbell and, 193
John Laurens and, 110-111
John Turner and, 195
Joseph Brant and, 138
mourning Butler's death and, 146
new martial player into the
    Bahamas and, 251
prisoner exchanges and, 113-114,
    196
restitution of the Loyalists' confis-
    cated estates and, 356
revenge killings near Toms River
    and, 352
slaves and, 358
subjected to "violence and plunder",
    36
taking refuge in Halifax and, 273
Tory privateers and, 262
William Brereton and, 107
William Caldwell and, 166
Wilmington as haven for, 51
Luxembourg Palace, 8

MacMillan, Margaret, xvi
Madras (Chennai), 312-314, 316, 318-
    322, 326, 328-329, 331, 333,
    335-337, 339, 399-400n21
Maham, Hezekiah, 81, 93-94, 96-97,
    102
Mahan, Alfred Thayer, 237
malaria, 14, 29, 42, 108, 312, 332
Manley, John, 284-286
Marine Anti-Brittanic Society, 251
Marion, Francis, 77, 80-81, 90-98,
    102-104, 107, 119, 122, 182,
    186, 346, 374-375n9
Maroons, 218
Marquess of Rockingham, 4
Marquis de Bouillé, 225-227, 231,
    233, 236, 238, 242, 246, 274
Marshall, John, 45, 207
Marten, Humphrey, 270-271
Martin, Alexander, 184, 186
Martin, Joseph, 187
Martinique, 216, 218-219, 226, 232-
    233, 237-239, 250, 335,
    388n22
Mathews, John, 116-117
Mathieu, Guillaume, 20
McArthur, Archibald, 206

McDonell, John, 147
McDowell, William, 30
McFall's Mill, 58
McGary, Hugh, 168, 170-172, 179, 188
McGillivray, Alexander, 206
McIntosh, Lachlan, 213
Medea, 337
Micmac Indians, 273
Middleton, Charles, 235, 391n11
Miller, Phineas, 121-122
Mingo Indians, 130, 149, 157
Miró, Esteban Rodríguez, 194-202
Miskito Coast, 245
Mississauga Indians, 208
Mississippi River, 127-128, 141, 164,
    177, 182, 189-191, 193, 196-
    201, 203, 206-207, 216
Mohawk Indians, 127-128, 132, 134,
    137-138, 172, 189, 208
molasses, 216, 346
Monck's Corner, 47, 88, 93, 102, 110
Moñino, José, 191
Monmouth, battle of, 17, 66, 82, 140,
    282
Monongahela River, 174
Moravian Church, 150
Moravian Indians, 150-153, 162
Moreno, Bonaventura, 302
More's Plantation, 55
Morris, Robert, 18, 120, 192, 348
Motte, Rebecca, 74
Moultrie, William, 45-46, 83-84, 91,
    99, 122
Mount Misery, 233
Murray, George, 294
Murray, James, 292-295, 344
Murray, John, 76
Muskingum River, 150

Natchez, 189-190, 192-193, 195-197,
    201
National Park Service, 203
Native Americans
    anti-Indian violence and, 134
    Cherokee Indians and, 54, 89, 91,
        99, 102, 129, 149, 167, 182-
        184, 186-187, 204, 207
    Chickasaws and, 149, 189-191, 193-
        194, 196-199, 202, 207-208
    Christian Indians and, 128, 149
    co-dependency with whites and,
        127

Creek Indians and, 36, 68-70, 89, 127-128, 149-150, 183, 187, 202-203, 207

Delaware Indians and, 130, 136, 149-151, 157, 159-160, 162, 169, 173, 179

Iroquois Indians and, 128, 130, 134-141, 149-150, 160, 167, 206-208

Mingo Indians and, 130, 149, 157

Mohawk Indians and, 127-128, 132, 134, 137-138, 172, 189, 208

Moravian Indians and, 150-153, 162

Oneidas and, 135, 138-139, 145, 147, 208-209

Quapaws and, 189-190, 198-200, 202

Seneca Indians and, 130, 160-161, 165

Shawnee Indians and, 127, 129-130, 136, 149-150, 157-160, 163-164, 167-169, 171, 177-183, 187, 205, 208

"Squaw War" and, 161

Trail of Tears and, 208

treaties and, 130, 137

Wyandots and, 149, 157

Naval Academy, 234

Negapatam, 313, 321, 330-331

Nelson, Horatio, 236, 246, 248-251, 305

New Ebenezer, 63, 68-69

New Mole, 296

New Orleans, 36, 189-190, 192-197, 201, 203

New Providence Island, 214, 251

New River, 129

Newton, Isaac, 231

New York City, British evacuation of, 360

New York Harbor, 360

Nippising nation, 183

North River, 33

North Sea, 234, 268

Oconee River, 69

O'Hara, Augustus, 11

O'Hara, Charles, 5-14, 18-21, 32, 35, 43, 50, 75-76, 83, 213-214, 243, 291, 308, 311, 324, 365n13

O'Hara, James, 9, 291

O'Hara's Battery, 214

Ohio River, 17, 127, 129, 152, 159, 167, 173, 177, 344

Ohio River Valley, 17

Ojibwa Indians, 270

Old Mole, 296

Old Tassel, 184

Oneidas, 135, 138-139, 145, 147, 208-209

Onondaga Indians, 133

Order of Malta, 324, 333

The Origin of Species (Darwin), 271

Paoli Massacre, 66

Parliament, 3-5, 22, 61, 79, 174, 207, 224, 243, 248, 304, 312, 318, 338, 345, 356

Patissier, Charles-Joseph, 332, 334-337

Patuxent River, 284

Paul, François Joseph (Comte de Grasse), 18, 25, 231-233, 236-242, 249, 260, 264, 266, 274, 325, 334

Pee Dee River, 29, 93, 97

Pégase, 267

Penobscot Bay, 275

Penobscot River, 35, 51, 274-275, 285

Pensacola, 189, 192-194, 196

Pequot War (1637), 133

Pickens, Andrew, 80, 186

Pigot, Hugh, 235

Plains of Abraham, battle of, 344

Polk, James, xv

Porto Novo, 320, 328-329, 335-336

Protector, 282-283

Provedien, 329, 334

Quakers, 33, 39, 140, 185

Quapaws, 189-190, 198-200, 202

Quarter House, 47, 81

Québec Act of 1774, 344

Quebec, 280-281

Resolution Island, 271

Rhode Island Army, 39

Rigaud, Louis-Philippe de, 239

Ritchie, William, 100

Roatán Island, 247

Rochambeau, Count de, 9, 16, 18-20, 232-233, 275, 365n8

Rock of Gibraltar, 221

Rodney, George Bridges, 223-228, 231-232, 234-235, 237-240, 242-244, 247, 260, 265, 279, 287, 299, 307, 321, 344, 347
Rogers, Josias, 280-281
Roosevelt, Theodore, 185-186, 205
Rose, John, 151, 153, 155-158
Ross, John, 141-142, 144-147
Royal Gazette, on Lauren's death and, 111
Royal George, 266, 393n14
Royal Society, 96
Rutherford, Griffith, 52-56, 58, 60, 80, 136, 182
Rutledge, Edward, 86, 392n16
Rutledge, John, 44

Sackville, George, 22
Sadras (Kalpakkam), 328
Saint-Cyr, Jacobo Dubreuil, 198-203
Saint-Domingue (Haiti), 216, 219, 225, 232-233
Saint Lawrence River, 143, 145
Saintes, battle of, 240-244, 260, 334
Saluda River, 101
Sandusky River, 158
Santee River, 29, 93, 96-97
Saratoga, battle of, 20, 90, 117, 138, 140, 222, 305, 345
Savannah, British evacuation of, 71-72, 118, 121
Savannah River, 60, 62-63, 68
Scammel, 276
Sceptre, 268, 271
Schaukirk, Ewald Gustav, 346, 353, 356
Schaw, Janet, 218, 222, 233
Schermerhorn, Symon, 137
Schoenbrunn, 150, 152
Schuyler, Philip, 139
Second Battalion, 41
Second Regiment, 91
Seeger, Pete, xv
Seillans, Marie-Thérèse de Perrot, 325
Seminoles, 203, 208
Seneca Indians, 130, 160-161, 165
Seven Years' War, 17, 39, 53, 89, 128, 135, 140-142, 155, 160, 170, 174, 177, 189, 216, 224, 226-227, 234, 268-269, 287, 297, 300, 322, 325, 335, 344

Severn, 270-271
Sevier, James, 187
Sevier, John, 184-188
Seymour, William, 81
Shakespeare, William, 231
Shannon, Alexander, 45
Shawnee Indians, 127, 129-130, 136, 149-150, 157-160, 163-164, 167-169, 171, 177-183, 187, 205, 208
Shay's Rebellion, 21
Shelby, Isaac, 185
Shenandoah Valley, 129
Sibyl, 287
Skidaway Island, 72
slaves, 13, 30-31, 36-37, 41, 48, 51, 60, 72, 75-78, 82, 85-87, 89, 93, 103, 107, 110, 114-117, 120, 175, 187, 189, 191, 195, 197-198, 201-202, 208, 215, 217-219, 229-231, 233, 243, 254, 262, 282-284, 353, 357-359; *see also* African Americans
Smith, Adam, 215-216
Smith, John, 133
Solomon Islands, 272
Sons of Liberty, 140, 365n13
South Carolina, 252, 261, 279, 282
Spanish Havana, 192
Spanish Omoa, 247
"Squaw War", 161
St. Clair, Arthur, 60, 63-64, 130
Stedman, Charles, 136
St. Eustatius (Statia), 221-228, 232-233, 235, 243, 245, 279
St. Francis River, 201
St. Helena Sound, 108
St. Kitts, 219, 233-234, 236-238, 268, 274
St. Kitts council, 219
Stock, William, 109-110
Stoddard, Noah, 276-277
Stono River, 29, 105
Stony Point, 66
Stuart, James, 335-339
Stuart, John, 167
Suffren, Pierre André de, 323-338
sugar, 30, 120, 215-219, 229-230, 233, 262, 283
Sullivan, John, 136, 139-140
Sumter, Thomas, 80

Tahourdin, William, 230-231, 389-
 390n7
Tar Bluff, 107-109, 377n20
Tecumseh, 208
Tender is the Night, 122
Thomas, John, 86
Thompson, Benjamin, 95-97, 346-347
Thomson, Charles, 5
Tierney, John, 157-158
Tilden, John Bell, 30
The Times, capture of Charles O'Hara
 and, 6
Tipu Sultan, 334, 337-338
Todd, John, 170-171
Todd, Levi, 170-171
Toles, Oliver, 101
Tories, xvii
 a "system of plunder and cruelty"
  practiced by, 52
 Alexander Gillon and, 251
 Alexander Leslie and, 71, 88, 113
 Anthony Wayne and, 68, 71-73
 attack on ninety Whigs and, 55
 David Fanning and, 56, 58, 98
 Francis Marion and, 92, 103
 Griffith Rutherford and, 52, 55
 Henry Clinton and, 140
 ill treatment of, 43-45, 54, 58, 120,
  359
 Indian atrocities and, 133
 James Jackson and, 63, 68-69
 John Butler and, 146, 166
 John Cropper and, 282
 John Laurens and, 106
 John Sevier and, 186
 Marine Anti-Brittanic Society and,
  251
 Marinus Willet and, 140
 Micajah Ganey and, 103
 Nathanael Greene and, 67, 113
 on Butler's death and, 146
 passing laws against and, 353, 359
 prisoner exchange and, 113
 Simon Girty and, 169
 slaves and, 87
 using dogs to track Tories and, 89
 Wheland raid and, 284
 Whig army in South Carolina and,
  53
 William Cunningham and, 98-102
 William Seymour and, 81

torture, 44-45, 51, 100-102, 133-134,
 152, 160-164, 214, 218-219,
 261, 315
Trail of Tears, 208
treaties
 Britain declaring war on Holland
  and, 223
 Central-American settlements and,
  247-248
 Chickasaw Nation and, 201
 Clark and Irvine's two-pronged
  expedition into Indian coun-
  try, 179
 David Fanning and, 98
 Francis Marion and, 103
 Franklin and Jay exchanging peace
  treaty documents in Passy
  and, 3
 George III and, 3
 giving Florida to Spain and, 59
 giving away Indian land and, 205-
  206
 Hyder Ali and, 314, 316
 Indian alliance and, 208
 Iroquois giving land up and, 130,
  135, 167, 208
 Jamaica and, 250
 Maroon freedom and, 218
 Micmacs and, 273
 Nathanael Greene and, 46, 120-121
 new power on Indian land in the
  Mississippi Valley and, 189
 reaching preliminary treaty and, 4-
  5, 201, 307, 355-357
 returning Bahamas to the British
  and, 253
 Seven Years' War (1763) and, 216
 Spain's war with Britain and, 291
 St. Kitts and, 233
 territorial disputes in Maine and,
  275
 treaty of alliance with France and,
  259
 Treaty of Mangalore and, 338
 Treaty of Paris (1783) and, 3-6, 206,
  307, 337, 355-356
 Treaty of Peace between Spain and
  Great Britain, 202-203
Trincomalee, 313, 321, 326-330, 332-
 333, 335-336
Trincomalee Harbor, 321
Trois Rivières, 65

Tubman, Harriet, 108, 376n14
Tullidiph, Mary, 32
Turk's Island, 249-250
Turner, Frederick Jackson, 129
Turner, John, 160, 180, 195
Turner, Jr., John, 161
Tuscarawas River, 150
Tybee Island, 71
Tydiman, Hester, 97

Umfreville, Edward, 269-271
United Brethren Church, 150
University of Leyden, 297
U.S. Constitution, 253
U.S. National Park Service, xvi
Ushant Island, 263, 265, 267, 308

Valley Forge, 45, 66, 139, 155, 207, 282
Vancouver, George, 288
Vashon Island, 288
Vashon, James, 287
Vaughan, John, 223, 228, 235
Videau Bridge, 94
Videau, Joseph Henry, 94, 375n21
Vietnam War, xv
Ville de Paris, 239-242
Villars, Luis de, 199-201
Vimeur, Donatien Marie Joseph de, 9, 16
von Rumford, Count, 347

Wadboo Creek, 102
Walley, Zedekiah, 282-283
Wambaw Creek, 96-97
Ward, George Atkinson, 99
War of 1812, 172, 181, 208, 281
War of the First Coalition, 6
Warren, Thomas, 81
Washington, George
  accepting implicit French terms and, 16
  African American soldiers and, 78
  attacking the Iroquois and, 139
  attack on Penobscot and, 275
  Battle of the Saintes and, 266
  besiege New York as "a probable operation" and, 5
  black soldiers and, 86
  Britain's new "pacific disposition" and, 346
  British evacuation of New York and, 359
  comments on Willett and, 140
  delaying the evacuation and, 354
  demanding Lippincott's extradition and, 352
  dismissing the Continental army and, 360
  ending the mutiny and, 349
  furlough of most of his army and, 356
  Great Dismal Swamp and, 29
  John Laurens fighting duel and, 83
  Laurens defeat in South Carolina and, 86-87
  learning military skills and, 39
  learning of Lauren's death and, 111
  mixed record as commander and, 17
  morale visit to the Mohawk Valley and, 147
  naming Greene quartermaster general and, 40
  naming John Laurens as Whig representative and, 19
  parole of prisoners and, 347-348
  preliminary peace treaty and, 355
  reinforcements sent to Greene and, 60
  returning escaped slaves and, 357
  views on Native Americans and, 130, 132
  Wayne's over-the-top personality and, 65
  wealth of, 17
  Willett's winter raid and, 147-148
  William Crawford and, 155
Wayne, Anthony, 36, 60, 63-73, 80, 118, 121-122, 208
Weems, Mason Locke, xvi
West Canada Creek, 145
West Florida, 189, 192-193, 203, 246, 251
West Indies, 21, 91, 102, 213-220, 223-224, 226, 229, 234, 237, 243-244, 249-250, 266, 268, 281, 285, 293, 299
West Point, 66, 117
Wheeling Creek, 173
Wheland, Jr., Joseph, 284
White Eyes (Koquethagechton), 136
White, Philip, 352

Whitney, Eli, 121
Wilks, Mark, 314, 319, 333-334, 336,
    399-400n21
Willett, Marinus, 139-148
William IV, 249
Williamson, David, 151, 155, 158-159
Wilmington, 24-25, 31, 35-36, 43, 47,
    50-55, 57-58, 75, 80, 104
Wolfe, James, 343-344
Wolf River, 195
Wood, James, 101
Woodmason, Charles, 184-185
Wraxall, Nathaniel, 243, 364n3
Wyandots, 149, 157

Yale University, 354
yellow fever, 29, 42, 281
York Factory, 269-271
York River, 13
Yorktown, 364n5
  America's reaction to surrender
      and, 23-24
  as "a hotbed of disease" and, 20
  British occupied peripheries and
      enclaves, 35
  Dutch reaction to Britain's defeat
      and, 23
  George III wanting to continue war
      and, 4
  Lord North's reaction to defeat
      and, 22
  Nathanael Greene's strategy and, 40
  O'Hara's retreat to, 76
  Paul, François Joseph (Comte de
      Grasse) and, 231, 233, 260
  Pierre André Suffren and, 325
  siege of, 14, 16, 20
  strategy to rendezvous in, 18-19
  surrender terms and, 19-20
  Washington's preparations for con-
      tinued fighting and, 25, 30

Zambo people, 245
Zane, Betty, 175-176
Zane, Ebenezer, 173-176, 384n9
Zane, Jonathan, 173
Zane, Silas, 173
Zeisberger, David, 149-153

CPSIA information can be obtained
at www.ICGtesting.com
Printed in the USA
LVHW03s0115231018
594492LV00002B/234/P